Understanding Dark Networks

Understanding Dark Networks

A Strategic Framework for the Use of Social Network Analysis

Daniel Cunningham, Sean Everton,
and Philip Murphy

ROWMAN & LITTLEFIELD
Lanham • Boulder • New York • London

Published by Rowman & Littlefield
A wholly owned subsidiary of The Rowman & Littlefield Publishing Group, Inc.
4501 Forbes Boulevard, Suite 200, Lanham, Maryland 20706
www.rowman.com

Unit A, Whitacre Mews, 26-34 Stannary Street, London SE11 4AB

British Library Cataloguing in Publication Data

Library of Congress Cataloging-in-Publication Data

Names: Cunningham, Daniel, author.
Title: Understanding dark networks : a strategic framework for the use of social network analysis / Daniel Cunningham, Sean Everton, and Philip Murphy.
Description: Lanham : Rowman & Littlefield, 2015. | Includes bibliographical references and index.
Identifiers: LCCN 2015042815 (print) | LCCN 2015046205 (ebook) | ISBN 9781442249431 (cloth : alk. paper) | ISBN 9781442249448 (pbk. : alk. paper) | ISBN 9781442249455 (Electronic)
Subjects: LCSH: Intelligence service—Methodology. | Social sciences—Network analysis. | Espionage. | Counterinsurgency. | National security.
Classification: LCC JF1525.I6 C87 2015 (print) | LCC JF1525.I6 (ebook) | DDC 302.3—dc23
LC record available at http://lccn.loc.gov/2015042815

♾™ The paper used in this publication meets the minimum requirements of American National Standard for Information Sciences—Permanence of Paper for Printed Library Materials, ANSI/NISO Z39.48-1992.

Printed in the United States of America

For Genevieve, Deanne, and Karen

Contents

List of Figures

List of Tables

Introduction

This book is about how social network analysis (SNA) can be used to gain a greater understanding of dark networks as well as help craft strategies that undermine them. Dark networks are often defined as covert and illegal networks (Milward and Raab 2006; Raab and Milward 2003), that is, groups that seek to operate in the dark by concealing their activities from authorities. The difference between light and dark networks is less an either/or proposition and more of a continuum. That is, networks lie on one continuum that runs from overt to covert and on another from legal to illegal (see Figure I.1). The term is typically used to refer to groups, such as terrorists (Cunningham, Everton and Murphy 2015), gangs (Bouchard and Konarski 2014), drug traffickers (Boivan 2014; Raab and Milward 2003), criminal organizations (Famis 2014), white collar conspiracies (Baker and Faulkner 1993; Faulkner and Cheney 2014), and so on, but it can refer to groups that most would consider "good," such as Żegota, the predominantly Roman Catholic resistance group that operated in German-occupied Poland from 1942 to 1945 (Tomaszewski and Webowski 2010); it was both covert and, at least from the perspective of the Nazis, illegal. Other networks may have elements of both light and dark networks. Be that as it may, for most of what follows the focus will be on those groups that are "traditionally" seen as dark networks.

Although social scientists have long considered the nature of dark networks (see, e.g., Baker and Faulkner 1993; Erickson 1981; Simmel 1950b), since 9/11, analysts have become increasingly drawn to the use of SNA as a tool for understanding dark networks, largely because of Valdis Krebs's (2002) analysis of the 9/11 hijacker network. For instance, Marc Sageman (2004) analyzed the network of 172 Islamic terrorist operatives affiliated with the global salafi jihad; Ami Pedahzur and Arie Perliger (2006) examined the nature of suicide attack networks; Stuart Koschade (2006) explored those

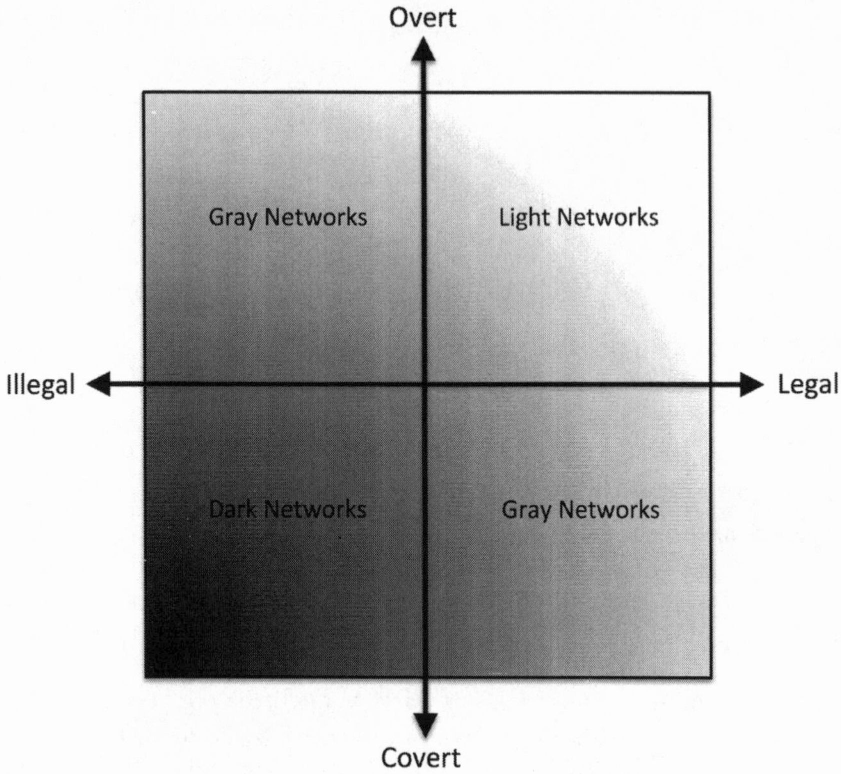

Figure I.1 Light and Dark Networks

involved in the first Bali bombing; and Ron Breiger and his colleagues (2011; 2013) have developed unique methods for examining terrorist groups. These, of course, are just a sample; several other studies exist (see, e.g., Asal and Rethemeyer 2008; Carley, Lee and Krackhardt 2002; Cunningham, Everton and Murphy 2015; Cunningham et al. 2013; Faulkner and Cheney 2014; Gerdes 2015; Magouirk, Atran and Sageman 2008; McCulloh and Carley 2011; Milward and Raab 2008).

Those who analyze dark networks are immediately confronted with three formidable difficulties—the dynamic and evolving nature of networks, the incompleteness of data, and the fuzziness of boundaries (Krebs 2002; Sparrow 1991). In terms of the first, consider how al-Qaeda's structure changed after the September 11 attacks. Prior to the attacks, it was a somewhat vertically integrated organization, at least at the command and control level, but after the U.S. invasion of Afghanistan, available evidence indicates that it has become far more decentralized (Raab and Milward 2003:425; Sageman 2008). The dynamic nature of dark networks also makes the gathering of timely, accurate, and complete data difficult (Krebs 2002; Sparrow 1991), which can have a substantial negative impact on the accuracy of SNA metrics (Borgatti, Carley and Krackhardt 2006). That said, there is a surprising amount of detailed information on dark networks, much of it in the open-source literature. The challenge for many analysts lies, not in finding data, but in sorting through it. Finally, determining the boundaries of dark networks can be exceedingly difficult. They are often connected through actors who function as brokers between these networks, which makes it difficult to know who is in and who is out. These problems are not unique to dark networks, but given that dark networks actively seek to remain hidden from prying eyes, they tend to be more acute. Does that mean we should abandon SNA as a means for gaining a better understanding of dark networks? No. In recent years, SNA has enhanced our understanding of how they organize themselves and offered potential strategies for their disruption (see, e.g., Everton 2012a; Gerdes 2015; Krebs 2002; Roberts and Everton 2011). We just need to be aware of its limitations.

At the time of this printing, the focus of much research has been somewhat narrow: namely, on a handful of metrics (e.g., centrality and brokerage) analysts can use to identify key players whose removal from the network will sufficiently fragment and disrupt it. Put somewhat differently, there appears to be a lack of awareness of the wide range of metrics available and the various strategies with which they can be matched (Roberts and Everton 2011). This book addresses this issue by considering how SNA can inform the crafting of a wide array of strategies for the tracking and disrupting of dark networks. It provides an introduction to SNA but embeds this within a strategic framework that considers both kinetic and nonkinetic (i.e., coercive and noncoercive) approaches to the tracking and disruption of dark networks (e.g., terrorist, insurgent, and criminal networks).

ORGANIZATION OF THE BOOK

The book is divided into four sections. The first consists of three chapters that introduce readers to SNA, the strategic uses of SNA to disrupt dark networks, and the collection, coding, and manipulation of social network data. After a brief historical overview, the first chapter examines what SNA is and is not and how it differs from other approaches. For example, SNA is often confused with social networking in general and social media (e.g., Facebook and Twitter) in particular. Although researchers can use SNA to analyze social media data, they are not the same. SNA also differs from standard statistical approaches in that SNA focuses on different types of relations between actors (e.g., friendship, kinship, and shared affiliation) rather than actors' attributes (e.g., race, gender, and religious tradition). The chapter also introduces readers to basic SNA terms, concepts, and assumptions so that they will not become lost in later chapters. Not all terms and concepts will be discussed here: only those that are necessary for readers to move forward. Others will be introduced as the book progresses, and a glossary is included as an appendix. Readers familiar with SNA will probably be able to skip this chapter.

The second chapter explores the strategic alternatives for tracking, disrupting, and destabilizing dark networks. Too often, analysts do not consider such a framework before estimating metrics, which can unfortunately lead to metrics driving strategy rather than the other way around (Roberts and Everton 2011). Because analysts often overlook several other important considerations prior to estimating network analysis measures, such as establishing clear network boundaries and creating a codebook that defines the various relationships being analyzed, chapter 3 discusses the "how-to" of collecting, coding, and manipulating of social network data. The failure to consider these factors prior to data collection and analysis, particularly in an operational environment, can cause significant problems relating to data management and quality, as well as any conclusions that analysts draw from the analysis of such data.

The book's second section introduces several "families" of metrics commonly used for exploratory network analysis: topography, centrality, clustering, brokerage, and blockmodeling; each chapter discusses how these metrics can be used in a strategic framework. The fourth chapter focuses on network topography. Networks differ from one another in terms of their overall structure or topography, and a network's topography has a strong impact on the behavior of its members and is related to its resilience and/or efficiency. We begin with a few basic metrics before turning to those that capture a network's level of centralization and interconnectedness. The fifth chapter explores the more common approaches for using patterns of ties to detect cohesive subgroups within social networks: components, cliques, k-cores, factions, and community detection algorithms. Components are the simplest form of subgroups, while cliques are the strictest. K-cores are groups of actors that are often nested within one another, while faction analysis and community detection algorithms seek to identify subgroups in which there are more ties within groups and fewer ties between groups than one would expect if the ties were randomly distributed through a network. Because different methods sometimes identify very different subgroups, the chapter concludes with guidance as to the differences and limitations of the various algorithms, along with how some approaches may be well suited to specific tasks and how others may be better for general inquiry and induction.

The next chapter introduces readers to algorithms that identify a network's central actors. Centrality is perhaps the most intuitive social network measure; however, what constitutes a central actor is based on the interests and assumptions of the analyst (Bonacich 1987; Everett and Borgatti 2005; Freeman 1979; Friedkin 1991). A central actor can be seen as someone who has numerous ties to other actors (e.g., degree centrality), as someone who has numerous ties to highly central actors (e.g., eigenvector centrality), as someone who is close to other actors in the network (e.g., closeness centrality), or as someone who lies on the shortest path between numerous pairs of actors in a network (e.g., betweenness centrality). Social network analysts also use centrality measures to identify prestigious actors in a network. These generally require the use of directed networks (see chapter 3), and we will introduce readers to several. The seventh chapter explores metrics closely related to centrality: bridges and brokers. Bridges are ties that span gaps in a social network, whereas brokers are the actors at either end of bridges. As we will see, however, what constitutes a broker and a bridge depends on one's definition and assumptions. Structural holes, which was developed by Ronald Burt (1992a; 1992b), is probably the best known "brokerage" algorithm (and often the most misunderstood), but there are others (e.g., cutpoints, cutsets, edge betweenness, and counts of how often individual actors sit between two other pairs of actors) that are often just as effective, sometimes more so.

The section's final chapter, positional analysis, introduces readers to a series of algorithms that seek to identify actors who hold similar positions within a network (e.g., the chief surgeons of different hospitals, the chairs of divinity school departments in different academic institutions, and the company commanders of Special Forces companies).Such actors may or may not have ties with one another, but the positional approach assumes that structurally equivalent actors are likely to behave in similar ways regardless of whether a tie exists between them or not. The set of actors who hold a similar position is termed a "block" and the process by which blocks are identified is referred to as blockmodeling. Unsurprisingly, analysts have developed a number of different types of algorithms for identifying structural equivalent actors and multiple algorithms within each of these types. We consider blockmodeling in this chapter and highlight its importance for understanding dark networks.

The book's third section consists of three chapters that focus on several confirmatory, and often underutilized, techniques for examining dark networks. Chapter 9 focuses on hypothesis testing techniques for analyzing social network data, including quadratic assignment procedure (QAP) and conditional uniform graphs (CUGs). The statistical analysis of social network data differs from standard statistical models in at least three important ways. First, standard models are designed to analyze random samples so that researchers can generalize their results to the population at large. By contrast, social network analysts generally analyze whole (i.e., complete, full) networks, so there is no need for a larger population for which to generalize. Second, standard models assume that observations are independent of one another, but a central assumption of SNA is that observations (i.e., actors) are interdependent and that these interdependencies profoundly impact actor behavior. Finally, standard models usually assume that the population variables follow a known statistical distribution (e.g., Gaussian, Poisson, and Logistic), but the distribution of social network data is seldom normal (i.e., Gaussian) and often unknown. Because of this, standard statistical models should not be used for testing hypotheses, but instead models should be used that specifically account for the interdependencies of social network data and allow for statistical inference.

Chapter 10 introduces exponential random graph models (ERGMs, also referred to as p* models), which provide analysts with a way to examine the internal (endogenous) and external (exogenous) social processes that give rise to a network's observed patterns (Harris 2014; Lusher, Koskinen and Robins 2013; Robins et al. 2007). ERGMs assume that observed social networks are built upon local patterns of ties, sometimes called micro-configurations, that are a function of local social processes, such that "actors in the network form connections in response to other ties in their social environment" (Lusher, Koskinen and Robins 2013:1). They are similar to the general linear models found in standard statistical packages (in particular, logistic regression models), except that they include important modifications in order to account for the dependencies between observations (Harris 2014; Lusher, Koskinen and Robins 2013; Robins et al. 2007). The basic approach for estimating an ERGM is to hypothesize as to what endogenous social processes gave rise to a particular network's global properties, and then build a model that takes these and other factors into account. Local processes are operationalized in terms of the various micro-configurations found within a network (e.g., edges, stars, and open and closed triads), while exogenous factors, such as race, gender, religious affiliation, and age, are modeled in order to capture various social selection processes, such as homophily or status.

In chapter 11, we explore methods for understanding changes in a dark network over time. The chapter begins with an overview of how longitudinal approaches have been used to understand dark networks over time. Next, it explores the panel data approach to analyzing dark networks known as stochastic actor-oriented models (SAOMs) (Snijders 2005; Snijders, Bunt and Steglich 2010; Van de Bunt, Van Duijin and Snijders 1999). They are similar to ERGMs, in that they assume that the observed network structure is, in part, a function of local patterns of ties that reflect endogenous social processes. Like ERGMs, they test whether a particular configuration occurs more frequently than one would expect, given the other configurations included in the model. They differ from ERGMs in that they are designed for longitudinal social network data and explicitly model the choices of actors, who "are assumed to control their outgoing ties and to make changes in these ties according to short-term goals and restrictions" (Snijders and Koskinen 2013:138). As the predecessor to ERGM models, there is a good deal of overlap in the interpretation and setup. We therefore focus on the additional advantages offered by this procedure.

The book concludes with a final chapter that summarizes key items outlined in previous chapters and discusses several "lessons learned" on which future research can build. In particular, it will draw from research and experience attained by working with practitioners who have actively countered dark networks. Finally, the book will contain three appendices: (1) one that provides codebooks and descriptions of the various data sets used throughout the book (2) another that contains a glossary of key terms and concepts, and (3) a third outlining the various analytic software packages used in producing the analyses contained in the book.

The monograph is largely nontechnical. There are plenty of resources for exploring SNA's mathematical and graph theoretical foundations (see, e.g., Brandes and Erlebach 2005; Jackson 2008; Lewis 2009; Wasserman and Faust 1994), so there is little need to repeat them here. Instead, this book focuses on the assumptions underlying the various metrics, as they apply to dark networks. Put bluntly, most (if not all) analysts exploring dark networks in an operational environment do not care, nor do they need to know, how to calculate betweenness or eigenvector centrality by hand; they do, however, need to know the assumptions underlying these and other forms of centrality so that they can appropriately evaluate the metrics they estimate. This is not to say that the book is completely devoid of equations. We have given in to the temptation from time to time. However, readers uninterested in the mathematics behind the algorithms can skip these equations without peril. In addition, rather than filling up pages illustrating how to visualize network data, estimate various types of centrality, or detect cohesive subgroups in UCINET, Pajek, NetDraw, R, or Gephi, we have included these at the book's companion website (https://sites.google.com/site/understandingdark-networks/). Worked examples are important, but we thought that in this case they detracted from the flow of the book.

ACKNOWLEDGMENTS

We have all contributed equally to the writing of this book. We divided up who wrote the first draft of each chapter, but by the end we had all read, edited, and contributed to each chapter. Thus, our names appear in alphabetical order. Numerous people are in our debt for the writing and completion of the book. It has benefitted from the suggestions of and conversations with several individuals, in particular, John Arquilla, Doug Borer, Ron Breiger, Kathleen Carley, Patrick Doreian, Karen Flaherty, Glenn Johnson, Gordon McCormick, Ian McCulloh, Daniel LeRoy, Malcolm Mejia, Brint Milward, Nancy Roberts, Rob Schroeder, Jörg Raab, and Greg Wilson. Students at the Naval Postgraduate School's Defense Analysis (DA) Department, who have spent years deployed dealing first-hand with dark networks, are not only inspirational, but they have also provided valuable insight over the years. Alex Stivala, Garry Robins, and Dean Lusher provided some much appreciated input and insight on the topic of exponential random graph modeling, and Jeffrey Spegal provided helpful feedback on an early draft. We also benefitted from the comments of several anonymous reviewers who made valuable suggestions as to how the manuscript could be improved. Finally, we would not have been able to write this book without the patience and support of our more-than-significant others: Deanne, Genevieve, and Karen. They have put up with the endless hours we have spent on writing and rewriting this manuscript, and it is to them that we dedicate this book.

Part I

INTRODUCTION TO SOCIAL NETWORK ANALYSIS

Chapter 1

Social Networks

It is relatively commonplace for analysts and researchers to raise the subject of networks and their importance for understanding and countering nonstate criminal, insurgent, or terrorist groups. However, although the topic has reached a level of acceptance, the practice of formally and rigorously analyzing such "dark" networks has only just begun to take hold. This may be due, in part, to the patterns of reluctance and acceptance that fields exhibit when confronted with relatively new paradigms of inquiry (Kuhn 1970), although a better explanation may lie in the perceived complexity and depth of the network analysis field, and the expected difficulty of training and transition from observational and descriptive tools to a greater reliance upon formal measurement and testing that is offered through the field of social network analysis (SNA). In this text, we proceed from the standpoint that SNA provides an opportunity for analysts, researchers, law enforcement, and warfighters to better break down and conceptualize the patterns of interdependency that regulate and drive dark networks. Think of SNA as a collection of useful, powerful, and specialized tools that were developed in order to better understand how social ties help to define, enable, and constrain the knowledge, reach, and capacities of people and other actors. When used in conjunction with reliable data collection, along with the guidance of subject matter experts, the formal analysis of social networks can provide a perspective that is otherwise unavailable with traditional methods.

It is important to keep in mind that SNA is not a panacea or magic bullet. Like any other tool, its efficacy is limited by the knowledge and skills of the user, so it is important for those interested in adopting network analytics into their repertoire to carefully consider the meaning and intent behind any network-related tools that they wish to use before applying or trying to gain inference from them. Blindly estimating a battery of centrality measures in hopes of identifying which of a network's members are most "important" can be very misleading without a careful consideration of what each of the measures mean and the context in which one is operating. However, when used properly, such measures can offer fairly quick and verifiable information that contributes to a deeper and more meaningful understanding of how a poorly perceived group operates and may offer either clues about how to proceed in gathering more information on a group or how they may be deterred or disrupted.

Even in its simplest form (i.e., sociograms or visualized networks), SNA can offer powerful new perspectives for those who already hold a great deal of knowledge about a particular group or organization. Analysts and researchers often have an intuitive understanding about the networks in which they are interested or tasked to analyze. They can usually explain nonrelational (i.e., attribute) information about their networks, such as the formal titles of individual actors, and they can argue which actors seem relatively "important" to the overall network. Army Special Forces (SF), for example, are often active in a diverse set of networks in their area of operation, including tribal, political, and organizational networks. The same goes for many other practitioners (e.g., other military, law enforcement) trying to understand and interact with various networks. They are often at an advantage to understand such networks given their tasks, deployments, and access to such networks. However, it is unlikely that even the most seasoned field analyst can account for more than a specific subset of network actors.

As humans our working memory is limited, and this restricts our ability to process and identify network patterns of more than a few people. In other words, no matter how much we think we know about a network, our cognitive abilities limit our ability to process and understand several important aspects of those networks. For example, it is difficult for most people to grasp and hold a full rendering of every actor and even a substantial portion of the relationships that constitute even a relatively small network that they know well. If you find this claim dubious, try the following exercise. Consider a network that you know well: your own "trust" network, made up of your friends and family members.

1. Using a pen draw an actor in the center of a blank sheet of paper to represent you.
2. Draw additional points on the piece of paper, one for each of your friends.
3. Next, draw a line to signify a relationship (i.e., friendship) between you and each of your friends, and then draw lines between any of your friends who are also friends with one another.
4. Next, superimpose your kin, or family, into that network. In other words, now draw actors that represent your family members.

5. Draw a line (i.e., kinship relationships) between your family members.
6. Finally, draw relationships (kinship or friendship) among your friends and family.

Now, take a moment and observe your network and consider a few questions. Did you remember all of your friends and family? Are you confident you mapped all friendship and kinship relations among the individuals in your network? Who is actually connected to whom? For example, do you have a sibling who is also friends with one or some of your friends? Are some of your family members also your friends? If you wish to verify whether you have a strong grasp of your trust network, try the exercise again in an hour or show your work to some friends and family members and see what they say. Now consider how much more difficult this exercise would be with a (dark) network that seeks to hide its activities from authorities. Moreover, it would be functionally impossible in the context of large networks, such as Twitter networks of groups like the Islamic State.

Tools, such as those offered through SNA and the related field of link analysis, provide a means to formally record a list of actors and the ties between them. What sets SNA apart is its ability to quantify, test, and predict various social phenomena within the network. The collection of theoretically grounded tools that comprise SNA is based on the assumption that actors' behavior (regardless of whether they are individuals, groups, or organizations) is driven by how they are linked to others and the networks in which they are embedded. Rather than requiring independence of observations—treating individuals, groups, or organizations as being unaffected by those around them, as we do when using frequentist statistics—SNA accounts for interdependence and operates under the assumption that people are social beings whose patterns of interaction play a strong role in what they do, say, and believe. Although some interactions occur randomly, many do not. Actors tend to interact with others for reasons that are socially determined, and repeated interaction can lead, among other things, to the emergence of social formations at the micro (e.g., individual), meso (e.g., group or subgroup), and macro (e.g., meta-network, institutions, nations) levels, which can be analyzed in their own right. Social interaction can drive group solidarity, reinforce norms of behavior symbols of group belonging (e.g., team mascots, gang colors, sacred religious symbols such as the Christian cross and the Jewish star, and national flags), and generate a sense of identity (Collins 2004; White 2008). Social networks are an important concept for understanding the needs, motivations, and capacities of individuals in a society. They help us make sense of their world, shape our preferences, and influence the choices we make (Passy 2003:23). Consequently, a primary goal of SNA has been to clarify those processes. Analysts studying dark networks must do this as well, but we operate under some special constraints—not the least of which is the clandestine nature of the groups we study.

The remainder of this chapter provides a brief overview of the field of SNA, as well as some basic information to help those who are less familiar with the field of SNA to get started. The term "network" has become relatively common of late. As such, the following section differentiates SNA from the concept of "networking," as well as some other techniques that bear some resemblance to the network approach. The next section provides a very brief accounting of the history of SNA before turning to some basic terms and their use in the field. This is followed by a discussion of the role of networks in human society.

1.1 THE UNIQUE ASPECTS OF SOCIAL NETWORK ANALYSIS

The term "social network analysis" is generally met with varying degrees of recognition and misidentification. For general audiences, it is frequently confused with social networking and social media analysis. Often when people hear the term, they hold the vague expectation that it has something to do with analyzing social media outlets such as Facebook or Twitter. The two are not the same, however. SNA is a set of theories and methods that were developed to understand social structure, while social media is user-generated content that can include text, pictures, videos, connections among users, and links to websites. Analysts can extract network data from social media platforms and subsequently use SNA to understand those social media networks (e.g., followers in a user-to-user Twitter network). The fact that relational data are inherently embedded in social media content, and therefore lend themselves to SNA, only adds to the confusion. That said, analysts can use SNA to analyze social media data with varying degrees of efficacy, but this is a relatively recent development and the value of such work has yet to be established.

The use of the term "networks" bears similar potential for confusion. Theoretical approaches to understanding the threats or opportunities posed by networks tend to focus upon the cases of decentralized, informal, and/or organic types of organizations, viewing hierarchies as centralized, formal, and/or bureaucratic (Arquilla and Ronfeldt 2001; Powell 1990; Powell and Smith-Doerr 1994; Ronfeldt and Arquilla 2001). Although such distinctions can be of use in some theoretical contexts, social network analysts consider all organizations to be networks. The hierarchies present in more formalized institutions are important for their own unique abilities, but they are networks nevertheless (Nohria 1992).

At the applied end of the analytic spectrum, those who understand analytics will also tend to conflate SNA with the fields they find most familiar.

Those whose experience resides in the experiential, descriptive, or other methods of qualitative inference will tend to focus on the visual depictions of how various entities relate to one another. Those who are more closely involved in quantitative aspects of analysis, such as statistics and agent-based modeling, will sometimes focus on the measurement or statistical aspects of the discipline. A better description of SNA lies somewhere between the two views.

Among many practitioners, the more common misconception is the conflation of SNA with link analysis. It is common for people who have used link analysis programs, such as Palantir or Analyst's Notebook, to believe they have conducted network analysis. This is partially due to the network visualization format that both programs use to search, sort, and present the relational data collected and stored within the program. The diagrams used in link analysis are mainly used for qualitative inquiry, with few, if any, metrics applied for the purpose of inference. Additionally, although both approaches map and analyze relationships among actors, the two approaches hold very different methodologies and, correspondingly, purposes. Link analysis has essentially developed into a method of interactively curating and querying a relational database. Link analysis diagrams are created to identify explicit connections between people, places, documents, and many other potential objects and entities (e.g., events, individuals, aliases, cars, bank accounts, and cell phones). The ties between them are used to explore and describe the environment surrounding a particular entity or set of entities. The notable difference between link analysis and social network diagrams is that the latter only focuses on ties between similar objects or entities, whereas the former does not.[1] Now consider how one of the simplest SNA measures, degree centrality, which is simply a count of the number of ties an actor has to other actors, is meaningful within the world of SNA but not link analysis. Restricting the focus of inquiry to the structure of ties between the same types of objects makes it possible to quantify various ways in which they are linked. However, counting the ties of actors in a link analysis diagram is essentially meaningless since the ties being counted are between different, and sometimes noninteracting, things.

Oddly enough, somewhat similar misconceptions about the qualitative nature of SNA arise from analysts who are more accustomed to quantitative analytics, especially those with a statistical background. It is not uncommon for statisticians to perceive SNA as being primarily qualitative and descriptive due to the frequent use of visualization as a tool for inference. However, such an assumption is needlessly reductive, though it is becoming less frequent in nature.

SNA differs from more traditional quantitative approaches (i.e., frequentist statistics), in that while the latter focuses on a random sample of actors and their attributes (e.g., age, gender, political preference, and education) and ignores or attempts to remove the broader pattern of social interactions in which they are embedded (e.g., at home, social gatherings, workplace, and centers of worship), SNA focuses on how these interaction patterns affect behavior. SNA does consider the role that attributes play but only in the context of how they predict or explain interaction patterns, and it typically sees interaction patterns as better explanatory variables of actor behavior than are attributes. Unfortunately, analyses of dark networks often limit their focus to actor attributes, which makes it difficult to explain actor behavior across social contexts (i.e., networks). For example, an actor holding a mid-level position in a terrorist group's communication network is unlikely to gain significant attention from the authorities due to his lack of formal prestige, but he may be a charismatic recruiter and creative operational planner because of his recruiting and operational ties. These behavioral differences can be difficult to reconcile with his unchanging gender, operational role, and status, but they may make sense in the context of the actor's structural relations across various contexts.

SNA, then, is best considered as a set of theories and techniques that make it possible to account for empirical content within social context. The tool set has been used to successfully explain a variety of behaviors due to its tendency to force researchers "to think in terms of constraints and options that are inherent in the way social relations are organized" (Raab and Milward 2003).

1.2 A BRIEF HISTORICAL BACKGROUND

The recognition of the role and power of networks is nothing new to the study of clandestine and covert groups. The idea of drawing associations between entities and other factors was first introduced in 1975 in the context of criminal organizations (Harper and Harris 1975). Whether they knew it or not, their proposal, an early version of link analysis, bore some characteristics of a much larger intellectual movement that had begun over half a century earlier and was beginning to undergo an initial two-decade revitalization and expansion in the 1960s (Freeman 2004). The initial kernel was planted by Georg Simmel ([1908] 1955; [1908] 1971), who argued that we must study patterns of interaction if we hope to understand social behavior. Simmel additionally offered penetrating insights into the nature of secret societies (1950b), the dynamics of dyads and triads (1950a; 1950c),[2] and drew links between modern individualism and increases in social complexity (Simmel [1908] 1955).

Simmel's insights remain influential to this day. Drawing upon his work, social psychologists have emphasized how pattern recognition shapes how we see and interpret the world (Heider 1946; Lewin 1951; Moreno 1953b), while social anthropologists have emphasized the relationship between social patterns and social structure (Nadel 1957; Radcliffe-Brown 1940). These efforts laid the groundwork for the later development of what we know today as SNA. Sociologist Harrison White and his students, such as Ronald Breiger, Bonnie Erickson, Ivan Chase, Mark Granovetter, Michael Schwartz, and Barry Wellman (Freeman 2004; Prell 2011; Scott 2013), were at the center of the field's revitalization at Harvard during the 1960s and 1970s. White drew upon his background in theoretical physics and enlisted his students to develop an approach that focused on social relations and the patterns that emerge from them. The discipline has continued to expand since that time (Freeman 2004; Prell 2011; Scott 2013). In recent years, physicists and other scientists have "discovered" the field, which has led to an increased interest in applying the tools and techniques of SNA to other fields and thereby building up and expanding the tools (Barabási 2002; Barabási and Albert 1999; Girvan and Newman 2002; Kleinberg 2000; Watts 1999a, 2004).

The 2001 terrorist attacks of September 11 were a major catalyst for applying SNA to dark networks. The effort began to take on momentum following Krebs's (2002) analysis of the 9/11 hijacker network. Afterward, researchers in the United States increasingly employed SNA for the tracking, disruption, and/or destabilization of terrorist networks (Reed 2007; Ressler 2006). A few of the many notable efforts include Sageman's (2003, 2004) analysis of the Islamic terrorist operative network affiliated with the global Salafi jihad (GSJ); Rodriguez's (2005) map of the March 11, 2004, Madrid bombing network; Pedahzur and Perliger's (2006) exploration of four suicide attack networks; and Koschade's (2006) analysis of the Jemaah Islamiyah cell responsible for the first Bali bombing.

Despite the great increase in work around analyzing dark networks, the largest contribution remains in the area of theory. Early on, Erickson (1981) refuted Simmel's (1950b) assertion that hierarchies provided a preferred structure for secret societies, finding instead that the ideal structure of dark networks are idiosyncratic, varying from network to network according to the group's level of risk aversion. Baker and Faulkner (1993) reached a similar conclusion, arguing that dark networks are driven more by the need to maximize security than efficiency, leading most to adopt decentralized structures, which allow for rapid adaptation in the face of problematic or rapidly changing environments (Arquilla and Ronfeldt 2001; Bakker, Raab and Milward 2011; Klerks 2001; Krebs 2002; Milward and Raab 2006; Powell 1985, 1990; Raab and Milward 2003; Ronfeldt and Arquilla 2001; Saxenian 1994; Saxenian 1996). Although the practice of researching dark networks has been ongoing for some time, the term was not coined until after 2001 (Bakker, Raab and Milward 2011; Milward and Raab 2006; Raab and Milward 2003).

1.3 A BRIEF INTRODUCTION TO NETWORK TERMS

Network analysis focuses on the study of relational structures. The networks themselves consist of a set of entities and the relationships between them. Another way to say this is that social networks are made up of *actors* and the *ties* between them (Wasserman and Faust 1994:21). The actor set—also referred to as a node or vertex set—in a network can take a variety of forms. Though they often represent individual people, they may also be used to represent groups, organizations, businesses, or even nonhuman entities such as websites, publications, or even improvised explosive devices (IEDs) (Childress and Taylor 2012).

Perhaps the most important aspect of the actors in a network is how they are tied to one another. Ties can vary in terms of type, direction, and strength, and they are taken to represent relationships or aggregate relationships. Examples of network ties include those that are affective, or sentiment based (e.g., friendship and liking), role based (e.g., kinship), resource or transaction related (e.g., business transactions and financial flows), derived through affiliation (e.g., participates in the same events, members of the same church, club, and terrorist group), behavioral (e.g., communication), formal (e.g., organizational hierarchy), cognitive (e.g., knows and thinks like), and so on (Wasserman and Faust 1994:18). Ties may exhibit direction (e.g., the flow of resources from one actor to another, where one actor communicates with another actor), and such ties are referred to as arcs. Ties that have no inherent direction (i.e., undirected) are referred to as edges. Due in large part to the covert nature of dark networks, tie direction can be difficult or impossible to ascertain; thus, they are frequently treated as being undirected. When appropriate, ties may also be characterized in terms of their strength, which can also vary on a continuum from strong to weak (Granovetter 1973, 1974). For example, strong ties are those between actors that have repeated and relatively intense interactions with one another, and weak ties connect actors who see one another occasionally or rarely. Alternatively, analysts may choose to value ties according to the number of different relationships that two actors share with one another. A common difficulty is determining what differentiates a tie from the numerous, random, and usually unrepeated encounters that actors experience on a daily basis. It is helpful to think of a tie as "a theoretical construction, abstracted by the analyst from the bulk of largely erratic streams of affections, encounters and interactions between a pair of actors, be they human beings, informal groups, formal organizations, or others" (Azarian 2005:37).

The simplest structures that may constitute a network are dyads (i.e., two actors), triads (i.e., three actors), and the patterns of ties between them. Such microstructures can reveal a great deal about the dynamics within the network, and they received much early attention from network analysts (Cartwright and Harary 1956; Heider 1946; Holland and Leinhardt 1976). Because dark networks are most frequently undirected, much of the nuance relating to dyadic and triadic variation is lost. But four triadic possibilities (Figure 1.1) remain with such data: (1) all three actors may be connected to one another; (2) none of the three actors are connected; (3) two of the three actors may be connected to one another, but not to the third; or (4) two edges are present connecting two actors through an intermediary third, but not directly to one another.

Three of the four triadic configurations in Figure 1.1 correspond with the concept of *transitivity* and are considered to be in "*balance*," where it is assumed that when there is a tie from A to B, and from B to C, that there will be a tie from A to C.[3] To determine whether a triad is in balance, treat null ties (i.e., the absence of a tie) as negative and edges as positive and multiply the three edge configurations. A positive product indicates that the triad is in balance (i.e., transitive), whereas a negative product indicates that the triad is unbalanced (e.g., intransitive) (see Cartwright and Harary 1956). Therefore, triads one, two, and three in Figure 1.1 are considered to be in balance, and triad four is considered to be in a state of unbalance. The unbalanced configuration—two edges and one null tie—is considered to be in a state of tension, with two actors that are connected only through an intermediary actor; although, as we will see in chapter 7 that the intermediary actor is in a position of brokerage (Burt 1992b; Granovetter 1973).

Bridges are ties that span gaps in a social network, and *brokers* are actors located at either end of such bridges. Both can be seen as being in a position to control the flow of resources through a network. In terms of Figure 1.2, the edges between actor 3 and actors 2, 4, 10, and 16 would be considered bridges and all five actors would be considered brokers. That said, because actor 3 acts as a broker between the other four actors, actor 3 is clearly in more of a position of brokerage than are 2, 4, 10, and 16.

In a manner similar to the bridge, outlined above, a *path* is defined as a *walk* (i.e., a sequence of actors and ties) in which no actor between the first and last actor of the walk occurs more than once, whereas the *path distance* between two actors is the number of steps between the two actors. In

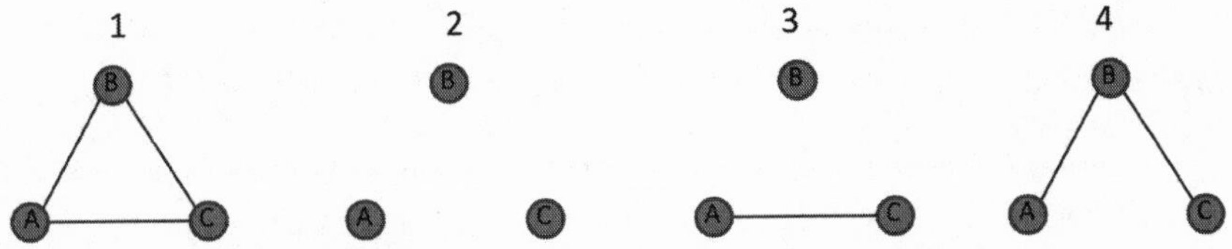

Figure 1.1 Triadic Possibilities

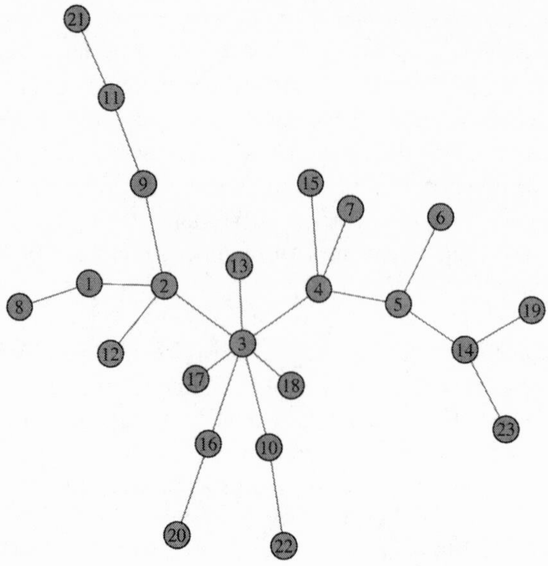

Figure 1.2 Hypothetical Social Network

Figure 1.2, you can trace a path from actor 9 to actor 12 through the actor 2, and the path from actor 6 to actor 4 through actor 5. In both cases the distance between the actors is two (i.e., two steps). It is quite common for numerous paths to exist between actors, some longer and shorter than others. The shortest path between two actors is known as a *geodesic*.

In undirected networks, the actors that can reach one another via a path are considered to be in the same *component*. Components are therefore sets of mutually reachable actors, in undirected networks. For directed networks, the direction of the relationship is an additional consideration. In such cases, all actors that are mutually reachable when following the direction of the relations form a *strong component*, and those that are mutually reachable when ignoring the direction of the relation forms a *weak component*. Networks may have multiple components, and in such cases they are referred to as being *disconnected*. The smallest component that a network can have is a single actor with no ties to other actors. Such actors are referred to as *isolates*.

While SNA focuses primarily on the pattern of ties between actors, most social network analysts do not completely ignore *attribute data*, which are characteristics of individual actors. If the actors in a network are individuals, then attribute data include things such as gender, race, ethnicity, years of education, income level, and age. If they are terrorist or criminal groups, then attribute variables can be those that measure area of operations, financial resources, number of members, and so on.

Other basic network terms and features to be aware of include network topography, which enumerates a network's size, configuration, and other salient aspects of its structure, such as its density and level of centralization; cohesive subgroups, which are clusters of well-connected actors within a network; roles and positions, which are structural regularities that are used to identify equivalent actor sets; or centrality measures, which may be used to measure various conceptualizations of importance for the actors in a network. Each of these concepts is dealt with at length in later chapters due to their particular frequency of use and value to social (and dark) network analysis.

1.4 BASIC ASSUMPTIONS

Although it is important to understand the methods that essentially constitute the field of SNA (see e.g., Granovetter 1979), it is more helpful for analysts to establish a strong command of the assumptions on which most SNA methods are built (Azarian 2005; Knoke and Yang 2007; Wasserman and Faust 1994). The following assumptions are interdependent and mutually reinforcing. Taken as a whole, they will provide insight into the origins of the methods covered in the remainder of this book. When internalized, they may provide a deeper understanding of social processes that may, in turn, aid in further development or innovation on the part of the analyst.

- Ties between actors function as conduits for the transfer or flow of information, sentiment, material and/or nonmaterial goods, or other resources (e.g., funds, supplies, information, trust, and enmity).
- Actors, along with their actions and motivations, are interdependent, rather than independent, with other actors.
- A network's social structure reflects enduring patterns of interaction between actors.
- An actor's position in the social structure impacts his or her beliefs, norms, and behavior.
- Repeated interactions between actors give rise to social configurations that take on a life of their own and cannot be reduced to constituent components even though actors remain dependent upon those components.
- Social networks are dynamic and responsive to changes in the actors, subgroups, and ties between actors.

When considering which ties (i.e., relationships) to include in a network, it is important to consider the purpose of the tie and its function within the network. As one of the two most basic building blocks of a network, ties also convey a particular meaning and context, depending upon their characteristics. This is because ties function as conduits. As such, they aid or impede the flow of various types of material and nonmaterial "goods," such as information, sentiment, financial resources, norms, diseases, opinions, or trust. In terms of dark networks, propaganda, finances, and weapons are all examples of material and nonmaterial goods that frequently flow throughout networks.

Ties can also convey benefits that are relatively intangible. For example, "there is a mountain of research showing that people with strong ties are happier and even healthier because in such networks members provide one another with strong emotional and material support in times of grief or trouble and someone with whom to share life's joys and triumphs" (Stark 2007:37). Similarly, feelings of trust and solidarity are also more likely to be shared across strong ties. For example, Krackhardt (1992), in a study of a Silicon Valley high-tech firm undergoing a unionization campaign, found that employees tended to rely on those with whom they were strongly tied in making their final decision. However, whereas strong ties may offer support, weaker ties may provide reach and access into the network (Onnela et al. 2007). Granovetter's (1973, 1974) study of how people found their current jobs found that, rather than using formal channels of job search, people were far more likely to have used their personal contacts, in particular, individuals whom they saw rarely or occasionally. These comparatively "weaker" ties connected them to groups distinct from their immediate social circles. As such, they formed bridges between groups and provided information and/or introductions that the job seekers could not otherwise access. Granovetter's work suggests, "that whatever is to be diffused"—whether it is job information, influence, resources, trust, etc.—it "will reach a larger number of people, and travel a greater social distance (i.e., path length), when passed through weak ties rather than strong" (Granovetter 1973:1366).

A key point to understanding and conceptualizing social networks is the assumption that *actors do not make decisions autonomously* (i.e., in isolation). To many, this may be a difficult concept to process, but it is critical to understanding why SNA can be so powerful. The crux of the argument is that people are substantially influenced by the behavior and choices of other actors around them—both directly and indirectly. This assumption differs substantially from a rational choice perspective where actors act independently of those around them. Studies such as Solomon Asch's (1951, 1955) social conformity experiments, Stanley Milgram's (1974) obedience to authority experiments, and Philip Zimbardo's (1972, 2000) prison experiment all highlight how the networks in which actors are embedded influence the choices they make. Being influenced by other actors is not limited to individuals. As John Meyer, Woody Powell, and Paul DiMaggio (and their numerous colleagues) have demonstrated, groups, corporations, and nation-states are no more likely to act autonomously than are individuals (see e.g., DiMaggio and Powell 1983; Meyer et al. 1997; Meyer and Rowan 1977; Powell and DiMaggio 1991). For example, organizations that interact with one another tend to become more like one another over time. This tendency is not driven primarily by concerns such as the bottom line, but rather that these organizations wish to maintain their legitimacy in the eyes of other similar organizations. "When an organizational practice or structure becomes commonly understood as a defining feature of a 'legitimate' organization of a certain type, organizational elites feel pressure to institute that practice or structure. If there is a cultural norm that says, 'In order for an organization to be a good organization, it must have characteristic X,' organizations feel pressure to institute characteristic X" (Chaves 1997:32–33).

It is not uncommon for social scientists to refer to the concept of *social structure*, by which they generally mean the social institutions that have become so embedded that they shape behavior. Social structures "constrain who is present, where they stand, what they can do, and how they are related to each other. This structure is as real as the buildings that people occupy" (Turner 2006:88). Although such structures may be "real" to those who are part of the system, they are notoriously ephemeral and difficult to measure, which is why many analysts find SNA so attractive. It allows analysts to capture social structures in terms of enduring patterns of ties between actors and thus provides a method for systematically and empirically studying the causes and consequences embedded in social structures (Degenne and Forse 1999).

Correspondingly, it follows that *actors' attitudes, beliefs, intentions, behavior, and even their identities are largely determined by their location in the social structure*. This assumption is at odds with what many of us moderns believe to be true (McAdam, Tarrow and Tilly 2001). The impact of social structure on actor behavior can be illustrated by examining what social scientists have learned about the process of conversion (recruitment) to religious and social movements. These studies show that people who are structurally (i.e., socially) close to a particular movement are much more likely to join that movement than are those who are not (Lofland and Stark 1965; McAdam 1988b; McAdam and Paulsen 1993; Snow, Zurcher and Ekland-Olson 1980; Stark and Bainbridge 1980). In other words, people seldom join groups randomly. Instead, they are more likely to join groups that are socially proximate to them. In other words, the structural location of actors is a large factor in determining which groups they will join and which ones they will not.

Given then that the repeated social interactions and social proximity comprise multiple forms of influence that exert themselves upon network members, it follows that *the pattern of ties extant in a network can take on the characteristics of a subsystem, effectively developing a "life of their own."*

This assumption makes explicit the idea that repeated interactions between actors can give rise to social formations (e.g., groups, formal organizations, and nations) that take on a life of their own, follow their own logic, and cannot be meaningfully reduced or explained by their constituent parts even though they remain dependent upon those parts (Clayton and Davies 2006; White 2008). Emergent properties of networks, such as the social formations that are products of interactions between actors, cannot be entirely explained by looking solely at the characteristics of those actors. Instead, they can be examined using SNA without needing to examine the network at a more atomic level.

The concept of emergent phenomena in networks depends largely upon the observation that the networks are social in nature and therefore nonstatic, which is why it is assumed that *networks are always changing as actors enter and leave the network and as ties form and dissolve*. Although social network analysts have always known this, historically, longitudinal network data have been difficult to come by and methods for their analysis were undeveloped (Wasserman and Faust 1994:730–31). This situation is beginning to change. Longitudinal network data and their analysis are becoming more common. Much of the analysis to date has been largely descriptive in nature, but the development of new approaches are allowing analysts to uncover the underlying processes that may be at work in particular networks (Breiger, Carley and Pattison 2003b; McCulloh and Carley 2011; Snijders 2005; Snijders, Bunt and Steglich 2010).

1.5 SOCIAL NETWORKS IN HUMAN SOCIETY

The concepts that drive the field of network analysis place a heavy emphasis on the manner in which networks and the processes that drive them, in turn, drive human—and organizational—actions. All of this can have the unfortunate effect of making network forces appear to be largely deterministic in nature. In many cases, this is merely a misconception, although, in some instances, determinism is a fairly close reflection of what the theories are meant to convey.

Emirbayer and Goodwin (1994:1424–36) identified three social network paradigms to which most social network analysts adhere: structural determinism, structural instrumentalism, and structural constructionism. The first, structural determinism, leaves no room for human agency or culture. It entirely ignores (or dismisses) the possible causal role that actors' beliefs, values, and commitments play in terms of social processes and historical change. The early writings of Harrison White (Boorman and White 1976; White, Boorman and Breiger 1976) reflect this view, as do those of the early network theorist, Bruce Mayhew (1980, 1981), for whom individuals are no more than biological machines (Smith 2010). Free will for structural determinists, in other words, does not exist.

By contrast, structural instrumentalism does allow room for human agency, but it tends to view it solely in terms of rational choice, instrumental action, and utility maximization. Roger Gould's (1991, 1993) masterful analyses of the Paris Commune and Nan Lin's (2001) work on social capital are examples of this, as are the numerous studies of religious phenomena by Rodney Stark and his colleagues (see, e.g., Finke and Stark 2005; Iannaccone, Finke and Stark 1997; Stark 1996, 2000; Stark and Bainbridge 1985; Stark and Iannaccone 1994). Given that ample evidence exists supporting the premise that actors do respond to incentives (see, e.g., Becker 1976; Berman 2009; Iannaccone 1994; Levitt and Dubner 2005), this perspective clearly improves on the previous one. Nevertheless, it is not without its weaknesses.

Structural constructionism, like structural instrumentalism, takes seriously the role of human agency, but unlike structural instrumentalism, it sees actors as motivated by additional concerns, such as norms, values, cultural commitments, and collective and individual identities. Adherents to this perspective hold that culture plays a role as well. Doug McAdam's studies of Freedom Summer (1986, 1988a) are examples of this approach, as are Harrison White's later writings (1992, 2008), with his emphasis on the importance of narratives, stories, and networks of meaning.

Why might this be important? The constraints and opportunities afforded to actors by the networks in which they are embedded cannot be considered apart from the cultural influences, normative commitments, and instrumental concerns of the actors involved. Some dark networks, such as drug cartels, may be motivated by instrumental concerns, whereas other networks, such as religious groups, may be motivated by normative ones. Thus, if we are to gain a better understanding of dark networks, then we need take into account the norms, values, cultural commitments that drive actors' preferences.

1.6 SUMMARY: LESSONS LEARNED

This chapter has provided an overview of social network analysis, how it differs from other analytic approaches, the basic terms and concepts that it employs, the key assumptions that underlie much, if not all, of what social network analysts do. These assumptions are provided to offer a glimpse into the background and motivations that inform network theory. These assumptions are more often implicit than explicit in the work of social network analysts, and may therefore be difficult to discern unless stated directly. The assumptions, basic terms, and—to some degree—the history of the field, provide the foundation for what we cover in later chapters. For instance, the various centrality metrics that we will examine provide analysts with a sense of actors' structural locations. Similarly, measures of density and centralization attempt to capture the overall structure of a social network. We will not always draw explicit ties between these assumptions and specific metrics, but hopefully they should become more and more obvious the longer you immerse yourself in this field. This chapter also took up the related issues of culture and human agency and what role they play in SNA. As we saw, not all social network analysts include human agency and culture into their causal models, but when it comes to crafting strategies for disrupting dark networks, such factors cannot be ignored. The crafting of strategies is the topic of the next chapter, to which we now turn.

1.7 QUESTIONS

1. Link analysis is the same as social network analysis.
   a. True.
   b. False.
2. In social network analysis, an actor can be
   a. An individual.
   b. A tribe.
   c. A country.
   d. An IED (improvised exploding device).
   e. All of the above.
3. Attribute data
   a. Are never used by social network analysts.
   b. Are nonrelational characteristics of individual actors in a network.
   c. Are also known as affiliation data.
   d. Are also known as asymmetric data.
   e. All of the above.
4. Social network analysis is a set of theories and techniques originally designed to understand social media.
   a. True.
   b. False.
5. All of the following are basic assumptions of social network analysis except
   a. Ties between actors function as conduits for the transfer or flow of information, sentiment, material and/or nonmaterial goods, or other resources (e.g., funds, supplies, information, trust, and enmity).
   b. Actors, along with their actions and motivations, are interdependent, rather than independent, with other actors.

c. An actor's position in the social structure impacts his or her beliefs, norms, and behavior.
d. Enduring patterns of interaction do not reflect social structure.

6. A *path* is defined as a *walk* (i.e., a sequence of actors and ties) in which no actor between the first and last actor of the walk occurs more than once.
   a. True.
   b. False.
7. The *path distance* between two actors is the number of steps between the two actors.
   a. True.
   b. False.

1.8 ANSWERS

1. False.
2. All of the above (e).
3. Are nonrelational characteristics of individual actors in a network (b).
4. False.
5. Enduring patterns of interaction do not reflect social structure (d).
6. True.
7. True.

1.9 FURTHER READING

For exploring the history of social network analysis, Linton C. Freeman's *The Development of Social Network Analysis: A Study in the Sociology of Science* (Vancouver, Canada: Empirical Press, 2004) is invaluable, as is his 2011 follow-up chapter, "The Development of Social Network Analysis—with an Emphasis on Recent Events," which appears in *The SAGE Handbook of Social Network Analysis*, edited by John Scott and Peter J. Carrington (Los Angeles and London: SAGE Publications Inc.).

There are a number of excellent introductions to social network analysis. A good place to start is Alexandra Marin and Barry Wellman's "Social Network Analysis: An Introduction," which is in the same edited volume as Freeman's. Indeed, the chapters in *The SAGE Handbook of Social Network Analysis* cover numerous aspects of social network analysis that readers may find interesting.

The "Bible" for doing social network analysis is, of course, Stanely Wasserman and Katherine Faust's *Social Network Analysis: Methods and Applications* (Cambridge, UK: Cambridge University Press, 1994). However, there are a number of excellent texts that cover more recent developments in the field:

- Stephen P. Borgatti, Martin G. Everett, and Jeffrey C. Johnson. 2013. *Analyzing Social Networks*. Thousand Oaks, CA: Sage Publishing—an excellent introduction that is especially valuable for users of UCINET (Borgatti and Everett are its current custodians).
- Wouter de Nooy, Andrej Mrvar, and Vladimir Batagelj. 2011. *Exploratory Social Network Analysis with Pajek*. Cambridge, UK: Cambridge University Press—another fine introduction that features worked examples from the software package, Pajek.
- David Easley and Jon Kleinberg. 2010. *Networks, Crowds and Markets: Reasoning About a Highly Connected World*. Cambridge and New York: Cambridge University Press—an introduction written by an economist and computer scientist.
- Robert A. Hanneman and Mark Riddle. 2005. *Introduction to Social Network Methods*. Riverside, CA: University of California, Riverside (published in digital form at http://faculty.ucr.edu/~hanneman/)—an online text that provides worked examples using UCINET.
- Charles Kadushin. 2011. *Understanding Social Networks: Theories, Concepts, and Findings*. Oxford and New York: Oxford University Press—an introduction by one of the giants in the field.
- Ian McCulloh, Helen Armstrong, and Anthony Johnson. 2013. *Social Network Analysis with Applications*. New York, NY: Wiley—an introduction that includes worked examples from the social network analysis package, Organizational Risk Analyzer (ORA).
- Christina Prell. 2011. *Social Network Analysis: History, Theory & Methodology*. London and Thousand Oaks, CA: SAGE Publications—a gentle introduction to social network analysis that also includes excellent discussion of recent developments.
- Garry L. Robins. 2015. *Doing Social Network Research: Network-based Research Design for Social Scientists*. London: SAGE—a book by one of the developers of the PNet suite of programs that estimate exponential random graph models (ERGMs or p*), which focuses on the how to conduct social network research.
- John Scott. 2013. *Social Network Analysis*. London and Thousand Oaks, CA: SAGE Publications Ltd—a classic introduction that is now in its third edition.

NOTES

1. A notable exception to this rule is the treatment of multimode networks.

2. A dyad is a pair of actors with a tie between them. A triad is a set of three actors that may or may not have ties between them.

3. It may help to think of transitivity (and balance) in terms of the following aphorisms: a friend of a friend is also a friend, an enemy of an enemy is a friend, and an enemy of a friend is an enemy. These sayings are reflective of the social forces that the concept of transitivity was designed to capture. When a triad is unbalanced, it is expected that such forces put a strain on the configuration until balance is achieved. For a broad introduction to this topic, see Wasserman and Faust (1994).

Chapter 2

Strategic Options for Disrupting Dark Networks

When one is confronted with the need to collect relevant information quickly, it helps a great deal to have a strong sense of the possible uses for that information. In the case of dark networks, it is all too often assumed that the information will be applied to the task of identifying high-value targets for the purpose of capture or elimination. Although such approaches may indeed serve to disrupt the network of interest, they also hold the potential to reconfigure the network to the point that any existing information is of questionable value for future analyses. To be sure, there are clear advantages to using kinetic approaches in terms of speed and symbolic value, but the costs in terms of casualties, community disruption, and retaliatory actions can be similarly immense. Given that there are trade-offs associated with any decision, it is important for analysts to consider potential options for countering dark networks as a natural accompaniment to analytic findings.

Perhaps the largest impediment for analysts who are interested in presenting potential options is the incredible dearth of work in the area of network disruption of this sort (Everton 2012a; Roberts and Everton 2011). Few attempts have been made to structure strategies for countering dark networks, and with few exceptions (*see*, e.g., Lempert et al. 2008), little or no research has compared alternative strategies with a view of balancing potential gains and costs. This brief but important chapter presents some of the options and decision points that are open to analysts working with dark networks. It begins by presenting a work-plan for integrating one or more strategic options for disrupting dark networks with the analysis of those networks. Next, it discusses hypothesis development as a critical element for developing a relevant analytic plan. The chapter then proceeds to distinguish between two broad approaches to countering dark networks: kinetic and nonkinetic.

The former involves aggressive and offensive measures designed to eliminate or capture network members and their supporters, while the latter involves the use of subtle, noncoercive means designed to reduce a network's effectiveness and impair their willingness to fight. The chapter concludes with a brief discussion of the analytic process and a reflection on the proper uses of social network analysis (SNA) in informing proposals for alternatives to disrupt covert and illegal networks.

2.1 CRAFTING STRATEGIES WITH SOCIAL NETWORK ANALYSIS

As with most analytic efforts, the returns gained from developing strategies that are based on network analysis are an almost direct result of the effort that went into them. This is important to keep in mind, as the task of strategy building is iterative, often involving both exploratory analysis and confirmatory analysis (i.e., hypothesis testing). Exploratory SNA "involves visualization and manipulation of concrete networks, whereas hypothesis testing boils down to numbers representing abstract parameters and probabilities" (de Nooy, Mrvar and Batagelj 2011:xxviii). The general process for crafting strategies to disrupt or otherwise counter dark networks hinges upon a focus on the context of network disruption. In a typical application, analysts will find themselves revisiting that context multiple times throughout the analytic process. A generalized outline for carrying this out is as follows:

1. Develop working hypotheses about network disruption
   a. Revisit background research regarding actors, their culture, and other factors
   b. Ask thoughtful analytic questions (exploratory and/or explanatory)
   c. Weigh the relative costs and benefits of various kinetic and nonkinetic actions
2. Identify, define, and record relationships of interest
   a. Create a codebook
   b. Identify boundaries
   c. Collect and record data
   d. Clean and format data
3. Analyze data and interpret results
   a. Select methods (descriptive or confirmatory analyses)
   b. Employ methods
4. Recast and present strategies for the disruption of the network
   a. Fuse with other data and information
   b. Make Recommendation

While we focus on each of these steps in more depth later, it is appropriate to discuss some of them briefly before proceeding. Also note this is not a strict, formal process, but rather a set of steps to guide analysts examining dark networks.

2.2 STRATEGIC OPTIONS FOR DISRUPTING DARK NETWORKS

Developing Working Hypotheses about Disruption

Before beginning any analyses, it is critical to establish a direction of research and workflow. It is not uncommon for particular scenarios to demand a particular response. At other times, analysts may possess greater leeway or leverage in developing one or more recommended options for disrupting a network. In such situations, they first need to develop working (i.e., tentative) hypotheses as to how best to disrupt the dark network they are analyzing. The environments in which the network operates and the individuals involved generally determine how these hypotheses are constructed. It is important that analysts not become too closely wedded to any of the hypotheses at this stage, as this is an iterative process, with ample opportunity for discovery and modification of initial expectations regarding the nature of the network and its members.

Hypotheses are falsifiable statements that may be tested for their veracity. As such, they should always be grounded in informed expectations. Analysts should therefore conduct a careful review of any available background information on the network, its constituent actors, the environment and culture in which it operates, and any other information that will provide useful background. Other venues for developing expectations include consultations with subject matter experts and examinations of analogous situations. The stopping point for the initial inquiry process will be dictated by the needs of the analysts. Analysts who already possess substantial subject matter expertise may wish to only spend some time reviewing notes or discussing the scenario with colleagues. Those new to the particular network, however, should spend a substantial effort on this portion of the work. The benefits will take the form of a reduction in the need to restart efforts or reformulate expectations.

Once analysts have built or refreshed their background knowledge, they are in a position to consider whether they intend to use kinetic or nonkinetic approaches or a combination of both, and then determine which relationships of interest best lend themselves to their chosen strategies.[1] Some, for example, may decide that the best approach is to target a network's financial ties, believing that shutting down or disrupting the flow of funds will result in greater disruptions down the line as it becomes difficult for the network to finance operations. Others may conclude that targeting a network's operational ties offers the best opportunity for disruption, assuming that without its key operatives, a network will not have the specific personnel necessary to carry out operations. Still others may seek to sow distrust among network members, with the expectation that inflamed interpersonal rivalries will cause the network to implode from within. Some may choose not to focus on a network's individual ties at all but instead on its formal and informal ties, arguing that it may be more efficient to disrupt a network by focusing on the groups and organizations that helped give rise to and currently sustain it. For example, in the fight against radical forms of Islam, analysts could identify central jihadi schools and build alternative schools nearby, ones that promote moderate forms of Islam and instruct students in subjects other than the memorization of the Qur'an (Roberts and Everton 2011). This would clearly constitute a long-term strategy, one that aims not so much at disrupting the network's current contours but one that aims to deprive it of a key resource. Analysts can then ask a host of analytic questions, either exploratory or explanatory, about their network once they have decided on their approach.

As one considers the options available in terms of network disruption, it becomes clear that each approach tends to demand a very different conceptualization of the network and the ties that define it. The strategy, or strategies, that analysts select will, therefore, govern the type of data that must be collected. Before beginning to collect data, or pulling data from an existing database on a dark network, researchers need to first develop working hypotheses as to how they plan to disrupt the network. Bypassing this stage in the research setup will either prevent what could have been promising strategies from being considered, or force the analyst to go back to the data collection stage at a later stage in the process.

Kinetic versus Nonkinetic

Of the two general approaches that may be applied to combating dark networks, the kinetic approach tends to receive more attention by far. This is largely due to the symbolic value that the capture or elimination of high-value targets achieves as it attracts headlines and generates popular support. Recall the media attention (and spontaneous celebrations across the United States) that the removal of Osama bin Laden engendered. The nonkinetic approach, which typically requires patience, usually attracts far less attention, partially because of its lack of newsworthiness, and partially because nonkinetic approaches often require subterfuge that would be compromised through media attention. Nevertheless, the former U.S. Special Operations Commander, Admiral Eric T. Olson, has invested attention and effort into shifting the emphasis away from kinetic, high-profile raids and toward the use of more nonkinetic approaches. He notes that while kinetic action may be "urgent and necessary" in the short run, he believes that it is merely "a holding action that buys time for" nonkinetic approaches to have their "effects" (quoted in Roberts and Everton 2011:4). Because of the importance that these two approaches play in counterinsurgency operations, both are explored here.

Table 2.1 summarizes these options. Of course, a single approach seldom will be sufficient to disrupt a major network. It is not uncommon for multiple strategies to be adopted, some focused on the short term, some on the long term. Moreover, analysts must take into account unanticipated second- (and third- and fourth-)order effects. For example, implementing a raid to capture an insurgent in an otherwise friendly neighborhood is its first-order effect, but a second-order effect may be to decrease support for the host nation government and increase support for the insurgents if done incorrectly. If the second-order effects of a successful but unpopular raid begin to outweigh the first-order benefits, the secondary effects should take precedence in the planning cycle. Analysts and decision makers must also remember the role of agency in social networks where actors respond and react to both endogenous and exogenous effects on the network. It is critical that analysts and decision makers avoid the trap of seeing actors simply as data points as opposed to the humans they represent. Clearly, commanders and policy officials must consider kinetic and nonkinetic actions, approaches, and most importantly effects together as a net positive or net negative in order to most effectively craft strategies for disrupting dark networks. Some of these trade-offs and n-order effects should become clear as we consider the various options.

Kinetic Approach

Kinetic operations target enemy combatants and their supporters with the goal of neutralizing, capturing, or eliminating high-value targets. As such, they are typically referred to as *targeting strategies* and can be pursued at various levels (e.g., individual, group, and organizational). The kinetic approach typically involves the removal of key actors or the severing of ties between such actors. When individuals are the target, such as the capture or elimination of Saddam Hussein, Abu Musab al-Zarqawi, or Osama bin Laden, the U.S.

Table 2.1 Strategic Options of Social Network Analysis

	Kinetic	*Nonkinetic*				
Strategies	Targeting	Track, Monitor	PsyOp	Information Operations	Rehabilitate/ Reintegrate	Institution Building
Level	Individual, Group, and Institutional					

military describes such operations as man-hunting (Marks, Meer, and Nilson 2005); when groups or organizations are the target, they are referred to as group or organizational targeting (Roberts and Everton 2011).

Nonkinetic Approach

Nonkinetic approaches seek to undermine dark networks with more subtle use of power. The goal is typically to secure the population's safety and support while weakening the enemy's influence and control (Galula [1964] 2006; Kilcullen 2010; McCormick 2005; Nagl 2005; Sepp 2005) and thereby having numerous and varied methods to accomplish this goal: tracking and monitoring, institution building, psychological operations (PsyOp), information operations (IO), and rehabilitation and reintegration programs. Like the kinetic approach, nonkinetic approaches can be applied at the individual, group, or organizational level.

Tracking and Monitoring

Although it may seem counterintuitive, sometimes the best strategy may be to only watch and wait. Because information on a particular dark network is often incomplete, rather than taking immediate action, it is sometimes better in the short run to track and monitor certain actors with the hope of improving our knowledge of the network, which will in turn improve the selection of strategies adopted down the road (Arquilla 2008). This approach can therefore actually call for relatively dynamic participation on the part of analysts, who may take an active part in identifying individuals, upon whom to focus resources. The metrics offered through social network analyses provide an exceptional fit for the task of selecting individuals, subgroups, organizations, and so on, that could lead to critical revelations about the parts of the network that still remain obscured.

Institution Building

The strategy of institution building is an approach used to undermine the network's legitimacy in the eyes of the local populace by performing reconstruction in war-torn communities and building goodwill in the process. This approach requires the active involvement of civil affairs forces that provide humanitarian and civic assistance and work in tandem with intergovernmental and interagency partners in the reconstruction process. The emphasis is on building healthy host-government institutions of governance, rule of law, economic development, and transportation infrastructure (Fridovich and Krawchuck 2007; Kilcullen 2009).

Psychological Operations (PsyOps)

Psychological operations are concerned with the dissemination of information for the purpose of influencing the emotions, perceptions, attitudes, objective reasoning, and ultimately the behavior of dark networks so that they are more aligned with one's goals and objectives during times of conflict and peace (U.S. Special Operations Command 2003). Approaches such as this are also employed to counter-adversary propaganda and to sow disaffection and mistrust among network members to reduce their will to fight and ultimately to induce their surrender. This strategy also includes tactics that attempt to set network members and/or subgroups against each other.

Information Operations (IO)

The information operations strategy uses integrated employment of electronic warfare and computer network operations to combat terrorism. In contrast to military doctrine (U.S. Director of Operations 2006), here psychological operations are separated from information operations because the latter puts a strong emphasis on technology-centric interventions that involve computer and other sophisticated electronic systems, while the former puts a strong emphasis on human factors. Examples include the disruption of fund transfers, the monitoring of charitable donations, the detection of money laundering, black market activity, and the drug trade. Activities also include interventions to compromise terrorists' cell phone and online connections and the use of these platforms to locate leaders and their followers.

Rehabilitation and Reintegration

A similar strategy involves providing the members of a network with a legitimate or productive role in society. The rehabilitation and reintegration strategy seeks to deplete dark networks of members and recruits by adding them back into civil society. An example is Singapore's counter-ideological program founded by Muslim scholars, which seeks to "correct" the thinking of its detainees and influence into the wider Muslim community by giving talks, disseminating publications, and hosting a website in order to "immunize" the minds of Singaporean Muslims against violent radical Islamist ideologies (Ramakrishna 2005, 2012). Similar rehabilitation programs also have been introduced in other countries such as Indonesia, Saudi Arabia, and Yemen (Boucek 2008; Fink and Hearne 2008; Horgan 2009), but it is unclear how effective they have been (Hwang, Panggabean and Fauzi 2013). If recent research on the effectiveness of U.S. faith-based prison programs to reduce recidivism is any guide, what may be necessary are "after care" programs that sort former detainees away from the networks that gave rise to their extremism in the first place and toward networks that support their new theological outlook (Johnson 2011). Indeed, Hwang et al. (2013:757) found that "the building of interpersonal relationships with those outside the jihadi circle, pressure from parents, and changing personal and professional priorities have all created positive pressures to encourage and reinforce disengagement." Defections inspired by this approach can be severely disruptive to clandestine networks that rely on the discretion of their members. Studies of insurgent groups have found that groups that keep defection to a minimum tend to be more successful than those that do not because defection can shut an insurgency down for months (Popkin 2007, cited in Berman 2009:29) because of the doubt it sows among insurgent leaders about how much information concerning operations has been compromised.

Informed Inquiry and Interpretation

Once an approach or a set of approaches has been selected, the analysts' data needs become much more apparent. These needs then drive the processes of creating a codebook, establishing network boundaries, and working with the resulting data (see chapter 3). The analysis and interpretation are similarly driven by the informational and contextual needs of the selected strategy. Social network metrics play an important role in making sense of a social network's dynamics. Analysts generally use a variety of descriptive metrics (rather than just one or two) in their attempts to gain an overall understanding of a network (see chapters 4–8). On other occasions, they may use more advanced statistical techniques (see chapters 9–11). These are not the only tools available to social network analysts, however. Network visualization is another helpful tool that can help us see patterns that may not be readily apparent by simply looking at tables of metrics (Brandes, Raab and Wagner 2001; Freeman 2000).[2] For example, a visualization that highlights the centrality of actors in a network may better illuminate the variation between actors than a corresponding table of centrality metrics. Little variation could lead analysts to conclude that it makes little sense to pursue a kinetic targeting strategy because there are several high-value targets. Or, sometimes, clustering algorithms provide multiple "solutions" as to the identity of subgroups within a network, and often the only way to decide between the various alternatives is through network visualization. In short, metrics and visualization are complementary parts of the SNA toolbox. Most network analysis programs either come with network mapping algorithms (e.g., Pajek, ORA, and Gephi) or integrate with network visualization programs that do (e.g., UCINET and NetDraw).

Crafting Strategies

At any point during the process of analysis and interpretation, it is appropriate to reevaluate the original hypotheses for their appropriateness to the selected strategies and to the data as well. Following Admiral Olson's observation that kinetic action is merely "a holding action that buys time for non-kinetic approaches to have their effects" (quoted in Roberts and Everton 2011:4), we may seek to implement a combination of kinetic and nonkinetic strategies. Or, if General Flynn is correct that kinetic attacks sometimes multiply enemies rather than decrease them (Flynn, Pottinger and Batchelor 2010), we may only consider nonkinetic strategies that will take longer to implement but may yield better results. The broader point is that SNA provides various ways of teasing out the nature of dark networks, which in turn provides us with valuable information as to what strategies may best disrupt them. Moreover, this process can result in information that should be subsequently fused with other types of analysis (e.g., geospatial and temporal) that can further inform recommendations to decision makers.

2.3 SUMMARY: LESSONS LEARNED

This chapter has presented a workflow for integrating strategy into analysis. In particular, it has outlined the role that SNA should play in the crafting of strategies for the disruption of dark networks. We began with a presentation of the workflow, followed by a brief overview and examples of how SNA may work in conjunction with crafting strategies for disrupting dark networks. This was followed by a more detailed discussion of the various strategic approaches and then moved to a very brief overview of the analytic process and how it recursively informs the hypotheses relating to potential strategies for disruption. Although the focus of the chapter remained concerned with how social network analysis can be useful for the crafting of strategic options within the kinetic and nonkinetic approaches, it also served the larger function of demonstrating how the process of conducting network analysis is not divorced from the larger goal of countering a dark network. Due to the practical focus of this chapter, the actual analysis process was sometimes given short shrift. The chapters that follow should more than make up for that and will greatly expand on the topic of analytic processes.

It should, however, be kept in mind that the use of SNA to support operations has its challenges. As noted in the preface, data on criminal groups, insurgencies, and terrorists can be difficult to collect and are often incomplete, meaning that analysts must use caution when crafting strategies. Another is that critics have challenged the use of SNA for military purposes, in particular, for targeting purposes (Kadushin 2005, 2012). This book shares this concern and reminds readers that not only may lethal targeting increase, rather than reduce, the level of violence, but also an emphasis on kinetic operations often neglects or minimizes SNA's use for rebuilding and rehabilitating purposes. Finally, the use of SNA to generate strategic options should not be confounded with decision-making. The latter depends on a whole host of issues—knowledge of context and local culture, and the assessment of risks, costs, and potential for unintended consequences, just to name a few (Moody 2005). SNA is a powerful tool, but it should not be seen as a silver bullet or substitute for other critical elements in the decision process. It can certainly inform decisions, but it should not determine them. That is why this book emphasizes the use of SNA for the *crafting* of alternative strategies for countering dark networks and how analytic results can help to inform which strategic decisions may be more promising.

2.4 QUESTIONS

1. Kinetic strategies can only be targeted at the individual level.
   a. True.
   b. False.
2. Nonkinetic strategies can be targeted at multiple levels.
   a. True.
   b. False.
3. Which of the following is not a nonkinetic strategy?
   a. Tracking and monitoring.
   b. Psychological operations.
   c. Kill and capture.
   d. Rehabilitation.
   e. All of the above are nonkinetic strategies.
4. Actor agency is an important factor to consider when using social network analysis to develop and implement strategic approaches against dark networks.
   a. True.
   b. False.
5. The application of social network analysis often can be an iterative process.
   a. True.
   b. False.
6. What below should drive the application of social network analysis to examine dark networks?
   a. Data collection.
   b. Strategy.

c. Analytic methods.
d. Data cleaning.
e. The software you are using.

2.5 ANSWERS

1. False.
2. True.
3. Kill and capture (c).
4. True.
5. True.
6. Strategy (b).

2.6 FURTHER READING

We highly recommend the series of articles by Jörg Raab and H. Brinton Milward that helped coin the term, "Dark Networks": "Dark Networks as Problems." *Journal of Public Administration Research and Theory* 13 (2003):413–39; "Dark Networks as Organizational Problems: Elements of a Theory." *International Public Management Journal* 9 (2006):333–60; and "A Preliminary Theory of Dark Network Resilience." *Journal of Policy Analysis and Management* 31 (2011 – with René M. Bakker):33–62.

Then there is the article by Nancy Roberts and Sean F. Everton—"Strategies for Combating Dark Networks." *Journal of Social Structure*, 12(2)—which forms the basis of the strategies outlined in this chapter (see also, Sean F. Everton, Chapter 2 of *Disrupting Dark Networks* (Cambridge and New York: Cambridge University Press, 2012)).

In addition, there are a number of excellent articles and books that explore the nature of dark networks and how they might be undermined:

- Kathleen M. Carley, Ju-Sung Lee, and David Krackhardt. 2002. "Destabilizing Networks." *Connections* 24:79–92.
- Luke Gerdes (ed.). 2015. *Illuminating Dark Networks: The Study of Clandestine Groups and Organizations*. New York and Cambridge: Cambridge University Press.
- Peter Klerks. 2001. "The Network Paradigm Applied to Criminal Organisations: Theoretical Nitpicking or a Relevant Doctrine for Investigators? Recent Developments in the Netherlands." *Connections* 24:53–65.
- Valdis Krebs. 2002. "Mapping Networks of Terrorist Cells." *Connections* 24:43–52.

- Marc Sageman. 2004. *Understanding Terror Networks*. Philadelphia, PA: University of Pennsylvania Press.
- Malcom K. Sparrow. 1991. "The Application of Network Analysis to Criminal Intelligence: An Assessment of the Prospects." *Social Networks* 13:251–74.

NOTES

1. In many cases, analysts will gravitate toward the focus of their organization, or in the case of military personnel, their Military Occupational Specialty (MOS). For example, Psychological Operations (PSYOP) military personnel will tend to focus on nonkinetic strategies to disrupt dark networks.

2. Some of the more common visualization algorithms include the Fruchterman Reingold (Fruchterman and Reingold 1991), Kamada-Kawai (1989), multidimensional scaling (MDS), and spring-embedded algorithms.

Chapter 3

Collecting, Coding, and Manipulating Social Network Data

Most analysts currently learn social network analysis (SNA) using available, ready-to-use data. Many, if not all, software packages such as UCINET, NetDraw, Pajek, ORA, and R either, come bundled with practice data, or they have companion websites that make such data available. Analysts can utilize these data to examine a host of network-related questions. In the real world, however, we have to conduct several important steps prior to analyzing dark networks, including the development of analytic questions, creating a coding scheme, and collecting, recording, and manipulating data. Knowing how to do these are important first steps in efficiently and effectively conducting SNA. Unfortunately, many analysts fail to give these steps proper attention prior to conducting analysis. Admittedly these steps can often be tedious and time consuming. The advancement of network tools and technologies, and the potential they provide, also leads many analysts to want to skip directly to analysis and presentation. The failure to take one's time and thoughtfully conduct these important steps prior to analysis, however, will not only reduce the effectiveness of the analysis but also lead to errors that could force analysts to spend additional time and resources repeating several steps during their analysis.

This chapter focuses on properly setting up a network analysis in a manner that saves time, frustration, and effort. It briefly presents a simple outline for the data collection process, followed by a more detailed discussion of the development of analytic questions before diving into the nuts and bolts of coding, collecting, recording, and manipulating data. It then considers how social network analysts specify a network's boundaries, the difference between personal (ego) and whole networks, the various types of social network data, and the variety of ways that network analysts collect social network data. Only after addressing each of these considerations will we be ready to collect, record, and manipulate actual social network data.

3.1 A PROCESS FOR DESIGNING AND COLLECTING NETWORK DATA

The process for collecting high-quality network data is deceptively simple. Although the steps outlined below are generally intuitive and straightforward, it is common to see people skip a step in a rush to getting their analysis up and running. Such "shortcuts" routinely require analysts to go back later in order to repair or reconstruct a faulty or poorly conceived data collection effort. The general process consists of the following:

1. Construct a set of analytic questions.
2. Decide on what you will need to know, at minimum, to answer the analytic questions.
3. Specify the boundaries for the network.
4. Keep a record of emerging data definitions in a codebook.
5. Select a method and tools to collect data.
6. Begin data collection.

The order of the above-listed items is somewhat flexible and is presented as a suggestion for how someone may wish to structure their inquiry. But, every network analysis is at least somewhat unique, as are the motivations behind that inquiry. Some may wish to start with a question and then select a particular network to which that question applies. Others may find more success in recursively readdressing many of these stages from time to time. It is a very rare case indeed, however, when the setup of a successful analysis does not begin with a question and end with collecting data.

3.2 ANALYTIC QUESTIONS

The development of an analytic question, or sets of questions, is a crucial step prior to conducting any type of analysis. SNA is no exception. As described in chapter 2, analysts should first decide whether they intend to recommend kinetic or nonkinetic strategies, which is a decision often based on the mission and the focus of the analyst or the analyst's organization. For example, a psychological operations team operating overseas or a domestic police unit will likely choose from nonkinetic approaches. Once that framework is established, they can ask a range of analytic questions, that when answered, can inform strategies they craft and the policies they recommend.

A nontrivial drawback of SNA comes in the form of the "bright, shiny object" factor. SNA has captured the attention of a cohort of people who understand that it can be an interesting and powerful tool, but do not understand how it works or what is involved in network inquiry. Generally speaking, SNA does hold the potential to reveal unique information about a group of entities and their various relationships. However, it is not enough to simply visualize a hastily constructed network in the hope that it will "reveal" something profound. Although revelations of this sort sometimes occur, they are rare and more typically just one of the additional benefits of a strategic and well-crafted analytic design.

The analytic question posed within a strategic framework should guide analysts through the "design," collection, and analytic phases of their examination. The failure to develop a clear analytic question, or sets of questions, will not only reduce the accuracy of the analysis, but it will also cost analysts significant time and resources during their analysis. For instance, analysts without access to existing data or a clear purpose in mind run the risk of collecting data irrelevant to the analysis, which will likely cause them to collect additional data down the road to correct for their initial error.[1] It is beyond the scope of this section to outline a comprehensive list of approaches for developing sound analytic questions. Readers new to network analysis should consider consulting the excellent texts written by Prell (2011), Borgatti et al. (2013), and Robins (2015) that, in addition to highlighting the importance of research design, dedicate sections to developing network-related research questions. That being said, analysts should consider a few things pertaining to the development of analytic questions.

The process a practitioner should follow in developing an analytic question differs somewhat from most scholarly network analysis studies, which are often driven by the intellectual interests of the researcher. To be sure, practitioners sometimes develop questions in the same manner, but in most cases they are chosen based on a particular incident (e.g., a shooting), information gap, or a superior's requirement. The fact that someone (or something) else is driving the question means there is room for several points of view about how to interpret the problem at hand. It is important, therefore, that analysts ensure that concepts embedded in the question are clearly defined before moving forward. For instance, a military commander may request that analysts examine a particular dark network's "support network" based on an information gap. The term "support network" is important, and its meaning should not be assumed. It is therefore the analysts' task to clarify what information is most important to defining and setting up the network to be analyzed. Does "support," in this case, indicate active, passive, or some combination of support? How should they define passive support versus active support? At what point does passive support become active support? These types of questions, which are similar to the types of questions scholars may ask during their research design, are particularly crucial for practitioners because they typically have to collect and analyze data with a host of other individuals (e.g., collectors), many of whom will have different conceptualizations or interpretations of the term "support" network.

Network analysts can ask a host of questions that fall within two general categories: exploratory and explanatory. The former are typically broader types of questions that take place at the early stages of analysis and will guide analysts through an exploration of new and unfamiliar data. These types of questions lead analysts to better understand the data at hand through a series of exploratory techniques and visualizations. Analysts can then use descriptive measures, such as those that fall within centrality or topographical approaches, to describe the "important" actors and/or the shape of the network. They cannot, however, safely make an argument about the underlying causes of that structure, or what characteristics contribute to actors becoming central, using only exploratory techniques and visualizations. For instance, analysts, using visualizations and common descriptive measures, may discover that a dark network exhibits high levels of clustering, but they cannot know whether the clustering is caused by a specific variable (e.g., transitive closure) or a set of variables (e.g., transitive closure combined with homophily). This is not to suggest that exploratory techniques are not useful, but rather that analysts and decision makers must be aware of the differences between exploratory and explanatory analysis and the types of answers they can provide. Chapters 4–8 provide several exploratory (or descriptive) techniques for examining dark networks. The following are examples of exploratory questions that analysts can ask at the early stages of their analysis (adapted from Everton 2012a:43):

- What is the network's overall structure? Does it exhibit characteristics (e.g., density, centralization, cohesion, fragmentation) that might indicate whether it is more or less effective than other networks?
- Are there some ties that appear to be more constitutive to the network than others (e.g., financial ties)? If so, is it possible and desirable to exploit the network at a different level (e.g., the charity network)?
- Are there any subnetworks within the larger network? Are there seams between them that can be exploited (e.g., drive a wedge between)? Can more peripheral subgroups be targeted for rehabilitation or redirection campaigns, or infiltration?
- Are there key actors or ties between actors whose removal or isolation (e.g., by being discredited) that will render the network less effective? If so, is it feasible to do so? Could there be any second-, third-, or fourth-order effects (e.g., causing the network to become more violent, generating hostility among the surrounding community) in pursuing such a policy? What about at the organizational level?
- Do some actors hold structurally equivalent positions in the network with other actors? Since such actors are essentially substitutable for one another, this could indicate potential emergent leaders or organizational

redundancies. That is, when a particular actor is removed, there is a strong probability that they will be replaced with a structurally equivalent actor. This could help identify a particular strategy's second-order effects.

- Are there key actors who could be targeted for the diffusion of misinformation or monitored in order to improve our knowledge of the network?
- Are there peripheral actors that could possibly be enticed to leave the network, making it more vulnerable to disruption or isolation?
- How has the network changed over time? What has previous research and case studies told us about how dark networks adapt to exogenous and endogenous shocks?

Explanatory questions are more specific and often arise from exploratory and qualitative analyses. Where exploratory questions can assist analysts with developing hypotheses, explanatory questions can help with testing them. For example, an analyst tasked with examining a specific insurgent group's recruitment network may notice in their data that many recent recruits are affiliated with particular academic institutions and political groups. Many analysts will be tempted to stop there and assume there is something about these academic and political institutions that is causing successful insurgent recruitment. That can be problematic. One reason is that the analyst cannot establish a *causal* relationship between successful recruitment and actor affiliation (academic and political institutions) without actually testing their hypothesis. A second, related reason is that additional relational and nonrelational (i.e., attributes) factors may be at play for which they need to control, such as the role of trust between existing members and new recruits. In other words, analysts should consider and simultaneously test several plausible effects to better understand network phenomena. Those familiar with basic statistics will be familiar with these problems and recognize they are not unique to network analysis.

Explanatory questions, often stated as formal hypotheses, generally require more thought than exploratory questions because analysts must first identify both independent and dependent variables. Networks can serve as independent or dependent variables (or both in some cases like QAP and MRQAP) depending on the question at hand. Independent variables, or explanatory variables, are those that help explain how the network or relations contribute to some behavior or outcome. For example, analysts can examine how a set of relations predicts another (Krackhardt 1988). Dependent, or outcome variables, can help analysts test questions about which independent variables (e.g., attributes, relations, and micro-tie structures) contribute to an observed network of interest. Recently, many scholars have utilized exponential random graph models (ERGMs or p*) and stochastic actor-oriented models to examine several generative processes of dark networks (Cunningham, Everton and Murphy 2015; Papachristos, Braga and Hureau 2012; Papachristos, Hureau and Braga 2013). Chapters 10–12 outline several explanatory techniques for examining dark networks, including ERGMs, along with several considerations for using statistical models with relational data, such as testing statistical significance. The following are a sample of potential explanatory questions that analysts can ask:

- Do certain types of relationships predict others in a particular context? For example, do close personal ties predict operational collaboration between dark network actors? Do kinship and friendship ties predict successful recruitment?
- What types of strategies help shape a network's overall structure? For instance, have specific kinetic or nonkinetic strategies contributed increasing centralization in particular dark network?
- What are the generative processes that led to a network's structure? Are these processes purely structural (i.e., endogenous)? Are they driven by actor-relation effects (i.e., attributes and relations)? To what extent are exogenous contextual factors, such as geospatial factors, contributing to an observed network structure?
- Does an observed dark network have a tendency toward network closure? In other words, is there a high probability that "friends of my friends are my friends?" (i.e., transitive closure).
- Are well-connected actors, or "popular actors," at an advantage in the formation of new ties (i.e., preferential attachment)? What does that mean for targeting certain key actors for a misinformation campaign?
- How do dark network actors choose their network partners? Is there a tendency for actors to select partners who share common characteristics with them (i.e., homophily)? If so, how does that tendency inform strategies, such as reconciliation and rehabilitation strategies or psychological operations?
- What role does physical proximity play in the formation of ties between dark network actors? Are there groups who share areas of influence and who are often at conflict with one another? Can the presence or absence of conflict between such groups lend itself to certain types of strategies?
- More importantly, which combinations of the processes above best describe the formation of an observed dark network?
- Can any of these processes be described as a longitudinal phenomenon?

3.3 SOCIAL NETWORK DATA

It is important to discuss the uniqueness of relational or social network data, before turning to an important step in network analysis, boundary specification. A difficulty facing social network analysts is that it is generally not possible to study extremely large social networks as well and completely as we do smaller networks, particularly with limited time and resources.[2] It would be very helpful if social network analysts could use sampling methods to collect social network data because that would allow us to generalize our findings to entire populations. In practice, however, sampling does not work for most forms of SNA. Imagine that we drew a random sample of 1,000 detainees or prisoners and questioned them to develop a list of their collaborators and identify the ties between them (granted, an unlikely scenario). Chances are that their co-collaborators would not be part of the original sample, which means that we would not have enough information about how these small clusters relate to one another, most of the people surveyed would not know one another, nor would they necessarily have colleagues in common.[3] Social network researchers have responded to this difficulty in two different ways. One approach actually uses sampling but focuses only on what social network analysts refer to as ego networks; the other, which is more common, analyzes what social network analysts call whole (or complete) social networks.

Ego Networks

An ego-centered approach focuses on an actor's (i.e., ego's)—immediate social environment: the set of actors (i.e., alters and neighbors) to which the actor has ties and the ties among them. There are generally two ways of obtaining ego network data. One way is to use whole (aka, complete, full) network data (see below) and then extract the ego networks of an actor or set of actors. For example, analysts may extract sets of persons of interest along with the individuals to whom they are connected (i.e., their ego network) from existing databases. The other way is to survey a random sample of individuals from whom ego network data are then collected. Each person surveyed is generally asked for a set of contacts (Burt 1984, 1985), using questions such as "Looking back over the last six months, who are the people with whom you discussed matters important to you?" After providing a list of contacts, they are then asked about the ties (if any) between their contacts (e.g., do they know one another, are they friends, and so on), as well as various attributes of the alters (e.g., gender, race, and education level). Needless to say, ties between an ego and his or her alters with different egos and their alters are not (and generally cannot be) recorded. This yields a data structure similar to that displayed in Figure 3.1. As one can see, only those ties within the ego network of the people sampled (i.e., Genevieve, Karen, and Deanne) are recorded, while the ties between their ego networks are not.

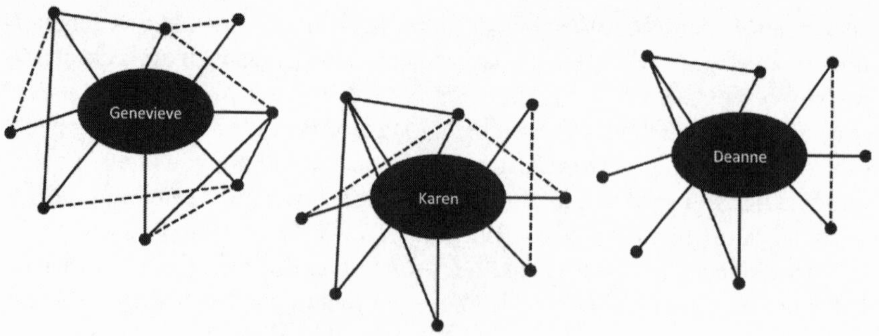

Figure 3.1 Hypothetical Ego Network

Although ego network data possess some limitations, they do lend themselves to certain types of analyses. Borgatti et al. (2013) note that ego network research can generally be broken down into two broad camps: the social capital camp and the social homogeneity camp. The former focuses on how success is a function of the resources and support an individual's ties provide him or her. The latter examines how an actor's ties influence his or her attitudes and behavior.

> In the social capital camp, the canonical research agenda is to investigate how achievement and success are a function of an individual's social ties, particularly how those ties enable access to resources and support. Given this connection, there is of course also an interest in how individuals acquire the network ties that they do. In the social homogeneity camp, there is a strong interest in how ego's ties determine ego's attitudes and behavior, with particular focus on the contagion mechanism—how the attitudes and behavior of ego's alters infect or influence ego's own attitudes and behavior. There is an equally strong interest in understanding how the characteristics of actors affect which actors become involved with each other, whether it is how firms choose alliance partners or persons choose their friends. (Borgatti, Everett and Johnson 2013:270)

One of the attractive features of ego-network data is that, if the data are collected randomly, the results can be generalized to the larger population from which the sample was drawn. In any case, it appears there is a lot of untapped potential in the application ego-network approaches to understanding dark networks.

Whole (Complete, Full) Networks

Early work in SNA focused on small, observable groups. For such networks to be considered a valid representation of the group, all relevant actors, and of the ties between them, must be present. With improvements in technology, it has become possible to capture information on a much larger scale, again, provided that full set of actors and the relationships between them are observable. In practice, analysts tend to subdivide data on complete networks into two general types: one-mode social network data (symmetric and asymmetric); and two-mode social network data.[4]

Symmetric (Undirected) One-Mode Network

One-mode networks, which are sometimes called an adjacency matrix, may be understood as containing a single set of actors (i.e., actors). Although actors can theoretically take the form of anything that can be defined, in a dark network they are generally more concrete. When possible, analysts will focus upon known entities (i.e., people) within a predefined group. Or, when such granular data are unavailable, an analyst may choose to collect network data at a more aggregate level, such as groups, families, tribes, organizations, corporations, or nation-states. It is not necessary for actors to even be human. In certain cases it may even be useful to represent and analyze networks of items that consist of various interrelated parts, origins, techniques, or uses—such as IEDs (Improvised Explosive Devices) (Childress and Taylor 2012) or key phrases. The ties between actors can take the form of friendship or kinship ties, material transactions such as business transactions, recruitment ties, and communication networks. These ties are often recorded as edges, especially when it is difficult or impossible to ascertain which actor initiated or sent the tie and which received it. An example of a symmetric one-mode network is the Koschade Bali I network (see Appendix A.2 for description), which is presented as a matrix in Figure 3.2 (created in UCINET). Note that that one-mode networks always result in square matrices because each actor appears as both a row and a column.

Asymmetric (Directed) One-Mode Network

At times, it may be possible to discern the direction that a tie travels and whether or not it is reciprocated. In such cases, it is possible to construct an asymmetric one-mode network. For an example of such a network, consider the formal relations among a sample of actors of the TFMC. Figure 3.3 presents a matrix consisting of 43 members and the individuals to whom they report in the mobile column's formal structure. In a matrix format, the actor sending the tie (i.e., source actor) is represented in the row and the receiver of the relationship (i.e., target actor) is listed in the column. For example, actor 1 reports to actor 14 in the TFMC's formal structure.

		1 Muklas	2 Amrozi	3 Imron	4 Samudra	5 Dulmatin	6 Idris	7 Mubarok	8 Azahari	9 Ghoni	10 Arnasan	11 Rauf	12 Octavia	13 Hidayat	14 Junaedi	15 Patek	16 Feri	17 Sarijo
1	Muklas	0	2	2	1	1	5	0	1	1	0	0	0	0	0	1	0	1
2	Amrozi	2	0	0	2	0	4	5	0	0	0	0	0	0	0	0	0	0
3	Imron	2	0	0	3	5	3	0	5	5	0	0	0	0	0	5	1	5
4	Samudra	1	2	3	0	2	5	2	2	2	2	2	2	2	2	2	0	2
5	Dulmatin	1	0	5	2	0	2	0	5	0	0	0	0	0	0	0	0	5
6	Idris	5	4	3	5	2	0	2	2	2	0	0	0	0	0	2	0	2
7	Mubarok	0	5	0	2	0	2	0	0	0	0	0	0	0	0	0	0	0
8	Azahari	1	0	5	2	5	2	0	0	5	0	0	0	0	0	2	1	2
9	Ghoni	1	0	5	2	5	2	0	5	0	0	0	0	0	0	5	1	5
10	Arnasan	0	0	0	2	0	0	0	0	0	0	2	2	2	2	0	0	0
11	Rauf	0	0	0	2	0	0	0	0	0	2	0	2	2	2	0	0	0
12	Octavia	0	0	0	2	0	0	0	0	0	2	2	0	2	2	0	0	0
13	Hidayat	0	0	0	2	0	0	0	0	0	2	2	2	0	2	0	0	0
14	Junaedi	0	0	0	2	0	0	0	0	0	2	2	2	2	0	0	0	0
15	Patek	1	0	5	2	5	2	0	2	5	0	0	0	0	0	0	1	5
16	Feri	0	0	1	0	1	0	0	1	1	0	0	0	0	0	1	0	1
17	Sarijo	1	0	5	2	5	2	0	2	5	0	0	0	0	0	5	1	0

Figure 3.2 Illustrative Example of Symmetric One-Mode Network

		1	2	3	4	5	6	7	8	9	10	11	12	13	14	15	16	17	18	19	20	21	22	23	24	25	26	27	28	29	30	31	32	33	34	35	36	37	38	39	40	41	42	43
1	1	0	0	0	0	0	0	0	0	0	0	0	0	0	1	0	0	0	0	0	0	0	0	0	0	0	0	0	0	0	0	0	0	0	0	0	0	0	0	0	0	0	0	0
2	2	0	0	0	0	1	0	0	1	0	0	1	0	1	0	0	1	0	0	0	1	0	1	0	0	0	0	0	0	0	0	0	1	1	0	0	0	0	0	1	0	0	0	0
3	3	0	0	0	0	0	0	0	0	0	0	0	0	0	0	0	0	0	0	0	0	0	0	0	0	0	0	0	0	0	0	0	0	0	0	0	0	0	0	0	0	0	0	0
4	4	0	0	0	0	0	0	0	0	0	0	0	0	0	1	0	0	0	0	0	0	0	0	0	0	0	0	0	0	0	0	0	0	0	0	0	0	0	0	0	0	0	0	0
5	5	0	0	0	0	0	0	0	0	0	0	0	0	0	0	0	0	0	0	0	0	0	0	0	0	0	0	0	0	0	0	0	0	0	0	0	0	0	0	0	0	0	0	0
6	6	0	0	0	0	0	0	0	0	0	0	0	0	0	0	0	0	0	0	0	0	0	0	0	0	0	0	0	0	0	0	0	0	0	0	0	0	0	0	0	0	0	0	0
7	7	0	0	0	0	0	0	0	0	0	0	0	0	0	0	0	0	0	0	0	0	0	0	0	0	0	0	0	0	0	0	0	0	0	0	0	0	0	0	0	0	0	0	0
8	8	0	0	0	0	0	0	0	0	0	0	0	0	0	0	0	0	0	0	0	0	0	0	0	0	0	0	0	0	0	0	0	0	0	0	0	0	0	0	0	0	0	0	0
9	9	0	1	0	0	0	0	0	0	0	0	0	0	0	0	0	0	0	0	0	0	0	0	0	0	0	0	0	0	0	0	0	0	0	0	0	0	0	0	0	0	0	0	0
10	10	0	0	0	0	0	1	0	0	0	0	0	0	0	0	0	0	0	0	0	0	0	0	0	0	0	0	0	0	0	0	0	0	0	0	0	0	0	0	0	0	0	0	0
11	11	0	0	0	0	0	0	0	0	0	0	0	0	0	0	0	0	0	0	0	0	0	0	0	0	0	0	0	0	0	0	0	0	0	0	0	0	0	0	0	0	0	0	0
12	12	0	0	0	0	1	0	0	0	0	0	0	0	0	1	0	0	0	0	0	0	0	0	0	0	0	0	0	0	0	0	0	0	0	0	0	0	0	0	0	0	0	0	0
13	13	0	0	0	0	0	0	0	0	0	0	0	0	0	0	0	0	0	0	0	0	0	0	0	0	0	0	0	0	0	0	0	0	0	0	0	0	0	0	0	0	0	0	0
14	14	0	0	1	0	0	1	1	0	0	0	0	0	0	0	0	0	0	0	0	0	0	0	0	0	0	0	0	0	0	0	0	0	0	0	0	0	0	0	0	0	0	0	0
15	15	0	1	0	0	0	0	0	0	0	0	0	0	0	0	0	0	0	0	0	0	0	0	0	0	0	0	0	0	0	0	0	0	0	0	0	0	0	0	0	0	0	0	0
16	16	0	0	0	0	0	0	0	0	0	0	0	0	0	0	0	0	0	0	0	0	0	0	0	0	0	0	0	0	0	0	0	0	0	0	0	0	0	0	0	0	0	0	0
17	17	0	0	0	0	0	0	0	0	0	0	0	0	0	0	0	0	0	0	0	0	0	0	0	0	0	0	0	0	0	0	0	0	0	0	0	0	0	0	0	0	0	0	0
18	18	0	0	0	0	0	0	0	0	0	0	0	0	0	1	0	0	1	0	0	0	0	0	1	0	1	1	0	0	0	0	1	0	0	0	0	0	0	0	0	0	0	0	0
19	19	0	0	0	0	0	0	0	0	0	0	0	0	0	0	0	0	0	0	0	0	0	0	0	0	0	0	0	0	0	0	0	0	0	0	0	0	0	0	0	0	0	0	0
20	20	0	0	0	0	0	0	0	0	0	0	0	0	0	0	0	0	0	0	0	0	0	0	0	0	0	0	0	0	0	0	0	0	0	0	0	0	0	0	0	0	0	0	0
21	21	0	0	0	0	0	0	0	0	0	0	0	0	0	0	0	0	0	0	0	0	0	0	0	0	0	0	0	0	0	0	0	0	0	0	0	0	0	0	0	0	0	0	0
22	22	0	0	0	0	0	0	0	0	0	0	0	0	0	0	0	0	0	0	0	0	0	0	0	0	0	0	0	0	0	0	0	0	0	0	0	0	0	0	0	0	0	0	0
23	23	0	0	0	0	0	0	0	0	0	0	0	0	0	0	0	0	0	0	0	0	0	0	0	0	0	0	0	0	0	0	0	0	0	0	0	0	0	0	0	0	0	0	0
24	24	0	0	0	0	0	0	0	0	0	0	0	0	0	0	0	0	0	0	0	0	0	0	0	0	0	1	0	0	0	0	0	0	0	0	0	0	0	0	0	0	0	0	0
25	25	0	0	0	0	0	0	0	0	0	0	0	0	0	0	0	0	0	0	0	0	0	0	0	0	0	0	0	0	0	0	0	0	0	0	0	0	0	0	0	0	0	0	0
26	26	0	0	0	0	0	0	0	0	0	0	0	0	0	0	0	0	0	0	0	0	0	0	0	0	0	0	0	0	0	0	0	0	0	0	0	0	0	0	0	0	0	0	0
27	27	0	0	0	0	0	0	0	0	0	0	0	0	0	0	0	0	0	1	0	0	0	0	0	0	0	0	0	0	0	0	0	0	0	0	0	0	0	0	0	0	0	0	0
28	28	0	0	0	0	0	0	0	0	0	0	0	0	0	1	0	0	0	0	0	0	0	0	0	0	0	0	0	0	0	0	0	0	0	0	0	0	0	0	0	0	0	0	0
29	29	0	0	0	0	0	0	0	0	0	0	0	0	0	0	0	0	0	1	0	0	0	0	0	0	0	0	0	0	0	0	0	0	0	0	0	0	0	0	0	0	0	0	0
30	30	0	0	0	0	0	0	0	0	0	0	0	0	0	0	0	0	0	1	0	0	0	0	0	0	0	0	0	0	0	0	0	0	0	0	0	0	0	0	0	0	0	0	0
31	31	0	0	0	0	0	0	0	0	0	0	0	0	0	0	0	0	0	0	0	0	0	0	0	0	0	0	0	0	0	0	0	0	0	0	0	0	0	0	0	0	0	0	0
32	32	0	0	0	0	0	0	0	0	0	0	0	0	0	0	0	0	0	0	1	0	0	0	0	0	0	0	0	0	0	0	0	0	0	0	0	0	0	0	0	0	0	0	0
33	33	0	0	0	0	0	0	0	0	0	0	0	0	0	0	0	0	0	0	0	0	0	0	0	0	0	0	0	0	0	0	0	0	0	0	0	0	0	0	0	0	0	0	0
34	34	0	0	0	0	0	0	0	0	0	0	0	0	0	1	0	0	0	0	0	0	0	0	0	0	0	0	0	0	0	0	0	0	0	0	0	0	0	0	0	0	0	0	0
35	35	0	0	0	0	0	0	0	0	0	0	0	0	0	1	0	0	0	0	0	0	0	0	0	0	0	0	0	0	0	0	0	0	0	0	0	0	0	0	0	0	0	0	0
36	36	0	0	0	0	0	1	0	0	0	0	0	0	0	0	0	0	0	0	0	0	0	0	0	0	0	0	0	0	0	0	0	0	0	0	0	0	0	0	0	0	0	0	0
37	37	0	0	0	0	0	0	0	0	0	0	0	0	0	0	0	0	0	0	0	0	0	0	0	0	0	0	0	0	0	0	0	0	0	0	0	0	0	0	0	0	0	1	0
38	38	0	0	0	0	0	0	0	0	0	0	0	0	0	0	0	0	0	1	0	0	0	0	0	0	0	0	0	0	0	0	0	0	0	0	0	0	0	0	0	0	0	0	0
39	39	0	0	0	0	0	1	0	0	0	0	0	0	0	0	0	0	0	0	0	0	0	0	0	0	0	0	0	0	0	0	0	0	0	0	0	0	0	0	0	0	0	0	0
40	40	0	0	0	0	0	0	0	0	0	0	0	0	0	0	0	0	0	1	0	0	0	0	0	0	0	0	0	0	0	0	0	0	0	0	0	0	0	0	0	0	0	0	0
41	41	0	0	0	0	0	1	0	0	0	0	0	0	0	0	0	0	0	0	0	0	0	0	0	0	0	0	0	0	0	0	0	0	0	0	0	0	0	0	0	0	0	0	0
42	42	0	0	0	0	0	0	0	0	0	0	0	0	0	0	0	0	0	0	0	0	1	0	0	0	0	1	0	0	0	0	0	0	0	0	0	0	0	0	0	0	0	0	0
43	43	0	0	0	0	0	0	0	0	0	0	0	0	0	0	0	0	0	0	0	0	0	0	0	0	0	0	0	0	0	0	0	0	0	0	0	1	0	0	0	0	0	0	0

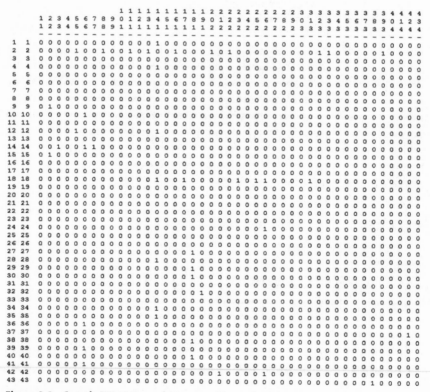

Figure 3.3 Sample TFMC Formal Structure Network Data

Analysts can potentially observe a host of other types of asymmetrical relationships in dark networks besides formal structures like the one depicted in Figure 3.4. It is possible, for example, to observe asymmetric communication, financial flow, and mentorship (technical and spiritual) relationships among dark network actors. Unfortunately, distinguishing tie direction in dark networks can prove challenging due to their covert nature, which often leaves analysts no choice but to treat ties as bidirectional (i.e., symmetric). The fact that it is unrealistic, to say the least, to expect that one could survey dark network actors about how they connect with others in their organization, serves to make this practice a common feature of the analysis of dark networks.

That being said, analysts should be encouraged to seek out directed data when possible. The collection of directed data, including asymmetric relationships, allows analysts to get additional—and potentially important—details about the nature of observed relationships by using basic visualizations and by applying techniques developed for directed data (e.g., strong components, hubs, and authorities). Take Figure 3.4, for instance, which presents a NetDraw-generated sociogram of the sample TFMC formal network. A few patterns emerge in the visualization, such as the central position of actors 2, 6, 14, and 18. The number of relationships in which actor 2 is embedded, however, can potentially overstate his importance if we ignore the direction of the ties. In fact, the direction of actor 2's relationships actually reflects

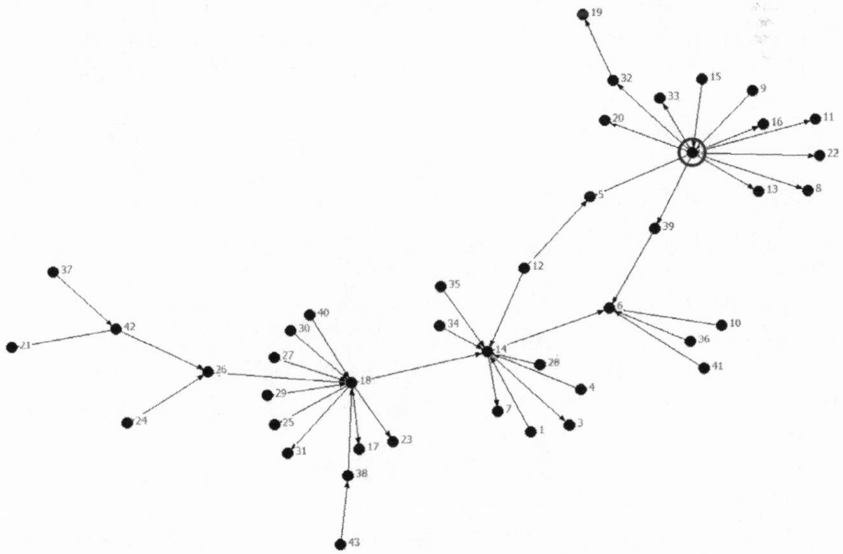

Figure 3.4 Sociogram of Sample TFMC Formal Structure Network Data

that he reports to many actors, which indicates he is subordinate to many other actors. This relatively simplistic example of a dark network highlights that we can lose potentially important details about dark networks using only undirected data.

Two-mode Networks

Two-mode networks differ from one-mode networks in a very important manner. Whereas one-mode networks consist of a single set of actors and the ties between them, two-mode networks consist of two sets of actors that have ties between, but not within, sets. Two-mode networks may therefore consist of two sets of different actors, one set of actors and one set of events or affiliations, or other combinations of actor types. But a critical feature of these networks is that there are no ties within each of the actor sets; there are only between actors of the two different sets. Two-mode networks are also referred to as affiliation networks, membership networks, dual networks, or hypernetworks. Each mode takes the form of a set of actors that either cannot have ties within the set—such as a set of job descriptions, events, or meetings—or the actors whose ties are difficult or impossible to discern otherwise, so their ties must be inferred through the actors in the opposing mode that they hold in common.

Examples of two-mode networks include membership in various organizations (e.g., terrorist, insurgent, or criminal), participation at particular events (e.g., robbery, terrorist attack, and meeting), and so on. Figure 3.5 presents an example of a two-mode network. It depicts a sample of actors in Noordin Top's network and the meetings in which actors participated. The actors are listed by row; the meetings (i.e., events) by column. As Figure 3.5 indicates, Abu Dujanah participated in meetings 1 and 2, while Abu Fida attended meetings 5, 6, and 13.

Note that in this matrix format, there is no possibility of recording how the various actors link to each other. Similarly, there is no provision for events to link to one another. This is by design. A NetDraw-generated sociogram of Noordin's meetings network appears in Figure 3.6. Note the difference between this one and the previous one-mode network example. Here, both sets of actors, individual members and meetings, appear together and are assigned different colors (or, in this case, shades of gray). The object of constructing a two-mode network is generally to infer latent or unobserved ties between actors in one set, given their participation or other links to the actors in the other set. We may therefore use the network as it is to investigate the role of meetings in the network, or convert the network from two modes to one in order to explore the connections that may be inferred between actors or between meetings.

		1 Meeting_1	2 Meeting_2	3 Meeting_3	4 Meeting_4	5 Meeting_5	6 Meeting_6	7 Meeting_7	8 Meeting_8	9 Meeting_9	10 Meeting_10	11 Meeting_11	12 Meeting_12	13 Meeting_13	14 Meeting_14	15 Meeting_15	16 Meeting_16	17 Meeting_17	18 Meeting_18	19 Meeting_19	20 Meeting_20
1	Abdul Aziz	0	0	0	0	0	0	0	0	0	0	0	0	0	0	0	0	0	0	0	1
2	Abdul Jabar	0	0	0	0	0	0	0	0	0	0	0	0	0	0	0	0	0	0	0	0
3	Abdul Malik	0	0	0	0	0	0	0	0	0	0	0	0	0	0	0	0	0	0	0	0
4	Abdul Rauf	0	0	0	0	0	0	0	0	0	0	0	0	0	0	0	0	0	0	0	0
5	Abdul Rohim	0	0	0	0	0	0	0	0	0	0	0	0	0	0	0	0	0	0	0	0
6	Abdullah Sunata	0	0	0	0	0	0	0	0	0	0	0	1	0	0	0	0	0	0	0	0
7	Abdullah Sungkar	0	0	0	0	0	0	0	0	0	0	0	0	0	0	0	0	0	0	0	0
8	Abu Bakar Ba'asyir	0	0	0	0	0	0	0	0	0	0	0	0	0	0	0	0	0	0	0	0
9	Abu Dujanah	1	1	0	0	0	0	0	0	0	0	0	0	0	0	0	0	0	0	0	0
10	Abu Fida	0	0	0	0	1	1	0	0	0	0	0	0	1	0	0	0	0	0	0	0
11	Abu Musab al-Zarqawi	0	0	0	0	0	0	0	0	0	0	0	0	0	0	0	0	0	0	0	0
12	Abu Roiroh	0	0	0	0	0	0	0	0	0	0	0	0	0	0	0	0	0	0	0	0
13	Abu Rusdan	0	0	0	0	0	0	0	0	0	0	0	0	0	0	0	0	0	0	0	0
14	Aceng Kurnia	0	0	0	0	0	0	0	0	0	0	0	0	0	0	0	0	0	0	0	0
15	Achmad Hasan	0	0	0	0	0	0	0	0	0	0	0	0	0	0	0	0	0	0	0	0
16	Ade Bahru	0	0	0	0	0	0	0	0	0	0	0	0	0	0	0	0	0	0	0	0
17	Aditya Tri Yoga	0	0	0	0	0	0	0	0	0	0	0	0	0	0	0	0	0	0	0	0
18	Adung	0	0	0	0	1	0	0	0	0	0	0	0	0	0	0	0	0	0	0	0
19	Agus Ahmad	0	0	0	0	0	0	0	0	0	0	0	0	0	0	0	0	0	0	0	0
20	Agus Dwikarna	0	0	0	0	0	0	0	0	0	0	0	0	0	0	0	0	0	0	0	0
21	Agus Puryanto	0	0	0	0	0	0	0	0	0	0	0	0	0	0	0	0	0	0	0	0
22	Ahmad Basyir	0	0	0	0	0	0	0	0	0	0	0	0	0	0	0	0	0	0	0	0
23	Ahmad Rofiq Ridho	0	0	0	0	0	0	0	0	0	0	1	1	0	1	1	1	0	1	0	0
24	Ahmad Roichan	0	0	0	0	0	0	0	0	0	0	0	0	0	0	0	0	0	0	0	0
25	Ahmad Sayid Maulana	0	0	0	0	0	0	0	0	0	0	0	0	0	0	0	0	0	0	0	0
26	Aip Hidayat	0	0	0	0	0	0	0	0	0	0	0	0	0	0	0	0	0	0	0	0
27	Ajengan Masduki	0	0	0	0	0	0	0	0	0	0	0	0	0	0	0	0	0	0	0	0
28	Akram	0	0	0	0	0	0	0	0	0	0	0	0	0	0	0	0	1	0	0	0
29	Ali	0	0	0	0	0	0	0	0	0	0	0	0	0	0	0	0	0	0	0	0
30	Ali Ghufron	0	0	0	0	0	0	0	0	0	0	0	0	0	0	0	0	0	0	0	0
31	Ali Imron	0	0	0	0	0	0	0	0	0	0	0	0	0	0	0	0	0	0	0	0
32	Amrozi	0	0	0	0	0	0	0	0	0	0	0	0	0	0	0	0	0	0	0	0
33	Andri Octavia	0	0	0	0	0	0	0	0	0	0	0	0	0	0	0	0	0	0	0	0
34	Anif Solchanudin	0	0	0	0	0	0	0	0	0	0	0	0	0	0	0	0	0	0	0	0
35	Apuy	0	0	0	0	0	0	0	0	0	0	0	0	0	0	0	0	0	0	0	0

Figure 3.5 Sample of Noordin Top's Meetings Network

A key assumption underlying the use of two-mode networks by social network analysts is that membership in an organization or participation in an event is a source of social ties. Why? Because people who join or participate in a common organization and/or event often share similar tasks and/or interests, and they are much more likely to interact with one another than two randomly selected people. That said, we need to be careful when using two-mode data. Just because two people participate in a common event or are members of the organization does not necessarily mean that a tie exists between them. It is very good practice to select actor sets where it can be plausibly argued that participants—or similar—would have a high probability of sharing a tie. For example, it is highly unlikely that every member of terrorist network, such as the Islamic State, actually knows one another. In the case of the Noordin data, however, the meetings were small and deliberately set. It is therefore likely that each of the participants either had the opportunity to meet, or already knew the others and ties can be logically inferred.

Analysts can derive one-mode networks from two-mode networks by multiplying the original two-mode matrix by its transpose. Although this procedure is relatively straightforward in terms of matrix algebra, it is

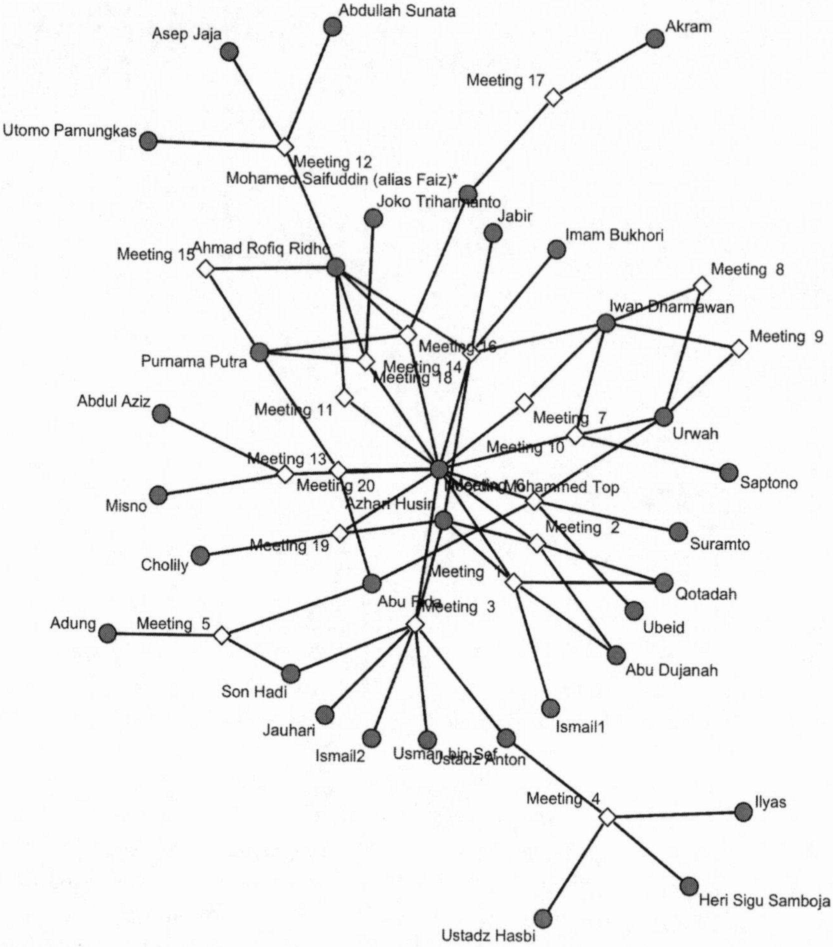

Figure 3.6 Sociogram of Noordin's Two-Mode Meetings Network (isolates hidden)

generally included as a common feature in SNA software. In most packages the function is referred to as "2-mode to 1-mode," although in the package, Organizational Risk Analyzer (ORA), (Carley 2001–2015) it is called "folding" a network. The product of such a procedure is a square frequency matrix, with the number of connections an actor has to the other mode given on the diagonal. The conversion from a two mode to a one mode can be performed for either of the two modes (i.e., rows and columns).

Consider the sample Noordin Top network depicted in Figures 3.5 and 3.6. We can create a new person-by-person network (i.e., rows and columns are people) where the cell values indicate the number of meetings in which each pair of actors participated. Figure 3.7, for instance, indicates that Ahmad

		1 Abdul Aziz	2 Abdullah Sunata	3 Abu Dujanah	4 Abu Fida	5 Adung	6 Ahmad Rofiq Ridho	7 Akram	8 Asep Jaja	9 Azhari Husin	10 Cholily	11 Heri Sigu Samboja	12 Ilyas	13 Imam Bukhori	14 Ismail1	15 Ismail2	16 Iwan Dharmawan	17 Jabir	18 Jauhari	19 Joko Triharmanto	20 Misno	21 Mohamed Saifuddin (alias Faiz)*	22 Noordin Mohammed Top	23 Purnama Putra	24 Qotadah	25 Saptono	26 Son Hadi	27 Suramto	28 Ubeid	29 Urwah	30 Usman bin Sef	31 Ustadz Anton	32 Ustadz Hasbi	33 Utomo Pamungkas
1	Abdul Aziz	1	0	0	0	0	0	0	0	0	0	0	0	0	0	0	0	0	0	0	1	0	1	0	0	0	0	0	0	0	0	0	0	0
2	Abdullah Sunata	0	1	0	0	0	1	0	1	0	0	0	0	0	0	0	0	0	0	0	0	0	0	0	0	0	0	0	0	0	0	0	0	1
3	Abu Dujanah	0	0	2	0	0	0	0	0	2	0	0	0	0	1	0	0	0	0	0	0	0	2	0	2	0	0	0	0	0	0	0	0	0
4	Abu Fida	0	0	0	3	1	0	0	0	0	0	0	0	0	0	0	0	0	0	0	0	0	2	1	0	0	1	1	1	1	0	0	0	0
5	Adung	0	0	0	1	1	0	0	0	0	0	0	0	0	0	0	0	0	0	0	0	0	0	0	0	0	1	0	0	0	0	0	0	0
6	Ahmad Rofiq Ridho	0	1	0	0	0	6	0	1	1	0	0	0	1	0	0	1	1	0	1	0	1	4	3	0	0	0	0	0	0	0	0	0	1
7	Akram	0	0	0	0	0	0	1	0	0	0	0	0	0	0	0	0	0	0	0	0	1	0	0	0	0	0	0	0	0	0	0	0	0
8	Asep Jaja	0	1	0	0	0	1	0	1	0	0	0	0	0	0	0	0	0	0	0	0	0	0	0	0	0	0	0	0	0	0	0	0	1
9	Azhari Husin	0	0	2	0	0	1	0	0	5	1	0	0	1	1	1	1	1	1	0	0	0	5	0	2	0	1	0	0	0	1	1	0	0
10	Cholily	0	0	0	0	0	0	0	0	1	1	0	0	0	0	0	0	0	0	0	0	0	1	0	0	0	0	0	0	0	0	0	0	0
11	Heri Sigu Samboja	0	0	0	0	0	0	0	0	0	0	1	1	0	0	0	0	0	0	0	0	0	0	0	0	0	0	0	0	0	1	0	1	0
12	Ilyas	0	0	0	0	0	0	0	0	0	0	1	1	0	0	0	0	0	0	0	0	0	0	0	0	0	0	0	0	0	1	0	1	0
13	Imam Bukhori	0	0	0	0	0	1	0	0	1	0	0	0	1	0	0	1	1	0	0	0	0	1	0	0	0	0	0	0	0	0	0	0	0
14	Ismail1	0	0	1	0	0	0	0	0	1	0	0	0	0	1	0	0	0	0	0	0	0	1	0	1	0	0	0	0	0	0	0	0	0
15	Ismail2	0	0	0	0	0	0	0	0	1	0	0	0	0	0	1	0	0	1	0	0	0	1	0	0	0	1	0	0	0	1	1	0	0
16	Iwan Dharmawan	0	0	0	0	0	1	0	0	1	0	0	0	1	0	0	5	1	0	0	0	0	3	0	0	1	0	0	0	3	0	0	0	0
17	Jabir	0	0	0	0	0	1	0	0	1	0	0	0	1	0	0	1	1	0	0	0	0	1	0	0	0	0	0	0	0	0	0	0	0
18	Jauhari	0	0	0	0	0	0	0	0	1	0	0	0	0	0	1	0	0	1	0	0	0	1	0	0	0	1	0	0	0	1	1	0	0
19	Joko Triharmanto	0	0	0	0	0	1	0	0	0	0	0	0	0	0	0	0	0	0	1	0	0	1	1	0	0	0	0	0	0	0	0	0	0
20	Misno	1	0	0	0	0	0	0	0	0	0	0	0	0	0	0	0	0	0	0	1	0	1	0	0	0	0	0	0	0	0	0	0	0
21	Mohamed Saifuddin (alias	0	0	0	0	0	1	1	0	0	0	0	0	0	0	0	0	0	0	0	0	2	1	1	0	0	0	0	0	0	0	0	0	0
22	Noordin Mohammed Top	1	0	2	2	0	4	0	0	5	1	0	0	1	1	1	3	1	1	1	1	1	13	3	2	1	1	1	1	2	1	1	0	0
23	Purnama Putra	0	0	0	1	0	3	0	0	0	0	0	0	0	0	0	0	0	0	1	0	1	3	4	0	0	0	0	0	0	0	0	0	0
24	Qotadah	0	0	2	0	0	0	0	0	2	0	0	0	0	1	0	0	0	0	0	0	0	2	0	2	0	0	0	0	0	0	0	0	0
25	Saptono	0	0	0	0	0	0	0	0	0	0	0	0	0	0	0	1	0	0	0	0	0	1	0	0	1	0	0	0	1	0	0	0	0
26	Son Hadi	0	0	0	1	1	0	0	0	1	0	0	0	0	0	1	0	0	1	0	0	0	1	0	0	0	2	0	0	0	1	1	0	0
27	Suramto	0	0	0	1	0	0	0	0	0	0	0	0	0	0	0	0	0	0	0	0	0	1	0	0	0	0	1	1	1	0	0	0	0
28	Ubeid	0	0	0	1	0	0	0	0	0	0	0	0	0	0	0	0	0	0	0	0	0	1	0	0	0	0	1	1	1	0	0	0	0
29	Urwah	0	0	0	1	0	0	0	0	0	0	0	0	0	0	0	3	0	0	0	0	0	2	0	0	1	0	1	1	4	0	0	0	0
30	Usman bin Sef	0	0	0	0	0	0	0	0	1	0	1	1	0	0	1	0	0	1	0	0	0	1	0	0	0	1	0	0	0	2	1	1	0
31	Ustadz Anton	0	0	0	0	0	0	0	0	1	0	0	0	0	0	1	0	0	1	0	0	0	1	0	0	0	1	0	0	0	1	1	0	0
32	Ustadz Hasbi	0	0	0	0	0	0	0	0	0	0	1	1	0	0	0	0	0	0	0	0	0	0	0	0	0	0	0	0	0	1	0	1	0
33	Utomo Pamungkas	0	1	0	0	0	1	0	1	0	0	0	0	0	0	0	0	0	0	0	0	0	0	0	0	0	0	0	0	0	0	0	0	1

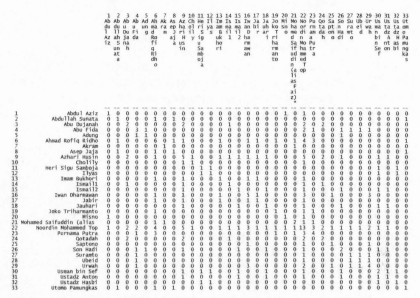

Figure 3.7 Matrix of Meetings Network Converted to One-Mode Network (isolates hidden)

Rofiq Ridho and Noordin Top attended four meetings together (see the corresponding cell of the two individuals—row 6 and column 22 [or row 22 and column 6]). Note we could have just as easily created a new meeting-by-meeting matrix to demonstrate how many participants each pair of events shared.[5] In any case, it bears repeating that analysts must account for the size of organizations or events contained in a two-mode network because larger organizations or events could skew the results of an analysis by making the possibility of a tie increasingly implausible. For instance, imagine a two-mode network where the rows are every high-tech worker in Silicon Valley and the columns are all of the high-tech firms in Silicon Valley. If we derived a one-mode network from the two-mode network, then every person who worked for, say, Apple, would have a tie with one another, but this is unreasonable. It is highly unlikely that every Apple employee knows every other Apple employee. The bottom line? We need to be careful when deriving one-mode networks from two-mode networks.

3.4 BOUNDARY WORK

An important concern in social network study is which actors to include in the network and which ones to exclude. Sometimes the boundary between who is in and who is not is relatively clear. Sometimes it is not. The goal should be "to find a set of actors with relatively good separateness from the rest of the world" from which we can draw reasonable conclusions (Erickson 2001:317). This is far easier said than done, however. Some researchers adopt the "vantage point of the actors themselves . . . [and] the network is treated as a social fact only in that it is consciously experienced . . . by the actors composing it" (Laumann, Marsden, and Prensky 1983:20). Actors and their ties are only included to the extent that other actors consider them to be part of the network (Knoke and Yang 2007:15). This is often referred to as the realist or emic approach (Laumann, Marsden and Prensky 1983). Others impose an a priori framework based on the analyst's theoretical concerns (Knoke and Yang 2007; Wasserman and Faust 1994). For example, a network analyst might be interested in examining the communication relations among leadership in a particular criminal group. In this analysis, the analyst might establish that only known members of the group who possess formal leadership positions will be included in the population. This approach is referred to as the nominalist or etic approach (Laumann, Marsden, and Prensky 1983).

These two approaches are then often refined by focusing on certain features of a network, such as the attributes of actors, types of relations, or participation in events (Laumann, Marsden, and Prensky 1983:22). Social network analysts who focus on the attributes of actors generally do so in one of two ways: either in terms of position (i.e., where a membership test refers to the presence or absence of some attribute, such as holding a position in a formal group) or reputation (e.g., one that draws on the judgments of knowledgeable informants for identifying participant actors). When social network analysts use a relational focus to determining network boundaries, they focus on a specific type of tie (or set of ties) between actors (e.g., friendship, kinship, and business). An example of this approach is Everton and Cunningham's (2015) examination of what they defined as Noordin Top's *Trust*, *Operational*, and *Combined* networks. Finally, some researchers use participation in a particular event or activity to select actors for a network study. Several excellent examples of this approach include Krebs's (2002) analysis of the 9/11 network, Koschade's (2006) examination of the 2002 Bali attack network, and Rodriguez's (2005) exploration of the 2004 Madrid bombing network.

Figure 3.8 combines these two dimensions into a single matrix to illustrate the array of possible approaches that researchers can use to define the boundaries of the network they are studying. What should be clear is that analysts are not limited to a single approach but rather can adopt approaches that combine two or more foci and land somewhere on the continuum between nominalist and realist strategies. What is ultimately important is not the approach taken but rather that the boundary of the network being analyzed is correctly specified. As with any empirical approach to studying social

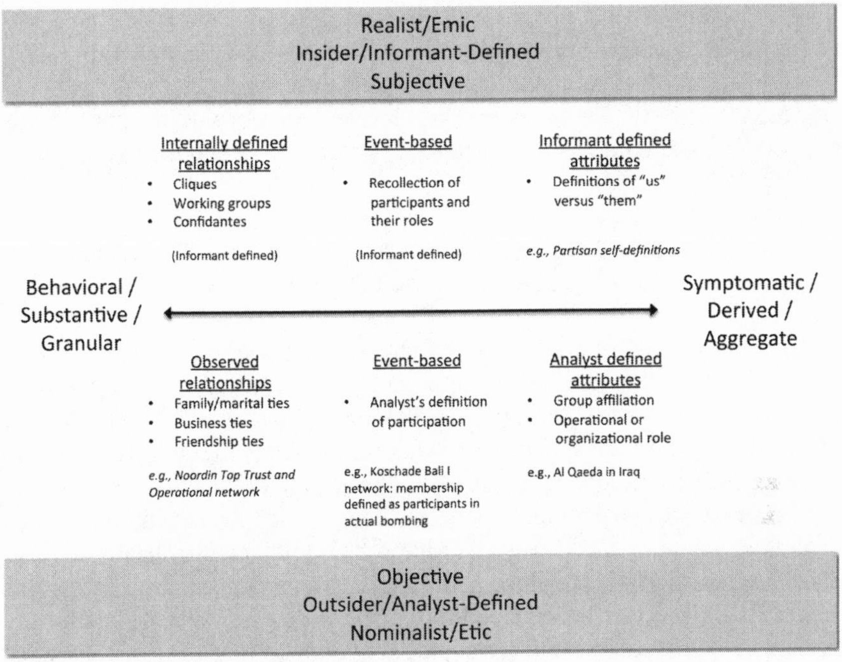

Figure 3.8 Boundary Specification Typology: Adapted from Laumann, Marsden, and Prensky (1983)

phenomena, misspecification can lead to erroneous conclusions, something we do not want to do when we are trying to track, disrupt, and/or destabilize a dark network. The questions below are a few of the essential questions that analysts should ask themselves as they develop their boundaries.

- Can I get access to the desired population? If so, then, it is up to the population to define itself (i.e., attributes, type of relation, events, or some combination). Access to detained terrorists or incarcerated gang members are two examples that would permit the realist approach. If not, then a nominalist approach is required, and analysts need to develop their own well-thought-out boundaries.
- If a nominalist approach is required, what do I think defines an actor's relevance to the analysis?
    - Are actors relevant because they possess some sort of characteristic (or set of characteristics), such as a certain role, organizational affiliation, and logistic function (i.e., attribute approach)?
    - Are actors relevant because they are embedded in a particular type (or types) of relationship (i.e., relational approach), such as operational ties within a specific dark network?

- Are actors pertinent because they participated in some event, such as a terrorist attack, or crime (i.e., event or activity-based approach)?
- Or, is it some combination of these items? For example, an analysis of the 9/11 financial network would combine a relational (i.e., financial network) focus with an event (i.e., 9/11) focus to set the boundaries.

3.5 CODING RELATIONAL AND ATTRIBUTE DATA: CODEBOOKS AND ONTOLOGIES

Relational data are a form of abstract data that serve to represent real-world interactions between actors. One of a network analyst's goals is to build, or utilize, a data set that is the best possible representation of the network they want to analyze. Analysts often have access to existing relational data (e.g., network data from colleagues from a previous deployment) in the form of unstructured documents that they can structure, such as text files or official reports, or structured data they can access from link analysis databases (e.g., Palantir and Analyst's Notebook). In some cases, existing data might be sufficient for the problem at hand, and assuming the data are "clean"—uniformly structured and verified—and are a good representation of the actual network of interest, little additional collection may be required. Unfortunately, that is often not the case, especially with dark network data.

Many analysts have to start from scratch and make a determination about which relationships and attributes they need to include in their analysis, either on their own or with the group in which they are working.[6] This determination must not only consider the strategic approach and the analytic question/hypothesis at hand, but also several other factors, such as the culture and context in which the network is embedded. For example, an analyst could argue that they should include *shared school affiliation* relationships in an analysis about dark network recruitment in Indonesia because militants have used schools in the past to recruit students; however, this type of tie might be irrelevant to an analyst examining the FARC, or one of its subcommands, in Colombia. Available time and resources are also important factors to consider. An analyst examining a terrorist group's *operational* network in a war-torn area, where operations are ongoing, may only have the time to collect a few types of ties among network actors. In any situation, it is critical that their choices are thought out carefully prior to investing time and resources into collection.

Once an analyst, or team of analysts, has identified the appropriate relational and nonrelational categories (i.e., the ontology) that will guide their collection, they must define them in order to make their reasoning clear to themselves in future iterations, and to make the definitions available to others who may wish to join in the analysis or apply the data at some future point. This is a critical step in the coding process, which is essentially the method of identifying and interpreting information, and subsequently categorizing that information to facilitate data analysis. A codebook is a document that clarifies the decisions made by the analysts who constructed the data set. At a minimum it includes detailed explanations of how the network's boundaries are defined, how each of the relationships that constitute a tie are defined, and the definitions of all additional variables included the data set. Additional details should also include the types of network data (e.g., one mode and two mode), the types of attributes included in the analysis (e.g., categorical and continuous), the coding scales (e.g., education level is coded in years completed vs. ordinal variables such as education and recorded as degree attained), and notes about vexing coding decisions and conflated definitions. Although codebooks are seldom discussed in existing social network literature, the practice of creating and maintaining them is a common feature of strong analytic work and failing to use them can make it difficult or impossible for analysts (and subsequent analysts) to use the data in the future (see Appendix 2 for the codebooks of the networks used in this book).

Codebooks are therefore indispensable reference guides that analysts construct during the coding process. They are especially helpful when it is necessary or efficient to carry out data coding and entry using a diverse or locationally distributed team. The definitions outlined in the codebook constitute the ontology of the investigation. If the definitions of the boundaries, ties, variables, and scales are well defined and adhered to closely by data coders, subjectivity will be greatly reduced, which, in turn, greatly increases the reliability of the coding and structuring processes. For instance, a team of analysts interested in monitoring and tracking a particular dark network's *financial* network will likely have different definitions and interpretations of what a *financial* relationship is between two actors in their context. One analyst may define presence of a financial tie between two actors as a "transfer of funds between two individuals," while a second may define it as "two actors who invest in the same stock." The point is that neither definition is necessarily better than the other. They are simply different. However, such a difference will result in two distinct data coding approaches, which will increase measurement error, as there are essentially two different tie variables that are being inconsistently recorded on top of one another. Worse, a situation of this sort does not only arise when more than one coder is working on data entry. It is not uncommon for a single analyst working in an operational environment to be inconsistent in his or her day-to-day coding if they are operating without the definitional reminders contained within a codebook.

The reliability advantages that codebooks make possible also transfer between rotations, deployments, or the arrival of new analysts. For example, analysts on a new deployment are more likely to build their own data set than to attempt to guess at how the data were previously defined and coded, using significant time and resources in the process. On the other hand, a clearly defined set of attributes and relationships in a codebook allows incoming analysts to further build upon the data set, or revise specific categories of relationships and attributes rather than abandoning the entire data set or database. As a case in point, major and common criticism of many existing software programs that have a built-in relational dimension is that they allow users to structure relational data without a clearly defined ontology.[7]

A good codebook provides specific and mutually exclusive definitions for each attribute and type of tie. For instance, one definition of a *communication* tie could be "the relaying of messages between individuals through some sort of electronic medium." Note that such a relationship does not explicitly include other types of relationships (e.g., friendship and kinship), and its specificity may lead data coders to ignore other, nonelectronic, forms of communication. A much looser definition may be "the relaying of messages in person and/or between two people who know one another," and could lead analysts to record a host of different relationships between two actors, including communication, meeting/event, and/or friendship, kinship, business, or other ties. The looser definition is much more expansive, but prone to inconsistent application, with some coders opting to record only known communications and others to record suspected communication, given some close relationship.

Rather than opting for an expansive definition of a particular type of tie at the outset of an investigation, it is good practice to break down the tie definition according to the analyst's degree of certainty. Following the example above, the analyst may choose to code known or observed communications separate from other relationships that would likely result in communications, such as friendship, kinship, or other close ties. The more specific and nonoverlapping the definitions are, the easier it will be for colleagues and later coders to follow. Additionally, and just as importantly, one can always go from specific to general, but never from general to specific with recorded data. Narrower definitions may always be combined into a larger, more general tie category. But looser definitions cannot be broken back down into narrower categories. The narrower definitions create more flexible data for the analyst.

Ultimately, an analyst's problem set should drive the development of a codebook and the relational and nonrelational information included in it. In terms of practical application, the scale or extent of a codebook will depend on how many analysts will be conducting the network analysis. A single analyst's codebook is likely to be less extensive and may include fewer attributes and relationships than an entire organization's codebook.

For example, a researcher looking at a specific terrorist group in northern Africa may include up to five or six relationships (e.g., kinship, business, trust, and primary solidarity group) and a dozen attributes in their analysis. On the other hand, an organization responsible for the entire region that employs a universal ontology for its team of analysts will likely need to define a greater number of relationships and attribute categories in order to account for its team's broader set of questions. This shared coding standard will also allow them to share and distribute the data collection effort, which is advantageous given the transnational (or trans-jurisdictional) nature of most dark networks.

3.6 COLLECTING SOCIAL NETWORK DATA

Social network analysts gather and collect social network data in a variety of ways. The most common are questionnaires, interviews, direct observation, and written records (Wasserman and Faust 1994:45–54), although not all of these are useful for dark network data collection. Still, it is useful to briefly consider the various approaches for collecting social network data in order to establish common practices in the field and to encourage the possibility of innovation through analogy.[8]

Questionnaires

Questionnaires are a common method for collecting social network data, especially when actors are individuals, although they are probably the least common method when it comes to collecting relational data on dark networks. Questions such as about who people consider to be their friends, to whom do they go to for advice, with whom they regularly communicate (e.g., talk face-to-face, e-mail, and telephone), and similar formats are used to investigate interpersonal interactions. Such data can be recorded either symmetrically or asymmetrically. Say, for instance, actor "A" considers actor "B" to be a friend, but "B" does not consider "A" to be a friend. In such a case, researchers can either record the data asymmetrically by considering the ties each actor "sends" or projects to their alters to be one-directional and in need of confirmation by their alter, or the tie may be considered symmetric by recording a reciprocated tie between two actors when anyone is identified by another as having that tie to them under the assumption that that type of tie, such as kinship, is something that must always be reciprocated by its nature. Analysts use various formats for collecting social network data using questionnaires; they fall under three broad categories: (1) roster vs. free recall, (2) free vs. fixed choice, and (3) ratings vs. complete rankings (Wasserman and Faust 1994:45). Readers interested in designing questionnaires for network analysis may also consult Borgatti et al. (2013:45–52) for a more complete description of the process.

Interviews

Social network analysts sometimes use interviews (either face-to-face or over the phone) to collect data (Wasserman and Faust 1994:48). In terms of practitioners, they often collect relational and attribute data via informal interviews and conversations with people in their area of responsibility. A soldier in the Philippines, for example, can collect relational data about dark network actors through a simple conversation with locals. Analysts can also create formal interviews with detained dark network actors. For example, a network researcher may interview captured insurgent actors and ask them a series of questions that produce relational data. Given the respondents' probable lack of motivation to produce complete or accurate information, however, such interviews should likely always be verified or supplemented through other methods (e.g., direct observation and written records).

Direct Observation

Another method for obtaining network data is for an observer to record any observed interactions that take place among actors in the network (Wasserman and Faust 1994:49). Dan McFarland (2004) used this approach to record student interaction patterns at two different high schools. An obvious drawback to direct observation is that in some situations interactions can be so numerous and occur so closely together that it becomes next to impossible to record all interactions. Then, of course, there is the problem of observer effects: Those being observed often alter their behavior when they are aware that their interactions are being recorded (Roethlisberger and Dickson 1939). Nevertheless, analysts of dark networks might find this approach useful when recording affiliation (i.e., two-mode) network data. For example, they can record which sites or events members of a particular dark network visit in connection with their participation with the network.

Written Records

Written records can be valuable sources of relational data. E-mails, memos, phone calls (if available), court proceedings, and situational and intelligence reports are just a few examples of sources from which one can determine ties between individual actors. At the organizational level, written records indicating actors who are members of multiple organizations (e.g., where the same individual is affiliated with two criminal organizations) may indicate ties between them. In terms of collecting relational data on dark networks, Sageman (2003, 2004, 2008) drew upon captured documents, trial transcripts, intercepted conversations, legal documents, and testimony notes in order to determine some of the ties among members of the global Salafi jihad. Several examples used throughout this book were largely drawn from written records, such as data on Noordin's terrorist network, which in turn drew in part on court records (International Crisis Group 2006, 2009a, 2009b, 2010).

Other Approaches

This is not meant as an extensive or exhaustive list of approaches to collecting social network data. Although it includes some of the more common methods of data collection, analysts are encouraged to explore analogous methods and innovate accordingly. Other forms of data collection include Delphi-type surveys, social media scraping, text matching from recorded statements, cognitive social structures, experiments, diaries, and small world research. As noted above, surveys are often used for collecting ego network data. When collecting cognitive social structure data, researchers ask respondents for their perception of other actors' network ties (e.g., "Who is friends with whom?", "Who seeks advice from whom?") (Krackhardt 1987a). Delphi method introduces the possibility of repeated polling and conversation among area experts for their insights into actors, events, and environments (Dalkey and Helmer 1963; Linstone and Turoff 1975). Social media and other publically available statements and conversations by and between actors may be used to seek patterns in communication or statements that could reveal latent or manifest ties. Social network analysts sometimes use experiments to observe the behavior of a set of actors in experimentally controlled environments (Bavelas 1950; Emerson 1962, 1972a, 1972b). They also ask people to keep diaries in order to capture a continuous record of people with whom they interact (Wasserman and Faust 1994:54). And finally they sometimes use variations on small-world network design (Korte and Milgram 1970; Milgram 1967; Travers and Milgram 1969) to estimate how many steps (i.e., degrees of separation) a respondent is from a randomly chosen target (Watts 1999b; Watts, Dodds and Newman 2003; Watts and Strogatz 1998).

3.7 RECORDING SOCIAL NETWORK DATA

The information gathered via one or more of the collection methods above must be formatted in a manner that is compatible for use in a social network analysis program. The process of recording social network data is often treated as being synonymous with the process of data coding; however, the two processes are not necessarily the same. As you may recall, coding is a process involving interpretation of information based on a series of definitions embedded in a codebook. Recording data, on the other hand, involves a set of techniques with which an analyst may structure the information into usable network data. For example, an analyst interested in identifying *trust* relationships among a set of actors must interpret, based on a codebook, what constitutes a trust tie. The analyst may then extract and format any data that was coded in a manner that falls within their definition into a structure that is usable for network analysis.

The process of coding and structuring relational data for dark networks is sometimes simplified or facilitated through the use of data management software such as Palantir and Analyst's Notebook. Such data management programs allow analysts to structure their data directly from within the software. Palantir, for example, has a built-in structuring feature (i.e., "tagging") that allows users to create entities (i.e., actors) as data objects and then establish relationships between entities based on the user's ontology. Programs of this sort may also have some rudimentary built-in SNA metrics that make these programs attractive to analysts who are unfamiliar with the extent of what is possible in SNA. Correspondingly, the main value of such programs for a social network analyst generally lies in data structuring, as they are not well designed for use with anything more than a very superficial analysis of a social network. The designers of these programs have therefore made provision for analysts to export data that have been coded and structured into one or more formats that are compatible with programs that have been specifically designed for social network analysis.[9]

Matrices

There is a wide variety of data formats that have been designed for social network data. One historically well-used data format is the *matrix representation* of a network, which may be imported into most network analysis packages. Matrices are, however, often tedious to construct, and impractical in operational environments and when working with large networks. Imagine having to create a matrix for a network consisting of 100 actors. Creating a matrix that size would require an analyst to fill out 10,000 cells (100 rows × 100 columns) for each type of relationship. It may therefore come as no surprise that simpler and more efficient formats have been developed to import data into network analysis programs.

Edgelists

Edgelists offer one of the more popular and efficient alternatives to creating data matrices. At its simplest, the edgelist data format generally consists of a file containing a two-column list of actors. Although edgelists may be either directed or undirected, in cases where the data are directed the actor "sending" the tie is given in the first column, and the actor "receiving" the tie in the second. For undirected edgelists, the actor pair is simply given as indicating a tie. This format is powerful, flexible, and nearly universal in its ability to be imported into various programs. But basic edgelists are somewhat limited in their ability to store additional data, such as the weight of individual ties and multiple types of relationship. A variety of edgelist variations have therefore been introduced to improve those shortcomings.

One of the most popular edgelist formats was developed for the program Pajek. The Pajek edgelist format—also referred to as the "dot net" (.net) format, or .net files—is comprised of two sections (Figure 3.8). The first provides information about actors (vertices), while the second contains information about the relationship(s) between actors. The actor information portion of the Pajek edgelist first indicates the number of vertices—or, in the case of two-mode data, the total number of vertices followed by the number of vertices in the first mode—followed by a numbered list of actor/vertex names. There are additionally three columns of numbers that record the x, y, and z coordinates last used to visualize the network. The relationship portion of the edgelist begins with information on whether the list represents arcs or edges, followed by two or three columns. The first two columns are numbers that correspond with the numbered list of actors. The actor in the first column is the source actor (i.e., sender) and the actor in the second is the target (i.e., receiver). The third column, when present, is a weight that indicates the strength of the tie between the pair of actors. It is possible to list multiple types of relationship in the relationship section, as well as other information such as time codes, vertex and line colors, and vertex shape indicators (Batagelj and Mrvar 2015).

Edgelists may be used to represent both one-mode and two-mode networks and can be saved in a host of different file types, including text (.txt), Excel (.xlsx), comma separated value (.csv), or Pajek (.net) files.[10] Programs such as UCINET, Pajek, and R (igraph and statnet) accept and store network data in this type of file format. Figure 3.9 depicts a portion of one-mode edgelist of the Koschade Bali I network as a text file that can be read into Pajek. Note that the actors (vertices) are listed first, followed by the edges between actors and the strength of the tie between them. Thus, we can see that Muklas (actor 1) has ties to actors 2 (Amrozi), 3 (Imron), 4 (Samudra), 5 (Dulmatin), 6 (Idris), 8 (Azahari), 9 (Ghoni), 15 (Patek), and 17 (Sarijo). The strength of most of these ties is equal to one, but Muklas's ties to Amrozi, Imron, and Idris equal, two, and five, respectively. Now compare this edgelist to the matrix in Figure 3.2. If you read across first row of the matrix (Muklas), you can see that his ties to others and the strength

```
*Vertices 17
  1 "Muklas"                        0.4192    0.6565    0.5000
  2 "Amrozi"                        0.6214    0.8500    0.5000
  3 "Imron"                         0.3141    0.4681    0.5000
  4 "Samudra"                       0.6063    0.4583    0.5000
  5 "Dulmatin"                      0.3367    0.3482    0.5000
  6 "Idris"                         0.4962    0.6510    0.5000
  7 "Mubarok"                       0.7168    0.8281    0.5000
  8 "Azahari"                       0.3955    0.4431    0.5000
  9 "Ghoni"                         0.3321    0.5601    0.5000
 10 "Arnasan"                       0.8500    0.4694    0.5000
 11 "Rauf"                          0.8469    0.3813    0.5000
 12 "Octavia"                       0.7514    0.1500    0.5000
 13 "Hidayat"                       0.8258    0.2966    0.5000
 14 "Junaedi"                       0.7983    0.2150    0.5000
 15 "Patek"                         0.3824    0.2357    0.5000
 16 "Feri"                          0.1500    0.2953    0.5000
 17 "Sarijo"                        0.4120    0.3094    0.5000
*Edges
  1    2 2
  1    3 2
  1    4 1
  1    5 1
  1    6 5
  1    8 1
  1    9 1
  1   15 1
  1   17 1
  2    4 2
  2    6 4
  2    7 5
  3    4 3
```

Figure 3.9 One-Mode Pajek (.net) Edgelist Format (Koschade Bali I Network)

of these ties are the same. Perhaps the most important difference between the two formats is that matrix formats contain both ties ("1s") and non-ties ("0s"), whereas edge lists include only ties. Consequently, edge lists tend to be smaller in size and thus more adept at handling large amounts of network data.

Analysts may also select from a variety of other edgelist formats to record their data. One example is shown in Figure 3.10. The basic concepts are the same for this format as those discussed above and shown in Figure 3.9. For instance, the relationships between actors are still established row by row. An important difference between this format and the one seen in 3.9 is that the one in Figure 3.10 allows analysts to record multiple relations between actors within the same file without having to be systematic. This can be done in two ways. The first method is to create two extra columns per row; one indicating the specific relationship between the two actors and the other indicating the direction of the relationship (Figure 3.9). This approach is often used in Gephi and it works best when analysts at least include "Source," "Target," "Type," and "Relationship" columns.[11]

	A	B	C	D	E	F
1	Source	Target	Type	Relationship		
2	Abdul Aziz	Noordin Mohammed Top	Undirected	Internal Comms		
3	Abdul Aziz	Azhari Husin	Undirected	Internal Comms		
4	Abdul Aziz	Misno	Undirected	Internal Comms		
5	Abdul Aziz	Said Sungkar	Undirected	Internal Comms		
6	Abdul Aziz	Misno	Directed	Mentor Supervisory		
7	Abdul Aziz	Misno	Directed	Mentor Technological		
8	Abdul Jabar	Noordin Mohammed Top	Undirected	Internal Comms		
9	Abdul Jabar	Farihin	Undirected	Internal Comms		
10	Abdul Jabar	Solahudin	Undirected	Kinship		
11	Abdul Jabar	Mohamed Islam	Undirected	Kinship		
12	Abdul Jabar	Farihin	Undirected	Kinship		
13	Abdul Malik	Akram	Undirected	Internal Comms		
14	Abdul Malik	Akram	Undirected	Kinship		
15	Abdul Rauf	Mohamed Ihsan	Undirected	Classmates		
16	Abdul Rauf	Sardona Siliwangi	Undirected	Classmates		
17	Abdul Rauf	Tohir	Undirected	Classmates		
18	Abdul Rauf	Abu Bakar Ba'asyir	Undirected	Classmates		
19	Abdul Rauf	Suramto	Undirected	Classmates		
20	Abdul Rauf	Abdullah Sungkar	Undirected	Classmates		
21	Abdul Rauf	Asmar Latin Sani	Undirected	Classmates		
22	Abdul Rauf	Mohamed Rais	Undirected	Classmates		
23	Abdul Rauf	Jabir	Undirected	Classmates		
24	Abdul Rauf	Andri Octavia	Undirected	Classmates		
25	Abdul Rauf	Ubeid	Undirected	Classmates		
26	Abdul Rauf	Baharudin Soleh	Undirected	Classmates		
27	Abdul Rauf	Andri Octavia	Undirected	Internal Comms		
28	Abdul Rohim	Ahmad Rofiq Ridho	Undirected	Friendship		
29	Abdul Rohim	Noordin Mohammed Top	Undirected	Internal Comms		
30	Abdul Rohim	Abu Bakar Ba'asyir	Undirected	Internal Comms		
31	Abdul Rohim	Fathurrahman al-Ghozi	Undirected	Internal Comms		
32	Abdul Rohim	Ahmad Rofiq Ridho	Undirected	Internal Comms		
33	Abdul Rohim	Abu Bakar Ba'asyir	Undirected	Kinship		
34	Abdullah Sunata	Asep Jaja	Undirected	Classmates		

Edgelist

Ready

Figure 3.10 Noordin Top Combined Network: Edgelist in Gephi

The second variation of an edgelist is depicted in Figure 3.11. This format, which is typically stored as Excel or CSV files, allows network analysts to build out several relationships across the columns by simply indicating the name of the relationship (or attribute) in the column header and the target actor of the relationship in the appropriate row-column cell. For instance, Abdul Aziz (column A, row 1) has an "internal communication" relationship with Azhari Husin (column F, row 1). The advantage of this format is that analysts can record their data, relational and nonrelational (i.e., attributes), into a single file as opposed to recording data in separate files, one for each type of relationship and one for attributes. As you can see in Figure 3.10, Abdul Aziz not only has an "internal communication" tie with Azhari Husin, but he also plays a role as a "Propagandist" (column B, row 1), he is a member of the Islamic Defenders Front (FPI) in Pekalongan (column C, row 1), and he uses "Computer-based" messages to communicate (column G, row 1). The subsequent rows (3–5) indicate Abdul Aziz is a "Resource Provider" (column B, row 3) and has "internal communication" ties with Misno (column F, row 3), Noordin Mohammed Top (column F, row 4), and

	A	B	C	D	E	F	G	H	I	J	K	L	M	N	O	P	Q	R	S	T	U
1	Source	Roles	Terrorist/I	Education	Classmate	Internal C	Comms M	Kinship	Training	Recruiting	Business a	Financial	Operation	Friendshi	Religious	Soulmate	Logistical	Mentor Id	Mentor Su	Mentor Technologi	
2	Abdul Azi	Propagand	Islamic Defenders Front (FPI) P			Azhari Hu	Computer-based						Bali II (Oct 05)		Pekalongan Pengaji		Material		Misno		
3	Abdul Azi	Resource Provider				Misno															
4	Abdul Aziz					Noordin Mohammed Top															
5	Abdul Aziz					Said Sungkar															
6	Abdul Jab	Bomber/ I	Jemaah Islamiyah (JI)			Farihin		Farihin					Bombing Attack on Philippine Ambassador in Jakarta (Aug 00)								
7	Abdul Jabar					Noordin Mohammed		Mohamed Islam													
8	Abdul Jabar							Solahudin													
9	Abdul Mal	Recruiter	Darul Islam (DI)			Akram		Akram			Tobacco B	Business					Transportation				
10	Abdul Malik											Money Transfer from unknown sources									
11	Abdul Rau	Resource	Ring Bant	Pondok N	Mohamed	Andri Octavia						Crime	Robbery To Raise Funds For Bali I (Aug 02)								
12	Abdul Rauf				Sardona Siliwangi								Bali I (Oct 02)								
13	Abdul Rauf				Tohir																
14	Abdul Rauf				Abu Bakar Ba'asyir																
15	Abdul Rauf				Suramto																
16	Abdul Rauf				Abdullah Sungkar																
17	Abdul Rauf				Asmar Latin Sani																
18	Abdul Rauf				Mohamed Rais																
19	Abdul Rauf				Jabir																
20	Abdul Rauf				Andri Octavia																
21	Abdul Rauf				Ubeid																
22	Abdul Rauf				Baharudin Soleh																
23	Abdul Roh	Liason				Abu Bakar Ba'asyir						Sales		Ahmad Rofiq Ridho			Material				
24	Abdul Roh	Propagandist				Ahmad Rofiq Ridho															
25	Abdul Rohim					Fathurrah	Videos														
26	Abdul Rohim					Noordin Mohammed		Abu Bakar Ba'asyir													
27	Abdullah :	Leader	KOMPAK Charity		Asep Jaja	Ahmad Rc	Computer-based		03 Mindanao Training			Money Transfer fron		Muzayin Abdul Wahab							
28	Abdullah :	Sympathi	KOMPAK Mujahidin			Ahmad Sa	Videos		Jul 04 West Ceram												
29	Abdullah Sunata		KOMPAK-Ambon Office			Akram			Oct 99 Waimurat, Buru Training												
30	Abdullah Sunata		KOMPAK-Waihong			Ali															
31	Abdullah Sunata					Asep Jaja															
32	Abdullah Sunata					Dulmatin															
33	Abdullah Sunata					Enceng Kurnia															
34	Abdullah Sunata					Harun															

Edgelist

Figure 3.11 Noordin Combined Network: ORA and Lighthouse Edgelists/"Simple Table"

Said Sungkar (column F, row 5).[12] A second advantage is that analysts can record multimodal networks in this format. For instance, network analysts can record person-to-person, person-to-organization, person-to-location, and person-to-resource relations all in the same file. ORA, with its meta-network approach, imports this file format seamlessly. The field-collection tool Lighthouse, which serves as an alternative to manually recording data, also allows collectors to structure their data in this format.

Nodelists

Nodelists provide another simple alternative to using matrices and edgelists. They are similar to the other formats in that they work row by row and left to right. In the example presented in Figure 3.12 (once again, the Koschade Bali I network), the actor in the first column represents the source actor, while the actors in the subsequent columns represent the target actors. The first row is Muklas, who is the source actor, and at a glance you can see that he has ties to actors 2 (Amrozi), 3 (Imron), 4 (Samudra), 5 (Dulmatin), 6 (Idris), 8 (Azahari), 9 (Ghoni), 15 (Patek), and 17 (Sarijo). Compare this with the edgelist in Figure 3.9 and the matrix in Figure 3.2. The simplicity of this approach, however, presents some limitations to network analysts, namely that these are only used for binary data, and the type of relationship by which actors are linked is not explicit with this format. This format is used primarily in UCINET.

In terms of practical application, the formats listed above are often recorded as asymmetric data where a source actor (i.e., rows in matrices, column A in edgelists) sends a relationship to a target actor (i.e., columns in matrices, remainder columns in edgelists). It would be ideal if the direction of ties within dark networks were easily observable. As noted earlier, though, the conditions under which dark networks are observed are seldom ideal. Take, for example, a hypothetical *business and finance* relationship between two dark network actors: actor A and actor B. In an optimal scenario, information about the direction of the relationship would be clear, such as actor A being observed as sending money to actor B. In reality, this information is often collected without specifying tie direction, which limits us to simply recording that actor A and actor B possess some sort of business or financial relationship. The question then becomes, do network analysts need to record both a relationship from actor A to actor B and a relationship from actor B to actor A because we have to assume the relationship is undirected due to a lack of information? The answer is no. Most network analysis programs have built-in features that allow analysts to symmetrize their data with very little effort. Such a procedure essentially recreates—or completes, if you will—the data set so that all relationships are made to be reciprocal. This approach

```
DL
N=17
FORMAT = NODELIST1 DIAGONAL PRESENT
ROW LABELS:
"Muklas"
"Amrozi"
"Imron"
"Samudra"
"Dulmatin"
"Idris"
"Mubarok"
"Azahari"
"Ghoni"
"Arnasan"
"Rauf"
"Octavia"
"Hidayat"
"Junaedi"
"Patek"
"Feri"
"Sarijo"
COLUMN LABELS:
"Muklas"
"Amrozi"
"Imron"
"Samudra"
"Dulmatin"
"Idris"
"Mubarok"
"Azahari"
"Ghoni"
"Arnasan"
"Rauf"
"Octavia"
"Hidayat"
"Junaedi"
"Patek"
"Feri"
"Sarijo"
LEVEL LABELS:
"Page 1"
DATA:
  1   2   3   4   5   6   8   9  15  17
  2   1   4   6   7
  3   1   4   5   6   8   9  15  16  17
  4   1   2   3   5   6   7   8   9  10  11  12  13  14  15  17
  5   1   3   4   6   8  17
  6   1   2   3   4   5   7   8   9  15  17
  7   2   4   6
  8   1   3   4   5   6   9  15  16  17
  9   1   3   4   5   6   8  15  16  17
 10   4  11  12  13  14
 11   4  10  12  13  14
 12   4  10  11  13  14
 13   4  10  11  12  14
 14   4  10  11  12  13
 15   1   3   4   5   6   8   9  16  17
 16   3   5   8   9  15  17
 17   1   3   4   5   6   8   9  15  16
1
```

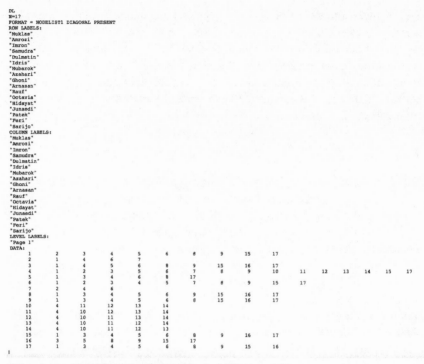

Figure 3.12 UCINET Node List (Koschade Bali I Network)

permits network analysts who wish to work with symmetric data to record the presence of a relationship only one time per relationship type.

As noted in the first chapter, although SNA focuses primarily on the pattern of ties between actors, it does not ignore actors' *attribute data*, which are nonrelational data that deal with actors' attitudes, roles, affiliations, behaviors, and so on. They are helpful to network analysts for a few important reasons. First, attributes provide additional context about networks and network actors. In an examination of a dark network's brokers, we may find several important actors in terms of the flow of information and resources throughout the network. The addition of attributes, such as the organizations to which they belong and the roles they serve, provides important information about those actors and potentially present reasons why those actors are relatively important within in the network structure. Second, attributes allow network analysts to use various techniques to better understand their network of interest. For example, an analyst interested in an Improvised Explosives Device (IED) network can extract and analyze a subset of actors from a larger dark network who possess bomb-making skills. We will explore some of these techniques throughout the rest of the book.

Generally speaking, attributes are recorded separately from relational data (the edgelists mentioned above being the exception). The specific manner in which an analyst records attribute data largely depends on the type of attributes included in the analysis. Network analysts can record categorical (qualitative) or continuous (quantitative) attributes. The former can be nominal, dichotomous, or ordinal. Nominal attributes contain two or more categories but do not have an intrinsic order. For example, a network may consist of many actors who possess several different organizational affiliations. Dichotomous attributes are those containing two categories. An example of this is whether an actor is a known felon ("1" or "Yes") or not ("0" or "No"). Ordinal attributes are two or more categories that have some inherent order, but not necessarily evenly spaced differences. Numbers should not be used in place of ordinal variables as though it were a continuous variable, as their values would be an inaccurate reflection of the original meaning. In the scenario where an analyst has access to dark network actors, the analyst could ask them if they liked the policies of the U.S. government and they could select from "I like them very much," "They're OK," or "I strongly dislike them." If the three ordinal categories were replaced with 1, 2, and 3, it could easily understate the—unmeasured—difference between liking very much and strongly disliking.

Examples of commonly used categorical attributes at the individual level are actors' roles and affiliations. At the organizational level, they may be the country (or countries) in which the organization operates or if an organization is listed on the Foreign Terrorist Organization List (yes or no). Continuous attributes, on the other hand, are represented by a numeric value (not a numeric category) and they can be broken down into interval or ratio attributes.[13] Examples of a commonly recorded continuous attribute are a criminal financier's income or an actor's betweenness centrality score (or any other metric output).

Fortunately, most network analysis programs allow users to record data directly into the program.[14] For instance, users can record attribute data directly into ORA's Editor Tab once they have imported network data. This section does not provide a detailed outline of the various import techniques available in the commonly used network analysis packages. Readers interested in a more detailed explanation of importing data can instead refer to Everton (2012a), de Nooy et al. (2011), McCulloh et al. (2013), or the user's manual for their program of choice. The appropriate technique is largely driven by the way in which the data were recorded and the analytic package that is going to be used to conduct the analysis. Fortunately, most SNA packages are compatible with one another (at least to some extent), which allows analysts to import data in one program and subsequently export their data to another. For example, an analyst comfortable with ORA may record data in the edgelist format seen in Figure 3.11. They may realize at some point that they need to export their data to utilize metrics or techniques only available in another package, such as UCINET. In most cases, analysts can transfer one-mode data between analytic programs without much trouble, provided they use the package's export function and know how data for the other package should be formatted. This process can be much more challenging with two-mode and attribute data and requires the analyst to follow specific steps, depending on the program from which they wish export their data and the program into which they want to import their data.

It is highly recommended, however, that analysts check their data to ensure they were transferred properly between the programs. It is common for different programs to have very different default methods for importing data. It is not uncommon to find that undirected data, once imported into another program, is being treated as though it is directed data. In other cases, default settings on the data import feature may treat recursive ties as an arc, an edge, or they may be omitted entirely, depending on the program. Additionally analyses with the same name may be implemented in slightly different manners or may have very different default settings from program to program. Analysts that take advantage of the export-import feature of network analysis programs should triple check their data and possibly run through one or more of their analyses once they have been successfully imported data into a new program.[15]

An important concern to network analysts is ensuring data are clean enough to conduct effective SNA. Several types of errors can occur during data collection and data recording processes even with a codebook. Common errors to look for are repeated actors based on misspellings and inappropriately coded relational and nonrelational data. It is, therefore, advisable to check for such errors before moving forward by examining the data in the data editor sections of the analytic package, or by visually examining the data using various network layouts. Time spent making sure that data are clean and ready to use will save many headaches later in the process.

3.8 COMBINING, AGGREGATING, AND PARSING NETWORKS

Up to this point we have focused on single types of relationships among actors: superior-subordinate, meetings, trust, financial, and so on. In the real world, however, actors are typically involved in more than one sort of a relationship (Hanneman and Riddle 2005). At the individual level, actors are embedded in several types of ties (e.g., friendship, kinship, operational, trust, and recruitment ties), and organizations are no different. Insurgent organizations, for example, often share material (e.g., weapons and money) and nonmaterial goods (e.g., ideology and information), and they even establish negative ties with one another through various types of conflicts, such as turf battles. More importantly, different types of ties can pressure actors to make conflicting choices (Pescosolido and Rubin 2000; Simmel [1908] 1955). Evidence from the wars in Afghanistan and Iraq, and the cartel wars in Mexico, highlight how dark network actors (individuals and organizations) often partner, shift alliances, and feud with others based on the relationships in which they are embedded and the context in which they are operating. However, little research on dark networks has accounted for the multirelational (i.e., multiplexity) nature of dark networks both at the individual and organization levels (Everton and Cunningham 2015; Roberts and Everton 2011).

The collection of multirelational data on dark networks is important from a practical point of view for a few reasons. The covert nature of dark networks makes it challenging to observe and collect relational data on them, which suggests that we can get a clearer picture of them by mapping as many relevant relationships as possible. A second reason is that once analysts have recorded and imported their data, they can focus on a set of relationships that can help them better understand the problem set at hand. For instance, an analyst with access to an existing data set, and who is tasked with analyzing a dark network's *operational* network, can select and analyze only relations that make up the best notion of operationally related ties in that context. The analyst may suggest logistical, training, and past-operational ties best define an operational network. What is crucial is that some thought is put into this decision because the definition of an operational network is likely to change across contexts and among network analysts. Another analyst, for example, could suggest the best definition of an operational network is the combination of logistic, training, past-operational, and communication ties. The addition of a single type of tie could change the results of the analysis, such as the overall structure and who the key players are, and ultimately the recommendations the analyst makes. Several approaches exist for working with multiple relationships embedded within a dark network, three of which we will consider here: combining (aka, stacking), aggregating, and parsing. We consider each of these in turn.

Combining (Stacking) Network Data

Combining or stacking networks is a commonly used technique available in most network analysis packages that allows analysts to store multiple network data as a set of actor-by-actor files (e.g., matrices), one for each type of relation. The individual networks (e.g., friendship and kinship) are essentially subfiles stored and embedded within a larger file.[16] The way in which data are combined and stored, however, varies across the different network analysis packages. Refer to the companion website for more detail on how individual programs differ in data stacking. Figure 3.13 presents a UCINET file partially depicting a stacked set of relations of the Noordin Combined Network.

Storing data in this manner is beneficial for a few reasons. First, it permits network analysts to easily store and manage their files. For example, an analyst working with multirelational data, such as friendship, kinship, and operational ties, can store all of these networks in the same file as opposed to storing and managing three different files. Second, analysts can "unpack" or extract specific relationships from stacked files if they choose to do so, which is something they cannot do after aggregating networks. Third, combining networks can facilitate the visual exploration of multiplex networks. One technique is to a color the ties of each of the combined networks by relationship type. For instance, this technique allows analysts to see which types of relations are important to the overall cohesiveness of a network. Figure 3.14 depicts the Noordin Combined classmate and friendship ties.[17]

Aggregating Network Data

A second option, aggregating networks, is a technique that creates a new network from a set of networks, including combined networks, by aggregating them into a single-valued network. Most network analysis programs provide analysts with several approaches for doing this with different levels of ease. A few of the commonly used options allow analysts to aggregate networks by adding them together (i.e., sum), assigning the minimum or maximum value of existing ties, taking the average value of relations, or by aggregating them based on binary values.[18] For example, a network analyst interested in examining a dark network's *communication* network may want to aggregate a series of stacked networks, such as formal relations with known phone conversations, by adding the two matrices together (i.e., the sum option). In this example, the values of each relationship have been recorded using binary values, which as you may recall, indicate whether a tie exists or not and they are typically recorded as a "1" for the presence of a tie and a "0" for the absence of tie. Two actors who have been observed communicating via phone and who maintain a formal relationship would, in this example, have a tie value/strength of "2" after aggregation.

Aggregating networks is a useful technique for a few reasons. Similar to stacking networks, it allows analysts to store and manage their data in a single file as opposed to multiple subfiles. The only issue with this is that once files are aggregated, they can no longer be "unpacked" or extracted because the aggregation process merges the networks into a single-valued network. In terms of the *communication* example, the analyst would no longer be able

DISPLAY

Input dataset: Noordin 139 - Combined Network (Stacked) (C:\Users\Sean\Dropbox\Casting More Light (Book)\Data\Noordin Top\UCINET Files\Noordin 139 - Combined Network (Stacked)

Matrix: Noordin 139 - Classmates

		1 Abd ul Azi z	2 Abd ul Jab ar	3 Abd ul Mal ik	4 Abd ul Rau f	5 Abd ul Roh im	6 Abd ull ah Sun ata	7 Abd ull ah Sun gka r	8 Abu Ba kar Ba 'as yir	9 Abu Du jan ah	10 Abu Fi da	11 Abu Mu sab al -Za rqa wi	12 Abu Ro iro h	13 Abu Ru sda n	14 Ace ng Kur nia	15 Ach mad Ha san	16 Ade Ba hru	17 Adi tya Tr i Y oga	18 Adu ng	19 Agu s A hma d	20 Agu s D wik arn a	21 Agu s P ury ant o	22 Ahm ad Bas yir	23 Ahm ad Rof iq Rid ho	24 Ahm ad Roi cha n	25 Ahm ad Say id Mau lan a	26 Aip Hi day at	27 Aje nga n M asd uki	28 Akr am	29 Ali	30 Ali Gh ufr on	31 Ali Im ron	32 Amr ozi	33 And ri Oct avi a	34 Ani f S olc han udi n	35 Apu y	36 Ard i W ibo wo	37 Ari s M una nda r	38 Ase p	39 Ase p J aja	40 Asm ar Lat in San i	41 Awa l P urn omo	42 Aym an al- Zaw ahr i	43 Azh ari Hu sin	44 Bah aru din So leh
1	Abdul Aziz	0	0	0	0	0	0	0	0	0	0	0	0	0	0	0	0	0	0	0	0	0	0	0	0	0	0	0	0	0	0	0	0	0	0	0	0	0	0	0	0	0	0	0	0
2	Abdul Jabar	0	0	0	0	0	0	0	0	0	0	0	0	0	0	0	0	0	0	0	0	0	0	0	0	0	0	0	0	0	0	0	0	0	0	0	0	0	0	0	0	0	0	0	0
3	Abdul Malik	0	0	0	0	0	0	0	0	0	0	0	0	0	0	0	0	0	0	0	0	0	0	0	0	0	0	0	0	0	0	0	0	0	0	0	0	0	0	0	0	0	0	0	0
4	Abdul Rauf	0	0	0	0	0	0	1	1	0	0	0	0	0	0	0	0	0	0	0	0	0	0	0	0	0	0	0	0	0	0	0	0	1	0	0	0	0	0	0	1	0	0	0	1
5	Abdul Rohim	0	0	0	0	0	0	0	0	0	0	0	0	0	0	0	0	0	0	0	0	0	0	0	0	0	0	0	0	0	0	0	0	0	0	0	0	0	0	0	0	0	0	0	0
6	Abdullah Sunata	0	0	0	0	0	0	0	0	0	0	0	0	0	0	0	0	0	0	0	0	0	0	0	0	0	0	0	0	0	0	0	0	0	0	0	0	0	0	0	0	0	0	0	0
7	Abdullah Sungkar	0	0	0	1	0	0	0	1	1	0	0	0	0	0	0	0	0	1	0	0	0	0	1	0	0	0	0	0	0	1	1	1	1	0	0	0	0	0	0	1	0	0	1	1
8	Abu Bakar Ba'asyir	0	0	0	1	0	0	1	0	0	0	0	0	0	0	0	0	0	1	0	0	0	0	1	0	0	0	0	0	0	0	0	0	1	0	0	0	0	0	0	1	0	0	0	1
9	Abu Dujanah	0	0	0	0	0	0	1	0	0	0	0	0	0	0	0	0	0	0	0	0	0	0	0	0	0	0	0	0	0	1	0	1	0	0	0	0	0	0	0	0	0	0	1	0
10	Abu Fida	0	0	0	0	0	0	0	0	0	0	0	0	0	0	0	0	0	0	0	0	0	0	0	0	0	0	0	0	0	0	0	0	0	0	0	0	0	0	0	0	0	0	0	0
137	Wawan Suprihatin	0	0	0	0	0	0	0	0	0	0	0	0	0	0	0	0	0	0	0	0	0	0	0	0	0	0	0	0	0	0	0	0	0	0	0	0	0	0	0	0	0	0	0	0
138	Wiwit	0	0	0	0	0	0	0	0	0	0	0	0	0	0	0	0	0	0	0	0	0	0	0	0	0	0	0	0	0	0	0	0	0	0	0	0	0	0	0	0	0	0	0	0
139	Zulkarnaen	0	0	0	0	0	0	1	1	0	0	0	0	0	0	0	0	0	0	0	0	0	0	0	0	0	0	0	0	0	1	0	1	0	0	0	0	0	0	0	0	0	0	1	0

Matrix: Noordin 139 - Friendship

		1 Abd ul Azi z	2 Abd ul Jab ar	3 Abd ul Mal ik	4 Abd ul Rau f	5 Abd ul Roh im	6 Abd ull ah Sun ata	7 Abd ull ah Sun gka r	8 Abu Ba kar Ba 'as yir	9 Abu Du jan ah	10 Abu Fi da	11 Abu Mu sab al -Za rqa wi	12 Abu Ro iro h	13 Abu Ru sda n	14 Ace ng Kur nia	15 Ach mad Ha san	16 Ade Ba hru	17 Adi tya Tr i Y oga	18 Adu ng	19 Agu s A hma d	20 Agu s D wik arn a	21 Agu s P ury ant o	22 Ahm ad Bas yir	23 Ahm ad Rof iq Rid ho	24 Ahm ad Roi cha n	25 Ahm ad Say id Mau lan a	26 Aip Hi day at	27 Aje nga n M asd uki	28 Akr am	29 Ali	30 Ali Gh ufr on	31 Ali Im ron	32 Amr ozi	33 And ri Oct avi a	34 Ani f S olc han udi n	35 Apu y	36 Ard i W ibo wo	37 Ari s M una nda r	38 Ase p	39 Ase p J aja	40 Asm ar Lat in San i	41 Awa l P urn omo	42 Aym an al- Zaw ahr i	43 Azh ari Hu sin	44 Bah aru din So leh
1	Abdul Aziz	0	0	0	0	0	0	0	0	0	0	0	0	0	0	0	0	0	0	0	0	0	0	0	0	0	0	0	0	0	0	0	0	0	0	0	0	0	0	0	0	0	0	0	0
2	Abdul Jabar	0	0	0	0	0	0	0	0	0	0	0	0	0	0	0	0	0	0	0	0	0	0	0	0	0	0	0	0	0	0	0	0	0	0	0	0	0	0	0	0	0	0	0	0
3	Abdul Malik	0	0	0	0	0	0	0	0	0	0	0	0	0	0	0	0	0	0	0	0	0	0	0	0	0	0	0	0	0	0	0	0	0	0	0	0	0	0	0	0	0	0	0	0
4	Abdul Rauf	0	0	0	0	0	0	0	0	0	0	0	0	0	0	0	0	0	0	0	0	0	0	0	0	0	0	0	0	0	0	0	0	0	0	0	0	0	0	0	0	0	0	0	0
5	Abdul Rohim	0	0	0	0	0	0	0	0	0	0	0	0	0	0	0	0	0	0	0	0	0	0	1	0	0	0	0	0	0	0	0	0	0	0	0	0	0	0	0	0	0	0	0	0

Figure 3.13 Partial View of Stacked Noordin Combined Network

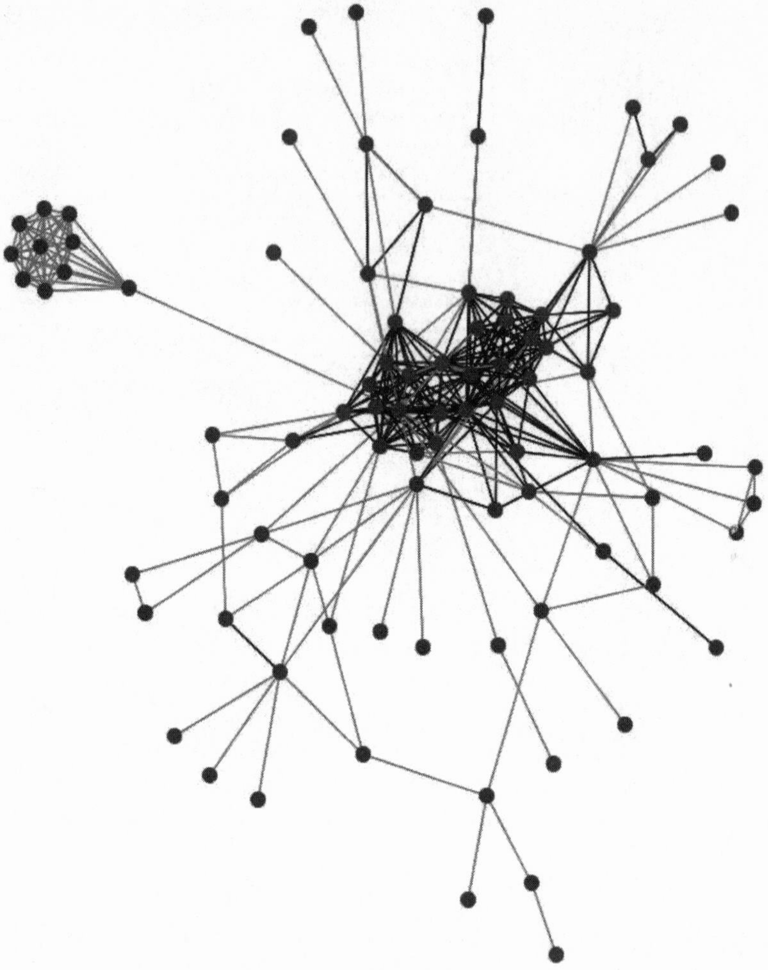

Figure 3.14 ORA Visualization of Stacked Noordin Combined Network: Classmates (Dark Gray Lines) and Friends (Light Gray Lines)

to distinguish between formal and phone call relations in the newly created aggregate file and are instead left with the meta-relationship, "communication." They can, of course, maintain the individual formal and the phone call subnetworks that they started with as a stacked file, or even as completely separate files, even after aggregation. A second benefit is that analysts can run metrics for a single aggregated network as opposed to running metrics for each network separately. Consider the *communication* network mentioned above. The analyst can only estimate metrics (e.g., centrality and topography) for the phone call and the formal networks separately until those relations are aggregated. An analysis on these separate files would produce results for each individual network and could result in specific actors who are central to the phone call network, but not the formal network (or vice versa). More importantly, they may not be fully accounting for the overall communication network by analyzing the formal and phone call networks separately. Figure 3.15 shows a symmetrized matrix of the aggregated Noordin Combined Network using the sum option in UCINET. For example, Abu Bakar Ba'asyir is tied with Abdullah Sungkar on three different types of relations.

Two additional issues are worth noting before moving on. The first is that network analysts working with multiple networks will often need to dichotomize (i.e., binarize) their data prior to or immediately after combining their networks of interest. This technique takes the value of the network's relationships and changes them to binary values (1s and 0s). As you will see in the later chapters, it is often necessary to dichotomize networks prior to running specific metrics. The second is that many actors are embedded in negative relations with others. Feuds between gangs, insurgent groups, sectarian militias, and terrorist organizations present challenging and important analytic questions for which analysts need to account. These scenarios also occur at the individual level. Analysts can record negative ties using the same techniques outlined in section 3.7 and they can combine them with other types of relationships using the approaches outlined above. Analysts need to consider, however, the effect that combining negative ties with positive ties will have on their analysis. For instance, a PSYOP officer who intends to disseminate a message to a network of interest will need to consider that the message may not flow between feuding actors (i.e., negative ties), which may reduce the effectiveness of the overall strategy in that context.

Parsing Network Data

As we noted above when discussing deriving one-mode from two-mode networks, just because two people are members of the same organization or attend the same event does not mean that they necessarily share a tie with one another. Thus, we may want to use some sort of threshold before concluding that a tie actually exists between two actors. Take the Noordin Logistical Place and Logistical Function networks as examples. These are two-mode networks in which some actors are associated with a location (i.e., city) where they carry out various logistical activities/functions, such as providing material support in terms of explosives, safe houses for meetings or hiding, transportation for the personnel or equipment, or weaponry for carrying out attacks. Although it may be a stretch to assume that two actors carrying out the same logistical function share a tie or that two actors carrying out logistical activities in the same city share a tie, it is not an unreasonable assumption

Input dataset: Noordin 139 - Combined Network (Aggregated) (C:\Users\Sean\Dropbox\Casting More Light (Book)\Data\Noordin Top\UCINET Files\Noordin 139 - Combined Network (Aggregated)

		1 Abd ul Azi z	2 Abd ul Jab ar	3 Abd ul Mal ik	4 Abd ul Rau f	5 Abd ul Roh im	6 Abd ull ah Sun ata	7 Abd ull ah Sun gka r	8 Abu Ba kar Ba 'as yir	9 Abu Du jan ah	10 Abu Fi da	11 Abu Mu sab al -Za rqa wi	12 Abu Ro iro h	13 Abu Ru sda n	14 Ace ng Kur nia	15 Ach mad Ha san	16 Ade Ba hru	17 Adi tya Tr i Y oga	18 Adu ng	19 Agu s A hma d	20 Agu s D wik arn a	21 Agu s P ury ant o	22 Ahm ad Bas yir	23 Ahm ad Rof iq Rid ho	24 Ahm ad Roi cha n	25 Ahm ad Say id Mau lan a	26 Aip Hi day at	27 Aje nga n M asd uki	28 Akr am	29 Ali	30 Ali Gh ufr on	31 Ali Im ron	32 Amr ozi	33 And ri Oct avi a	34 Ani f S olc han udi n	35 Apu y	36 Ard i W ibo wo	37 Ari s M una nda r	38 Ase p	39 Ase p J aja	40 Asm ar Lat in San i	41 Awa l P urn omo	42 Aym an al- Zaw ahr i	43 Azh ari Hu sin	44 Bah aru din So leh
1	Abdul Aziz	0	0	0	0	0	0	0	0	0	0	0	0	0	0	0	0	1	0	0	0	0	0	0	0	0	1	0	0	0	0	0	0	0	1	0	1	0	0	0	0	0	0	2	1
2	Abdul Jabar	0	0	0	0	0	0	0	0	0	0	0	0	0	0	0	0	0	0	0	0	0	0	0	0	0	0	0	0	0	0	0	0	0	0	0	0	0	0	0	0	0	0	0	0
3	Abdul Malik	0	0	0	0	0	0	0	0	0	0	0	0	0	0	0	0	0	0	0	0	0	0	0	0	0	0	0	3	0	0	0	0	0	0	0	0	0	0	0	0	0	0	0	0
4	Abdul Rauf	0	0	0	0	0	0	1	1	0	0	0	0	0	0	0	0	0	0	0	0	0	0	0	0	0	0	0	0	0	1	1	1	4	0	0	0	0	0	0	1	0	0	1	1
5	Abdul Rohim	0	0	0	0	0	0	0	2	0	0	0	0	0	0	0	0	0	0	0	0	0	0	2	0	0	0	0	0	0	0	0	0	0	0	0	0	0	0	0	0	0	0	0	0
6	Abdullah Sunata	0	0	0	0	0	0	0	0	0	0	0	0	0	0	0	0	0	0	0	0	0	0	4	0	1	0	0	1	2	0	1	0	0	0	0	0	1	1	5	0	0	0	0	0
7	Abdullah Sungkar	0	0	0	1	0	0	0	3	1	0	0	0	0	0	0	0	0	1	0	0	0	0	2	0	0	0	1	0	1	2	1	1	1	0	0	0	0	0	0	1	0	0	1	1
8	Abu Bakar Ba'asyir	0	0	0	1	2	0	3	0	0	0	0	0	0	0	0	0	0	1	0	0	0	0	1	0	0	0	0	0	0	0	0	0	1	0	0	0	0	0	0	1	0	0	1	1
9	Abu Dujanah	0	0	0	0	0	0	1	0	0	0	0	0	0	0	0	0	0	0	0	0	0	0	0	0	0	0	0	0	0	1	0	1	0	0	0	0	0	0	0	0	0	0	5	0
10	Abu Fida	0	0	0	0	0	0	0	0	0	0	0	0	0	0	2	0	0	2	1	0	0	0	0	0	0	0	0	0	0	0	0	0	0	0	1	0	0	0	0	0	0	0	1	1
11	Abu Musab al-Zarqawi	0	0	0	0	0	0	0	0	0	0	0	0	0	0	0	0	0	0	0	0	0	0	0	0	0	0	0	0	0	0	0	0	0	0	0	0	0	0	0	0	0	0	0	0
12	Abu Roiroh	0	0	0	0	0	0	0	0	0	0	0	0	0	0	0	2	0	0	0	0	0	0	0	0	0	0	0	0	0	0	0	0	0	0	1	0	0	0	0	0	0	0	0	0
13	Abu Rusdan	0	0	0	0	0	0	0	0	0	0	0	0	0	0	0	0	0	0	0	0	0	0	0	0	0	0	0	0	0	0	0	0	0	0	0	0	0	0	0	0	0	0	0	0
14	Aceng Kurnia	0	0	0	0	0	0	0	0	0	0	0	0	0	0	0	0	0	0	0	0	0	0	0	0	0	0	0	2	0	0	0	0	0	0	0	0	0	0	0	0	0	0	0	0
15	Achmad Hasan	0	0	0	0	0	0	0	0	0	2	0	0	0	0	0	0	0	2	1	0	0	0	0	0	0	0	0	0	0	0	0	0	0	0	1	0	0	0	0	0	0	0	2	1
16	Ade Bahru	0	0	0	0	0	0	0	0	0	0	0	2	0	0	0	0	0	0	0	0	0	0	0	0	0	0	0	0	0	0	0	0	0	0	1	0	0	0	0	0	0	0	0	0
17	Aditya Tri Yoga	1	0	0	0	0	0	0	0	0	0	0	0	0	0	0	0	0	0	0	0	0	0	0	0	0	1	0	0	0	0	0	0	0	3	0	3	0	0	0	0	0	0	1	1
18	Adung	0	0	0	0	0	0	1	1	0	2	0	0	0	0	2	0	0	0	0	0	0	0	0	0	0	0	0	0	0	0	0	0	0	0	0	0	0	0	0	0	0	0	0	0
19	Agus Ahmad	0	0	0	0	0	0	0	0	0	1	0	0	0	0	1	0	0	0	0	0	0	0	0	0	0	0	0	0	0	0	0	0	0	0	1	0	0	0	0	0	1	0	2	1
20	Agus Dwikarna	0	0	0	0	0	0	0	0	0	0	0	0	0	0	0	0	0	0	0	0	0	0	0	0	0	0	0	0	0	0	0	0	0	0	0	0	0	0	0	0	0	0	0	0
21	Agus Puryanto	0	0	0	0	0	0	0	0	0	0	0	0	0	0	0	0	0	0	0	0	0	1	0	0	0	0	0	0	0	0	0	0	0	0	0	0	0	0	0	0	0	0	2	0
22	Ahmad Basyir	0	0	0	0	0	0	0	0	0	0	0	0	0	0	0	0	0	0	0	0	1	0	0	0	0	0	0	0	0	0	0	0	0	0	0	0	0	0	0	0	0	0	0	0
23	Ahmad Rofiq Ridho	0	0	0	0	2	4	2	1	0	0	0	0	0	0	0	0	0	0	0	0	0	0	0	0	0	0	0	0	0	0	0	0	0	0	0	0	0	0	1	0	0	0	2	2
24	Ahmad Roichan	0	0	0	0	0	0	0	0	0	0	0	0	0	0	0	0	0	0	0	0	0	0	0	0	0	0	0	0	0	0	0	0	0	0	0	0	0	0	0	0	0	0	0	0
25	Ahmad Sayid Maulana	0	0	0	0	0	1	0	0	0	0	0	0	0	0	0	0	0	0	0	0	0	0	0	0	0	0	0	0	0	0	0	0	0	0	0	0	0	0	0	0	0	0	0	0
26	Aip Hidayat	1	0	0	0	0	0	0	0	0	0	0	0	0	0	0	0	1	0	0	0	0	0	0	0	0	0	0	0	0	0	0	0	0	2	0	1	0	0	0	0	0	0	1	1
27	Ajengan Masduki	0	0	0	0	0	0	1	0	0	0	0	0	0	0	0	0	0	0	0	0	0	0	0	0	0	0	0	0	0	0	0	0	0	0	0	0	0	0	0	0	0	0	0	0
28	Akram	0	0	3	0	0	1	0	0	0	0	0	0	0	2	0	0	0	0	0	0	0	0	0	0	0	0	0	0	0	0	0	0	0	0	0	0	0	0	0	0	0	0	0	0
29	Ali	0	0	0	0	0	2	1	0	0	0	0	0	0	0	0	0	0	0	0	0	0	0	0	0	0	0	0	0	0	1	1	0	0	0	0	0	1	0	1	0	0	0	0	0
30	Ali Ghufron	0	0	0	1	0	0	2	0	1	0	0	0	0	0	0	0	0	0	0	0	0	0	0	0	0	0	0	0	1	0	4	4	1	0	0	0	0	0	0	0	0	0	2	0
31	Ali Imron	0	0	0	1	0	1	1	0	0	0	0	0	0	0	0	0	0	0	0	0	0	0	0	0	0	0	0	0	1	4	0	3	1	0	0	0	2	0	1	0	0	0	1	0
32	Amrozi	0	0	0	1	0	0	1	0	1	0	0	0	0	0	0	0	0	0	0	0	0	0	0	0	0	0	0	0	0	4	3	0	1	0	0	0	0	0	0	0	0	0	2	0
33	Andri Octavia	0	0	0	4	0	0	1	1	0	0	0	0	0	0	0	0	0	0	0	0	0	0	0	0	0	0	0	0	0	1	1	1	0	0	0	0	0	0	0	1	0	0	1	1
34	Anif Solchanudin	1	0	0	0	0	0	0	0	0	0	0	0	0	0	0	0	3	0	0	0	0	0	0	0	0	2	0	0	0	0	0	0	0	0	0	3	0	0	0	0	0	0	1	1
35	Apuy	0	0	0	0	0	0	0	0	0	1	0	1	0	0	1	1	0	0	1	0	0	0	0	0	0	0	0	0	0	0	0	0	0	0	0	0	0	0	0	0	0	0	1	3
36	Ardi Wibowo	1	0	0	0	0	0	0	0	0	0	0	0	0	0	0	0	3	0	0	0	0	0	0	0	0	1	0	0	0	0	0	0	0	3	0	0	0	0	0	0	0	0	1	1
37	Aris Munandar	0	0	0	0	0	1	0	0	0	0	0	0	0	0	0	0	0	0	0	0	0	0	0	0	0	0	0	0	1	0	2	0	0	0	0	0	0	0	1	0	0	0	0	0
38	Asep	0	0	0	0	0	1	0	0	0	0	0	0	0	0	0	0	0	0	0	0	0	0	0	0	0	0	0	0	0	0	0	0	0	0	0	0	0	0	0	0	0	0	0	0

Figure 3.15 Aggregated Noordin Combined Network

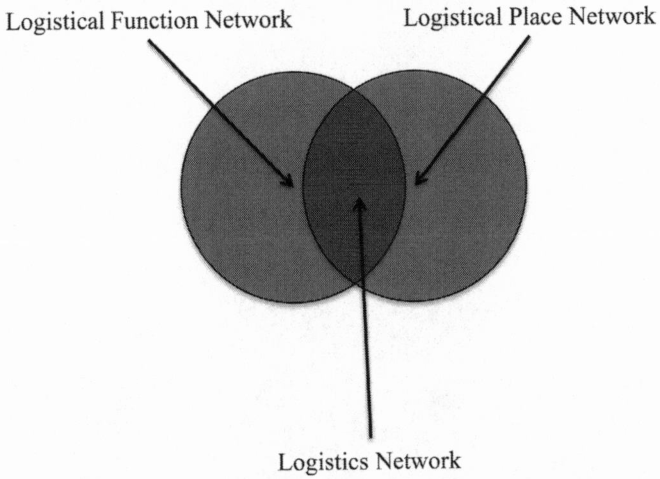

Figure 3.16 Parsing of Noordin Logistical Function and Logistical Place Networks

that a tie exists between two actors if they share the same logistical location and function. For example, if two actors are located in Poso and both handle transportation functions, then we could argue that a "logistics" tie exists between them. Figure 3.16 captures this approach to parsing network ties.[19]

3.9 SIMPLIFYING NETWORKS

Finally, let us consider a few techniques for simplifying networks and extracting subnetworks from the larger network. When working with large social networks, it is sometimes difficult to make sense of the pattern of ties. In such situations, being able to shrink a network or extract a subset of a network can aid the analysis process. In particular, these techniques can be useful when you want to examine a subset of a network or to see if there are patterns among the data that are not immediately observable when the network is visualized in its entirety. Take, for example, the Noordin Combined Network presented in Figure 3.17. In the left panel the actors are colored by logistical functions, whereas in the right the actors are colored by status (i.e., alive, dead, and incarcerated). What is clear is how unclear the network is. It is difficult to make sense of the network based solely upon the visualization. It is tightly bunched together, and difficult to detect whether any subclusters have formed. In such situations that network simplification may be in order. Two approaches are worth discussing.

The first technique, extracting relationships from a larger network, is helpful when working with multiple relationships. As previously mentioned, dark

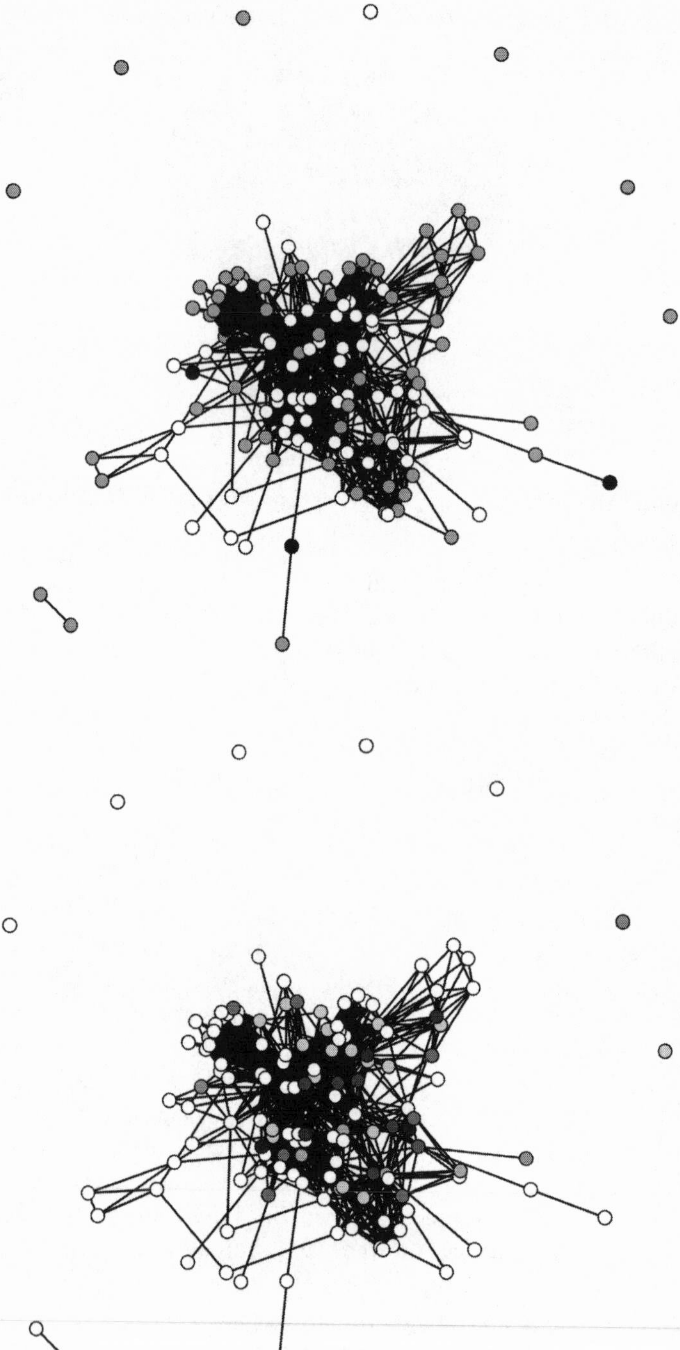

Figure 3.17 Noordin Combined Network by Logistics Function (Left) and Status (Right)

network actors are typically embedded in multiple relations and at some point we may want to examine a specific set of relationships, such as an *operational* network. We can extract or filter operational-type relations from a larger network and subsequently stack and/or combine that subset of relationships for analysis. Everton and Cunningham (2015), for instance, extracted a series of relationships from a much larger data set to combine and analyze longitudinally Noordin Top's *Trust*, *Operational*, and *Combined* networks. Analysts can also extract actors based on specific attributes. The same analysis examined only actors who were "Alive and Free" during each month of the network's existence. Figure 3.18 presents Noordin's Alive and Free Network that was extracted from the Noordin Combined Network. While the entire combined network includes 139 actors, the alive and free network includes only 64.

Analysts can also use attributes to simplify networks. This simplification technique combines actors into an aggregate set of actors in terms of a specific attribute. This process is often referred to as collapsing or reducing a

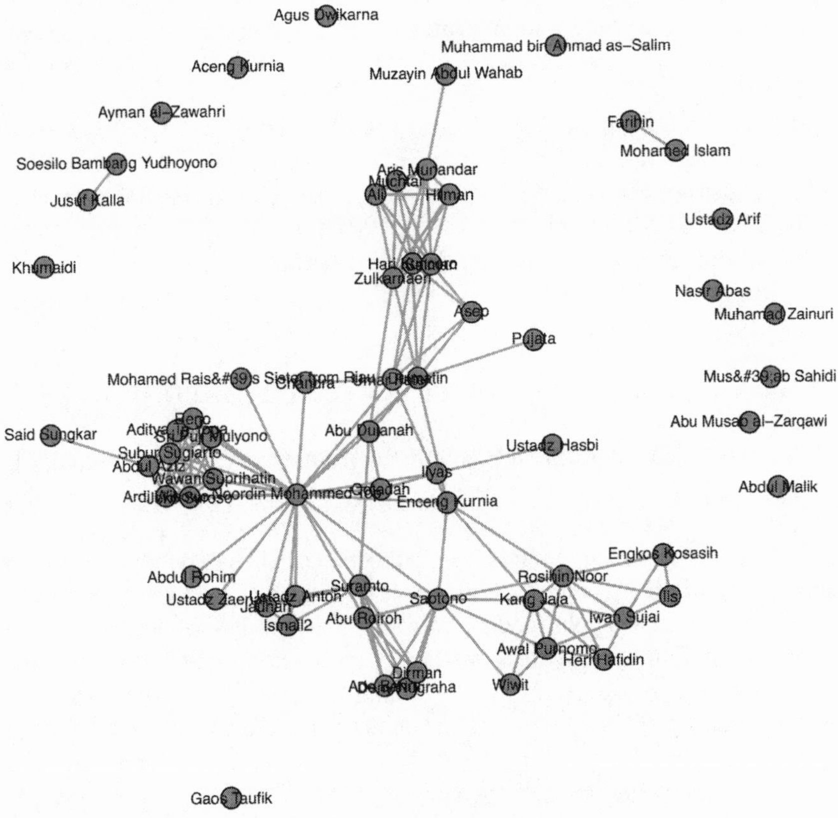

Figure 3.18 Noordin Combined Alive and Free Network

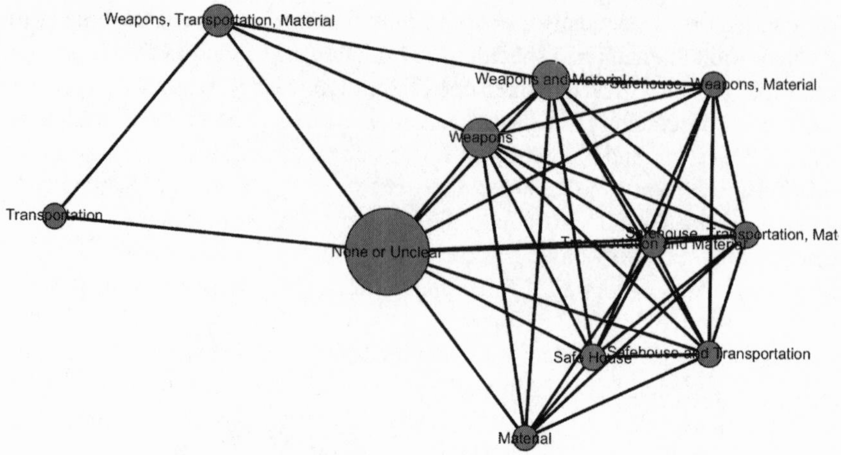

Figure 3.19 Noordin Combined Network Collapsed by Logistical Function

network. Once an analyst simplifies a network by an attribute, all the actors who share that attribute will be represented by a single actor. The relationships among the actors will represent the ties of the actors from which the collapse actors were created. For instance, Figure 3.19 depicts Noordin Top's operationally related network (operational, training, and communication ties) collapsed by logistical function in ORA. As the figure demonstrates, an advantage of this technique is that it can provide a macro-level view of network while highlighting central (and peripheral) logistical functions to the network. In fact, analysts can simplify actors by any attribute, including role and organizational affiliation, to get a different view of the dark network.

3.10 SUMMARY: LESSONS LEARNED

We have covered a considerable amount of ground in this chapter. We began by considering the importance of developing a set of analytic questions that should guide one's analysis of a dark network. In particular, they should guide researchers through the design, collection, and analytic phases of their analysis. We then turned to the importance of codebooks and why they should guide analysts during the coding process. The definitions outlined in the codebook, if followed properly by data coders, will reduce subjectivity and help improve consistency during the coding and structuring processes. Next we explored the different types of social network data. As we saw, network data are generally broken down into two primary types: ego network data and whole (or complete, full) network data. Both have their strengths and weaknesses, although in this book we will be primarily illustrating methods for analyzing whole network data. This was followed by a short discussion of determining a network's boundary. As we saw, this is often more art than science, but the ultimate goal is "to find a set of actors with relatively good separateness from the rest of the world" from which we can draw reasonable conclusions (Erickson 2001:317). We then turned our attention to the various methods of collecting and recording social network data. No single approach is always the right approach. The approaches that analysts use should fit the context in which they find themselves. Finally, we illustrated how social network data can be aggregated, combined, parsed, and simplified. Analysts typically need to manipulate network data in various ways in order to tease out underlying patterns that are not always immediately observable.

3.11 QUESTIONS

1. Which of the following are ways of collecting social network data?
   a. Interviews.
   b. Historical documents.
   c. Direct observation.
   d. Diaries
   e. All of the above
2. There is only one way to record social network data.
   a. True.
   b. False.
3. One-mode networks
   a. Consist of one set of actors and one set of events.
   b. Consist of two sets of actors.
   c. Are also known as affiliation networks.
   d. Only exist in our minds.
   e. Consist of a single set of actors.
4. Two-mode networks
   a. Consist of one set of actors and one set of events.
   b. Consist of two sets of actors.
   c. Are also known as affiliation networks.
   d. All of the above.
   e. None of the above.
5. Attribute data
   a. Are never used by social network analysts.
   b. Are nonrelational characteristics of individual actors in a network.
   c. Are also known as affiliation data.
   d. Are also known as asymmetric data.
   e. All of the above.

6. Codebooks are reference documents that typically include all of the following information except
   a. Definitions of relationships and attributes.
   b. Coding schemes.
   c. The software used for analysis.
   d. Modes of relational data.
   e. Notes on vexing coding decisions.
7. The process of structuring or tagging data is the same as coding data.
   a. True.
   b. False.
8. Exploratory questions allow social network analysts to make casual relationships between variables.
   a. True.
   b. False.
9. The establishment of network boundaries refers to a process of selecting actors to include in a study based on their geographical locations.
   a. True.
   b. False.

3.12 ANSWERS

1. All of the above (e).
2. False.
3. Consist of a single set of actors (e).
4. All of the above (d).
5. Are nonrelational characteristics of individual actors in a network (b).
6. The software used for analysis (c).
7. False.
8. False.
9. False.

3.13 FURTHER READING

As one can guess from this very long chapter, conducting social network research requires patience and an attention to detail. Although there are numerous sources out there, one of the best (and most recent) is Garry L. Robins's recent book *Doing Social Network Research: Network-based Research Design for Social Scientists* (London: SAGE Publications, 2015). Charles Kadushin explores some of the ethical dilemmas facing social network analysts in Chapter 11 of his book, *Understanding Social Networks: Theories,*

Concepts, and Findings (Oxford and New York: Oxford University Press, 2012). Analysts may also want to explore some of the following readings:

- Stephen P. Borgatti, Martin G. Everett, and Jeffrey C. Johnson. 2013. Pp. 24–88 (Chapters 3–5) in *Analyzing Social Networks*. Thousand Oaks, CA: SAGE Publishing.
- Stephen P. Borgatti and Jose-Luis Molina. 2005. "Toward Ethical Guidelines for Network Research in Organizations." *Social Networks* 27:107–17.
- Sean F. Everton. 2012. Pp. 365–83 (Chapter 12) in *Disrupting Dark Networks*. New York and Cambridge: Cambridge University Press.
- Rebecca Goolsby. 2005. "Ethics and Defense Funding: Some Considerations." *Social Networks* 27:95–106.
- Edward O. Laumann, Peter V. Marsden, and David Prensky. 1983. "The Boundary-Specification Problem in Network Analysis." Pp. 18–34 in *Applied Network Analysis*, edited by Ronald S. Burt and Michael Minor. Beverly Hills, CA: Sage.
- Ian McCulloh, Helen Armstrong, and Anthony Johnson. 2013. Pp. 189–201 (Chapter 8) in *Social Network Analysis with Applications*. New York, NY: Wiley.
- Christina Press. 2011. Pp. 59–92 (Chapter 3) in *Social Network Analysis: History, Theory & Methodology*. London and Thousand Oaks, CA: SAGE Publications.
- Stanley Wasserman and Katherine Faust. 1994. Pp. 28–66 (Chapter 2) in *Social Network Analysis: Methods and Applications*. Cambridge, UK: Cambridge University Press.

NOTES

1. In practice, the specificity of an analyst's question will largely depend on the amount of time they have to conduct the analysis, along with their access to relational data. For example, it is likely an analyst with limited time and without access to existing relational data will choose a very specific question, so they can reduce the amount of relational data they must collect and subsequently analyze. On the other hand, an analyst with unlimited time and access to an existing database will likely start off with much broader sets of questions they can explore before making a recommendation. This reflects the unique trade-offs many practitioners face with completeness and the amount of time they have for analysis.

2. The increasing popularity to study "big data," including social media networks (e.g., Twitter), has demonstrated new, exciting techniques to collect network data electronically and automatically. The collection of these data is not the focus of this chapter and research on these data remains a work in progress.

3. Granted, the ability to survey dark network actors in this form, and for them to identify those actors, is highly unlikely.

4. We use the term "whole network" rather than "complete network" because the latter term can be confused with complete graphs, which are graphs where all possible ties are present.

5. We could also create an organization-by-organization network if we were working with a two-mode affiliation network. The ties between organizations in this case would indicate which organizations share an actor in terms of membership.

6. In fact, this is likely the case for many readers whose organizations have not begun integrating social network analysis into their toolbox of analytic methods.

7. Some may argue flexibility in designing ontologies and not confining analysts to strict definitions is an advantage, given that most problem sets are complex and require flexibility. Our argument, however, is less about flexible ontologies and more about consistency in relational data. We have too often seen inconsistent data sets disregarded as unhelpful and subsequently dismissed due to the absence of a set of clear data standards outlined in a codebook. Moreover, we recommend that analysts who default to link analysis should still use codebooks because they can directly affect the quality of the data regardless of their analytic methods. We have noted several commands trained in social network analysis revert to link analysis but maintain higher-quality data by establishing a codebook.

8. For a more in depth but relatively brief summary of various methods for collecting social network data, see Prell (2011:68–74).

9. This process is often not as straightforward as it seems. Users often have to prep and/or reformat their data prior to exporting them. In many cases, they may have to conduct additional data cleaning and reformatting after their export.

10. The specific analytic package in which an analyst is going to conduct analysis will in part drive the type of edgelist that should be used. For instance, some of ORA's older versions (up-through version 2.3.6) allow users to create edgelists like the one seen in Figure 3.11. The same exact format cannot be imported into Gephi, however.

11. Gephi also requires a nodelist. A significant amount of materials exist showing analysts how they can build out structured data sets using node and edgelists for the various analytic packages.

12. Note additional relationships and attributes exist in the data set, but are not shown for demonstration purposes. For example, Abdul Aziz has mentorship relationships with actors such as Misno.

13. Interval attributes are typically measured on a continuum and the values are based on intervals. Ratio attributes contain the added condition that a 0 of that attribute indicates there is none of that attribute.

14. Some network analysis packages, such as UCINET and Pajek, require number codes for categorical attributes, which means they have to be recorded that way. An example of this could be organizational affiliation where a "1" indicates "Organization 1," a "2" designates "Organization 2," etc.

15. For example, Pajek reads network data exported from UCINET as arcs, which could be problematic if you are analyzing undirected data. Additionally, igraph does not automatically import tie strength values in .net files.

16. The networks also must be one-mode networks that each consists of the same set of actors, in its entirety.

17. It is often difficult to visually represent multiple relations between actors when relations are stacked. For example, some pairs of actors appear to be connected solely by "Organizational Affiliation" ties but they may be also connected via superior-subordinate or collaboration ties. Consequently, it is recommended that analysts also toggle between relations to observe patterns in stacked networks.

18. The minimum value option combines two or more networks by the minimum value of the relationships between pairs of network actors (i.e., dyads). The maximum takes the opposite approach and combines ties based on the highest value between pairs of network actors. The average takes the average of the tie values and the binary option indicates a "1" for pairs who have a tie and a "0" for those who do not. Finally, the sum option, as seen in the example above, adds the tie values together. For example, actor A and actor B have two different types of relationships, such as kinship and friendship. The value (or strength) of their kinship tie is "3" and the value of their friendship tie is "1." The tie value for actor A and B after combining these networks would be the following for each option: minimum=1; maximum=3; average=2; binary=1; and sum=4.

19. The two-mode networks need to be first converted to one-mode networks before carrying out these operations.

Part II

EXPLORATORY SOCIAL NETWORK ANALYSIS

Chapter 4

Topographical Features of Dark Networks

This chapter emphasizes the value of exploring network topography (e.g., level of density and centralization) as one of the first steps in descriptive analysis. Understanding such basic information about a network under analysis can reveal some fundamental information about the network's capacities and resiliency. Networks that lie on the extremes of various measures of network topography (e.g., very dense or very sparse) are less effective, meaning they cannot operate and maintain operational security, than those that lie somewhere in between (Everton 2012b). Ultimately, a network's topography should inform the crafting of strategies to disrupt dark networks. That is, prior to beginning more involved analyses such as detecting subgroups or identifying key actors, analysts need to determine how cohesive and centralized the network is overall. Topography provides information about a network's aggregate structure, which is in many ways as important as its component parts. This argument is based on research that suggests dark networks face trade-offs in terms of their overall structure; those that lie on the topographical extremes sacrifice efficiency for security, or vice versa. For example, some research suggests centralized networks are better for mobilizing people and resources (McCormick 2005; McCormick and Owen 2000); however, centralized networks might be vulnerable to disruption with the removal of central actors. This trade-off has implications for the development of strategies to counter dark networks, and ultimately the effects they may have on a network's structure and performance.

The chapter begins by considering a few basic metrics: network size, average distance, and diameter. Table 4.1 provides a summary of them, noting their formal explanation, their potential interpretation, and certain caveats

Table 4.1 Summary of Size, Diameter, and Average Distance

Measure	*Formal Explanation*	*Potential Interpretation(s)*	*Caveat(s)*
Size	A count of the number of actors in a network.	Knowing a network's size is important when interpreting measures sensitive to it, such as density, or diameter. Size also gives analysts an indication of how a network is growing or shrinking.	Metric outputs are dependent upon network size. Also, the manner in which an analyst sets an examination's boundaries may not reflect the actual size of a network.
Average Distance	The average length of all the shortest paths (geodesics) between all actors in a network.	All things being equal, dark networks with relatively shorter average path distances may be able to diffuse information quicker than networks with relatively longer average path distances.	Shorter average path distances do not necessarily mean information is going to travel quickly throughout a network (or slowly in networks with larger average distances). Some actors may withhold information from their neighbors, etc.
Diameter	The longest of all the shortest paths (geodesics) that traverse the network.	A relatively large diameter in a dark network could indicate that it is decentralized, given the greater number of steps it takes to get from one end to the other. Information may also take longer to traverse from one end of a network to the other.	Network diameter is a function of network size, which suggests that larger networks may have a larger diameter than smaller ones. This in turn has implications for comparing networks of different sizes, or over time.

to keep in mind when using them. We then turn to metrics used for measuring the centralization of networks. These include the standard measures of centralization, as well as alternative measures, such as variance and standard deviation. Summaries of these are presented in Table 4.2. Metrics related to interconnectedness are discussed next; these include density, cohesion (fragmentation), compactness (breadth), the clustering coefficient, and the E-I index and are summarized in Table 4.3. It is important to keep in mind that the metrics summarized in Tables 4.1 through 4.3 does not represent an exhaustive list of topographical metrics. Many more exist. The ones that are discussed, however, include some of the more popular ones employed by network analysts. It is also important to note that they are all descriptive in nature and should not be seen as substitutes for more fine-grained analyses. Rather, they speak to general traits of the network as a whole.

Table 4.2 Summary of Centralization Measures

Measure	*Formal Explanation*	*Potential Interpretation(s)*	*Caveat(s)*
Centralization	The standard measure of centralization uses the variation in actor centrality within the network to measure the level of centralization. More variation yields higher network centralization scores, while less variation yields lower scores. Formally, it is the ratio of the actual sum of differences in actor centrality over the theoretical maximum, yielding a score somewhere between 0.0 and 1.0.	Centralization indicates how centralized, or decentralized, a dark network is, which sheds light onto the potential trade-offs a network may have to make. A specific index needs to be interpreted in light of the type of centrality measure on which it is estimated. For example, a network with high degree centralization could indicate that one or a few actors are relatively active (i.e., possess a lot of ties), while others are not.	Many new network analysts confuse centrality and centralization. The former is about identifying central actors; the latter is about the distribution of a centrality score throughout an entire network.
Variance	Variance is the average of the squared differences between each actor's centrality score and the mean (*average*) centrality score. Network analysts can obtain variance scores for many types of centrality, including variance for degree, betweenness, and closeness.	Variance indicates how centralized, or decentralized, a dark network is, which sheds light onto the potential trade-offs a network may have to make. The variance needs to be interpreted in light of the centrality measure on which it is estimated. For example, a network with high levels of variance in terms of closeness centrality could indicate that one, or a few, actors have relatively high levels of accessibility to other actors, while others have very little.	Variance, standard deviation, and centralization can provide somewhat different interpretations about the nature of a network's level of centralization.
Standard Deviation	The standard deviation for a particular centrality measure is the square root of the variance.	Standard deviation indicates how centralized, or decentralized, a dark network is, which sheds light onto the potential trade-offs a network may have to make. Standard deviation needs to be interpreted in light of the centrality measure on which it is estimated. For example, a network with high levels of variance in terms of betweenness centrality could indicate that one, or a few, actors have relatively high levels of brokerage potential, while others do not.	Variance, standard deviation, and centralization can provide somewhat different interpretations about the nature of a network's level of centralization.

Table 4.3 Summary of Selected Interconnectedness Measures

Measure	*Formal Explanation*	*Potential Interpretation(s)*	*Caveat(s)*
Density	Density is formally defined as the total number of observed ties in a network divided by the total possible number of ties in that network. The output ranges from 0 to 1.	Indicates how interconnected a dark network is, which sheds light onto the potential trade-offs it may have to make. For example, a dark network's focus on recruitment via strong ties may limit its ties to outsiders who might have valuable resources and information.	It should not be used to compare networks of different sizes.
Average Degree	This measure is formally defined as the sum of ties in a network divided by the number of actors in the network.	Average degree indicates how interconnected a dark network is, which sheds light onto the potential trade-offs it may have to make.	Networks that adopt a cell-like structure can be locally dense but globally sparse, which a measure like average degree cannot, at least by itself, capture.
Fragmentation (Cohesion)	This measure is equal to the ratio of all pairs of actors that are connected, that is, actors that can either directly or indirectly reach one another.	Similar to density and average in that it indicates a network's level of cohesiveness (in this case, the lack thereof), which can highlight some of the potential trade-offs it may have to make.	This measure indicates the *lack* of network cohesiveness, which means the results should be read that way. Analysts should also remember the role of agency when comparing fragmentation scores over time.
Breadth (Compactness)	This measure is similar to fragmentation except that the score is weighted by the average path distance between all pairs.	Similar to fragmentation in terms of a network's level of cohesion; however, it adds the element of path distance to the fragmentation score, thus providing a different angle into the potential trade-offs a dark network may face.	This measure indicates the *lack* of network cohesiveness, which means the results should be read that way. Analysts should also remember the role of agency when comparing fragmentation scores over time. Not available in every social network analysis package.
Global Clustering Coefficient	The sum of each actor's clustering coefficient divided by the number of actors within the network.	Indicates how interconnected a network is, which highlights some of the potential trades of network may have to make.	Some software packages estimate the coefficient differently.
E-I Index	This measure indicates the ratio of ties a group has to nongroup members (i.e., external) and to group members (i.e., internal). The index equals 1.0 for groups that have all external ties; a group with all internal ties will get a score of -1.0; and if there are an equal number of internal and external ties, the index equals 0.0.	Indicates a network's balance of internal and external ties by accounting for internal and external density, which highlights potential trade-offs the network has to make.	It is likely most dark networks will be largely internal. Not available in every social network analysis program.

4.1 BASIC TOPOGRAPHICAL METRICS

Basic network metrics—network size, average distance, and diameter—are valuable for their ability to provide information about an entire network in aggregate. As aggregate measures, topographical information provides analysts with basic insight into the network's potential in terms of capacity and performance, and adds context that aids in the interpretation of other measures that may take place further down the analytic pipeline. Network size is simply a count of the number of actors (i.e., actors) in a network. It can have a nontrivial effect on the output and interpretation of several measures discussed below. For example, traditional measures of density are essentially meaningless if they are used to compare networks that differ even moderately in size. The second reason, which may be a bit more intuitive to those new to network analysis, is that size provides a straightforward measure of fluctuation in the growth or depletion of dark networks over time. A dark network that consistently grows in membership is likely to be recruiting successfully, while ineffective ones will likely shrink over time. Network analysts should be aware, however, that the size of dark network under examination may reflect the way that an analyst sets the boundaries of the network and may not necessarily capture the true size of a dark network (see chapter 3).

The next measure—average distance—places more emphasis on the ties between actors than on the actors themselves. Average distance is measured as the average length of all the shortest paths (i.e., geodesics) between all actors in a network, and it provides an indication of the potential speed with which information could spread through a network. All things being equal, resources and information should diffuse faster through networks with lower average distance than those with a higher average distance. Although it is a measure of a network's *potential* efficiency, it provides analysts with implications about the potential for carrying out a successful deception campaign that will rely on the spread of disinformation through a network. We would normally expect such a campaign to function better in the context of networks with lower average distances; however, since networks are dynamic—changing over time—their average distance will almost certainly vary over time, suggesting that timing is critical. We will revisit this theme of network dynamics in chapter 11 (longitudinal networks models).

Another measure of how relationships function in a network—network diameter—equals the network's longest geodesic. It may indicate how dispersed a network is. As we will discuss below, decentralized networks are expected to be better suited to solving nonroutine, complex, and/or rapidly changing problems or challenges. Because of the value that they generally place on adaptability, dark networks are probably more likely to be decentralized than they are hierarchical, particularly when their goal is to maintain operational security (Arquilla 2009). A network's diameter also could be used as a supplementary measure to the centralization measures we discuss in more detail below. That is, networks with large diameters may be more decentralized than those with small ones. However, since network diameter is, in part, a function of network size (all else being equal, the diameters of larger networks are longer than those of smaller networks), we should use diameter carefully when comparing networks of different sizes. That said, provided that changes in network size do not change substantially from one time point to another, both average distance and network diameter can provide useful information about how a network's structure develops longitudinally.

These basic topographical measures, and the manner in which they vary, highlight some trade-offs that dark networks may face, and they provide evidence of the potential of a given network. It is important to keep in mind, however, that these relationships are not always clear cut. The information should therefore be interpreted as evidence of potential, rather than a manifest certainty. For example, a network with a relatively large diameter—an indication that it may be decentralized—may in fact be more adaptable than centralized dark networks (i.e., networks with small diameters). Similarly, relatively dispersed structures could have difficulty spreading information among its members, such as religious edicts or new rules and regulations. The same goes for average distance. A network with a relatively small average path distance could be vulnerable to deception campaigns; however, small average path distance could also allow the network to quickly nullify the effect of disinformation, as well as providing it with the advantage of rapid dissemination of important information among network members, such as operationally related information. To get a better feel for how these measures vary according to the structure of the network, in Table 4.4 we provide

Table 4.4 Size, Diameter, and Average Path Distance

Network	*Size*	*Diameter*	*Average Path Distance*
Afghan Network			
Combined (Positive)	91	5	3.001
Kinship	91	7	4.337
Geographic Movement	91	5	2.152
Sentiment (Positive)	91	4	1.811
Sentiment (Negative)	91	7	3.445
Anabaptist Leadership Network	67	9	3.393
FARC TFMC	445	9	4.071
Koschade Network	17	3	1.588
Noordin Top Network			
Combined	139	6	2.302
Communications	139	8	3.120
Operations	139	5	2.198
Trust	139	7	3.270

the basic topography measures of the various networks that we examine in this book. As the table indicates, the networks used in this vary in terms of size, diameter, and average path distance although the variation in average path distance is probably not as great as one might expect. Still, it should be clear that these networks are quite different from one another.

4.2 NETWORK CENTRALIZATION

The operational efficiency of dark networks is largely affected by their ability to mobilize people and resources (McCormick 2005; McCormick and Owen 2000). Some believe it is positively associated with centralization (Baker and Faulkner 1993; Morselli 2009) because they more effectively mobilize people and resources because centralization facilitates efficient decision-making processes (Enders and Jindapon 2010). This, in turn, enhances strategic planning and creates accountability and standards among network members (Tucker 2008). Centralized networks can also facilitate efficiency in the transfer of resources due to shorter path lengths between leaders and other network members (Lindelauf, Borm and Hamers 2009). Thus, it is unsurprising that several relatively successful dark networks have been centralized around charismatic leaders. For example, Enders and Sandler (2006) suggest that the centralized nature of Aum Shinrikyo in the 1990s enhanced its ability to launch a sarin gas attack on the Tokyo subway, while the decentralized structure of al-Qaeda has reduced its ability to attain and launch a CBRN attack.[1] To be sure, many of these analyses have been largely qualitative in nature and lack standard social network analysis (SNA) measures.[2] They, do, however, suggest that centralization is often positively associated with the command and control of dark networks.

Centralization can be a mixed blessing, however. Research suggests that less centralized organizations can adapt quicker to rapidly changing environments (Arquilla 2009) and are less vulnerable to the removal of key members (Bakker, Raab and Milward 2011; Sageman 2003, 2004). Many dark networks, in particular, terrorist networks, are often assumed to adopt cellular and distributed forms of network structure (Carley, Reminga and Kamneva 2003), which allows them to adjust to a rapidly changing environment (Kenney 2007). Moreover, less centralized networks are more likely to withstand shocks, such as the removal of a key member, because much of the remaining network goes untouched and is capable of continuing on. However, dark networks that are too decentralized may find it difficult to mobilize resources. They may also run the risk of having individuals or small cells go "rogue" and conduct operations not aligned with their operational interests (Cronin 2009).

All this suggests that an optimal level of centralization exists for dark networks, and it is likely that this optimal level will change over time. One could argue that dark networks will shift toward the centralized side of the continuum when operational efficiency, such as the mobilization and the transfer of resources, is its primary focus (e.g., just prior to an attack). On the other hand, they may decentralize when operational security, or adaptability, takes precedence, such as in the aftermath of an operation. In addition, network centralization is almost certainly a function of environmental context (Everton 2012b). In relatively friendly environments where adaptability is less crucial and the risk for losing key actors is low, covert networks will probably be more centralized. However, if the environment becomes more hostile, they will likely move toward the decentralized end of the spectrum. For example, anecdotal evidence suggests that prior to 9/11 al-Qaeda was somewhat centralized, but after it came under attack, it adopted a much more decentralized organizational structure (Sageman 2008). In any case, these factors suggest cross-sectional analyses are ill equipped to fully understand network dynamics.

Measures: Centralization, Variance, and Standard Deviation

Network centralization, variance, and standard deviation are all measures that researchers use to determine a network's level of centralization. The standard measure of centralization uses the variation in actor centrality within the network to measure the level of centralization. More variation yields higher centralization scores, while less variation yields lower scores. Formally, centralization equals

$$C = \frac{\sum Cmax - C(n_i)}{max \sum Cmax - C(n_i)} \tag{4.1}$$

where *Cmax* equals the largest centrality score for all actors and $C(n_i)$ is the centrality score for actor n_i, and $max \sum Cmax - C(n_i)$ is the theoretical maximum possible sum of differences in actor centrality. In other words, network centralization is the ratio of the actual sum of differences in actor centrality over the theoretical maximum, yielding (like density) a score somewhere between 0.0 and 1.0. In general, the larger a centralization index is, the more likely it is that a single actor is very central while the other actors are not (Wasserman and Faust 1994:176); thus, they can be seen as measuring how unequal the distribution of individual actor values are. Because network centralization scores are based on the type of centrality estimated (e.g., degree, betweenness, closeness, and eigenvector), we need to interpret them in light of the centrality metric estimated. For example, degree centrality counts the number of ties of each actor; thus, we would expect that degree centralization will capture the extent to which a single actor possesses several ties while other actors do not. By contrast, a centralization measure based on betweenness centrality, which measures the extent to which actors lie between other actors in the network, could indicate the degree to which a single actor is in a brokerage position.

An alternative centralization measure recommended by Coleman (1964), Hoivik and Gleditsch (1975), and Snijders (1981) is the variance (S^2) of actor centrality scores found in a network (see also Wasserman and Faust 1994:177, 180–181), although the standard deviation (S) is the preferable expression of this measure since it is expressed in the original unit of measure (Hamilton 1996:72–73).

$$S^2 = \frac{\left[\sum_{i=1}^{n}(C(n_i) - \bar{C})^2\right]}{n} \tag{4.2}$$

$$S = \sqrt{\frac{\left[\sum_{i=1}^{n}(C(n_i) - \bar{C})^2\right]}{n}} \tag{4.3}$$

Those familiar with standard statistics will recognize these equations as standard measures of variance and standard deviation. The variance (4.2) equals the sum of the squared differences between each actor's centrality score ($C(n_i)$) and the average centrality score ($\bar{C}$), while the standard deviation (4.3) is simply the square root of the variance.[3] Comparing equations, one can see that they differ in that while centralization (4.1) uses the difference between the network's largest centrality score and each actor's centrality score to estimate variance in actor centrality, variance (4.2) and standard deviation (4.3) use the difference between the network's mean centrality score and each actor's centrality score. Thus, while both attempt to capture the level of variance in centrality scores, they look to different baseline reference points (i.e., largest centrality score vs. average centrality score) for comparison.[4]

Network Centralization Scores

Tables 4.5 and 4.6 present the centralization measures of the various networks examined in this book. As you can see there is considerable variation in the level of centralization across networks. This illustrates why one should not assume that all networks are "decentralized" or "hierarchical." Instead, analysts should be asking themselves, what is the relationship between the network's level of centralization and its efficiency? Does the network's level of centralization highlight any structural vulnerability? For example, if we

Table 4.5 Network Centralization Scores

Network	*Degree Centralization (%)*	*Closeness Centralization (ARD) (%)*	*Betweenness Centralization (%)*	*Eigenvector Centralization (%)*
Afghan Network				
Combined (Positive)	26.80	46.22	37.28	56.37
Kinship	24.87	39.88	27.01	98.33
Geographic Movement	15.59	35.02	2.77	67.68
Sentiment (Positive)	2.95	8.82	0.21	84.77
Sentiment (Negative)	6.84	22.63	3.8	71.27
Anabaptist Leadership Network	16.46	30.38	19.75	34.43
FARC TFMC	7.49	36.30	14.53	35.11
Koschade Network	53.75	53.95	49.99	27.37
Noordin Top Network				
Combined	46.22	63.08	24.17	32.78
Communications	35.76	66.16	47.84	68.38
Operations	38.08	62.59	12.87	38.11
Trust	18.60	46.91	16.98	40.71

Table 4.6 Network Standard Deviation Scores

Network	*Degree Standard Deviation (Normalized)*	*Closeness Standard Deviation (ARD) (Normalized)*	*Betweenness Standard Deviation (Normalized)*	*Eigenvector Standard Deviation (Normalized)*
Afghan Network				
Combined (Positive)	5.320	6.607	6.789	11.101
Kinship	3.531	8.298	5.156	12.890
Geographic Movement	2.993	6.335	0.375	13.295
Sentiment (Positive)	0.822	1.228	0.035	14.274
Sentiment (Negative)	1.823	4.773	0.702	13.671
Anabaptist Leadership Network	5.165	7.403	5.109	11.238
FARC TFMC	1.265	8.573	1.110	6.497
Koschade Network	18.198	9.850	11.829	16.060
Noordin Top Network				
Combined	9.049	13.873	2.417	7.944
Communications	4.252	12.750	4.308	9.385
Operations	7.784	17.508	1.613	8.679
Trust	4.702	13.269	2.360	10.323

conclude that it is moderately centralized and operating highly efficiently, then we may want to adopt a strategy that leads it to become even more centralized and thus reducing its overall effectiveness.[5]

Although centralization and standard deviation measure network centralization in different ways, they tend to correlate relatively highly with one another.[6] This relationship is captured in the graphs presented in Figure 4.1,

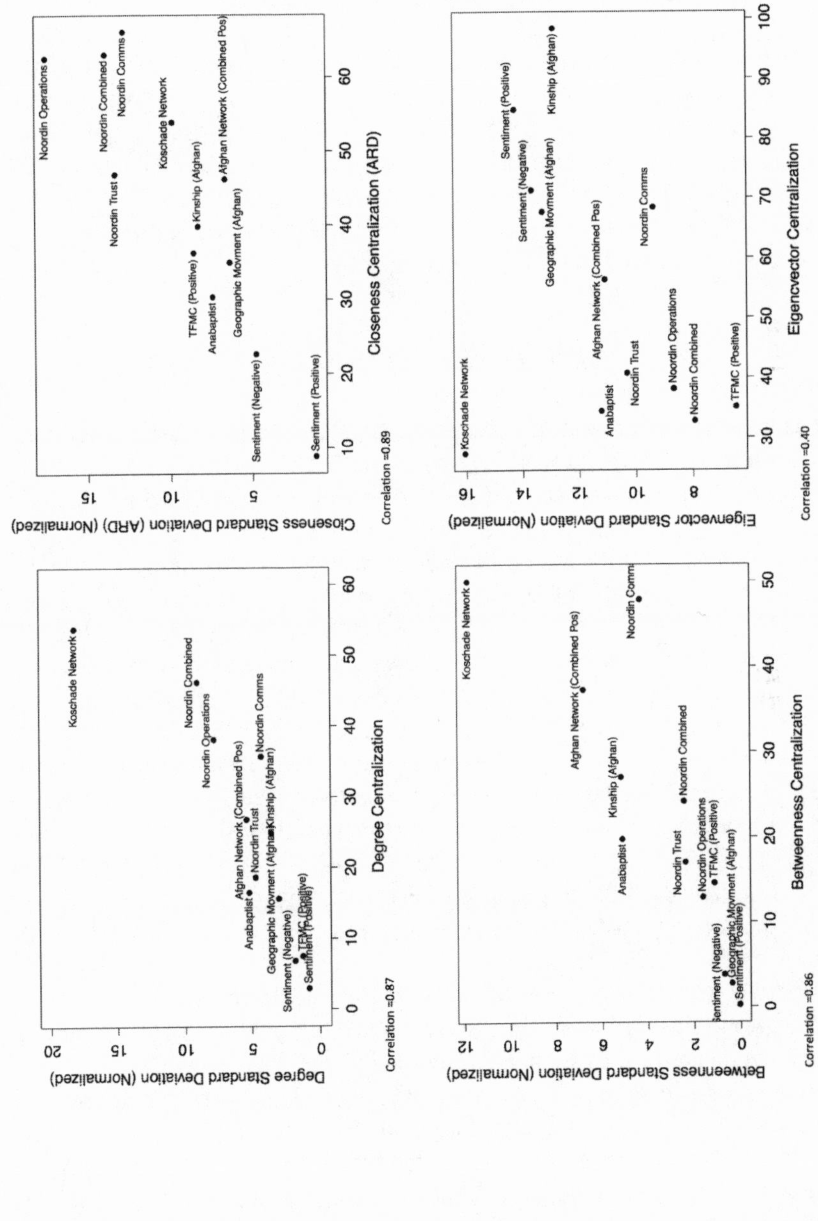

Figure 4.1 Comparison of Centralization and Standard Deviation Scores

which plot centralization (x-axis) by standard deviation (y-axis) for each of the four measures of centrality. Degree centralization by degree standard deviation is plotted in the graph in the upper left; closeness centralization by closeness standard deviation is plotted in the graph in the upper right; betweenness centralization by betweenness standard deviation is plotted in the graph in the lower left; and eigenvector centralization by eigenvector standard deviation is plotted in the graph in the lower right. In the first three plots (degree, closeness, betweenness) there is a high-level correlation between the two types of measures. All are greater than 0.800, which is quite high, especially by social scientific standards.[7] Only the correlation of eigenvector centralization by eigenvector standard deviation is somewhat modest at 0.403. The plots also illustrate what we noted earlier: namely, that networks vary greatly in terms of centralization.

4.3 NETWORK INTERCONNECTEDNESS

There is little debate that groups recruit primarily through their social ties. For instance, Lofland and Stark's (Lofland and Stark 1965; Stark 1996) study of conversion to the Unification Church discovered that those who ultimately joined tended to be those whose ties to group members exceeded their ties to nonmembers. Similarly, Stark and Bainbridge (1980) found that while the door-to-door efforts of Mormon missionaries were relatively unsuccessful, when missionaries met non-Mormons in the homes of Mormon friends, they enjoyed a success rate close to 50 percent. This was primarily because such meetings occurred only after lay Mormons had built close personal ties with these non-Mormons and essentially brought them into their networks. A meta-analysis by Snow and his colleagues (Snow, Zurcher and Ekland-Olson 1980) and McAdam's (1986) examination of the 1964 Freedom Summer campaign uncovered a similar dynamic: successful social movements recruit primarily through their social ties (Snow, Zurcher and Ekland-Olson 1980:791). And, finally, Sageman's (2004) analysis of the global Salafi jihad (GSJ) discovered that 83 percent of members were recruited through friendship, kinship, or mentorship ties.

Because security is a primary concern for dark networks, they tend to recruit along lines of trust (i.e., strong ties) (Passy 2003). In fact, not doing so can be dangerous, as Ramzi Yousef, one of the 1993 World Trade Center bombers, learned the hard way. As long as he recruited through strong ties, he successfully evaded the authorities, but when he enlisted an unfamiliar South African student, his luck ran out. After Yousef asked the student to take a suspicious package to a Shiite mosque, the student called the U.S. embassy, which led to Yousef's arrest and later extradition to the United States (Sageman 2004:109–10).

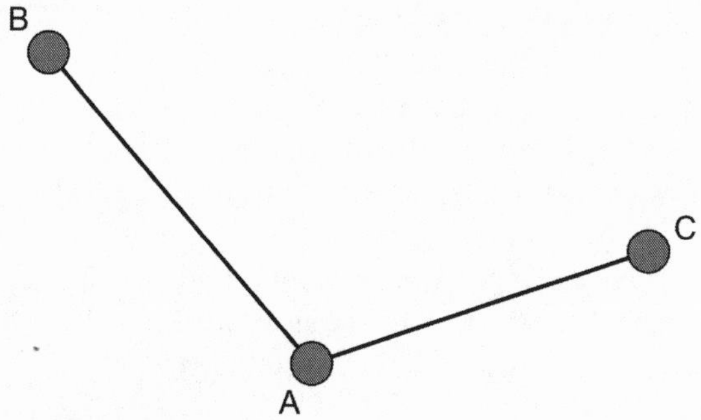

Figure 4.2 Granovetter's Forbidden Triad

Recruitment through strong ties suggests that the networks will become increasingly dense over time as ties form between previously unlinked actors. This is due to the phenomenon known as Granovetter's (1973) "forbidden triad" (Figure 4.2). Granovetter argued that this triad would not continue to exist for long because if actor A has a strong tie to both actors B and C (i.e., A interacts regularly with both), eventually B and C will meet and form a tie (Holland and Leinhardt 1976). It may be a weak or strong, but it will form nonetheless (Rapoport 1953a, 1953b; Rapoport and Horvath 1961), leading to an increase in the group's overall internal density.

Dense networks consisting of numerous strong ties bring an important benefit to dark networks: They minimize defection because the network can better monitor the behavior of its members (Finke and Stark 2005; Granovetter 2005), appropriate solidary incentives (McAdam 1999 [1982]; Smith 1991), and solve coordination problems (Chwe 2001). It should come as little surprise that dark networks that minimize defection are generally more successful than those that do not. In fact, they often "prefer" having members killed over having them defect because "if one activist decides to defect, the whole organization is vulnerable to the defector's subsequent actions" (Hafez 2004:40), which often leads them to alter their plans and lie low until they think it is safe (Berman 2009).

Concerns over security not only cause members of dark networks to recruit primarily through their strong ties, but it also leads them to limit their ties with outsiders in order to minimize the presence of countervailing influences (e.g., ideas and people) that could challenge the group's worldview. However, while limiting external ties can increase a group's security, dark networks that are entirely isolated are unlikely to sustain their movement over the long term (Jackson et al. 1960) because they need ties to other groups and individuals in order to access important information and other material and nonmaterial goods (e.g., weapons, materials, and new recruits). As others have noted, external ties are vital for any group or organization attempting to survive in a rapidly changing environment (Uzzi 1996, 2008; Uzzi and Spiro 2005), and this is simply more acute for dark networks because not only do they face a constantly shifting environment, but also one that is hostile at that.

All this suggests that, once again, an optimal level of interconnectedness exists for dark networks. They cannot afford to be too interconnected (i.e., too provincial), nor can they prefer to be too sparse (i.e., too cosmopolitan) (Everton 2012b). As with centralization, this level will almost certainly be a function of the environment in which the network operates and is likely to change over time as the goals of the network change.

Measures: Density, Average Degree, Cohesion, and the Clustering Coefficient

Multiple measures are available for measuring a network's interconnectedness with density and average degree being the most common. Network density (*d*) is measured as the total number of ties divided by the total possible number of ties:

$$d = \frac{L}{n(n-1)/2} \tag{4.4}$$

where *L* refers to the actual number of ties in a network and *n* to the number of actors in the network. Because each actor can potentially be connected to all other actors, in an undirected network, such as we have here (i.e., where ties are reciprocal), the total possible number of ties equals $n(n-1)/2$. In practical terms, what this means is that network density scores range from 0.0 to 1.0. In networks with a density of 0.0 (or 0.0%), no ties exist between actors, while in networks with a density of 1.0 (or 100.0%), all possible ties exist between actors. It is very important to remember that the formal measure of density is inversely related to network size (i.e., all else being equal, the larger the network, and the lower the density) because the number of possible lines increases exponentially as actors are added to the network, while the number of ties that each actor can plausibly maintain tends to be limited. That is why social network analysts often turn to average degree, which is simply the sum of each actor *i*'s degree centrality, C_j^{DEG},[8] divided by the number of actors, *n*, in the network:

$$\bar{\bar{C}}^{DEG} = \frac{1}{n}\sum_{i=1}^{n} C_i^{DEG} \tag{4.5}$$

Even average degree has its limitations, though, because a network that adopts a cell-like structure can be locally dense but globally sparse, which a measure like average degree cannot, at least by itself, capture.

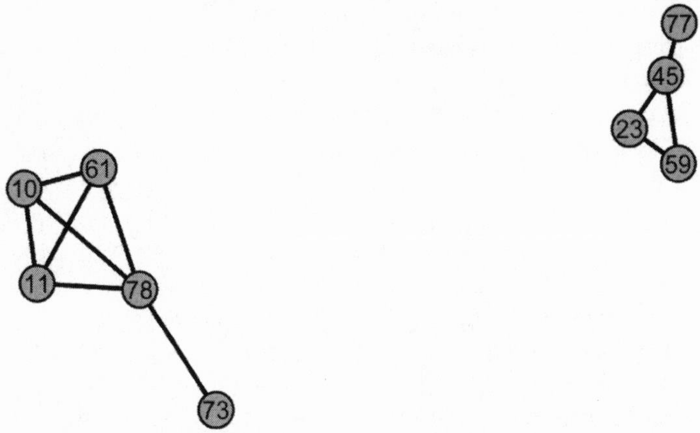

Figure 4.3 Connected and Unconnected Pairs

Network cohesion, as the nomenclature implies, measures a network's cohesiveness (or lack thereof). It equals the ratio of all pairs of actors that are connected, that is, actors that can either directly or indirectly reach one another; network fragmentation is the additive inverse of network cohesion and equals the proportion of all pairs of actors that are unconnected. Figure 4.3 illustrates what we mean by connected and unconnected pairs. Consider actor 77. It is connected directly to actor 45 and indirectly to actors 23 and 59. It is not connected, however, either directly or indirectly to actors 73, 61, 78, 11, or 10. Thus, actors 77 and 23 are considered a connected pair, while actors 77 and 73 are not (i.e., they are an unconnected pair)

Formally, cohesion, given a matrix R where $r_{ij} = 1$ if i can reach j and $r_{ij} = 0$ if i cannot, it is defined as follows (Borgatti, Everett and Johnson 2013):

$$C^{COH} = \frac{\sum_{i \neq j} r_{ij}}{n(n-1)} \tag{4.6}$$

Compactness is similar, except that the score is weighted by the average (path) distance between all pairs of actors, where d_{ij} is the path distance between i and j if i can reach j and 0 otherwise (Borgatti, Everett and Johnson 2013):

$$C^{COM} = \frac{\sum_{i \neq j} (1 / d_{ij})}{n(n-1)} \tag{4.7}$$

The two scores are identical when the distance between all instances of i and $j = 1$, but when the path distance between i and j is greater than 1, compactness is lower than cohesion. Both sets of measures could prove useful for understanding how a network has changed over time as well in the crafting of strategies. For instance, if analysts were seeking to determine the degree to which different scenarios will fragment a particular network, they could estimate before and after measures of cohesion/fragmentation. In fact, the SNA package, UCINET (Borgatti, Everett and Freeman 2002b), reports a series of scores for each actor in the network that indicate the degree of network fragmentation, the degree of distance-weighted network fragmentation, the change in network fragmentation, the change in distance-weighted network fragmentation, the percent of change in fragmentation, and the percent of change in distance-weighted fragmentation if a particular actor is removed from the network.[9] In our analysis, we use both the standard and distance-weighted measures.

The *global* clustering coefficient (Watts 1999a; Watts and Strogatz 1998), also known as average ego-network density (Davis 1967; Marsden 1987), is estimated by first taking the ego network of each actor (i.e., each actor's ties to other actors—aka, as an actor's "alters"—and the ties between them) and then calculating the density of each ego network (but not including ego or ego's ties in the calculation—that is, only the ties between ego's alters are used). This is known as the *local* clustering coefficient:

$$C_i^{CC} = \frac{p_{kj}}{k_i(k_i - 1)/2} \tag{4.8}$$

where p_{kj} equals the number of ties between actor i's alters, and $k_i(k_i - 1)/2$ equals the maximum number of ties that can exist between i's alters. Thus, if actor i has k_i alters, then at most $k_i(k_i - 1)/2$ ties can exist between them, and the density C_i is the ratio of actual to possible ties among i's alters. The *global* clustering coefficient is the same as the average level of clustering in the network, $\bar{C}^{CC}$, which equals the sum of each actor's clustering coefficient, C_i^{CC}, divided by the number of actors, n, in the network:

$$\bar{C}^{CC} = \frac{1}{n}\sum_{i=1}^{n} C_i^{CC} \tag{4.9}$$

Analysts need to be aware that software packages differ in how they estimate the global clustering coefficient. Some only calculate a local clustering coefficient (i.e., ego-network density) for actors with two or more alters, and then divide the sum by the number of actors with a clustering coefficient and not by the number of actors in the network. This is generally not an issue in networks with few isolates, but in sparse networks, it can be. It can mislead one into thinking that a network is more clustered than it actually is. We can illustrate this in the network maps presented in Figure 4.4. The global clustering coefficient (as calculated by UCINET and Pajek) for the two networks

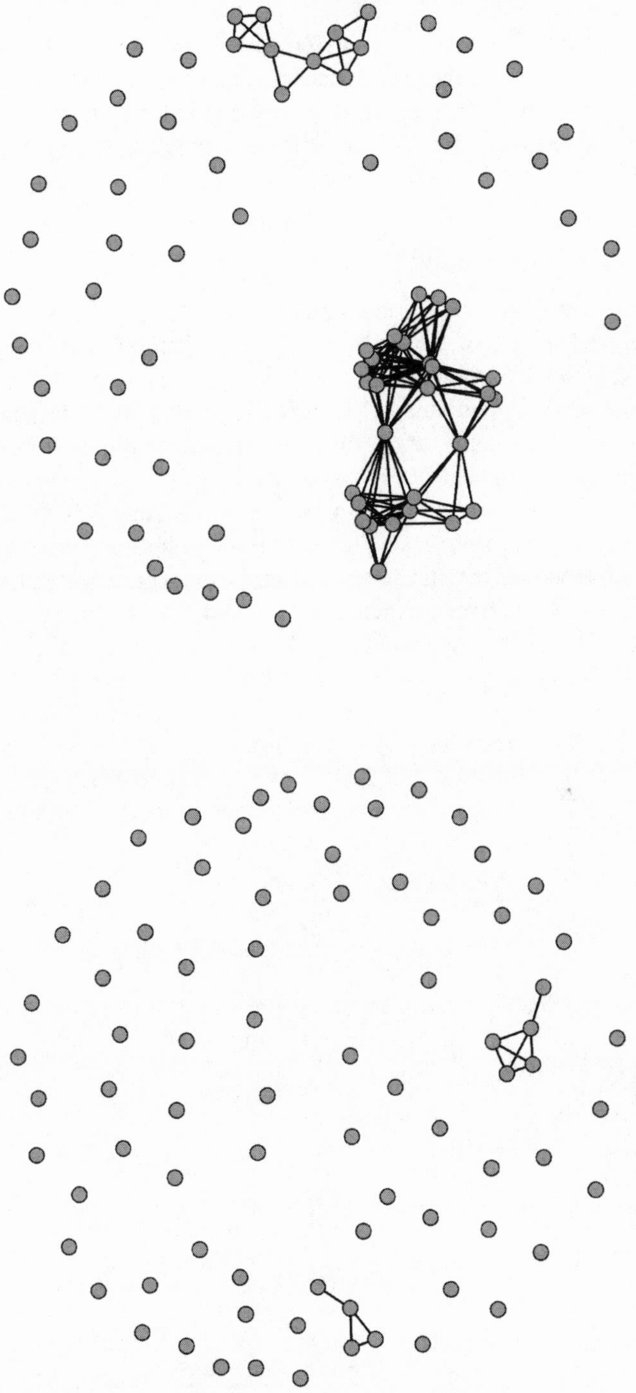

Figure 4.4 Comparing Clustering Coefficients

is nearly identical (0.833), but the one at the top of the figure is clearly less interconnected than the network at the bottom. Why? Because UCINET and Pajek divide the sum of the local clustering coefficients by the number of actors with ties to two or more actors. If they divided the sum by the number of actors in the network, then the clustering coefficients of the two networks equal 0.074 (left) and 0.401 (right), respectively.

Network Interconnectedness Scores

Table 4.7 presents the various measures of interconnectedness for the networks analyzed in this book. As with the centralization measures outlined in Tables 4.5 and 4.6, there is considerable variation across the networks. This variation is also illustrated in Figure 4.5, which plots the average degree for each of the networks by the various measures of cohesion presented in Table 4.7.

A notable attribute of the graphs presented in Figure 4.5 is that although the various measures are clearly correlated with one another, the correlations are probably not as strong as one might expect. The relatively low level of correlation between average degree and density (0.398) is largely due to the fact that, as we mentioned above, network density is sensitive to network size. Compare, for instance, the density and average degree scores for the Combined Afghan Network and the FARC TFMC presented in Table 4.7. The average degree scores of the two networks are relatively the same, but the density of the FARC TFMC is much lower because the Combined Afghan Network consists of 91 actors, while the FARC TFMC

Table 4.7 Network Interconnectedness Measures

Network	*Density*	*Average Degree*	*Cohesion*	*Compactness*	*Clustering Coefficient*
Afghan Network					
Combined (Positive)	0.038	3.407	1.000	0.373	0.417
Kinship	0.023	2.110	0.726	0.212	0.216
Geographic Movement	0.014	1.275	0.067	0.037	0.646
Sentiment (Positive)	0.004	0.370	0.009	0.006	0.238
Sentiment (Negative)	0.010	0.913	0.083	0.033	0.278
Anabaptist Leadership Network	0.081	5.343	1.000	0.376	0.447
FARC TFMC	0.009	3.888	0.357	0.101	0.784
Koschade Network	0.463	7.412	1.000	0.723	0.899
Noordin Top Network					
Combined	0.110	15.137	0.874	0.434	0.703
Communications	0.033	4.489	0.744	0.276	0.540
Operations	0.081	11.209	0.537	0.279	0.814
Trust	0.041	5.698	0.569	0.212	0.619

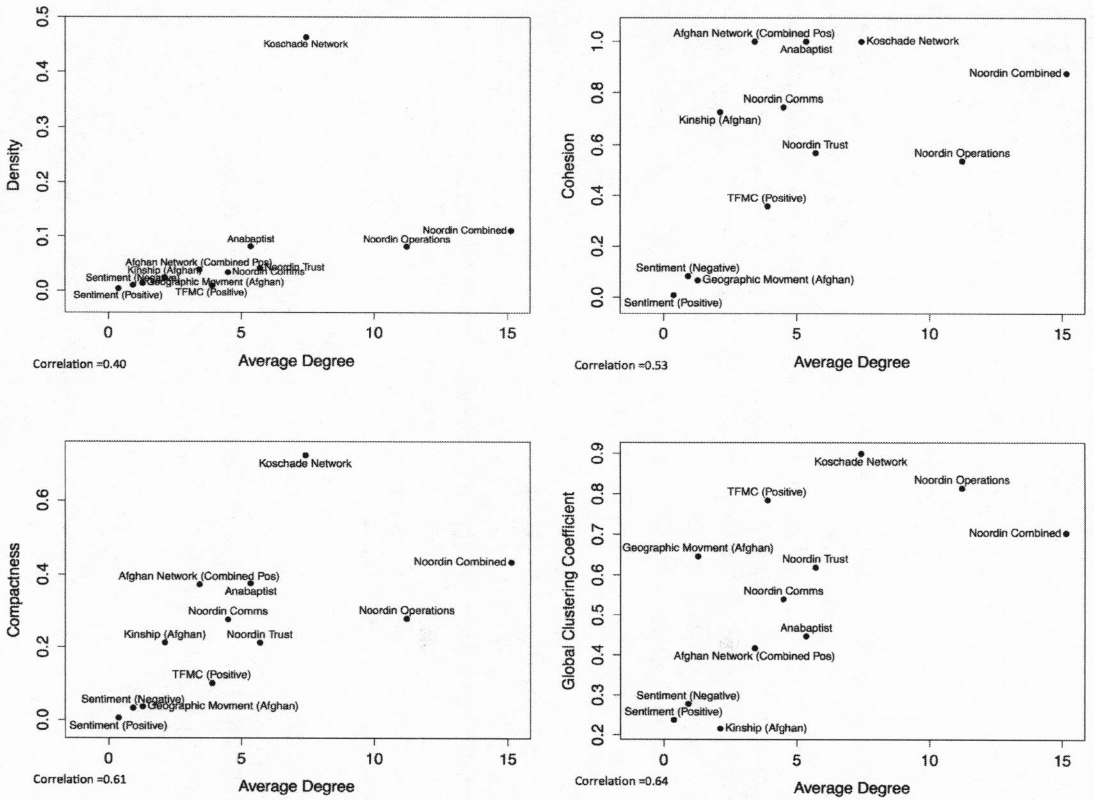

Figure 4.5 Comparing Measures of Cohesion Across Various Networks

has 445 actors. Still, the correlations between average degree and the other interconnectedness measures are not nearly as high as those we saw between the centralizations scores.[10] This reflects the simple fact that the interconnectedness measures are calculated quite differently from one another and highlights why it is critical for analysts to consider multiple measures before drawing any definitive conclusions. The one way that these graphs are similar to the centralization graphs is the variance in scores across networks. Dark networks clearly vary in terms of the level of interconnectedness.

Internal and External Ties

Up to this point, all of the measures discussed in this chapter only capture a network's internal connectedness. However, Krackhardt's (1994) E-I Index offers an alternative for taking external ties into account as well. The measure is a ratio of ties a group has to nongroup members, and to group members, thereby taking into account both external and internal ties:

$$\frac{E-1}{E+1} \tag{4.10}$$

where E equals the number of external ties and I equals the number of internal ties. Thus, if a group has all external ties, the index equals 1.0; if it has all internal ties, the index equals −1.0; and if there are an equal number of internal and external ties, the index equals 0.0. We expect a dark network's E-I index to be less than those of light networks, all else being equal. Indeed, we expect it to always be negative. Take, for instance, the Noordin network pictured in Figure 4.6. The gray actors are actors who are members of Noordin's network, while the white actors are actors who are individuals with ties to Noordin's network, but who are not actual members. The E-I index for the network equals –0.422, which indicates that it has more internal than external ties. Whether this is more or less than other networks is an open question, one that we could explore if other network data included information on members and nonmembers.

4.4 SUMMARY: LESSONS LEARNED

In this chapter, we have considered a number of different measures of network topography and have seen that networks can vary widely in terms of their topography. Some can be quite interconnected, while others can be quite sparse. Some can be very centralized, while others can be quite decentralized. We have also noted that effective networks can be neither too dense nor too sparse and neither too centralized nor too decentralized. We have

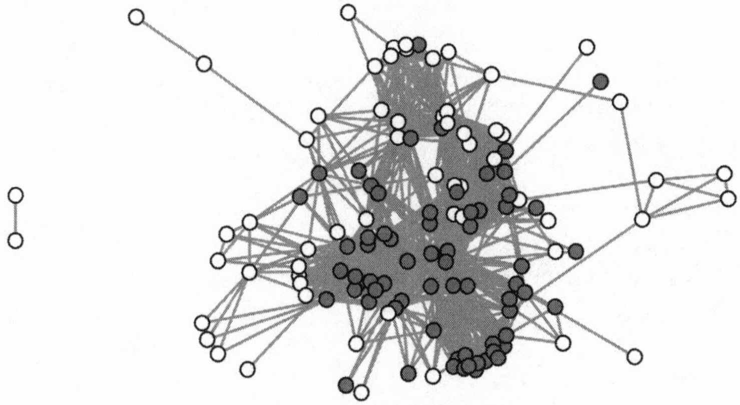

Figure 4.6 Noordin Network—Members (Gray) and Nonmembers (White)

also seen that no single topographical structure is optimal for every situation. Dark networks make trade-offs based on their goals, and they have to react to the strategic approaches implemented against them, both of which lead to changes in the overall structure.

Perhaps the most important takeaway from this chapter is that analysts need to first explore a dark network's overall topography before jumping to analyses that seek to identify key actors. Strategies focused on central actors and brokers often fail to account for the effect (s) that they will have on the overall network. Network analysts must recognize that key actors are embedded in a larger network, which means strategies to counter dark networks may prove unsuccessful or produce unintended consequences, depending on the network's structure and the context in which it operates. Consider, for example, a kinetic strategy that targets a key actor in the FARC TFMC for removal. As we saw above, however, the FARC TFMC appears to be relatively decentralized centralized network (at least when compared to the other networks examined in this book). This suggests that it is likely to survive such an operation and that an alternative strategy may be in order. In short, because dark networks do not assume simple, predictable structures, and because key actors are embedded in larger network structures, analysts need to first explore the topographical makeup of the dark networks they are examining. Such an approach will almost always lead to better decision-making.

4.5 QUESTIONS

1. Which of the following metrics would you use to measure the interconnectedness of a network?
   a. Average Distance.
   b. Average Degree.

   c. Diameter.
   d. Standard Deviation.
2. Which of the following metrics would you use to measure the centralization of a network?
   a. Average Distance.
   b. Average Degree.
   c. Diameter.
   d. Standard Deviation.
3. In some circumstances, average path distance may indicate the extent to which a dark network is distributed.
   a. True.
   b. False.
4. Which of the following is correct?
   a. Density equals the total number of actors in a network.
   b. Density equals the total number of ties in a network.
   c. Density equals the total number of ties in a network divided by the total number of possible ties.
   d. Density equals the total number of ties in a network divided by the total number of actors.
5. Which of the following statements is correct?
   a. Density and centralization measure different dimensions of a network's topography
   b. Unlike average degree centrality, we can use density to compare the interconnectedness of networks of different size.
   c. There is only one measure of centralization.
   d. The global clustering coefficient can only be used to compare the interconnectedness of networks of the same size.
6. Topographical measures, backed by context, can help social network analysts identify potential trade-offs that dark networks face.
   a. True.
   b. False.
7. Topographical measures are explanatory measures that allow social network analysts to make causal statements about dark networks.
   a. True.
   b. False.
8. When should we use average degree centrality instead of network density?

4.6 ANSWERS

1. Average Degree (b).
2. Standard Deviation (d).

3. True
4. Density equals the total number of ties in a network divided by the total number of possible ties (c).
5. Density and centralization measure different dimensions of a network's topography (a).
6. True.
7. False.
8. We should use average degree centrality rather of network density when we are comparing networks of different size.

4.7 FURTHER READING

There are a number of helpful discussions of network topography (aside from ours, of course). See, for instance, Chapter 9 in Borgatti, Everett, and Johnson's *Analyzing Social Networks* (Thousand Oaks, CA: SAGE Publishing, 2013), Chapter 8 in Christina Prell's *Social Network Analysis: History, Theory & Methodology* (London and Thousand Oaks, CA: SAGE Publications, 2011), and Chapter 3 in McCulloh, Armstrong, and Johnson's *Social Network Analysis with Applications* (New York, NY: Wiley, 2013). Chapters 4 and 5 in John Scott's *Social Network Analysis* (London and Thousand Oaks, CA: SAGE Publications Ltd., 2013) offer an excellent, nontechnical introduction. Finally, see Sean Everton's discussion of the relationship between network topography and dark network efficiency in "Network Topography, Key Players and Terrorist Networks" (*Connections* 31:12–19, 2012). Readers may also be interested in the following:

- Albert-László Barabási. 2002. *Linked: The New Science of Networks*. Cambridge, MA: Perseus Publishing.
- Albert-László Barabási and Eric Bonabeau. 2003. "Scale-Free Networks." *Scientific American* 288(5):60–69.
- Wouter de Nooy, Andrej Mrvar, and Vladimir Batagelj. 2011. Pp. 71–77 in *Exploratory Social Network Analysis with Pajek*.
- Robert A. Hanneman and Mark Riddle. 2005. "Connection and Distance" and "Embedding" (Chapters 7 & 8) in *Introduction to Social Network Methods*.
- Stanley Milgram. 1967. "The Small-World Problem." *Psychology Today* 1:61–67.
- Jeffrey Travers and Stanley Milgram. 1969. "An Experimental Study of the Small World Problem." *Sociometry* 32:425–43.
- Duncan J. Watts. 1999. *Small Worlds: The Dynamics of Networks Between Order and Randomness*. Princeton, NJ: Princeton University Press.

• Duncan J. Watts. 2003. *Six Degrees: The Science of a Connected Age.* New York: W. W. Norton & Company

NOTES

1. Other examples of successful centralized covert networks include Pablo Escobar's drug trafficking network and Peru's Sendero Luminoso (Shining Path).

2. One notable exception is Koschade's (2006) analysis of the first Bali Bombing network.

3. Because the sum of the differences always equals zero, we first square the differences. Squaring the differences eliminates negative values and gives us a measure of the magnitude of variation around the mean. However, because the variance is expressed in squared units (e.g., centrality^2) its interpretation is not intuitive. Taking the square root of the variance (i.e., the standard deviation) returns us to the original measurement scale and provides a more intuitive unit of measure (e.g., centrality). Think of standard deviation as the average difference between the measure for each actor and the middle (mean) for the measure.

4. One last set of measures worth noting is Krackhardt's (1994) graph theoretical measures of hierarchy. These can be quite informative, but they are intended for directed data, and to date, most SNA data collected on dark networks have been undirected, which is why we do not consider Krackhardt's measures at any length in this book.

5. This could have the added bonus of making the network more vulnerable to the removal of key actors from the network (Everton 2012b).

6. It is possible, however, that a network analyst could get results where centralization and standard deviation results appear to contradict one another.

7. Correlation coefficients range from −1.00 to 1.00, where −1.00 indicates perfect negative correlation and 1.00 indicates perfect positive correlation. Generally, social scientists are fairly happy when correlation coefficients are greater than 0.20 (or −0.20).

8. See chapter 6 for the equation used for calculating degree centrality.

9. These measures can be very useful to examine dark networks; however, network analysts should remember of the role of human agency in social networks. In other words, there is going to be a reaction for every action against a dark network. Once an actor's neighbors are removed, it is very likely that they will behave differently, such as forming or dissolving relationships, and changing their operating procedures. These reactions will ultimately change the structure of the network under examination.

10. The correlations between density, cohesion, and the global clustering coefficient are lower than those between average degree, cohesion, and the global clustering coefficient, while the correlation between density and compactness is higher than the correlation between average degree and compactness.

Chapter 5

Detecting Subgroups in Networks

One of the more engaging aspects of working with structural analysis is the ability to decompose a network into smaller units according to their patterns of interaction. Social network analysis (SNA) offers a set of tools to identify regularities in a network's structure that are generally taken to indicate communities of people who influence one another closely, or frequently enough to develop a distinct subculture within the network or organization (Frank and Yasumoto 1998). The implications are immense. The ability to parse dark networks into distinct subentities brings with it the option of mapping the subcultures and potential rivalries and the access points between them.

Much of what makes subgroups important in the eyes of network analysts is the interaction that they imply. Intimate interaction, be it through frequency, intensity, or proximity, amplifies the peer effect that governs people's actions and constraints (Wasserman and Faust 1994). In other words, "social interaction is the basis for solidarity, shared norms, identity, and collective behavior, so people who interact intensively are likely to consider themselves a social group" (de Nooy, Mrvar and Batagelj 2011:61). Distinct pockets of interacting actors may therefore imply the presence or potential of relatively distinct subcultures with—again, at least somewhat—distinct motivations, goals, or perspectives. Because the interest in subgroups within social networks is long-standing, there has been a good deal of innovation around how subgroups may best be identified. It would be incorrect to assume that there is one "best" method for determining subgroups. Rather, it is best to consider each method to be a unique definition of what it means to be a part of a subgroup.

In this chapter, we present five of the options that are available to analysts interested in exploring and isolating subgroups—each one offers a somewhat unique viewpoint on how to identify a subgroup. When selecting between these methods, analysts should consider the implications of each algorithm in

Table 5.1 Summary of Selected Subgroup Measures

Measure	*Formal Explanation*	*Potential Interpretation(s)*	*Caveat(s)*
Weak Components	Subgroups of actors who can reach one another either directly or indirectly.	Help analysts identify the largest components within a network for further analysis. These are disconnected "islands."	Applies to both undirected and directed data. Often not very useful in a well-connected network.
Strong Components	Subgroups in which each pair of actors is connected by a directed path and no other actor can be added without destroying its connectedness.	Allow analysts to identify the largest components for further analysis, but they also allow analysts to see the potential flow of material and nonmaterial goods within the subgroup.	Applies only to directed data. These are not available in every social network analysis program.
Cliques	A maximal subset of three or more actors where each actor is directly connected to all other actors.	These are largely nested subgroups within larger communities, and within the larger network. The dense nature of cliques highlights potential trade-offs for dark networks.	Actors can belong to more than one clique, which often makes identifying distinct subgroups impossible (i.e., where each actor is assigned to one and only one subgroup). Several alternative clique algorithms exist to ease the restrictions that each actor is directly connected to one another.
K-cores (Wasserman and Faust 1994)	A maximal group of actors, all of whom are connected to some number (*k*) of other group members.	These are nested subgroups based on each actor's degree centrality. The distribution of higher k-cores may indicate insights about the distribution of power throughout networks (i.e., assuming connectedness indicates levels of actor power [see chapter 6]) throughout a network.	Actors of the same core do not necessarily have to be connected to one another. Not available in every social network analysis program.
Factions	Compares an actual network with an idealized factional one, and then assesses the extent to which the former "fits" the latter.	The extent to which an observed network "fits" an idealized factional network highlights potentially structural vulnerabilities between "factions" in a dark network.	Analysts can draw from numerous measures to identify factions. Not available in every social network analysis program.

Table 5.1 (cont. . .)

Girvan–Newman (2002)	Similar to faction analysis in that subgroups are defined as having more ties within and fewer ties between groups than would be expected in a random graph of the same size with the same number of ties. Focuses on edge betweenness.	Helps analysts identify larger communities, or relatively dense clusters, within dark networks, which highlights potential seams, or vulnerabilities, between those communities.	Calculated differently than other community detection algorithms because it begins an iterative process by calculating edge betweenness and subsequently removing the tie with the highest score. Although the approach is intuitive, it tends to exhibit poor sensitivity with dense networks. Not available in every social network analysis program.
Clauset, Newman, and Moore (2004)	Similar to faction analysis in that subgroups are defined as having more ties within and fewer ties between groups than would be expected in a random graph of the same size with the same number of ties. An agglomerative method that begins by treating each actor as a cluster unto itself.	Also helps analysts identify larger communities, or relatively dense clusters, within dark networks, which highlights potential seams, or vulnerabilities, between those communities.	Calculated differently than other community detection algorithms because it begins by treating each actor as a cluster unto itself. Not available in every social network analysis program.
Walktrap (Pons and Latapy 2005)	An agglomerative clustering approach that models a random walker who would tend to remain in dense part of a network (i.e., communities) since there are fewer paths out than within. Actors are merged into subgroups according to their similarity, estimated through random walks.	Also helps analysts identify larger communities, or relatively dense clusters, within dark networks, which highlights potential seams, or vulnerabilities, between those communities.	Tends to exhibit better sensitivity in dense networks than other community detection models, except for Spinglass. Not available in every social network analysis program.
Spinglass (Reichardt and Bornholdt 2006)	Based on a physics model of glass cooling to a rigid structure, actors are treated as being in one of several spin states at the start, but tend to want to match the state of their neighbors as the model anneals.	Also analysts identify larger communities, or relatively dense clusters, within dark networks, which highlights potential seams, or vulnerabilities, between those communities.	Spinglass tends to exhibit greatest sensitivity, especially in dense networks, but is also somewhat slower in execution. Not available in every social network analysis program.

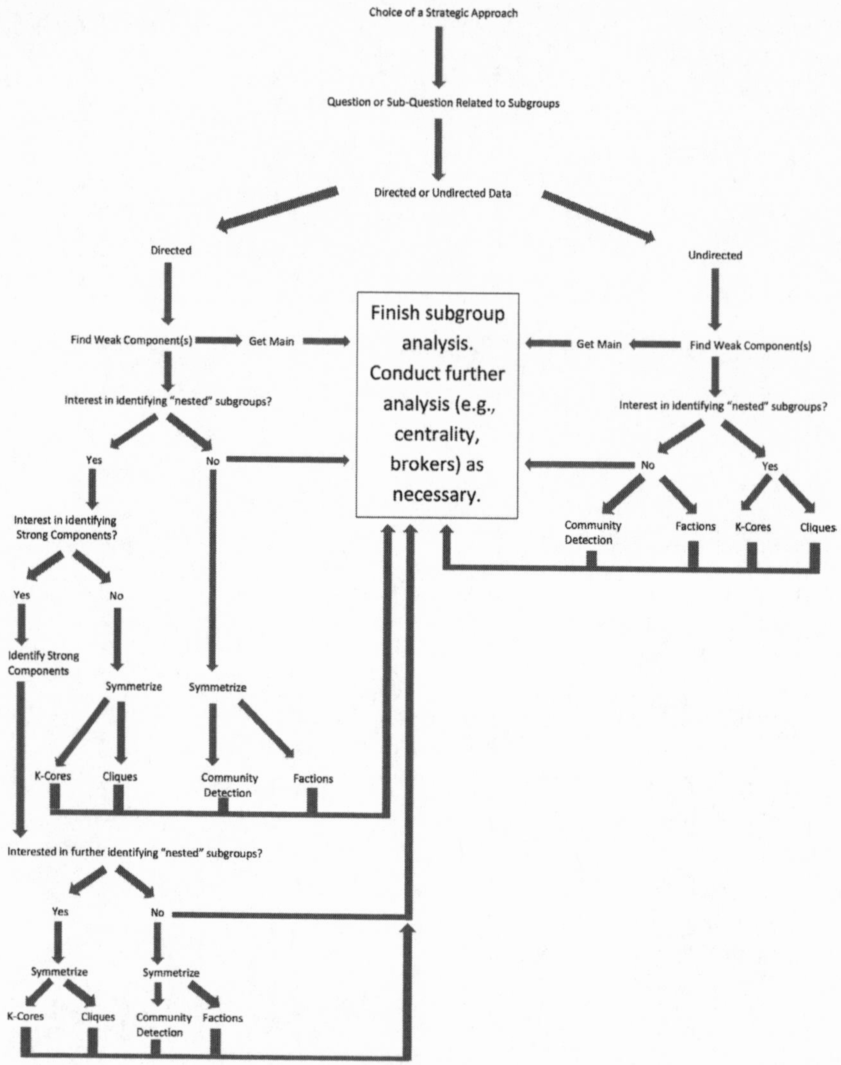

Figure 5.1 Subgroup Analysis Flow Chart

terms of what it captures and whether it best suits the needs of the situation the analyst is exploring or the strategic option they hope to inform. Table 5.1 summarizes the measures described in this chapter, while the flowchart that follows (Figure 5.1) seeks to provide general guidance about how to approach subgroup analysis, most of which will be discussed in detail throughout the chapter's sections. We will then return to a discussion of this approach in the final section.

5.1 COMPONENTS

Some of the easiest subgroups to identify are components. The type of component in which an actor is embedded depends on the type of data with which an analyst is working (i.e., directed or undirected). In undirected networks, components are composed of all actors that can reach one another via a path. The actors in each component can reach only the other actors in that component and not those from other components. If there is only one component in the network (i.e., every actor in the network may be reached by every other actor via a path), then the network is considered to be connected.

Directed networks, on the other hand, provide the opportunity for two conceptualizations of what constitutes a component, each of which depends upon how we honor the direction of the arc or ignore it altogether. The less restrictive definition is referred to as a weak component. Weak components function in a manner similar to undirected components in that they ignore the direction of the tie. A weak component, therefore, consists of all actors within directed network that are reachable by the others in the component, by *ignoring the direction* of ties in the network. By contrast, the more restrictive definition is that of the strong component. Strong components consist of only actors within a network that are *mutually reachable* by all others in the component by following a directed path. That is, there must be a directed path *in each direction* connecting every pair of vertices to qualify as a strong component.[1]

To better understand the concept of components, take the network in Figure 5.2 as an example (de Nooy, Mrvar and Batagelj 2011:77). The network contains three strong components—(1) Tyrone, (2) Max, and (3) Wes, Inigo, and Andre—and two weak components—(1) Tyrone and (2) Max, Wes, Inigo, and Andre. Max, Wes, Inigo, and Andre do not constitute a strong component because if you follow the directions of the arrows, you cannot "walk" from Wes, Inigo, or Andre to Max. They do, however, constitute a weak component because anyone can walk to anyone else if the direction of the arrows is ignored (Tyrone, of course, cannot reach any of them and is not part of the weak component). Thus, while strongly connected networks are also weakly connected, not all weakly connected networks are strongly connected.

Figure 5.2 also illustrates that weak components within a given network are (by definition) isolated from one another (unless, of course, there is only one), which suggests that attempting to identify components in a well-connected and undirected network may not be a good use of one's time. Instead, a quick glance at a network map will do the trick, such as the Koschade Bali I network (Figure 5.5) illustrates. It is undirected, and all actors are connected either directly or indirectly, so the entire network constitutes a single component. Analysts do not need an algorithm to tell them that.

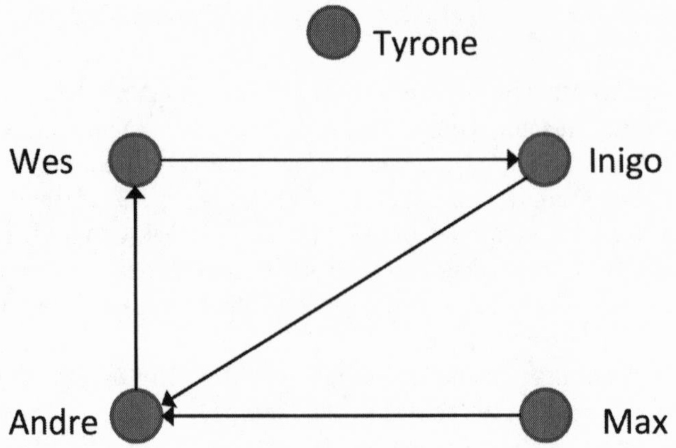

Figure 5.2 Simple Unconnected Directed Network (adapted from de Nooy et al. 2011:77)

When faced with a disconnected network, however, component analysis can be a useful first step before conducting additional analyses. An assessment of the components in a network is generally undertaken in order to subset the network into its main (i.e., largest) component, to extract various components to analyze separately, or to simply characterize the network according to how well connected it may be. With directed networks, an analyst may choose to extract a strong component if they are analyzing it in light of a fairly specialized situation, such as an evaluation of a communication network in which all actors are assumed to be readily able to communicate in either direction. Weak components in a directed network are important to analysts who would like to take the entire component into account for further analyses. Take, for instance, the TFMC network presented in Figure 5.3. A number of isolates are present, along with several small components of sizes two and three, which are shaded gray, plus the largest weak (main) component, which is colored black. Though the entire network consists of 445 actors, the main component only includes 226 actors. With large networks such as this, it is often easier and more illuminating to extract and analyze the network's main component. That, in fact, is the approach we adopt for the remainder of this chapter when analyzing TFMC network.

Network analysts may want to apply component analysis (strong and weak) for several reasons. An important reason, as alluded to before, is that network analysts may want to extract the main component (undirected or directed relations) of a dark network before conducting additional analysis and refining strategic options to counter the network. As mentioned in chapter 1,

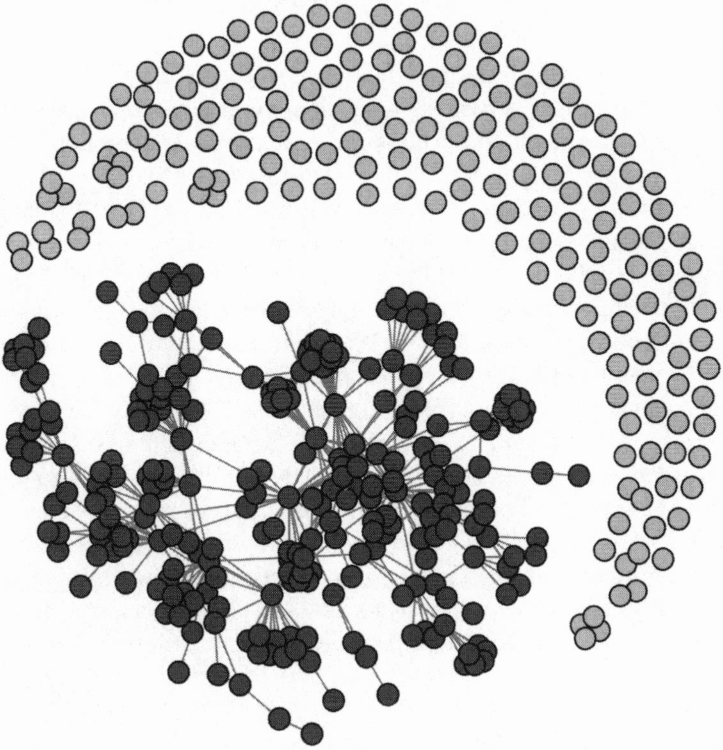

Figure 5.3 FARC TFMC Network

one of the assumptions of SNA is that ties serve as channels for the flow of material and nonmaterial goods and resources. We cannot assume, therefore, that information and resources will flow between disconnected components (i.e., "islands"). For instance, it is unlikely that information inserted as a part of a misinformation campaign against the TFMC (Figure 5.3) will transfer between disconnected components (i.e., gray and black components). This means that practitioners have the greatest potential to reach the most actors if the misinformation is inserted into the main component. Network analysts working with directed data can extract a strong component and follow the potential for resource or information flow throughout the network if they are analyzing it in light of a fairly specialized situation. Weak components in a directed network are important to analysts who would like to take the entire component into account for further analyses, regardless of some actors' inability to return communication, trade, or whatever else is flowing through the network.

5.2 CLIQUES

The most restrictive clustering algorithm is clique analysis; cliques are defined as a maximal subset of three or more actors where each actor is directly connected to all other actors (in other words, the density of a clique is 100%).[2] Figure 5.4 presents a simple illustration of two cliques (adapted from de Nooy, Mrvar and Batagelj 2011:85). Charlie, Dan, Eleanor, and Frank are members of clique A, while Alan, Bella, and Charlie are members of clique B. Neither Alan nor Bella can be members of clique A because although they have ties to Charlie, they do not have ties to Dan, Eleanor, and Frank. For similar reasons, Dan, Eleanor, and Frank cannot be members of clique B. Note that Charlie is a member of both cliques, and some analysts consider clique count as a measure of an actor's centrality. However, the fact that actors can belong to more than one clique often makes identifying distinct subgroups impossible (i.e., where each actor is assigned to one and only one subgroup) and one reason why many analysts shy away from clique analysis. Another is because of the requirement that each clique member be tied to every other member, a requirement that does not always reflect reality. Consequently, social network analysts have developed a number of alternative clique algorithms (e.g., *n*-cliques, *n*-clans, and *k*-plexes) that relax the

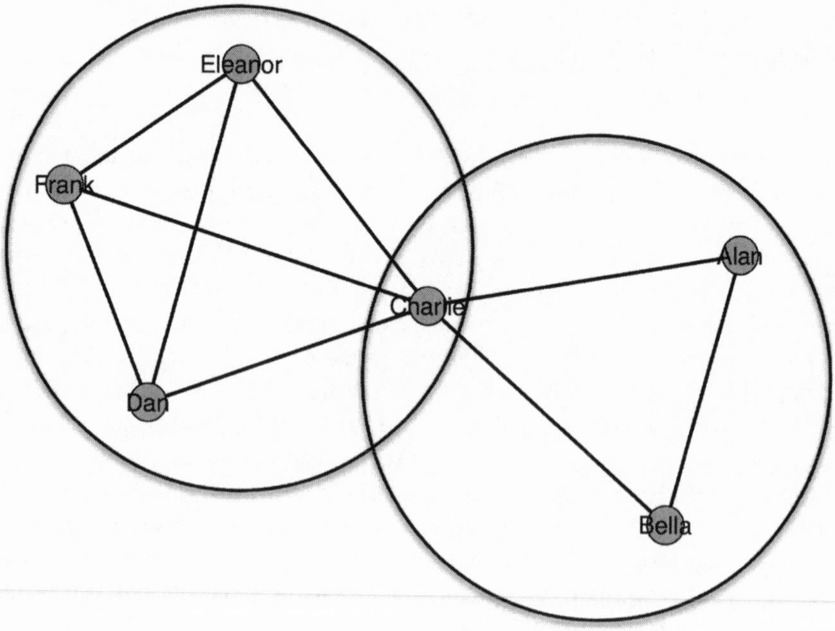

Figure 5.4 Cliques Illustration

assumption that each member of a clique has a tie to every other member.[3] Each of these were created in order to better capture the definition of belonging to a friendship group, and some, such as n-cliques (Reed and Segal 2006), have been used in reference to dark networks. These clique generalizations remain seldom used, in light of the many alternative existing algorithms for assessing community structure. The original concept of a clique, however, remains in use and has been extended.

One of the more innovative approaches to clique analysis is the bimodal approach developed by Martin Everett and Steve Borgatti (1998), which examines the actors and the cliques to which they belong as a two-mode network. Consider, for example, the Koschade Bali I network, which is presented in Figure 5.5. It contains six cliques, ranging in size from four to eight actors, with Samudra being a member of five cliques. If we were to circle all of the cliques, the diagram would be so cluttered that it would become nearly impossible to detect any discernible patterns.

However, when we examine it as a two-mode network, as we do in Figure 5.6,[4] certain patterns present themselves. For example, not only is Samudra's centrality obvious, but so is the centrality of cliques #1 and #2, which consist of eight and seven actors, respectively, six of which are members of both: Muklas, Imron, Samudra, Idris, Azahari, and Sarijo. One could hypothesize that these six individuals wield far more power than other

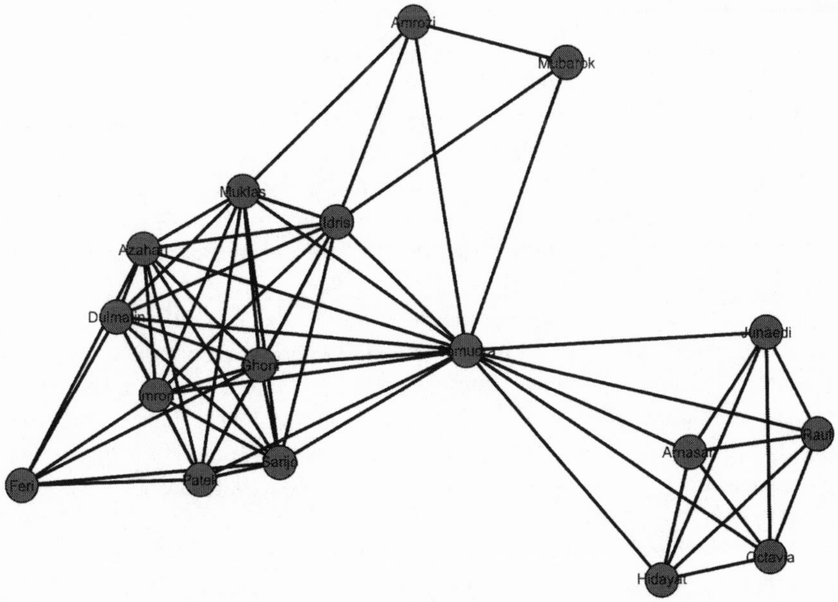

Figure 5.5 Koschade Bali I Network

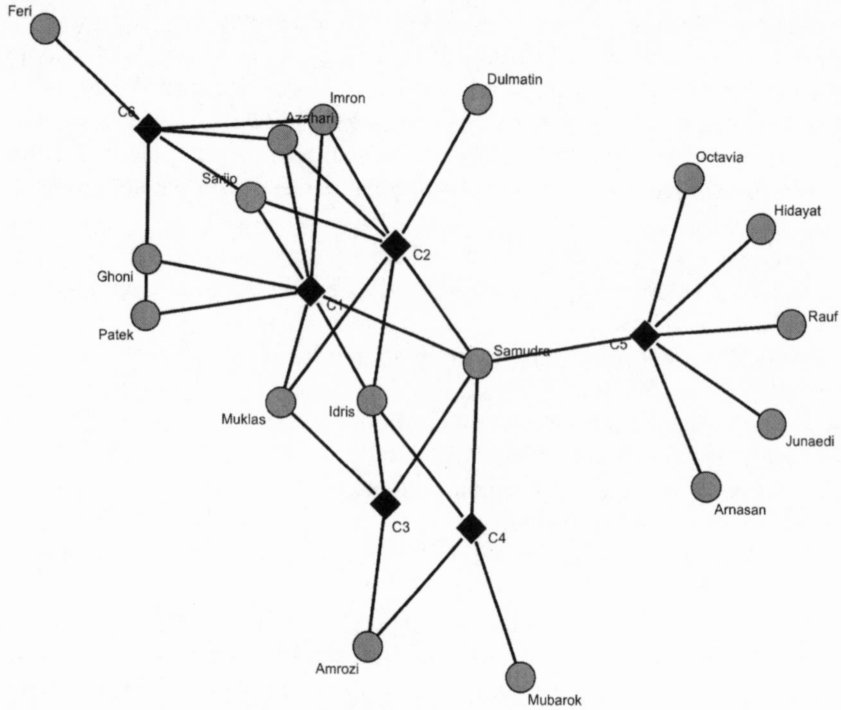

Figure 5.6 Koschade Bali I Actor-by-Clique Network

members of the network. Additional information gathering would be needed, of course, but it is a hypothesis worth exploring.

Another approach is to identify the largest clique in a network (in this case, #1) and assume that its eight members represent the core of the network (in addition to the six mentioned in the previous paragraph, Ghoni and Patek). Since core members are far less likely to leave or defect from a network than are peripheral members (Popielarz and McPherson 1995; Stark and Bainbridge 1980), then if we were considering implementing a reconciliation strategy that offered amnesty to those who leave the network, we would probably not want to target these individuals. Alternative strategies focused on the core, such as misinformation campaigns or the capture/arrest of core members, also could be relatively effective approaches to countering dark networks. The completeness of cliques (i.e., density) suggests that misinformation could spread efficiently throughout the core of a network regardless of which actors serve as seed actors for the spread of misinformation. As suggested in chapter 4, relatively dense networks (or subnetworks such as cliques) are also potentially vulnerable to the arrest or capture of core members because they are (by definition) connected to all other actors within the clique, which increases the likelihood that captured actors have information on all the other core actors.

As maximally dense sets of interconnected actors, cliques are arguably strong representations of subgroups within a network, but their use can also be very unsatisfying at times. Since any three actors that are connected to one another and no one else will constitute a clique, the vast majority of cliques will be uninformative in relation to emergent cultures. Those cliques that are large enough to attract the attention of analysts tend to be few, and it is common for their membership to overlap. In fact, it is not at all uncommon to find multiple actors in the network who are members of numerous overlapping cliques. Though measures such as clique overlap are able to capture this feature, it is difficult to interpret such overlaps in terms of cohesive subgroups. The fact that multiple cliques overlap does not necessarily indicate that the overlapping clique structure will resemble what the analyst would envision as a cohesive subgroup. So, while cliques remain a useful method of divining the densest subgroups in a network, most tend to be small and plentiful throughout most networks. The cliques that are large can be meaningful reflections of working cells, leadership structures, or other meaningful microstructures that are characterized by their intensity. However, larger cliques tend to occur rarely and may not match larger, more loosely combined structures upon which the analyst may also wish to focus. For these and other reasons, additional approaches have since been developed to fill the gap left by some shortcomings of clique analysis.

5.3 CORES

Another way to envision cohesive subgroups is in terms of aggregating actors that share the most concentrated patterns of interaction (de Nooy 2011:61). This makes intuitive sense given those who interact the most with one another are more likely to develop social or functional commonalities than with those with whom they are sparsely or indirectly connected. In a manner that is similar to cliques, the emphasis is on identifying dense pockets—or cores—of actors who are in direct contact with most others in the core. The procedure is operationalized as the *k*-core approach. Formally, a *k*-core is a maximal[5] group of actors, all of whom are connected to some number (*k*) of other group members (de Nooy 2011:82; Wasserman and Faust 1994:266–67). It therefore follows that all actors in a 2-core must possess two or more ties to all other actors in the 2-core, all actors in a 3-core must possess three or more ties to all other actors in the 3-core, and so on. As a result, higher *k*-cores are nested within lower *k*-cores in a manner that is similar to a topographical map. Though, with *k*-cores, the inner nested contour lines that would normally signify peaks actually signify localized pockets of relatively high density in the network that are surrounded by other bands of decreasing values of density outside the cores.

The nested pattern allows for some generalization of what should be considered as a cohesive subgroup. Thus, actors in a 4-core may also be included as members of a 3-core, actors in a 3-core are also members of a 2-core, and so on. The reverse is not necessarily true, however. Not all actors in a 2-core are members of a 3-core, and not all members of a 3-core are members of a 4-core. To expediently extract subgroups through *k*-core analysis, remove only the dense cores, or successively remove the lowest *k*-cores until the network begins to fragment. As the lower valued cores are removed, islands of density will generally emerge, revealing the areas of greatest social or other activity in the network.

The subgroups identified through *k*-core analysis, due in part to its focus on density, do not necessarily constitute a viable cohesive subgroup (de Nooy 2011:83). This is illustrated in Figure 5.7 where the 3-core (white actors) is composed of two distinct groups. One consisting of Harry, Emma, Ronald, and Al; the other consisting of Tom, Luc, Fen, and Bella. This is not necessarily a limitation of *k*-core analysis, however. For example, if we were to

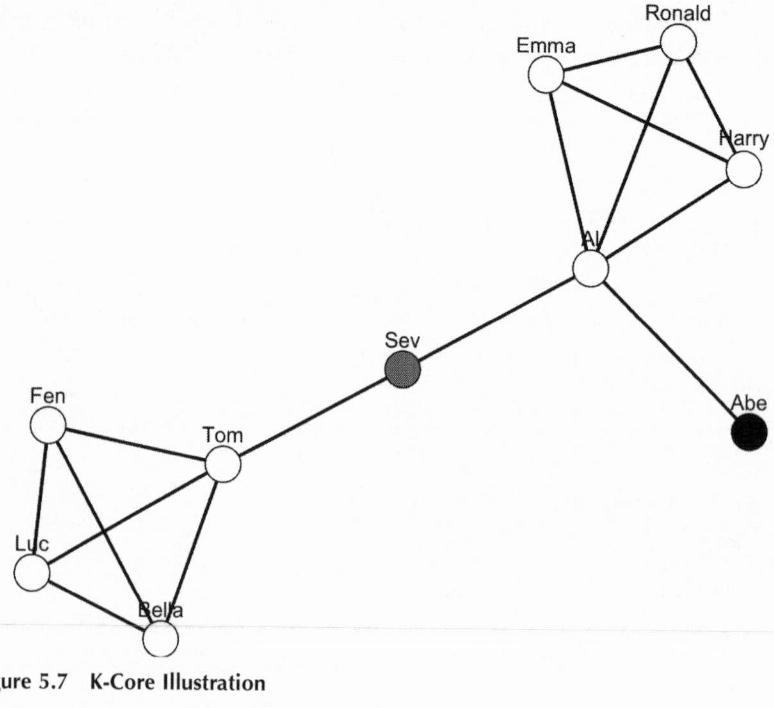

Figure 5.7 K-Core Illustration

extract the 3-core (i.e., remove the 1- and 2-cores), we would be left with what is better describes as two distinct groups. In fact, it is possible that Harry, Emma, Ronald, and Al want nothing to do with Tom, Luc, Fen, and Bella (and vice versa). It is for that reason that *k*-core analysis is ill suited for an exercise that has the purpose of identifying actors who are in a position of brokerage between the two groups. Faction analysis and community detection algorithms should instead be considered for such a purpose.

It may also be of benefit to point out that the highest-valued *k*-core in a network does not necessarily reflect the highest centrality score in the network. This may be illustrated by using the simple example of a hypothetical network in which the measure of degree centrality for one actor is ten, but none of the other actors in the network have a degree centrality higher than four. The highest *k*-core cannot be a 10-core, because every actor in a 10-core would have to be tied to 10 other actors. However, if there were three other actors with a degree centrality of four, then the highest possible *k*-core for that network would be a 4-core.

Now consider the Koschade Bali I network (Figure 5.8). It contains a 3-, 5-, 6-, and 8-core. The 8-core consists of nine individuals—Samudra, Idris, Muklas, Dulmatin, Imron, Azahari, Ghoni, Patek, and Sarijo—all of whom, except Dulmatin, are members of the largest clique. This provides additional support to the idea discussed earlier that these individuals represent

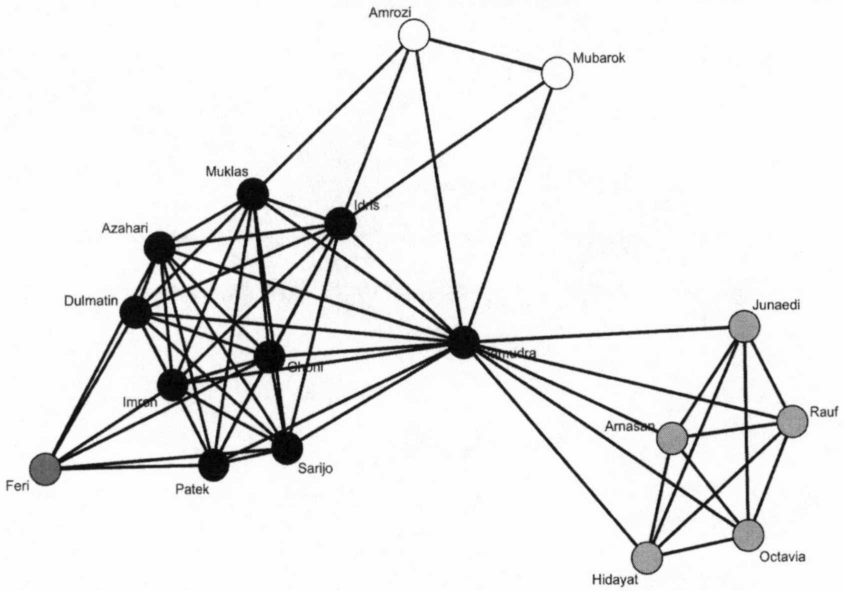

Figure 5.8 K-Cores of the Koschade Bali I Network

the core of the network and are the least likely individuals to defect. According to these findings, the individuals most likely to respond to offers of amnesty are probably Amrozi and Mubarok, who are members of the 3-core, as well as clique #4, which is the network's smallest clique and is located on the periphery of the network (see Figure 5.6).

Turning to a more complex example, Figure 5.9 presents the results of the *k*-core analysis of the FARC TFMC network. Here the *k*-cores range from a 1-core to an 18-core. Members of the 1-core are colored white, members of the 2- through 11-*k*-core are colored gray, and members of the 18-core are colored black (there are no 12- through 17-cores). Although the highest *k*-core does not lie at the center of the network, its members are almost certainly less likely to defect. The presence of just one high-value core reveals the FARC TFMC network to be a core-periphery structure. As such, there appear to be no competing substructures and the densest activity is located in the core. Of particular interest, therefore, may in this case be members of the 1-core, most of which lie on the periphery of the network. These may be individuals that could be targeted for either defection or information.

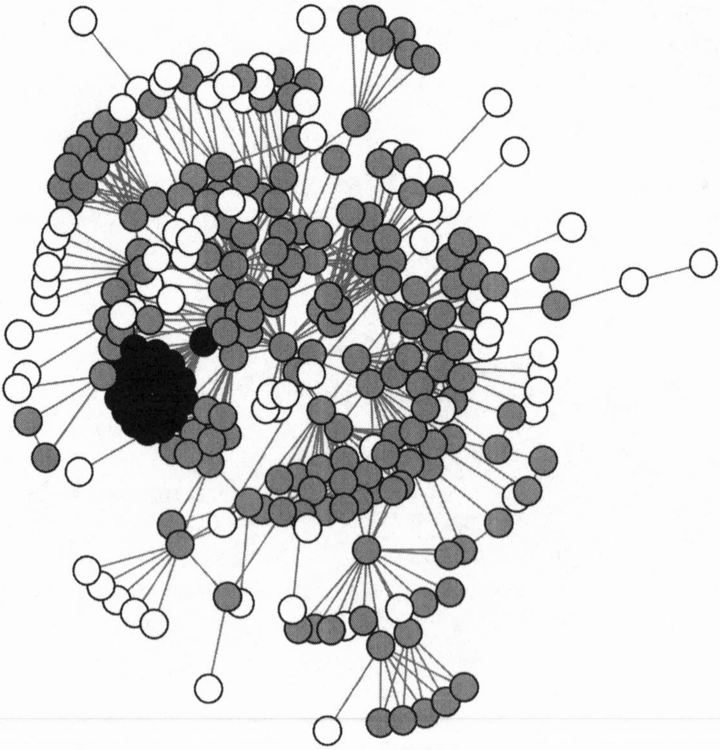

Figure 5.9 K-Cores of the FARC TFMC

K-cores can be helpful in revealing the densest areas of activity in a given network. At times, this can be very helpful for revealing areas of greatest redundancy, interaction, or activity in a particular network. That said, some aspects of *k*-core analysis will fail to match with the concept of cohesive subgroups. For example, there is a tendency for *k*-cores to not identify subgroups that are readily apparent through a visual examination of the visualized network. Similarly, the core levels that are identified by the algorithm do not necessarily constitute a single, uniform group. For these and other reasons, analysts may wish to consider closely what *k*-cores do well: identify dense regions in a graph. Though this is meaningful for finding a structure within the overall network, it may also work well as a supplement to work performed using other community structure approaches. In particular, the *k*-core procedure is likely one of the most efficient means of "drilling down" to the densest elements of each of subgroups extracted using one of the methods mentioned subsequently—Factions, Newman, Spinglass, or Walktrap. Such a procedure would reveal only the most connected regions of various groups within a network, if such information applies to the task at hand.

5.4 FACTIONS

Those who are unsatisfied with what *k*-core analysis reveals may find the factions algorithm to be a more satisfying alternative. Like *k*-cores, the faction algorithm employs density as the defining characteristic of its process, though it differs in how density is applied to the problem of identifying subgroups. The concept of a faction is that of highly interconnected groups that share no connection with one another. This concept can certainly be appealing to an analyst who is interested in the idea of turning elements of a given network against one another. As satisfying as it may appear to be, however, the faction aspect of the method is merely a metaphor that describes the ideal state that the algorithm seeks to replicate through a network sorting and optimization approach. The idea is to classify (sort) each actor into one of a user-specified number of subgroups. Each of the resulting subgroups should ideally be densely interconnected within subgroups but with few, if any, ties between subgroups. This is frequently a useful method of assessing whether there is structural evidence of subgroups that appear to be present in the network.

The procedure for parsing a network in terms of factions requires analysts to first specify the number of factions that they wish to derive from the network. The number may be arbitrarily selected, but it is much better practice for analysts to base their estimate on what they already know about the network. Ideally, such information would not only come from background knowledge, reports, or the expectations of field agents, but it is also common practice for analysts to base their estimate on their assessment of the visualized network. For example, an examination of the network in Figure 5.10 clearly indicates that there are two subgroups present in the network although, in this particular case, simply assessing these as components—or any of the other subgroup analyses for that matter—would yield the same result. Perhaps a better example is the Koschade Bali I network (Figure 5.8). Analysts examining it may begin by specifying two groups, and, after considering the result, may then consider increasing the number of groups in hopes of improving the "fit."

Goodness of fit for the faction algorithm is measured through a comparison between the result provided through the faction procedure and the ideal manifestation of how a faction "should" look. As mentioned earlier, the ideal faction model is that of some number of groups, where the members of each group share ties with one another, but do not share ties with members of other groups. Figure 5.10 presents an idealized factionalized network.

Carrying out a faction analysis of the network that is visualized in Figure 5.10 in UCINET yields the output presented in Figure 5.11. What one may normally think of as "goodness of fit" is presented by UCINET in terms

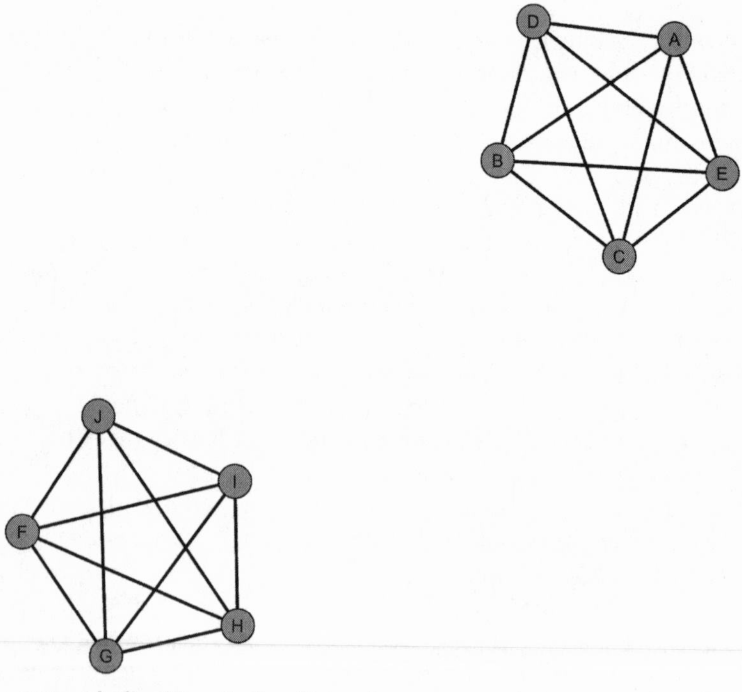

Figure 5.10 Idealized Two-Faction Network

```
ucinetlog1.txt - Notepad
File Edit Format View Help
FACTIONS
--------------------------------------------------------

Number of factions:                          2
Measure of fit:                              Hamming
Input dataset:                                ()

Initial proportion correct: 1.000

...Badness of fit: 0.000
...Badness of fit: 0.000
...Badness of fit: 0.000

Final proportion correct: 1.000

Group Assignments:

   1:  F G H I J
   2:  A B C D E

Grouped Adjacency Matrix

                     1
           6 7 8 9 0   1 2 3 4 5
           F G H I J   A B C D E
          ----------------------
   6 F |   1 1 1 1 |           |
   7 G | 1   1 1 1 |           |
   8 H | 1 1   1 1 |           |
   9 I | 1 1 1   1 |           |
  10 J | 1 1 1 1   |           |
        ------------------------
   1 A |           |   1 1 1 1 |
   2 B |           | 1   1 1 1 |
   3 C |           | 1 1   1 1 |
   4 D |           | 1 1 1   1 |
   5 E |           | 1 1 1 1   |
         -----------------------
```

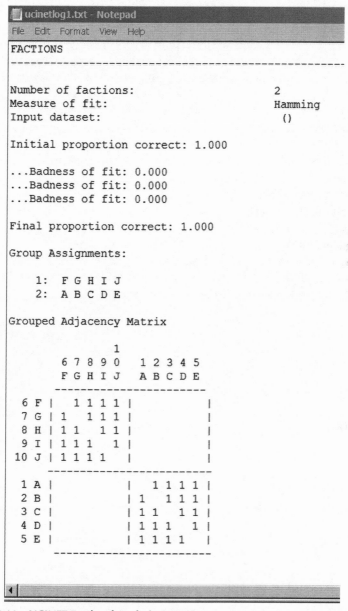

Figure 5.11 UCINET Factional Analysis Output

of "badness of fit" and "final proportion correct." Each measure presents essentially the same information, with badness of fit calculated as the number of ties that do not match the "ideal" faction model and final proportion correct calculated as the percentage of ties that do match the ideal. Therefore, lower badness of fit and higher proportion correct each indicates a better fit. In this example, the badness of fit score is "0" and the proportion correct is 100 percent, each of which indicates a perfect fit. It is very uncommon to see measures close to these when working with real data; analyses such as these are generally reserved for finding or assessing subgroups that are not nearly so obvious.

The remainder of the output describes the network in terms of "blocks" that are expressed as a grouped adjacency matrix, described further in chapter 8. The rows and columns of the data matrix have been rearranged to conform to what is expected of the ideal model, while minimizing error (badness of fit). As you can see, all possible the ties are present within the blocks (i.e., groups) along the diagonal and no ties are present in the off-diagonal blocks. A density table at the bottom of the output (not shown) is another way of assessing how well the actual network compares to the idealized one. In this case, the density of each block along the diagonal is 100%, while the density of the off-diagonal blocks is 0%, which is what we would expect.

Now consider the network in Figure 5.12 where two distinct groups clearly exist but one tie is present across the groups that should not be in an idealized factional network (i.e., tie between C and G):

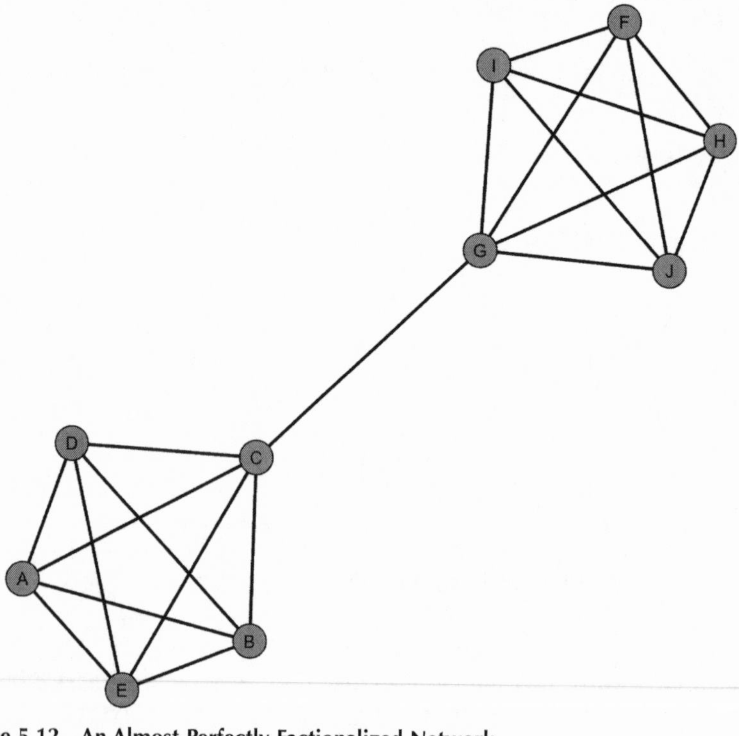

Figure 5.12 An Almost-Perfectly Factionalized Network

The results of the factional analysis for the network presented in Figure 5.13 paint a slightly different picture than the results in Figure 5.11. The badness of fit score is 2 because of the tie between actors G and C. Note that UCI-NET counts this error twice, which reflects the fact that it treats the network as directed rather than undirected. The presence of the two errors lowers the

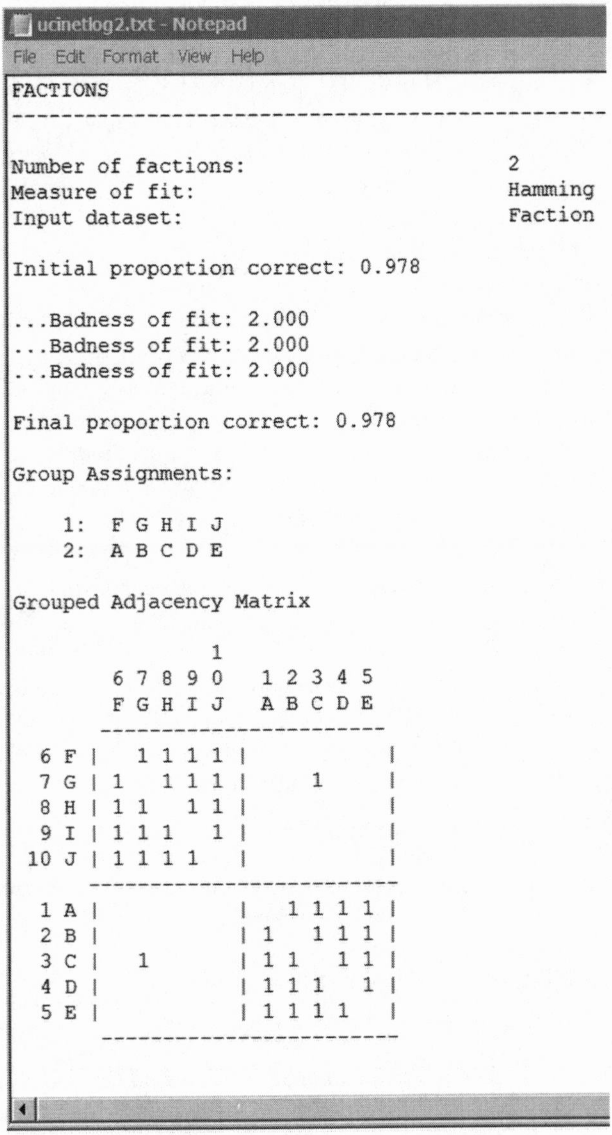

```
ucinetlog2.txt - Notepad
File  Edit  Format  View  Help
FACTIONS
------------------------------------------------

Number of factions:                          2
Measure of fit:                              Hamming
Input dataset:                               Faction

Initial proportion correct: 0.978

...Badness of fit: 2.000
...Badness of fit: 2.000
...Badness of fit: 2.000

Final proportion correct: 0.978

Group Assignments:

    1:  F G H I J
    2:  A B C D E

Grouped Adjacency Matrix

                  1
          6 7 8 9 0   1 2 3 4 5
          F G H I J   A B C D E
        -----------------------
   6 F |    1 1 1 1 |           |
   7 G | 1    1 1 1 |     1     |
   8 H | 1 1    1 1 |           |
   9 I | 1 1 1    1 |           |
  10 J | 1 1 1 1    |           |
        -----------------------
   1 A |            |   1 1 1 1 |
   2 B |            | 1   1 1 1 |
   3 C |   1        | 1 1   1 1 |
   4 D |            | 1 1 1   1 |
   5 E |            | 1 1 1 1   |
        -----------------------
```

Figure 5.13 UCINET Faction Analysis Output

proportion correct to 97.8% (88/90) and is illustrated in the grouped adjacency matrix.

Factional analysis is generally used as an exploratory device to detect subgroups, examining the results from several iterations where we vary the number of factions in order to see which number of subgroups yields the best fit. UCINET actually offers numerous measures of fit, including Hamming, phi, modularity, and entailment. Of those, we will use the first three. *Hamming* is the conventional measure and the one illustrated before. *Phi* measures the correlation between the actual data matrix and an idealized one where the density of the diagonal blocks is 100% and the density of the off-diagonal is 0%. *Modularity* is a measure developed by Mark Newman (2006) that compares the ties within and across blocks to what one would expect in a random graph of the same size and having the same number of ties. Formally, it is the fraction of internal ties in each block less than the expected fraction if they were distributed at random but with the same degree sequence. It compares the actual network with a random network of the same size (i.e., number of actors) and the same number of ties. It is the same measure used to evaluate the fit of community detection groups. UCINET has implemented a variation on the modularity measure, Q-prime, which normalizes the modularity score in comparison to the maximum possible score given the number of groups detected in the network. For instance, the maximum modularity score in a network with only two groups is 0.500. Thus, if an analysis yields a modularity score of 0.450, then the normalized modularity score (or Q-prime) would equal 0.900.

The results of a faction analysis of the Koschade network are presented in Table 5.2, and they are somewhat mixed.[6] Hamming, phi, and modularity suggest that three faction subgroups provide the best fit. On the other hand, normalized modularity indicates that two provide the best fit. This situation, and situations like it, strongly suggests that more information is necessary in order to make a decision on how many subgroups should be extracted from the Koschade network. In this case, knowledge about the actors in the network and a visual inspection of the 2-, 3-, and 4-group partitions were used to select the number of groups that best seemed to fit. Figure 5.14 presents the Koschade network partitioned into three factions. A two-faction partition

Table 5.2 Faction Analysis of Koschade Bali I Network

Number of Factions	*Hamming (Proportion)*	*Phi (Correlation)*	*Modularity*	*Modularity (Normalized)*
2	0.820	0.659	0.293	0.586
3	0.893	0.786	0.298	0.447
4	0.864	0.771	0.283	0.377

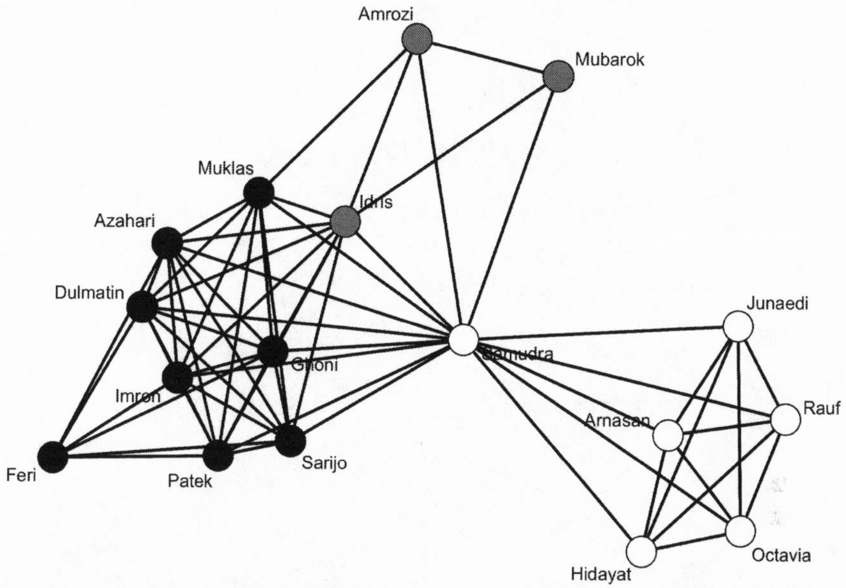

Figure 5.14 Faction Analysis of Koschade Bali I Network

does not separate Idris, Amrozi, and Mubarok into a different subgroup. Note that faction analysis groups Samudra with different actors than did k-core and clique analysis.

Because faction analysis is an iterative process, it can be quite time consuming to analyze large networks because knowing approximately how many factions with which to begin can be difficult. That is why with large networks it is often best to begin with the community detection algorithms discussed in the next section in order to estimate the approximate number of factions. Indeed, that is what we did here. Three community detection algorithms—Girvan–Newman (2002); Clauset, Newman, and Moore (2004); and Spinglass (Reichardt and Bornholdt 2006)—partitioned the network into 17 subgroups. Another—Walktrap (Pons and Latapy 2005)—partitioned the network into 33 groups. Since three out of the four identified 17 subgroups, we began our analysis by estimating measures of fit for 17 partitions and then increased and decreased the number of partitions one at a time. Interestingly, the Walktrap algorithm yielded a similar solution as the Hamming measure of fit, which detected 51 subgroups. However, when using modularity, our faction analysis identified only 14 or 15 subgroups (depending on whether one uses raw or normalized modularity). The two solutions are presented in Figures 5.15 and 5.16.

In our opinion, the analysis that used modularity as a measure of fit provides appears to provide a more convincing solution. Visually, more of the

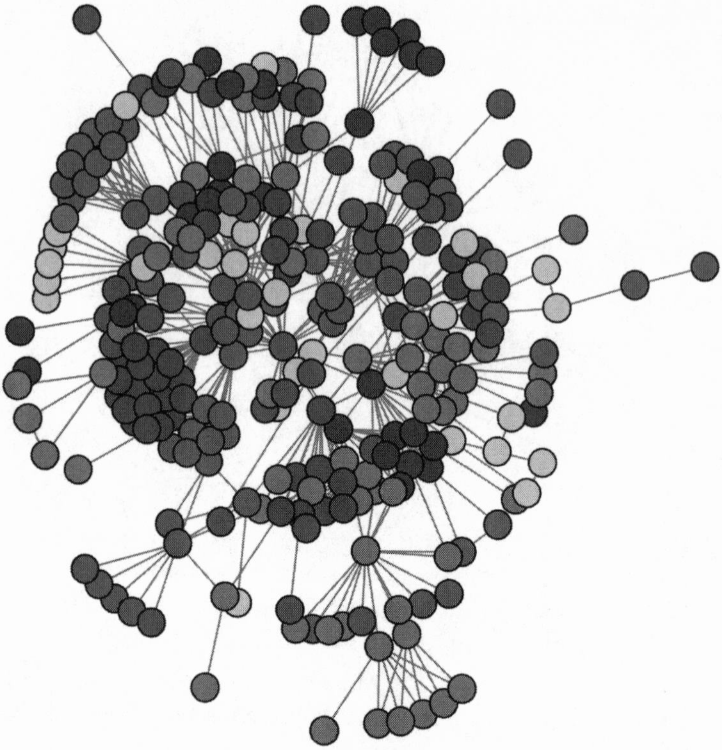

Figure 5.15 Faction Analysis of FARC TFMC using Hamming Measure of Fit (51 Factions)

subgroups (as represented by shading) in Figure 5.17 appear to reflect actual cohesive subgroups (i.e., they are located next to one another) as compared to the subgroups in Figure 5.16. In Figure 5.16, actors that are members of the same subgroup (i.e., they are the same shade) are often located at some distance from one another (e.g., on opposite sides of the graph). To be sure, the subgroupings in Figure 5.17 are not perfect, but they appear to be a better reflection of "real life."

5.5 COMMUNITY DETECTION

One of the better-received aspects of physicists entering the field of network analysis is the development of community detection algorithms that are fast and efficient enough to quickly parse even very large networks, often in an intuitive manner. Of these, perhaps the most readily recognizable are those developed by Mark Newman and his colleagues (Clauset, Newman and

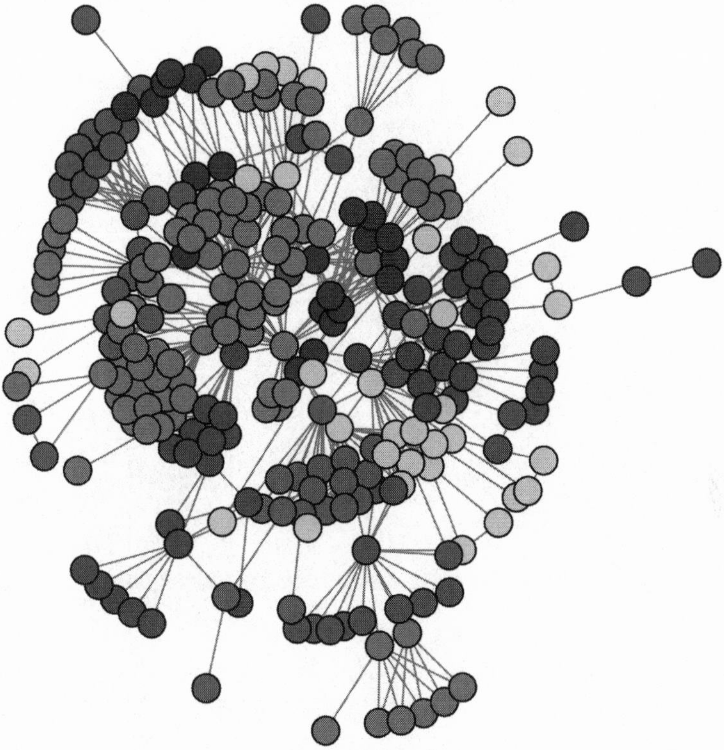

Figure 5.16 Faction Analysis of FARC TFMC using Modularity Measure of Fit (14 Factions)

Moore 2004; Girvan and Newman 2002; Newman 2004), who envisioned an approach similar to that of faction analysis, defining subgroups as having more ties within and fewer ties between groups. The popular Girvan–Newman algorithm (2002) is the most widely implemented and generalized of the three. The other two—the fast greedy algorithm (Newman 2004) and the Clauset, Newman, and Moore algorithm (2004)—are optimized for use with very large networks.

In contrast to the top-down approaches presented earlier in the chapter, the Girvan–Newman algorithm uses a bottom-up divisive approach. Whereas the algorithms presented thus far have generally operated from the standpoint of aggregating actors according to their similarity, the Girvan–Newman focus is upon iteratively locating and removing edges that connect the *least similar* pairs of actors, *dis*aggregating them, in effect. Key to this process is the notion of edge betweenness, which is similar to (actor) betweenness, except that it measures the extent to which each edge (i.e., tie) lies on a shortest path between all pairs of actors in the network. An edge with high betweenness is

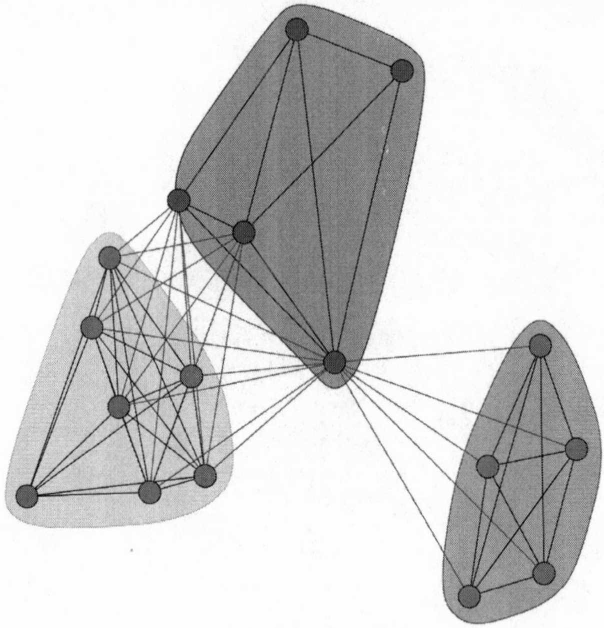

Figure 5.17 Community Detection Analysis of Koschade Bali I Network

similar to a bridge that connects two large populated cities that are separated by a river. The shortest path from some point in one city to any one point in the next is very likely to cross that bridge or another. If all of the bridges were to be removed, then the cities would be divided into separate units.[7]

The Girvan–Newman algorithm operates in a manner that is similar to the bridge example. It iteratively seeks out the edge with the highest edge betweenness score—those edges that form a bridge between communities—and removes it before recalculating edge betweenness scores for the remaining edges for use in the next iteration. As more of the high-betweenness edges are removed, the network will begin to break apart into smaller components. Each time the removal of an edge causes the network to break into separate clusters, the algorithm calculates a modularity score (Q) as a measure of the quality of the division of the network. Higher values of Q are interpreted as reflecting relatively better representations of community structure in the network. As a relative scale, analysts will compare the modularity scores calculated as various components are separated out. The highest value of Q attained during the process is usually, but not always, taken as the optimal division of the network. With this and other divisive algorithms, analysts may also consider the interpretability of the network in light of its attributes and other information. Ultimately, it is their responsibility to review the various configurations that this or any other algorithm produces and determine and defend their interpretation of the "best" representation of community structure for a given network. Other community detection algorithms that have gained attention in the network science community include the Walktrap (Pons and Latapy 2005) and Spinglass (Reichardt and Bornholdt 2006).

Each algorithm will tend to produce results that are often somewhat unique from the others, which can make conducting subgroup analysis somewhat confusing for new network analysts. For instance, in analyzing the Koschade network Girvan–Newman identified seven subgroups, Clauset, Newman, Moore identified three, Walktrap identified five, and Spinglass identified three. The normalized modularity scores were 0.274, 0.488, 0.343, and 0.291, respectively. Thus, Figure 5.17 presents the results from the Clauset, Newman, and Moore algorithm. The figure also highlights one of the options available in the igraph R package: The ability to draw convex hulls around each of the subgroups in order to aid in interpretability.

Figure 5.18 presents the results of a community detection algorithm analysis for the TFMC network. As noted earlier, all the algorithms identified 17 groups except for Walktrap, which identified 22. The normalized modularity score for the Girvan–Newman algorithm was 0.813; for Clauset, Newman, and Moore, 0.788; Walktrap, 0.776; and Spinglass, 0.828. Thus, the figure presents the results from the Spinglass algorithm. The demarcation between the various groups is not nearly as clear as with the Koschade network, but that is not surprising since larger networks are typically more complex than smaller networks. In fact, one of the major benefits of using community detection algorithms on real-world dark networks, which are typically complex, is that it is often too difficult to properly identify and demarcate clusters using only visualizations as our guide.

5.6 SUMMARY: LESSONS LEARNED

In this chapter we have explored five sets of algorithms for detecting cohesive subgroups: components, cliques, cores, factions, and community detection algorithms. This list certainly does not exhaust our options; there are several others we have not considered. However, we do consider the ones we covered in to be among the most useful. What should be clear by now is that we may have to use multiple algorithms before we succeed in detecting cohesive subgroups. Of course, when working with small groups, we can often detect them visually; however, as groups become larger, it becomes increasingly necessary to turn to algorithms in order to identifying subgroups.

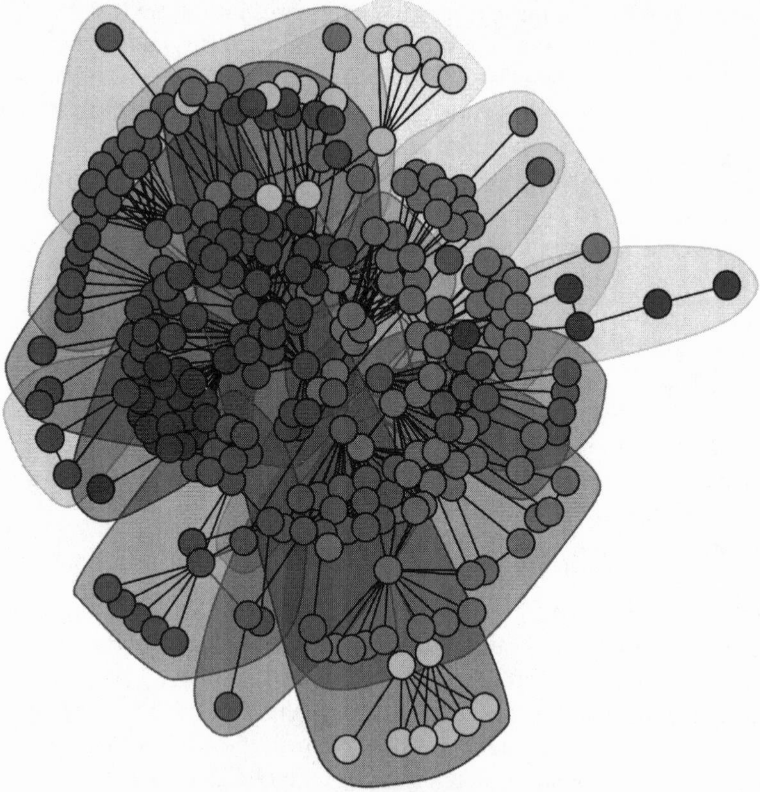

Figure 5.18 Community Detection Analysis of FARC TFMC

Indeed, it is probably best to follow a consistent approach for identifying a dark network's subgroups (see the flow chart at the beginning of the chapter). The first decision we need to make, which is largely driven by our chosen strategic approach and the environmental context, is whether we are looking for nested subgroups or not. If we are, then k-core, clique, or strong component analysis are probably the best approaches. As mentioned earlier, certain strategic options lend themselves to the identification of nested subgroups. For example, a PSYOP team interested in implementing a misinformation campaign against a dark network containing a clique should be able, at least theoretically, to insert information at any point or actor within that clique to sow seeds of distrust among that subgroup's members. Furthermore, the completeness of cliques suggests that misinformation should have a greater likelihood of spreading throughout the entire subgroup.

If we are not looking for nested subgroups, then faction analysis or community detection algorithms are probably the best choice. One approach that covers a range of strategic options (kinetic and nonkinetic) is to identify seams between communities or factions within a dark network that may serve as crucial bridges or highlight important brokers between clusters. We may want to consider strategies that sow seeds of distrust that promotes infighting among the various subgroups, which could lead the network to fragment or implode. As social movement scholars have noted, infighting can lead to a decline of an insurgency or movement (McAdam 1999 [1982]). Of course, the network could respond by taking new steps to evade authorities and making it hard to track and monitor. Or, it could form and/or sever ties with other actors (both in and outside of the network), which would cause its structure to change and render our network map of it out of date.

Another approach would be to extract one or more of the subgroups in order to conduct a more focused analysis. As we saw earlier, extracting the largest component prior to conducting further analysis allows us to focus on the bulk of the network while ignoring smaller portions of the network on which a strategy will likely have less impact. Similarly, we may identify a subgroup that contains several actors of interest, such as key leaders, logisticians, and recruiters that we could extract and conduct additional analyses outlined in this book. In fact, this technique is frequently used to examine extremely large online networks, such as Twitter networks, where running metrics on the entire network is computationally challenging (see, e.g., Schroeder, Everton and Shepherd 2012). A simple example is depicted in Figure 5.19, which presents the largest subgroup of the TFMC detected using the Spinglass algorithm. As one can clearly see, most of the actors in this subgroup are tied together because of a single individual: Agent 342, suggesting that further analysis of his role in the network may be warranted.

The identification of cohesive subgroups can often be quite tricky for those new to SNA. The application of these algorithms, and the subsequent interpretation of the results, may require some getting used to because they seem less intuitive than illuminating other important network characteristics, such as central actors (chapter 6) or brokers and bridges (chapter 7). For instance, we saw in section 5.6 “Community Detection” that different community detection algorithms provided the best answer for two different dark networks, namely the Koschade network (Figure 5.17) and the TFMC network (Figure 5.18). Nonetheless, these algorithms (and the others mentioned in this chapter) can be crucial in the proper identification of network clusters and critical weaknesses between them regardless of the strategic approach at hand. We cannot rely solely on visualizations given the complex nature of some dark networks. In other words, the algorithms covered in this chapter provide a useful approach for examining crucial elements of a larger

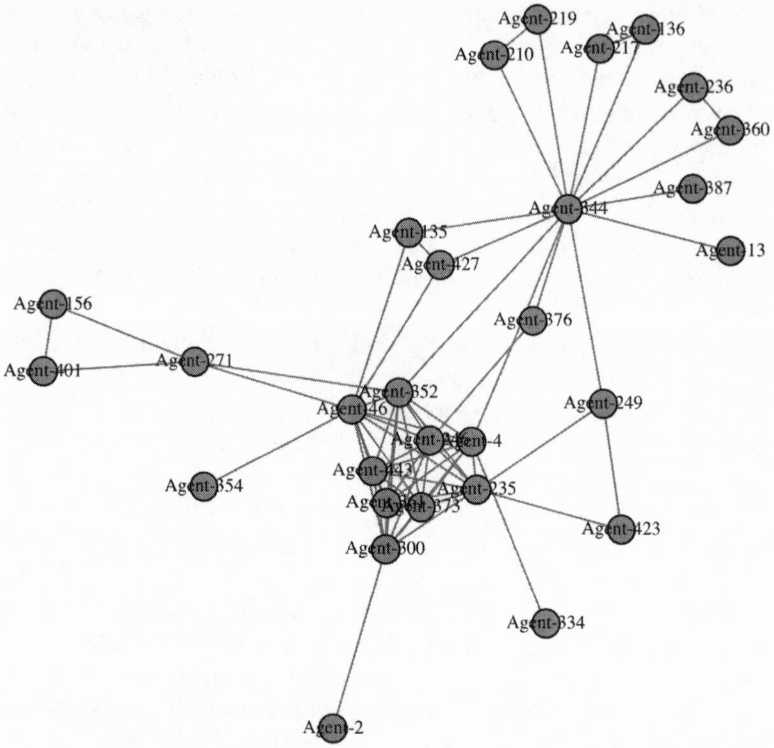

Figure 5.19 Largest FARC TFMC Subgroup

dark network, which will facilitate a better understanding of a network, and ultimately, better inform the decision-making process.

5.7 QUESTIONS

1. Which of the following is a community detection algorithm?
   a. Faction analysis.
   b. Clauset, Newman, and Moore.
   c. K-core analysis.
   d. Clique analysis.
   e. Component analysis.
2. Which of the following statements regarding cliques is true?
   a. Cliques are the least restrictive type of clustering algorithm.
   b. Cliques require every actor to have a tie to every other actor.
   c. Cliques are the same as components.

   d. Clique analysis is probably the most widely used algorithm for detecting subgroups in networks.
   e. Cliques are also referred to as social circles.
3. Component analysis is a useful technique for identifying and removing the largest cluster in a network.
   a. True.
   b. False.
4. Strictly speaking, which of the following are types of components?
   a. Weak.
   b. Clique.
   c. Strong.
   d. K-core.
5. Community detection algorithms automatically identify actors who have the same norms, ideas, and beliefs.
   a. True.
   b. False.
6. Which of the following does not necessarily produce viable cohesive subgroups?
   a. Weak Components.
   b. Cliques.
   c. K-cores.
   d. Factions.
   e. Newman groups.
7. Actor attributes are rarely used to supplement structural approaches for identifying cohesive subgroups.
   a. True.
   b. False.
8. Which of the following do social network analysts use to determine the level of fit a clustering of a network?
   a. Hamming
   b. Phi
   c. Modularity
   d. Badness of fit
   e. All of the above.

5.8 ANSWERS

1. Clauset, Newman, and Moore (b).
2. They require every actor to have a tie to every other actor (b).
3. True.
4. Weak (a) and Strong (c).

5. False.
6. K-cores (c).
7. False.
8. All of the above (e).

5.9 FURTHER READING

Two good places to start are works by Borgatti et al. (*Analyzing Social Networks,* Thousand Oaks, CA: SAGE Publishing, 2013) and Prell (*Social Network Analysis: History, Theory & Methodology*, London and Thousand Oaks, CA: SAGE Publications, 2011) respective chapters on subgroups. Wasserman and Faust's (*Social Network Analysis: Methods and Applications*. Cambridge, UK: Cambridge University Press, 1994) chapter on cohesive subgroups (chapter 7) is also helpful although it does not reflect more recent developments. Readers may also want to consider the following readings:

- Wouter de Nooy, Andrej Mrvar, and Vladimir Batagelj. 2011. Pp. 77–96 (chapter 3) in *Exploratory Social Network Analysis with Pajek.*
- Martin G. Everett and Stephen P. Borgatti. 1998. "Analyzing Clique Overlap." *Connections* 21:49–61.
- Kenneth A. Frank. 1995. "Identifying Cohesive Subgroups." *Social Networks* 17:27–56.
- Scott D. Gest, James Moody, and Kelly L. Rulison. 2007. "Density or Distinction? The Roles of Data Structure and Group Detection Methods in Describing Adolescent Peer Groups." *Journal of Social Structure* 8(1): http://www.cmu.edu/joss/content/articles/volume8/GestMoody/
- Michelle Girvan and Mark E. J. Newman. 2002. "Community Structure in Social and Biological Networks." *Proceedings of the National Academy of Sciences USA* 99(12):7821–26.
- Robert A. Hanneman and Mark Riddle. 2005. "Cliques and Sub-groups" (chapter 11) in *Introduction to Social Network Methods.* Riverside, CA: University of Riverside: http://www.faculty.ucr.edu/~hanneman/nettext/C11_Cliques.html.
- John Scott. 2013. Pp. 99–120 (chapter 6) in *Social Network Analysis*. London and Thousand Oaks, CA: SAGE Publications Ltd.

NOTES

1. A path is a walk (i.e., a sequence of actors and ties) in which no actor between the first and last actors of the walk occurs more than once.

2. Here, the term maximal means that no other actor can be added to the subnetwork without destroying its defining characteristic, which in this case means that each actor must be tied to each other actor in the network.

3. We will not discuss alternative clique algorithms in this book. Readers interested in learning more about these alternatives can consult Wasserman and Faust (1994).

4. Calculated using UCINET (Borgatti, Everett and Freeman 2002b) and visualized using the R sna package (Butts 2014).

5. Maximal, in this case, is defined as a set to which no other actor can be added without destroying its defining characteristic. For *k*-cores, the minimum number of ties that each actor must have in order to belong to a particular *k*-core is the defining characteristic.

6. A dichotomized version of the Koschade network was used for this analysis.

7. We return to the notion of edge betweenness in chapter 7 as a method for identifying bridges in a network.

Chapter 6

Identifying Central Actors in Networks

Centrality is perhaps the most intuitive set of social network analysis metrics and one of the oldest concepts in social network analysis. Notions that certain actors are more central than others can be traced at least as far back as Jacob Moreno's (1953a) conception of sociometric stars (Wasserman and Faust 1994:169). Its formal properties have been tested experimentally (Bavelas 1948, 1950; Cook and Emerson 1978; Cook et al. 1983; Cook, Gillmore and Yamagishi 1986; Cook and Whitmeyer 1992; Emerson 1962, 1972a, 1972b, 1976; Leavitt 1951), and scholars such as Linton Freeman (1977, 1979), Phillip Bonacich (1972, 1987), Noah Friedkin (1991), and Steve Borgatti and Martin Everett (e.g., Borgatti 2005; Borgatti and Everett 2006; Everett and Borgatti 2005) have refined and expanded the measures of centrality available to analysts. The great work of these scholars, along with the intuitiveness of centrality as a concept, is a major reason why practitioners, and the software they use, regularly incorporate basic centrality measures in their normal use of social network analysis (SNA). Centrality functions better as a conceptual category than as a concept. This is largely due to wildly differing interpretations of what it means to be central or important in a network. The richness of the concept has therefore been preserved as numerous researchers have chosen to "conceptualize centrality in a variety of ways" (Bonacich 1987; Borgatti 2005; Borgatti and Everett 2006; Freeman 1979). "A central actor can be seen as an actor who has numerous ties to other actors (e.g., degree centrality), as an actor who has numerous ties to highly central actors (e.g., eigenvector centrality, hubs and authorities), as an actor who is close (in terms of path distance) to other actors in the network (e.g., closeness centrality), or as an actor who lies between numerous pairs of actors in a network (e.g., betweenness centrality)" (Everton 2012).

This variety of centrality definitions makes it possible for analysts to select the version of centrality that best corresponds with what they are seeking to discover in a particular network. The centrality measures covered in this chapter are by no means the only ones available, but they are among the most commonly applied and, as such, they constitute a useful—and fairly deep—starting point for analysts interested in exploring the concept. We begin our presentation with a discussion of best practices for applying what many treat as a ubiquitous concept to dark network data. We argue that best results are obtained from deciding on what central should mean in a particular network *before* calculating any measures. We then continue with a discussion of the measures themselves. In so doing, we follow a modified form of Freeman's (1979) classification of centrality into three general families: frequency-based measures, distance-based measures, and path-based measures (Borgatti and Everett 2006). Freeman's classification system helps to clarify some of the more important similarities and differences between various measures. Discussions of centrality are immediately followed by a similar treatment on the closely related concept of prestige. The chapter concludes with examples of what centrality measures may reveal about the actors in a network.

6.1 WORK-PLAN FOR CENTRALITY CALCULATIONS

Because of their ubiquity and ease of calculation, it is altogether too easy to calculate centrality measures without prior consideration for their contextual meaning, their relation to the problem being investigated, or their limitations given the context or type of network data that is being analyzed. It is not uncommon for those who are new to network analysis—and even many with experience in the field—to calculate a battery of centrality measures and then attempt to use them for inference, regardless of whether the measures they have run may be poorly suited to the data or the question at hand. Once the output has been produced it becomes far too tempting to justify the "importance" of a few actors based upon a handful of high centrality scores. Unless, however, those measures meaningfully relate to the question that analysts are hoping to resolve *and* are appropriate for use with the data they are analyzing, such a finding is more likely to be a false trail than a genuine discovery. It is critical to keep in mind that centrality measures are diverse because they each carry a very specific meaning. As with most of other network analytic procedures mentioned in this book, each measure was developed to capture a unique understanding of centrality or to function with a specific type of network data. Each was designed with a particular scenario or data type in mind. However, with enough manipulation and frequently with no manipulation at all, it is typically possible to get a computer to generate any centrality measure on any data. But, the fact that it is possible to produce output should not be taken to mean that the measures are appropriate or that the results are meaningful. A best practice is therefore for analysts to first consider the information they hope to gain about the actors in a network in order to assemble a list of metrics relevant to that information. The first priority for any analyst is to discuss or consider the object of the analysis. If the work is being performed in support of operations, relate the analysis back to the strategy or strategies that it is intended to support (see chapter 2). If the analysis is for research, then consider what you hope to uncover about the actors in the network. What does "important" mean in the context of the network and the environment in which it resides? Who, or what type of person, is being sought?

The importance of central actors should be evident through their position of prominence, power, direct or indirect influence, brokerage, access, or some combination of those characteristics. The strategy being supported, or the type of role, or other analytic goal should drive the analyst's decision on which measures of centrality are most appropriate to access. Restricting a centrality analysis to just the relevant measures will help to avoid the problematic tendency to include irrelevant measures in an assessment. Table 6.1 provides an overview of a selection of centrality measures that are frequently associated with power in a network. Similarly, Table 6.2 provides as assortment of measures that reflects various notions of prestige. These tables are a good place to start the process of selecting measures that are relevant to the analyst's goals.[1] A more detailed description in the sections that follow should then be consulted for further clarification on how the measure functions and what it was designed to indicate. The progression from considering the question and environment at hand, to isolating the types or profiles of actors that are worth considering, to selecting appropriate measures will not only aid in narrowing the selection of measures to run, but it will also increase the validity of the analysis. The simple act of deliberately selecting measures that are meaningful to the topic will also aid in demystifying just what analysts are hoping to interpret, provided they have taken the time to familiarize themselves with the meaning of the measure and how it is calculated in advance of applying them.

6.2 CENTRALITY AND POWER

Frequency-based Measures

The way a particular centrality measure is calculated is the best indication of how it is meant to function and what it is intended to indicate. One of the simplest examples is degree centrality (Freeman 1979). Degree measures

Table 6.1 Summary of Selected Centrality Measures in the Context of Power (Undirected Networks)

Measure	*Short Explanation*	*Possible Interpretation(s) of Power*	*Caveat(s)*
Frequency-based Measures			
Degree Centrality (Freeman 1979)	Count of an actor's ties.	Actor activity; Direct influence or power, or ability to be influenced by others.	In some cases, well-connected actors are the result of biased collection. In others, it can be difficult to identify a single, or a few, potentially powerful actors using degree on well-connected networks (or subnetworks, such as cliques).
Eigenvector Centrality (Bonacich 1972a)	Weights an actor's centrality by the centrality scores of its neighbors.	Indirect influence or power; Potential social capital.	In well-connected networks (or subnetworks, such as cliques), it is often difficult to identify a single, or a few, potentially powerful actors.
Distance-based Measures			
Closeness Centrality (Freeman 1979)	The average geodesic distance from an actor to every other actor in the network.	Actor levels of accessibility to others, and to material and nonmaterial goods.	Not designed for use with disconnected networks. Pay close attention to program defaults and options for dealing with undefined distances. They can change how the results should be interpreted.
Average Reciprocal Distance (ARD) (Borgatti 2006)	Similar to closeness; however, the calculation of this metric allows it to be used with disconnected networks.	Actor levels of accessibility to others, and to material and nonmaterial goods.	Not available in several social network analysis programs.

Table 6.1 (cont. . .)

Reach Centrality (Sade 1989)	Counts the number of actors each actor can reach in *k* steps or less.	Actor levels of accessibility to others, and to material and nonmaterial goods.	Not available in several social network analysis programs.
Information Centrality (Stephenson and Zelen 1989)	Takes into account all paths between two actors and assigns them weights based on their lengths.	Actor levels of accessibility to others, and to material and nonmaterial goods.	Not available in several social network analysis programs.
Path-based Measures			
Betweenness Centrality (Freeman 1979)	How often each actor lies on the shortest path between all pairs of actors.	Brokerage potential; Gatekeepers; Boundary Spanners	Betweenness assumes a desire for efficiency. Actors, resources, and information may not always follow shortest path.
Flow Betweenness (Freeman, Borgatti, and White 1991)	Assumes that actors will use all pathways between them in proportion to the length of the pathways.	Brokerage potential (information flow, specifically)	Not available in every social network analysis program.
Proximal Betweenness Centrality (Borgatti 2006)	Estimates the proportion of all geodesics linking two actors that pass through a particular actor who is the second to last actor on the geodesic.	Brokerage potential	Not available in every social network analysis program.
Fragmentation Centrality (Borgatti 2006)	Estimates several "fragmentation" effects on a network if an actor is removed.	Brokerage potential (network fragmentation, specifically)	Not available in every social network analysis program.

Table 6.2 Summary of Selected Centrality Measures in the Context of Prestige (Directed Networks)

Measure	*Short Explanation*	*Possible Interpretation(s) of Prestige*	*Caveat(s)*
Indegree Centrality (Wasserman and Faust 1994)	Count of direct *incoming* ties.	Highly sought after (resources, wisdom)	Accounts only for direct incoming ties, but not indirect relations.
Outdegree Centrality (Wasserman and Faust 1994)	Count of direct *outgoing* ties.	Highly active; Distributor of material and/or nonmaterial goods	Accounts only for direct incoming ties, but not indirect relations.
Input Domain (Lin 1976)	Counts all people by whom someone is chosen whether directly or indirectly (can be restricted to actors within a certain number of steps).	Direct as well as indirect prestige.	Does not distinguish between "close" actors and actors "far away," which is a limitation in well-connected networks. Also, not available in several social network analysis programs.
Proximity Prestige (Wasserman and Faust 1994)	Accounts for all actors within an actor's input domain but weights closer neighbors higher than distant neighbors.	Direct as well as indirect prestige.	Not available in several social network analysis programs.
Reach Centrality (Sade 1989)	Counts the number of actors each actor can reach (or be reached) in k steps or less.	Direct as well as indirect prestige.	Very similar to input (and output) domain. Also, not available in several social network analysis programs.
Hubs and Authorities (Kleinberg 1999)	A good *hub* is an actor that points to many good *authorities*, and a good *authority* is one that is pointed to by many good *hubs*.	Major network connectors (hubs); Potential influence on network hubs (authorities).	Provides two scores (i.e., hub and authority scores). Also, this algorithm provides same scores as Eigenvector when run on undirected networks. Also considered as a frequency-based measure of power.

popularity, measured as the direct influence of an actor on others, or the number of others that directly influence a particular actor. It can be interpreted in several ways depending on the context of the analysis. Because social network analysts assume that actors are interdependent, and also that ties serve as channels for the flow of material and nonmaterials goods, actors that are embedded in a relatively greater number of relationships have the potential to influence or be influenced by the actors to whom they are connected. For example, if "actor A" communicates with 10 actors in an undirected, binary dark network, and "actor B" communicates with 5, then the former is arguably more active in the network, and has a greater potential to spread information or get information than "actor B" does. When working with binary (i.e., dichotomized) network data, the calculation is simply a count of an actor's ties (equation 6.1). Raw (i.e., nonnormalized) degree centrality is calculated as follows:

$$C_i^{DEG} = \sum_{j=1}^{n} x_{ij} \tag{6.1}$$

The calculation of degree is performed for each actor in the network. Equation 6.1, therefore, reads as the degree centrality for a given actor (i) being equal to the sum of all ties from i to other actors (x_{ij}), where the value of the tie is equal to one (i.e., a tie is present, or not equal to zero (0)). Because degree centrality depends on network size (n), degree centrality's maximum value is $n - 1$ (i.e., where an actor has a tie to every *other* actor in the network). However, interacting with a few actors in a small network may well indicate greater influence or power than interacting with many actors in a very large network. It is therefore generally advisable to normalize the measure to show the magnitude of the degree measure, relative to the size of the network in which it resides. Normalization makes it possible to compare the measure across different-sized networks. It is defined formally as

$$C_i^{NDEG} = \frac{\sum_{j=1}^{n} x_{ij}}{n-1} \tag{6.2}$$

where the numerator is an actor's raw degree score (equation 6.1) and the denominator is network size minus the actor. Comparing the two formulas, one can see that there is no difference between degree (equation 6.1) and normalized degree (equation 6.2), except that the value for degree will be a raw count of ties and the value for normalized degree will be the proportion relative to the total possible ties an actor could have in the network. This is the same basic procedure that the normalization of other centrality measures will take—the output is scaled, relative to potential values a particular measure could take.

If you are examining valued network data, then degree centrality may also take into account the sum of the values of an actor's ties. While researchers often prefer estimating degree centrality with binary data (i.e., they want the count of each actor's ties), it can be useful to examine valued data if, for example, the value of each tie is a measure of tie strength. In other words, if two actors, "A" and "B," both have five ties, but most or all of A's are strong ties, while most or all of B's are weak ties, A will have a higher degree centrality score—less power—than B. But, even when considering valued ties, the focus remains on direct ties and has the downside of missing the effect of having indirect ties. To measure the effect of indirect ties, an analyst should consider using eigenvector centrality.

Eigenvector centrality, like degree centrality, can be interpreted in several ways. One interpretation is the level of indirect power of an actor in a network. Take, for example, an undirected, operational network that includes of three relatively well-connected actors (i.e., degree centrality), namely, actors "A," "B," and "C." In this network, these three actors are all operationally connected to 20 other actors, meaning they have operated with 20 other actors within the network. However, say the alters of actors "A" and "B" each have operated with five other actors. The actors to whom actor "C" is connected have each collaborated with 15 other dark network actors. Which actor appears to have the most indirect, structural power in the network? The answer is "C" because the actors to whom he is connected are relatively more "powerful" (i.e., they each have 15 ties) than those of actors "A" and "B" (5 ties each).

Eigenvector centrality (Bonacich 1972, 1987) is a frequency-based measure (Borgatti and Everett 2006) because, like degree centrality, it takes into account the number of ties an actor has to others. It differs in that it assumes that ties to highly central actors are more important than are ties to peripheral ones, so it weights an actor's initial degree centrality by the degree centrality of its neighbors. Formally, if A is an adjacency matrix (i.e., a one-mode network), then we can allow for this effect by making actor i's centrality proportional to the average of the centralities of i's neighbors:

$$C_i^{EIG} = \frac{1}{\lambda}\sum_{j=1}^{n} A_{ij}x_j \tag{6.3}$$

where λ is a constant and i's associated eigenvalue; the largest eigenvalue is generally preferred (Bonacich 1987). Normalized eigenvector centrality is the scaled eigenvector centrality divided by the maximum difference possible, expressed as a percentage (Borgatti, Everett and Freeman 2002b):

$$C_i^{NEIG} = \frac{\frac{1}{\lambda}\sum_{j=1}^{n} A_{ij}x_j}{C_{Max}^{EIG}} \tag{6.4}$$

Kleinberg's (1999) "Hubs and Authorities" measure, which was developed to rank web pages, is based on the same assumption as eigenvector centrality and, in fact, produces identical scores with undirected networks. Google's Page Rank algorithm is also a variant of eigenvector centrality (Austin 2011; Brin and Page 1998). One advantage that it has over eigenvector centrality is that, like Hubs and Authorities, it can be applied to directed networks, which are often useful for measuring an actor's prestige within a network. The Hubbel and Katz (and Taylor) (Hubbell 1965; Katz 1953; Taylor 1969) influence measures are in many ways precursors to eigenvector centrality; quite early on, in fact, Bonacich noted the similarity of Hubbell's equation and the definition of an eigenvector (Bonacich 1972). Bonacich's power (or beta) centrality is similar to his eigenvector centrality, except that it introduces a parameter that allows researchers "to vary the degree and direction (positive or negative) of the dependence on each unit's score on the score of other units" (Bonacich 1987:1173). In other words, when the parameter is a negative value, an actor's score is higher when it is connected to actors with low power; and when the parameter is a positive value, an actor's score is higher when it is connected to actors with high power.

Distance-based Measures

The uniting feature of frequency-based measures is their focus on the importance of the frequency (count) with which an actor has ties to others in the network. They therefore assume that such "counts" represent a characteristic that is important for determining an actor's centrality or power. By contrast, distance-based measures begin with the assumption that relative differences in the length of the paths between actors constitute an important or defining factor in determining an actor's centrality and power. It is to an overview of distance-based measures that we now turn.

Underlying distance-based measures is the concept that actors who are relatively close to others in terms of path length possess a certain form of structural power within a network. One argument is that actors who are close to others have relatively greater access, not only to other actors in the network, but also to material and nonmaterial goods present within the network. For example, in a terrorist "communication" network, information has to travel only relatively short distances to reach actors with high values of distance-based measures such as closeness centrality. In other words, actors scoring highly in closeness centrality will have opportunities to access information from not only those the actors around them, but also many other actors who are considered outside of their neighborhood because, on average, they are relatively close to all other actors in the network. This could indicate, depending on the context, that actors with high values of distance-based measures like closeness hold the potential to be the critical actor on which misinformation campaigns can be implemented. This is not to say, however, that such actors are guaranteed access to information (or any other material or nonmaterial good), nor does it mean that they will necessarily spread it once they have access to information. So it is often prudent to access multiple actors with high values in this area.

The best-known distance-based measure is Freeman's (1979) closeness, which reflects the distance from each actor to every other actor in the network. Freeman's closeness—or, more appropriately, "farness"—measure is technically a distance or farness measure, rather than a closeness measure. It is simply the sum of all geodesic (i.e., shortest path) distances between each actor and all other actors in the network,

$$C_i^{FAR} = \sum_{j=1}^{n} d_{ij} \tag{6.5}$$

Because most analysts operationalize the concept of distance from the point of view of immediate proximity, and therefore greater influence, farness is much more frequently expressed in terms of "closeness," which is calculated as the inverse of the farness score (equation 6.6), where, in either of which,

$$\sum_{j=1}^{n} d_{ij}$$

represents the sum of all the geodesic distances between pairs of actors i and j.

$$C_i^{CLO} = \frac{1}{\sum_{j=1}^{n} d_{ij}} \tag{6.6}$$

$$C_i^{NCLO} = \frac{n-1}{\sum_{j=1}^{n} d_{ij}} \tag{6.7}$$

This closeness score is typically "normalized" so that a score of 1.00 indicates that an actor is one step away from every other actor in the network, while scores nearing 0.00 are approaching the maximum distance possible from every other actor in the network. Normalized closeness (equation 6.7) is the ratio of the number of other actors in a network (i.e., $n - 1$) over the sum of all geodesic distances between the actor and all other actors in the network. Placing the number of actors in the network in the numerator successfully normalizes the score because $n - 1$ provides the minimum farness score actors can obtain if they are one step away (i.e., they are adjacent) from every other actor in the network. Thus, an actor's closeness score will equal 1.00 if they are one step away from all other actors in the network; it will equal 0.50 if they are, on average, two steps away, and so on.

Freeman closeness technically cannot be calculated when a network is disconnected (i.e., multiple components) because the distance between two disconnected actors is undefined and potentially infinite. One way to use Freeman's measure with a disconnected network, then, is to first extract the network's largest weak component (also known as its "main" component), which is an approach discussed in the previous chapter. Another is to assign a default distance to instances where the distance is undefined. For example, UCINET allows users to set the distance to equal the number of actors in a network, the maximum distance plus one, missing, or zero.

Freeman's closeness measure is not the only distance-based measure available, however. One alternative measure that avoids the problems associated with disconnected networks is average reciprocal distance (ARD), which sums and averages the reciprocal distance between all actors. ARD is attractive because it can be used without special considerations for transforming disconnected networks or modifying the algorithm in the presence of undefined distances (Borgatti 2006):

$$C_i^{RD} = \sum_{j=1}^{n} \frac{1}{d_{ij}} \tag{6.8}$$

Note the similarity between this measure and Freeman's raw closeness score (equation 6.6). In both the cases, the geodesic distance between actors is included in the denominator. However, with Freeman's measure, the distances are summed first before being placed in the denominator, but since infinite distances cannot be summed (at least in ways that provide meaningful results), the calculation becomes impossible. With ARD, however, the reciprocal of the distances is calculated first and then summed, and since the reciprocal of infinity is conventionally set to zero, it may be included in the summation and thus allows it to be used with disconnected networks. ARD is also probably a better approach than using Freeman's measure to calculate the closeness centrality for actors included in the main component (and setting the scores of all others in the network to zero) because, with ARD, all network actors and those that are located in clusters (but just not the largest cluster/component) receive a score of greater than zero. ARD is normalized by taking the average of the sum of the reciprocal distances:

$$C_i^{ARD} = \frac{\sum_{j=1}^{n} \frac{1}{d_{ij}}}{n-1} \tag{6.9}$$

This is because ARD reaches its maximum value when an actor is adjacent to all other actors in the network (i.e., when it equals $n - 1$), which means that its normalized score will equal 1.00 when it is one step away from every other actor in the network. Currently, UCINET and R:statnet offer the only implementations of ARD, which means ORA, Pajek, and Gephi users (along with those using Palantir and Analyst's Notebook) should extract a network's main component and use Freeman's closeness measure.

Reach (or *k*-path) centrality (Sade 1989) is yet another distance-based measure, as it counts the number of actors each actor can reach in k steps or less. When $k = 1$, the resulting score is the same as degree centrality; when it equals $n - 1$ (i.e., the size of the network less 1, which is its maximum value), the resulting score (when it is normalized) equals ARD closeness centrality plus one. One other closeness measure is Stephenson and Zelen's (1989) information centrality, which attempts to estimate the information contained on all paths originating with each actor. It takes into account all paths between two actors (including but not limited to the geodesics) and assigns them weights based on their lengths.

Path-based Measures

Path-based measures can provide a different point of view about which actors in a dark network are "powerful." One interpretation of path-based measures is the concept of brokerage. Take, for example, a simple triad in which insurgent "B" sits on a direct path between two other insurgents, actors "A" and "C," who are not directly connected. Say "actor A," who is hypothetically a powerful financier and an experienced weapons dealer, has guns and money he wants to get to insurgent "C," who has a growing reputation of carrying out successful attacks against government forces. In order for "A" to get those materials to "actor C," the former is required to transfer those materials through "actor B." This scenario provides "actor B" with control, or brokerage potential, over the flow of those materials, which implicitly provides "B" with a structural advantage in this triad over insurgents "A" and "C." The challenge, and a reason why network analysts leverage path-based measures, is that identifying potential brokers in real-world networks is significantly more complicated than in this example. Chapter 7 will discuss several additional algorithms that more specifically identify actors playing different types of brokerage roles. This section, however, covers a more generalized *potential* for actors to involve themselves in brokerage, bottlenecks, stress, or power.

Betweenness centrality is perhaps the best-known path-based measure. It differs from frequency- and distance-based measures in that it assumes that an actor is in a position of potential power over any two other actors when it lies on the shortest path (i.e., geodesic) between them in a given network.

"Loosely described, the betweenness centrality of a node is the number of times that any actor needs a given actor to [most efficiently] reach any other actor" (Borgatti and Everett 2006:474). Formally, if we let g_{ij} indicate the number of geodesics from actor *i* to actor *j* and g_{ikj} indicate the number of geodesic paths from actor *i* to actor *j* that pass through actor *k*, then the betweenness centrality of an actor may be expressed as

$$C_i^{BET} = \sum_i \sum_j \frac{g_{ijk}}{g_{ij}} \quad (6.10)$$

Therefore, betweenness centrality measures actor *k*'s share of all shortest paths from actor *i* to actor *j*, summed across all choices of actors *i* and *j*:

$$C_i^{NBET} = \frac{\sum_i \sum_j \frac{g_{ijk}}{g_{ij}}}{\frac{(n-1)(n-2)}{2}} \quad (6.11)$$

Because an actor's betweenness centrality is a function of the number of pairs of actors in a network, we can normalize it by dividing through by the number of pairs of actors that do not include actor *k*, which equals $(n - 1)(n - 2)/2$ (Equation 6.9).

A weakness of betweenness centrality is that there is no guarantee that two actors will always follow the shortest path between them. They may choose another path, even if it is longer and less efficient. Flow betweenness centrality (Freeman, Borgatti and White 1991) takes this possibility into account and assumes that actors will use all pathways between them in proportion to the length of the pathways. It measures the proportion of the entire flow between two actors that occurs on paths of which a particular actor is a part. In other words, each actor's flow betweenness score captures the extent to which each actor is involved in all of the flows between all other pairs of actors in the network (Hanneman and Riddle 2011:366–67).

Proximal betweenness estimates the proportion of all geodesics linking two actors (e.g., "A" and "C") that pass through a particular actor (e.g., "B") who is the second to last actor (i.e., the penultimate actor) on the geodesic. In other words, on the geodesic that runs from actor A to C and passes through B, B would be considered the penultimate actor if the tie between B and C is the last edge of the geodesic. Proximal betweenness can therefore be thought of as a measure of the number of times an actor occurs in a penultimate position on a geodesic.

One last path-based centrality measure worth noting is fragmentation centrality, which calculates a series of scores for each actor in the network that indicates (1) what will be the network fragmentation; (2) what will be the distance-weighted network fragmentation; (3) what will be the change in network fragmentation; (4) what will be the change in distance-weighted network fragmentation; (5) what will be the percent change in fragmentation; and (6) what will be the percent change in distance-weighted fragmentation if they are removed from the network.

Summary

This section introduced readers, albeit in a somewhat technical manner, to a handful of centrality measures in the context of identifying potentially "powerful" actors within dark networks. It is also important, as we alluded to before, to understand potential interpretations of the results that these measures produce. The bad news for those new to network analysis is that no single interpretation exists for each measure; it will depend on the context, the type of data, etc. That said, a few possible and practical interpretations exist that can guide analysts in the right direction. Table 6.1, which was presented at the beginning of the chapter, summarizes some of the potential interpretations for the centrality measures that we have discussed so far along with a few other items that network analysts should consider.

Analysts should approach the concept of measuring power within dark networks somewhat critically. This statement, of course, is not a critique of the algorithms or the work of the prominent scholars who developed them. It simply means that each measure is only a potential, structural indicator of some element of power within a dark network. One reason of this, as alluded to in chapter 3, is that the results of these measures are largely dependent upon the data on which they are applied. For instance, a data set built around high-valued targets, meaning collection efforts focused on those individuals, will likely reinforce the notion that high-valued targets are structurally important (i.e., central in the one or more of the measures listed later). Moreover, network analysts can often gain additional insights into central actors when directed data are available, which is why social network analysts have developed a series of centrality measures, specifically to analyze directed networks. Among these measures are centrality metrics that provide insights into another important network concept: actor prestige.

6.3 CENTRALITY AND PRESTIGE

For social network analysts, the concept of prestige may be operationalized as either those to whom the most is given, or as those who give the most. Directed networks allow an analyst to view actors in the role of either givers or receivers of ties. In that light, indegree centrality, which is the count of incoming ties, provides a fair measure of prestige. For example, a member of a dark network to whom people go to for advice (e.g., a mentor) could be seen as enjoying higher levels of prestige than those who are sought only seldom for advice. Alternatively, if we were looking at the flow of money and other financial resources through a dark network, then outdegree might be a better measure of prestige. As we will see, there are several other measures of prestige. But indegree (and outdegree) centrality is typically the place where analysts start. Indegree centrality, as you may have guessed, is calculated in a similar fashion to degree centrality except it adjusts for directionality where X_{+i} is the sum of 1's in column i. Formally,

$$C_i^{INDEG} = \sum_{j=1}^{n} x_{ij} = x_{+i} \tag{6.12}$$

Normalized indegree is also calculated in the same manner as normalized degree centrality.

$$C_i^{NINDEG} = \frac{\sum_{j=1}^{n} x_{ij} = x_{+i}}{n-1} \tag{6.13}$$

In short, the numerator is an actor's raw indegree score and the denominator is the number of actors in the network minus the actor. Outdegree, on the other hand, is slightly different, in that X_{i+} indicates the sum of 1s in the row i (6.12). The equation for normalized outdegree centrality contains network size minus the actor in the denominator (6.13).

$$C_i^{OUTDEG} = \sum_{j=1}^{n} x_{ij} = x_{i+} \tag{6.14}$$

$$C_i^{NOUTDEG} = \frac{\sum_{j=1}^{n} x_{ij} = x_{i+}}{n-1} \tag{6.15}$$

As de Nooy, Mrvar, and Batagelj (2011) note, indegree centrality is a somewhat limited prestige measure because it only considers direct choices. Consequently, social scientists have developed alternative measures to estimate actor prestige, such as input domain and proximity prestige. Input domain is a measure of prestige that counts all people by whom someone is chosen, whether directly or indirectly. The larger a person's input domain, the higher his or her prestige. Equation 6.14 states that input domain is the sum of distances from actor j to actor i divided by the number of actors (I) who can reach actor i.

$$N_i^{INDOM} = \sum \frac{d(n_j, n_i)}{I_i} \tag{6.16}$$

Unfortunately, in a well-connected network, an actor's input domain contains all or almost all other actors, so it does a poor job of distinguishing between actors. One solution is to assume that choices by closer actors (in terms of path length) are more important than they are from distant actors and restrict the input domain to neighbors at a prespecified maximum distance chosen by the analyst. For example, Christakis and Fowler (2009) have argued that a person's influence ceases to have a noticeable effect on others beyond three degrees of separation,[2] so they might argue that the influence that each manager has in terms of the advice does not extend beyond a path length of three (i.e., an advisee of an advisee of an advisee). Thus, we could restrict the input domain to 3 steps or less.

The choice of a maximum distance from neighbors within a restricted input domain can sometimes appear arbitrary, however. Proximity prestige overcomes this by taking into account all actors within an actor's input domain but weighting choices by closer neighbors higher than those of distant neighbors. In other words, a choice by a close neighbor contributes more to an actor's proximity prestige than does a choice by a distant neighbor. This helps analysts avoid the problem we ran into earlier with unrestricted input domain (i.e., in a well-connected network, unrestricted input domain does a poor job of distinguishing between actors). At the same time, however, because proximity prestige takes into account the choices from distant actors, they are not entirely discounted as they might be with restricted input domain. Consequently, many distant choices may contribute as much as a single close one. To calculate proximity prestige, we divide the unrestricted (and normalized) input domain size by the average distance.

$$N_i^{PROXPRES} \frac{I_i / (g-1)}{\sum d(n_j, n_i) / I_i} \tag{6.17}$$

Reach centrality, which was discussed in the previous section, is similar to proximity prestige when applied to directed network data. It counts the number of actors each actor can reach (or be reached) in k steps or less. When k =1, the resulting score is the same as degree centrality, which means that if we are analyzing a directed network, the resulting scores will equal indegree and outdegree centrality. When $k = n$–1 (i.e., the size of the network less 1, which is its maximum value), its raw score equals the total number of actors that can be reached in n – 1 (i.e., k) steps; so, the resulting raw scores equal the total direct and indirect choices each actor receives (or sends if we are focusing on outdegree). This is similar to what Pajek refers to as an actor's input (or output) domain.

Finally, hubs and authority scores are potentially useful for measuring prestige. If you recall, the hubs and authorities algorithm was initially designed to rank web pages. A good *hub* was defined as one that points to many good *authorities*, and a good *authority* is one that is pointed to by many good *hubs* (Kleinberg 1999). Thus, in terms of prestige, it allows analysts to not only take into account the number of ties an actor receives (i.e., an authority) but also weigh those ties by whether the actor that is sending the tie (i.e., a hub) also sends ties to other prestigious actors in the network.

Summary

This section introduced readers to a handful of centrality measures in the context of identifying potentially "prestigious" actors within dark networks, which means they should think carefully about how they want to measure it structurally. For example, is the identification of actors to whom many others seek out central to the analysis? Or, does the analysis not only require us to consider the central actors, but also the structural prestige of their neighbors? The measures discussed in this section can provide unique insights into central actors because they are designed for directed data. It is possible for an actor to appear powerful if we ignore the direction of the relations making up the network, but it may turn out that the actor is not necessarily prestigious. For example, as we briefly discussed in chapter 3, an actor with 10 connections in a sparse operational network may appear powerful at first, but a closer look may highlight that the actor reports to all of the actors to whom he is connected and, therefore, unlikely a prestigious, operational expert.

This section, like the previous one, also provided a somewhat technical approach to understanding various centrality measures in the context of prestige. Table 6.2 offers a few possible and practical interpretations that can guide analysts with interpreting prestige in dark networks. Again, readers should approach the concept of prestige somewhat critically. The metrics that social network analysts use to identify prestigious actors are only indicators of potentially prestigious actors. For instance, one could argue that an actor is prestigious if they have a relatively high number of incoming ties in a "mentorship" network in which many other actors seek out that actor for advice and weapons training; however, an actor with a relatively high indegree centrality score in a "enemies" network in which many other actors want that actor dead would not necessarily possess high levels of prestige. In other words, the results of these measures largely depend upon the type of network on which they are applied.

6.4 THE APPLICATION OF CENTRALITY MEASURES TO UNDERSTAND DARK NETWORKS

The preceding sections provided a handful of useful centrality measures for undirected and directed networks. We now turn to the Noordin Top and the TFMC networks to illustrate how social network analysts can use some of these centrality measures to understand dark networks. We begin by examining centrality in the context of power on four of Noordin Top subnetworks (communication, trust, operational, and combined), all of which consisted of actors who were "Alive and Free" as of early 2010.[3] We follow this with a basic exploratory analysis of the TFMC's network to identify potentially prestigious network actors. This network consists of active members through 2011 and a series of directed relationships that arguably could indicate influence within the network, namely, communication, and superior–subordinate ties. In both the examples, we follow simple scenarios in which a strategic approach, a reconciliation and rehabilitation approach for the Noordin network, and PSYOP approach for the TFMC, presents a question we can explore about each dark network. These questions, in turn, help us select the appropriate centrality measure to apply to each network.

The rehabilitation and reintegration strategy seeks to reintegrate dark networks, or at least many of its members, back into civil society. As mentioned in chapter 2, it is unlikely that central actors in a dark network (i.e., those who are likely members of the network's core) will participate in such a campaign, which suggests we may want to focus on a network's peripheral actors. One potential question, then, is which individuals within the network's periphery could be approached about reconciling with the government and rejoining society? Figure 6.1 depicts the main component of the "Alive and Free" combined network (generated in NetDraw) consisting of communication, trust, and operational ties.[4]

One measure that we can use to examine this question, in conjunction with observing the network visually, is degree centrality because it allows us to identify actors with relatively few connections who are, or at least appear to be, less embedded within the network's core. Specifically, we will use normalized degree centrality because it allows us to compare networks of different sizes, which is the case here. For example, the trust network consists of 14 actors and the communication network consists of 20. Figure 6.2 shows the combined network (using NetDraw) with the actors sized by normalized degree centrality; however, because we are interested in identifying peripheral actors, or less connected ones, the actors of interest in this example are the relatively smaller ones.

Table 6.3 summarizes the results for the "top-ten" actors who possess the fewest number of ties and, therefore, have the lowest normalized degree

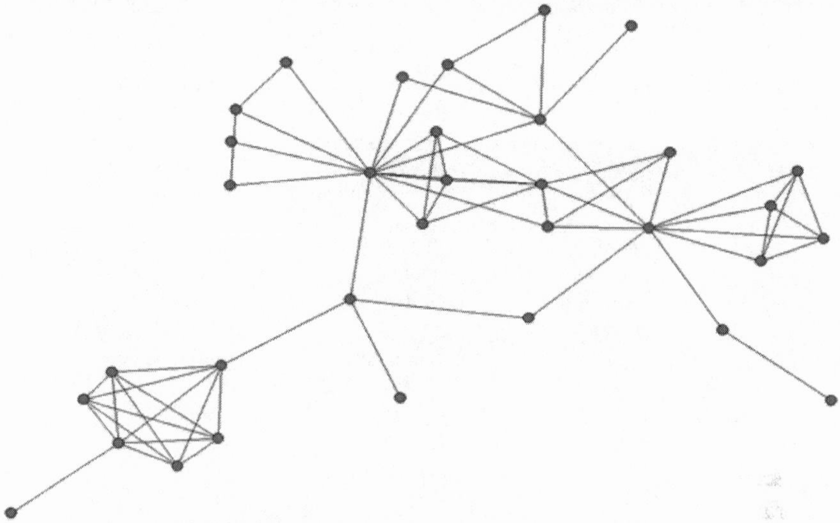

Figure 6.1 Main Component of Combined Network

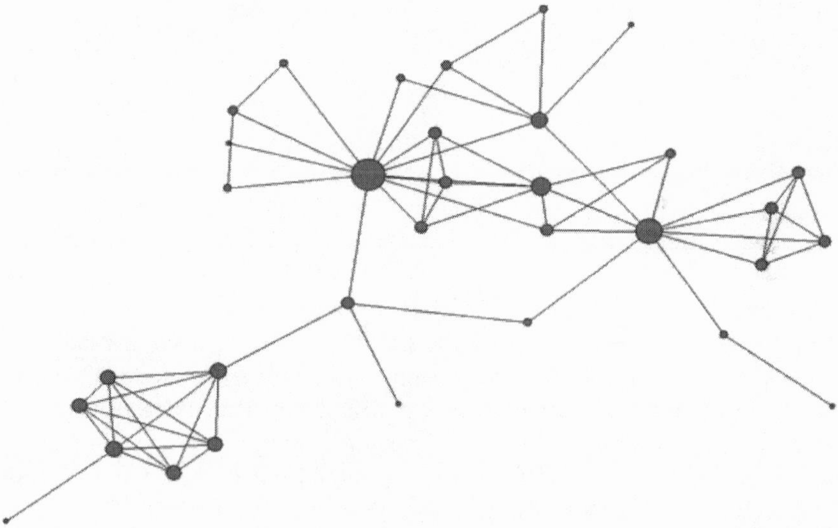

Figure 6.2 Noordin Combined Network with Actors Sized by Normalized Degree Centrality

centrality scores.[5] In some cases, more than 10 are listed because several had the same scores, in which case, they are listed in alphabetical order.[6] The results suggest that there are a handful of actors lying on the periphery of the various Noordin networks—in particular, Aceng Kurnia, Asep, Khumaidi, Muhamad Zainuri, and Muzayin Abdul Wahab—who might be candidates

Table 6.3 Noordin Combined Network Rankings for Normalized Degree Centrality

Communication	*Trust*	*Operational*	*Combined*
Abdul Malik (5.26)	Abu Fida (7.69)	Ustadz Hasbi (6.25)	Aceng Kurnia (3.13)
Aceng Kurnia (5.26)	Aceng Kurnia (7.69)	Mus'ab Sahidi (12.5)	Asep (3.13)
Hilman (5.26)	Chandra (7.69)	Ustadz Zaenal (12.5)	Khumaidi (3.13)
Khumaidi (5.26)	Hilman (7.69)	Chandra (18.75)	Muhamad Zainuri (3.13)
Marwan (5.26)	Khumaidi (7.69)	Said Sungkar (18.75)	Muzayin Abdul Wahab (3.13)
Mus'ab Sahidi (5.26)	Qotadah (7.69)	Abu Fida (25.00)	Abdul Malik (6.25)
Ustadz Zaenal (5.26)	Umar Burhanuddin (7.69)	Abu Roiroh (25.00)	Marwan (6.25)
Abu Fida (10.53)	Abdul Malik (15.38)	Ade Bahru (25.00)	Mus'ab Sahidi (6.25)
Chandra (10.53)	Ismail2 (23.08)	Ahmad Rofiq Ridho (25.00)	Qotadah (6.25)
Qotadah (10.53)	Jauhari (23.08)	Deny Nugraha (25.00)	Ustadz Hasbi (6.25)
Ustadz Hasbi (10.53)	Ustadz Anton (23.08)	Dirman (25.00)	Ustadz Zaenal (6.25)
		Ismail2 (25.00)	
		Jauhari (25.00)	
		Ustadz Anton (25.00)	

for reconciliation and/or rehabilitation. The next step in the process would be to gain a contextual understanding of these actors, such as their potential willingness to reconcile with the government. These same individuals could, of course, be targeted in conjunction with one of the other strategies discussed in chapter 2, such as a PSYOPs or misinformation campaign. Ultimately, whatever strategies we recommend, they should reflect the environment in which they will be implemented.

Figure 6.3 depicts the main component of TFMC network, specifically the "influence" network, which consists of communication and superior–subordinate ties, some of which are reciprocal. Looking at this, a question that analysts might ask is, "Which individuals within the network have the greatest structural potential to pass misinformation to other members of the network?" One could argue that outdegree centrality is an ideal measure for identifying such actors because it allows us to capture the flow of information from central actors to many other actors. Specifically, it allows us to assess

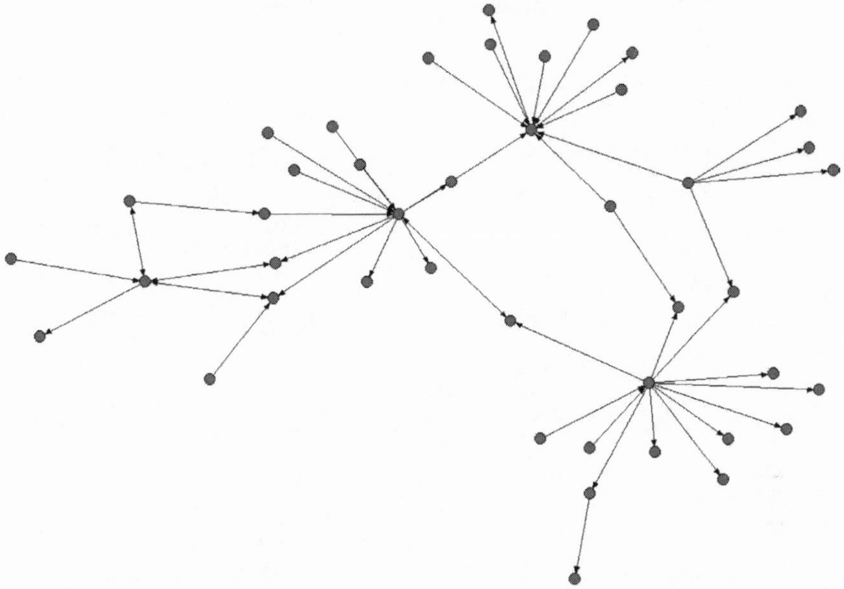

Figure 6.3 TFMC "Influence" Network

which actors report to and communicate with many other actors. Figure 6.4 reproduces the network pictured in Figure 6.3, except that the actors vary in size in terms of normalized outdegree centrality.

Table 6.4 summarizes the normalized outdegree centrality scores for the top-ten actors in the TFMC's "influence" network.[7] Although we have anonymized the network, we have included two additional columns in order to provide additional information about the actors and the actors with whom they communicate or report to.[8] The results suggest that there are a handful of candidates who might be "receptive" to a PSYOP campaign.[9] Instructively, we probably would not have identified all of the actors included in the table as potentially influential if we had relied solely on their attributes. Several of the top-ten actors are "low-ranking" actors, such as actors 2 and 18, who are a sub-leader and militia member, respectively. What this highlights is how centrality analysis can help identify important actors who might otherwise go unnoticed be of their role (or other attribute) in a network.

What these two examples illustrate is the importance of beginning with a strategy and then choosing the appropriate centrality metrics(s) given the network being analyzed and the environment in which it is embedded. Still, network analysts may want to consider a series of centrality measures for exploring their network of interest because the questions and topics they explore are often fairly broad. For instance, an analyst supporting PSYOPs

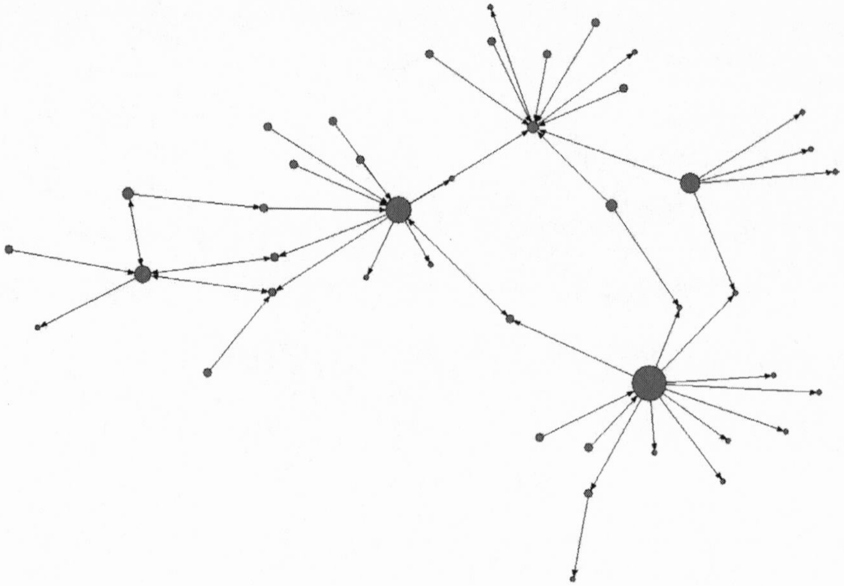

Figure 6.4 TFMC "Influence" Network with Actors Sized by Normalized Outdegree Centrality

Table 6.4 TFMC Influence Network Rankings for Normalized Outdegree Centrality

Actor	*Formal Role/Titles(s)*	*Role(s) of Neighbors*
Actor 2 (23.81)	Sub-Leader; Recruiter	Guerrilla; High-Level Leader; Militia Member
Actor 18 (16.67)	Militia Member	Guerrilla; Militia Member; Sub-Leader
Actor 6 (11.9)	High-Level Leader	High-Level Leader; Militia Member; Sub-Leader
Actor 42 (9.52)	Guerrilla	Militia Member; Sub-Leader
Actor 12 (4.76)	Sub-Leader; Recruiter	High-Level Leader
Actor 14 (4.76)	High-Level Leader	Column Medic; High-Level Leader; Radio Operator
Actor 43 (4.76)	Militia Member	Militia Member; Guerrilla
18 Tied (2.38)		

might be tasked to identify a dark network's "influential actors," but does influence mean brokerage potential (betweenness)? Does it stem from having numerous ties (degree)? Some actors might score high in terms of the former but not in terms of the latter (or vice versa). Take, for example,

Table 6.5 Noordin Combined Network: Comparison of Normalized Degree and Betweenness Centrality Scores

Normalized Degree	*Normalized Betweenness*
Usman bin Sef (40.63)	Usman bin Sef (48.32)
Umar Burhanuddin (31.25)	Akram (41.63)
Son Hadi (21.88)	Umar Burhanuddin (36.66)
Ahmad Rofiq Ridho (18.75)	Hilman (31.45)
Aris Munandar (18.75)	Ahmad Rofiq Ridho (15.86)
Hilman (18.75)	Abdul Malik (13.31)
Ali (15.63)	Son Hadi (9.04)
Muchtar (15.63)	Aris Munandar (6.25)
Umar2 (15.63)	Marwan (6.25)
Zulkarnaen (15.63)	Abu Fida (3.6)

Table 6.5, which presents the top-ten ranked actors of the Noordin Combined Network in terms of normalized degree and betweenness centrality. One can see that while some actors, such as Usman bin Sef and Umar Burhanuddin, score relatively high in both measures, other actors, such as Ali, Muchtar, and Zulkarnaen, do not. Thus, we have to ask ourselves, “What constitutes an influential actor in this network?” The answer is not always obvious.

6.5 SUMMARY: LESSONS LEARNED

In this chapter we have explored perhaps the most intuitive and one of the oldest of social network analysis metrics. We have seen that a central actor can be seen as someone who has numerous ties to other actors (e.g., degree centrality), who has numerous ties to highly central actors (e.g., eigenvector centrality, hubs and authorities), who is close to other actors (e.g., closeness centrality), or who lies on the shortest path between other pairs of actors (e.g., betweenness centrality). In addition, we briefly explored a handful of measures that we can use with directed networks in order to identify prestigious actors.

Put simply, network analysts have a wide range of centrality measures at their disposal, but we need to be circumspect in our use of them, taking time to consider which characteristic of power (or prestige) we are trying to measure. An understanding of the specific context in which the dark network operates is a crucial part of this process. Moreover, we should not consider them in isolation of other measures. Instead, we need to incorporate them into a larger analytic package that includes insights from the topographical analysis of the network, the identification of cohesive subgroups within the network, and the environmental context in which the network operates. Both the Noordin and the TFMC examples above leveraged basic component analysis prior to identifying central actors. Finally, as we emphasize throughout this book, strategy should drive our choice of metrics, not the other way around. Unfortunately, the default option is often to identify central actors without taking into account strategic considerations. Not only can this lead to the inappropriate use of centrality measures, but it can also limit our ability to ask the types of questions that need to be asked about how to undermine the dark networks we are examining. For example, analysts often fail to recognize that the arrest of a central actor may have little or no effect on the performance of a decentralized dark network. The bottom line? Centrality is a useful concept that can lead to insights of dark networks, but network analysts must consider how their strategies will affect the larger network before relying on centrality alone.

6.6 QUESTIONS

1. Which of the following measures the extent to which actors lie on the shortest path between other actors?
   a. Degree centrality.
   b. Hubs and Authorities.
   c. Closeness centrality.
   d. Betweenness centrality.
   e. Proximity Prestige.
2. Which of the following measures is considered a measure of power?
   a. Hubs and Authorities.
   b. Indegree centrality.
   c. Closeness centrality.
   d. Proximity Prestige.
   e. Input Domain.
3. Which of the following measures is considered a measure of prestige?
   a. Degree centrality
   b. Betweenness centrality

c. Closeness centrality
d. Hubs and Authorities
e. Eigenvector centrality

4. In the following network (see figure below), what is the degree centrality of actor 1?

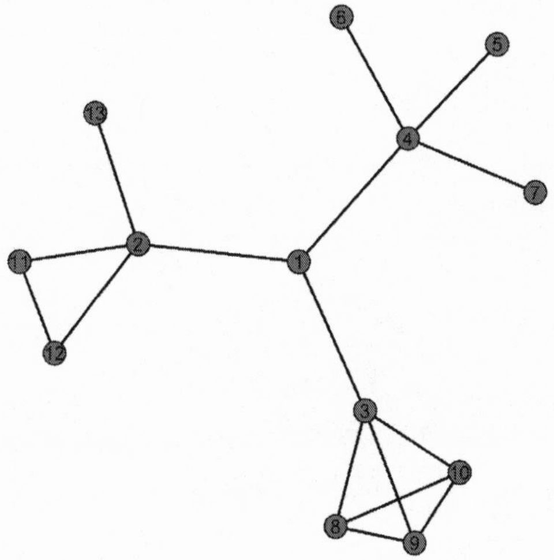

a. One.
b. Two.
c. Three.
d. Four.
e. Five.

5. What about actor 3 (see figure above)?

a. One.
b. Two.
c. Three.
d. Four.
e. Five.

6. Which actor do you think scores highest in terms of betweenness centrality in the figure above?

a. One.
b. Two.
c. Three.
d. Four.
e. Five.

7. Social network analysts should state central actors are “potentially” important in some aspect as opposed to claiming that those actors are, in fact, important.
   a. True.
   b. False.
8. Which of the following are “distanced-based” centrality measures?
   a. Closeness Centrality.
   b. Average Reciprocal Distance.
   c. Reach Centrality.
   d. Degree Centrality.
9. Which of the following are “frequency-based” centrality measures?
   a. Closeness Centrality.
   b. Betweenness Centrality.
   c. Degree Centrality.
   d. Eigenvector Centrality.

6.7 ANSWERS

1. Betweenness centrality (d).
2. Closeness centrality (c).
3. Hubs and Authorities (d).
4. Three (c).
5. Four (d).
6. One (a)—see the same graph from above, below, except that the size of the actors varies in terms of betweenness centrality.

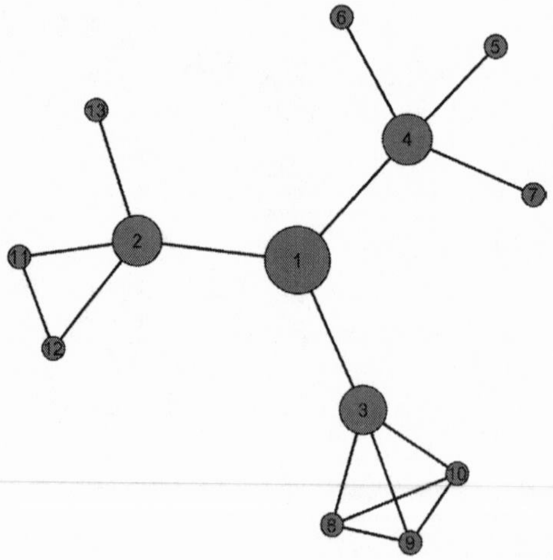

7. True.
8. Closeness Centrality (a); Average Reciprocal Distance (b); Reach Centrality (c).
9. Degree Centrality (c); Eigenvector Centrality (d).

6.8 FURTHER READING

The literature on centrality is voluminous, which can make it somewhat daunting. It is probably best to begin with an overview of the topic before moving on to the more specialized articles and chapters. Thus, we recommend beginning with Wasserman and Faust's (*Social Network Analysis: Methods and Applications*. Cambridge, UK: Cambridge University Press, 1994) chapter on centrality and prestige (Chapter 5) and then at least one of the following: Chapter 10 in Borgatti, Everett, and Johnson's *Analyzing Social Networks* (Thousand Oaks, CA: SAGE Publishing, 2013), Chapter 4 in Christina Prell's *Social Network Analysis: History, Theory & Methodology* (London and Thousand Oaks, CA: SAGE Publications, 2011), and Chapter 2 in McCulloh, Armstrong, and Johnson's *Social Network Analysis with Applications* (New York, NY: Wiley, 2013). Then, if you have not had enough, you may want to consider the following:

- Stephen P Borgatti. 2005. "Centrality and Network Flow." *Social Networks* 27:55–71.
- Stephen P Borgatti and Martin G. Everett. 2006. "A Graph-Theoretic Perspective on Centrality." *Social Networks* 28:466–84.
- Phillip Bonacich. 1987. "Power and Centrality: A Family of Measures." *American Journal of Sociology* 92:1170–82.
- Martin G. Everett and Stephen P. Borgatti. 2005. "Extending Centrality." Pp. 57–76 in *Models and Methods in Social Network Analysis*, edited by Peter J. Carrington, John Scott, and Stanley Wasserman. New York: Cambridge University Press.
- Linton C. Freeman. 1979. "Centrality in Social Networks I: Conceptual Clarification." *Social Networks* 1:215–39.
- Jon Kleinberg. 1999. "Authoritative Sources in a Hyperlinked Environment." *Journal of the ACM* 46:604–32.

NOTES

1. These tables are not intended to serve as an exhaustive list of potential interpretations for each measure. In terms of the "Caveats (s)" column, the issue of "collection

bias" aforementioned applies to every measure listed below even though it is only emphasized for degree centrality. Moreover, the "Caveat (s)" column does not provide an exhaustive list of potential limitations in terms of interpreting each metric. Rather, it is meant to highlight one or two that are particularly relevant for each measure.

2. Christakis and Fowler's method for estimating this effect has been persuasively challenged on mathematical and statistical grounds (Cohen-Cole and Fletcher 2008; Lyons 2011).

3. All three of these networks are binary and undirected.

4. We limit our visualizations to the "Combined" network for demonstration purposes.

5. We applied normalized degree centrality to main component of each of the four networks (i.e., without isolates and other smaller components) for illustrative purposes. One could make the case that strategies should only be applied to main components of disconnected networks because they are more likely to have a greater impact on the overall network than if applied to smaller, isolated components. That said, we recognize that this specific strategy, a reconciliation and rehabilitation campaign, could be also effective on those not tied into the core part of the network.

6. It is extremely important to observe the metric results when analyzing central actors. Too often, network analysts pick an arbitrary set of ranked actors, such as the "top-10," for a particular centrality measure and fail to compare each actor's scores. Analysts should consider the following questions, how much more central are the top-2 actors versus the next 7? Do any of those top-10 actors have the same score? Do actors falling outside of the top-10 have similar scores to the top-ranked actors?

7. It is possible that a different centrality measure might be better for the same question in a different context.

8. Note that some actors report to or communicate with several actors who possess a specific role/title. For example, actor 2 communicates with multiple militia members.

9. It is worth pointing out that the highest-ranked actors are substantially more central than are the others. For instance, actor 2's normalized outdegree score (23.81) is more than twice as much as the third and fourth ranked actors, actors 6 (11.90) and 42 (9.52).

Chapter 7

Brokerage within Networks

The previous chapter introduced betweenness centrality as an indication of an actor's potential to affect the flow of comparatively more resources than others in the network. Generally speaking, this is the concept of brokerage. Brokers hold the potential to control, restrict, modify, or otherwise intercede in or affect the transfer of goods or information through at least a portion of the network. This chapter explores the notion of brokerage in more depth in order to highlight what the concept may offer for the analysis of dark networks. We begin with a brief discussion of how the topic of brokerage may be approached when analyzing dark networks. In so doing, we include summary tables to aid in the navigation through some of the various measures available to the analyst.

A deeper discussion of the various means that are available for understanding, analyzing, and isolating brokerage in a network can be broken into five general topics: cutpoints, key players, bridges, structural holes, and affiliations. We consider each in turn. The concept of cutpoints—actors whose removal will fragment the network—is presented first (section 7.2); not as a means for attacking a network, but instead as an indication of the brokerage potential that such positions imply (Wasserman and Faust 1994:112–15). However, while this approach is intuitively appealing, it is often difficult to find actors whose removal disconnects a well-connected network. On the other hand, *sets of actors* (cutsets) with the same characteristic of disconnecting or substantially fragmenting a network on their removal can be much more common (Borgatti 2006). Applying what is known as the key player approach identifies such cut sets, and we will examine the approach in section 7.3. Somewhat similar to the cutpoint and cutset idea is that of measuring the degree to which a tie functions as a bridge within the network (Freeman 2011; Girvan and Newman 2002). A discussion of how bridges may be conceptualized and applied in dark networks is presented in section 7.4.

Next, in section 7.5, we turn to the related concepts represented by Ron Burt's (1992a, 1992b) notion of structural holes, which builds upon Mark Granovetter's (1973, 1974, 1983) work on weak ties. Burt argues that actors who sit astride structural holes—gaps in the structure of the network—are in a better position for brokerage. All of the approaches mentioned above contain the implicit assumption that identifying brokers and the ties that bind them is largely determined by the cohesive subgroups of which they are (and are not) a part. Section 7.6 introduces an algorithm that explicitly brings these two aspects together. The Gould–Fernandez algorithm assumes that brokerage is a function of the different groups with which actors are affiliated; thus, not only does it require network data, but it also requires attribute data indicating the specific groups to which people belong. Although Girvan–Newman is not covered in depth in this chapter, it is covered more thoroughly in chapter 5, in the discussion of methods for identifying subgroups. This chapter concludes with examples of how we can apply the concept of brokerage in the context of a dark network.

7.1 ANALYZING BROKERAGE IN DARK NETWORKS

Network analysts have a range of measures from which they can choose to identify potential brokers within dark networks. Analysts should take time to consider which characteristic of brokerage they are truly trying to identify in network actors. An understanding of the specific context in which the dark network operates is a crucial part of this process. Moreover, as we emphasize throughout this book, a network analyst's strategic approach, along with their specific question, should drive which metrics they should use. The choice of a brokerage measure is no exception. For instance, an analyst focused on a misinformation campaign should explore one of Borgatti's reach indices as opposed to his key player measures focused on fragmentation. Regardless of which measure they choose to apply, network analysts should be able to defend why they chose to apply that particular brokerage measure (or set of measures) on dark network data, as well as what it contributes to the analysis.

Similar to centrality measures, analysts conducting exploratory analysis should consider incorporating brokerage into larger analyses that include measures from other metric categories, such as network topography and cohesive subgroups. For instance, many network analysts will simultaneously conduct community detection and brokerage analysis to identify potential brokers between clusters. If they so choose, network analysts can use partitions created from community detection algorithms, or some other types of clustering algorithms, to represent actor affiliations when using Gould and Fernandez's approach. Like with centrality, however, many network analysts often default to identifying potential brokers without considering other network characteristics. This tendency is partly due to the intuitiveness of identifying "important" individuals (e.g., brokers and central actors) who are involved, or are suspected to be involved, in nefarious activities. However, analysts should remember that brokers are embedded within larger networks consisting of interdependent actors, so they should strongly resist the urge to focus solely on these potentially important individuals and consider the larger picture (especially during an exploratory phase) of how such actors fit within a dark network of interest.

At the point that analysts are ready to consider brokerage in a network, the context and goals for the analyst should already be clear. Those aspects will therefore constitute a filter that will help analysts select one or more brokerage measures or indicators that are appropriate to their work. Table 7.1 provides an overview of the methods covered in this chapter. This list is by no means exhaustive. It is possible to use other approaches—such as community detection, as mentioned above—to aid in identifying potential brokers in a network. Provided they have achieved command of the concept, an analyst is limited only by their inventiveness and their knowledge of the programs they are using.

7.2 CUTPOINTS, BI-COMPONENTS, AND BRIDGES

In some cases, it may be possible to identify actors that are critical to the integrity of the network. Such actors occupy a starkly apparent position of brokerage due to their potential as a facilitator or choke point for the flow of anything through the network. Although the implication is fairly clear, however, the terminology for identifying such actors tends to be somewhat disparate. These actors may be alternately referred to as cutpoints (UCINET, NetDraw, sna), cut-vertices (Pajek), articulation points (UCINET and Pajek), or boundary spanners (ORA). A simple example is presented in Figure 7.1, which presents the Koschade Bali I network that we have explored in previous chapters. Samudra (colored white) is a cutpoint because his removal would disconnect the network into two separate components. Most dark networks, however, are not this straightforward and often contain several cutpoints.

Closely related to the notion of cutpoints is the concept of bi-components. Bi-components are essentially the converse of cut points, in that they refer to those parts of a network that are invulnerable to the removal or isolation of a single actor. A bi-component constitutes a set of actors that has no cutpoint because every pair of actors in the set has two or more independent paths between them. Thus, in a bi-component no actor completely controls the flow of resources between two other actors because there is always an alternative path through which resources can flow, even if the removal of an actor interrupted a path. This built-in redundancy explains why bi-components tend to

Table 7.1 Summary of Selected Brokerage Metrics

Measure	*Short Explanation*	*Possible Interpretation(s)*	*Caveat(s)*
Cutpoints (cut-vertices, articulation points, and boundary spanners) (Wasserman and Faust 1994)	Actors whose removal disconnects a network. An actor is either a cutpoint or not.	Actors with the potential to control the flow of information and/or resources at some scale (i.e., between two actors, and between clusters).	It is uncommon for networks to contain a single actor whose removal disconnects the network. Also, not all cutpoints are equal in terms of the effect of their removal, and cutpoint analysis does not indicate which actor's removal would be the most disruptive. In fact, the removal of some cutpoints (particularly those on the periphery) may have little or no effect on a dark network's performance.
Key Players—Fragmentation (Borgatti 2006)	Fragmentation score is calculated prior to and after the removal of each of each cutset. The set whose removal most increases network fragmentation is considered optimal.	An optimal set of actors that, when removed, either completely disconnects a network or fragments it to an extent that the flow of information and/or resources across the network is impeded. Implicit in this explanation is that actors within a critical set have relatively high brokerage potential.	A set of key players that fragment a dark network may not be the optimal set for diffusing information. Not all software packages include this measure, and some of those that have produced inconsistent results.
Key Players—Distance-weighted Fragmentation (Borgatti 2006)	Similar to the "Fragmentation" measure except, average distance is used in place of fragmentation. The optimal actor set is defined as those whose removal most lengthens the average distance (in terms of path length) between all pairs of actors in the network.	An optimal set of actors that, when removed, not only fragments a network, but also creates greater distances (on average) for nonmaterial and material goods to travel. Implicit in this explanation is that actors within a critical set have relatively high brokerage potential.	A set of key players that fragment a network may not be the optimal set for diffusing information. Not all software packages include the key player algorithms.

Table 7.1 (cont. . .)

Key Players—Percent Actors Reached (Borgatti 2006)	The proportion of distinct actors that can be reached by the set of key actors.	An optimal set of actors to diffuse information and/or resources within a network. Implicit in this explanation is that actors within a critical set have relatively high brokerage potential.	A set of key players to diffuse information may not be the optimal set for fragmenting the network. Not all software packages include the key player algorithms.
Key Players—Reach Index (Borgatti 2006)	Weights the "Percent Actors Reached" by the path distance between the set of key actors and all other actors in the network.	An optimal set of actors to diffuse information and/or resources within a network. Implicit in this explanation is that actors within a critical set have relatively high brokerage potential.	A set of key players to diffuse information may not be the optimal set for fragmenting the network. Not all software packages include the key player algorithms.
Edge Betweenness Centrality (Freeman 2011; Girvan and Newman 2002)	A high value of edge betweenness indicates that an edge resides within many geodesics between pairs of actors.	Edges with high edge betweenness centrality are bridge-like ties, implying the opportunity for brokerage.	Not available in some social network analysis programs.
Constraint (i.e., structural holes) (Burt 1992a, 1992b)	Each actor's constraint is based on the types of triads in which they are involved, weights this by the number of ties in which an actor is involved, and then sums the resulting calculations.	Maintaining ties is expensive. Actors with low constraint have a competitive advantage in terms of brokerage potential over actors with relatively higher constraint.	In terms of visualizing Burt constraint, smaller actors indicate relatively higher brokerage potential, which is contrary to most other measures. In other words, smaller is better unless one calculates and visualizes its additive inverse.
Brokerage Roles (Gould and Fernandez 1989, 1994)	This measure identifies five types of brokerage based on the triads in which each actor is involved along with their affiliations, and those of their neighbors.	Identifies Coordinators, Gatekeepers, Representatives, Itinerant Brokers/ Consultants, and Liaisons.	Intended for directed data, so there is no distinction between Gatekeepers and Representatives when applied to undirected network data. Not available in many social network analysis programs.

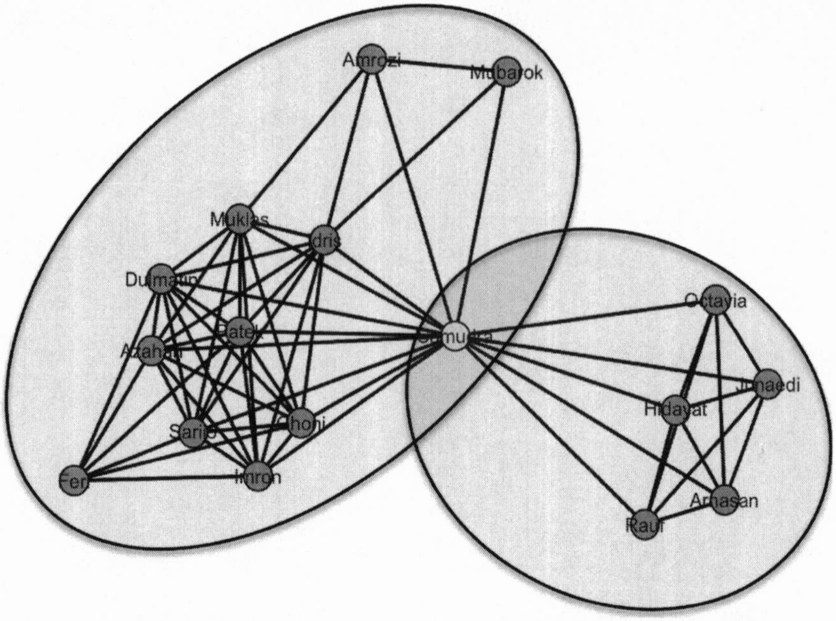

Figure 7.1 Bi-components and Cutpoints (white actor), Koschade Bali I Network

be more cohesive than strong or weak components. In the Koschade Bali I network, there are two bi-components, both of which are circled in Figure 7.1. You may be wondering how Samudra can belong to both bi-components if, by definition, bi-components are not supposed to include a cutpoint? The answer is that a bi-component does not include a cutpoint if you only look at the bi-component itself and ignore the rest of the network. For instance, if you only look at the bi-component on the right, Samudra's removal will not disconnect it. All of the actors within the bi-component still will be able to reach one another. The same is true with the bi-component on the left. What makes Samudra unique, at least in this network, is that he belongs to more than one bi-component. In fact, that is another way to locate cutpoints. They are actors that belong to two or more bi-components.

Generally, the definition of a bi-component is limited to a group of *minimum size three* that are without a cutpoint. However, bi-components of size two can be of special interest because they represent ties in the network that, if removed or dissolved, will disconnect the network. Put differently, a bi-component of size two is a *bridge* in a network. No bridges exist in the Koschade network, but we can illustrate this concept with the Noordin Trust Network, presented in Figure 7.2 (created in Gephi). There are actually 27 bi-components of size two or greater in the Noordin Trust Network, so we have only circled those of a size two that are neither isolated edges nor pendants.

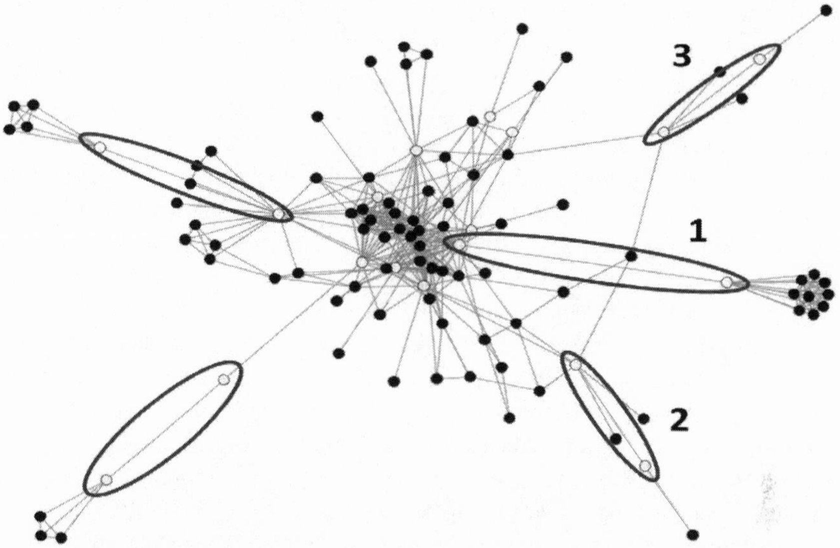

Figure 7.2 Bridges and Cutpoints, Noordin Top Trust Network (isolates hidden)

As you can see, in each case, the severing of these ties would disconnect the network, more in some cases than in others. For example, the dissolution of the tie/bridge on the middle-right side of the network (#1) would disconnect ten actors from the network, whereas with the dissolution of either of the other two ties/bridges on the right of the graph (#2 and #3) would (in each case) only disconnect two actors. Information such as this can prove strategically useful because it is sometimes easier to sever—or functionally sever—a tie in a dark network (e.g., feeding misinformation into a network so that two people stop trusting one another) than it is to remove an actor. These ties are also important for the implication of the brokerage or filtering that they represent. All information that flows from the network core to the cluster at the end of bridge one (#1) is essentially filtered, embellished, or otherwise colored by the bridge along which it traveled. That makes the resulting product of such an exchange somewhat more predictable, provided enough is known about the actors that constitute the endpoints of the bridge.

7.3 KEY PLAYERS (CUTSETS, CRITICAL SETS)

Although intuitively appealing, the identification of cutpoints is often impracticable. It is predicated on the assumption that there exists a single actor whose removal disconnects the network. In actual practice, however, many of the networks that an analyst will encounter will be well connected. Analysts have, therefore, developed alternative measures that generalize the cutpoint approach, which identify an optimal set of actors that, when removed, either completely disconnects the network, or maximally fragments it to the extent that the flow of resources (e.g., communication) across the network is increased or impeded. This, however, is not simply a matter of removing a set of the most central actors in a network. This is largely because highly central actors often reach or connect the same actors and groups, making their ties highly redundant.

Borgatti (2006) has developed algorithms that are specifically designed for identifying an optimal *set of actors* whose removal either *disconnects or significantly fragments* a network.[1] The cutset algorithms employ two variations on the measure of network disaggregation: fragmentation and distance-weighted fragmentation. The standard measure of fragmentation gauges the amount to which various sets of actors fragment the network when they are removed (discussed in chapters 4 and 6). The set whose removal results in the greatest increase in the level of fragmentation is considered optimal. The alternative measure, distance-weighted fragmentation, identifies the optimal set of actors whose removal most lengthens the average distance (in terms of path length) between all pairs of actors in the network.

Figure 7.3 presents the results of a key player analysis of the Noordin Top Trust Network. It plots the increase in fragmentation (both regular and distance-weighted) by the number of key players removed from the network. As you can see, the level of fragmentation continues to increase as additional people are removed from the network although the increase in the distance-weighted fragmentation is far more muted than the increase in the standard measure of fragmentation. How is one to know what the size of the cutset should be? That decision is a function of available resources, the likelihood that the key players can be removed the network, and the desired level of network fragmentation. Complete network fragmentation is probably neither desirable nor attainable. As we can see from the graph below, the removal of a cutset of size 10 increases the level of fragmentation by over 40 percent. That may be more than enough.

For those occasions when fragmentation is not the goal, Borgatti has developed a similar algorithm to locate sets of actors "that are optimally positioned to quickly diffuse information, attitudes, behaviors or goods and/or quickly receive the same" (Borgatti 2006:22). These are the actors who could potentially reach the greatest number of other actors in the network. As with fragmentation, two variations of the reach algorithm have been developed: the percent of actors reached and the reach index. The percent of actors reached measures the proportion of distinct actors that a set of actors can reach, whereas the reach index weights this proportion by the path distance between the set of key actors and all other actors in the network.[2] Figure 7.4 plots the reach (both regular and distance-weighted) by the number of key

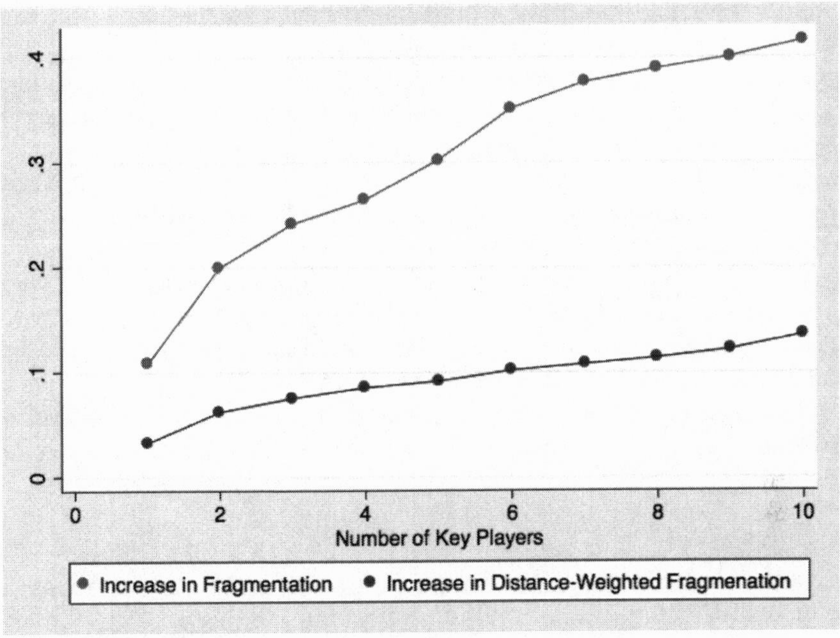

Figure 7.3 Key Player Analysis (Fragmentation)

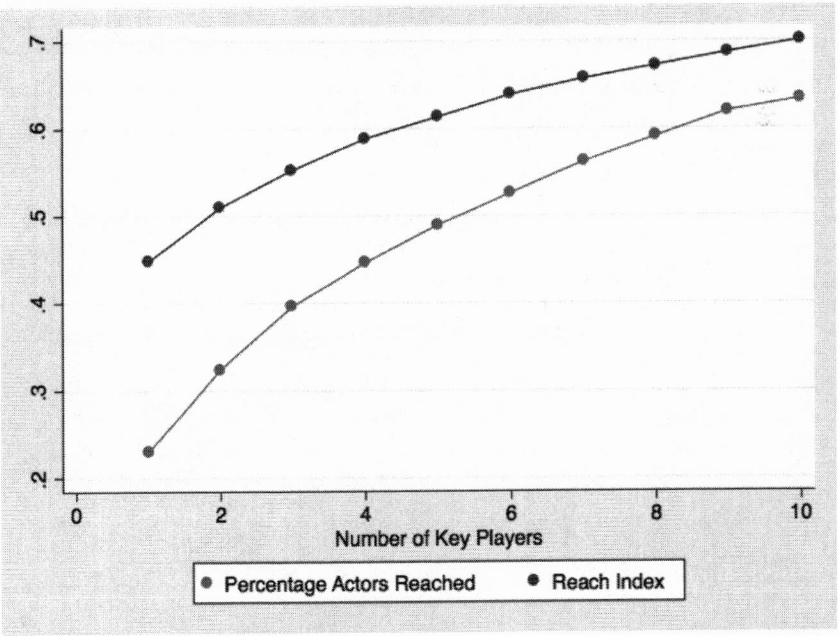

Figure 7.4 Key Player Analysis (Reach/Diffusion)

players targeted for the diffusion of (mis)information and the like. As you can see, the level of reach continues to increase as additional people are targeted. But unlike the two fragmentation algorithms, these are quite similar to one another. Like the fragmentation algorithms, the ideal size of a reach cutset is a function of available resources, the likelihood that the key players can be targeted, and the desired level of reach. In the case of the Noordin Top Trust Network, there is an upper bound to the level of reach attainable (0.78) as there are 30 isolated actors in the network.

Figure 7.5 presents network maps of the Noordin Top Trust Network with key players colored white. We have hidden the actors' names in order to make it easier to see the key players. The maps located on the left indicate the fragmentation (top) and distance-weighted fragmentation (bottom) cutsets, while the maps located on the right indicate the reach (top) and distance-weighted reach (bottom) cutsets. In all four cases, the cutsets are a size of

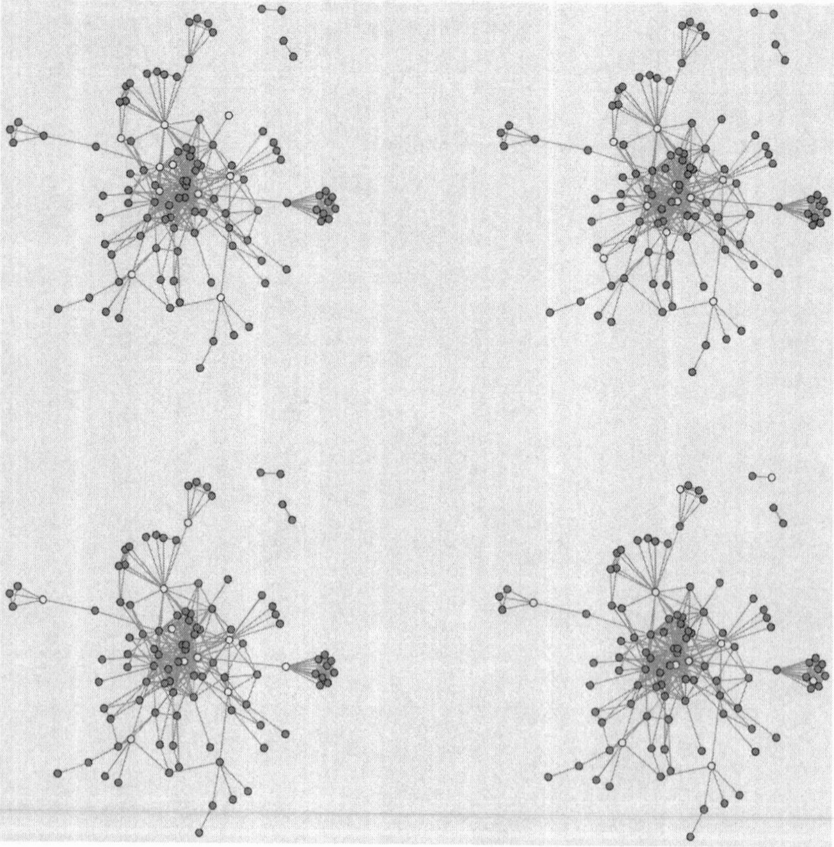

Figure 7.5 Key Players, Noordin Trust Network (isolates and labels hidden)

10 actors. The primary takeaway is that the cutsets are not always the same. The actors that are ideal to remove in order to fragment the network are not necessarily the same as those that are ideal to target for the diffusion of misinformation. Similarly, the cutsets will often differ between the standard and distance-weighted versions of the fragmentation and reach algorithms. Thus, analysts cannot use these algorithms blindly but instead must employ them from within a strategic framework that makes the ultimate desired outcome clear.

7.4 BRIDGES AND NETWORK FLOW

Just as it is often unlikely for a well-connected network to contain a cutpoint, it is also unlikely that such a network would include a tie whose removal will disconnect it. Thus, it is often more useful to turn to algorithms that help us identify ties whose removal could potentially disrupt the flow of resources through a network. Here we consider one such measure, edge betweenness centrality, which was built specifically around the concept of edge betweenness. As noted in chapter 5, the Girvan–Newman algorithm uses edge betweenness centrality to identify which edges to remove in order to detect subgroups in a network. The assumption lying behind the algorithm is that ties with high values of edge betweenness are more likely to span gaps in the social structure than are those whose edge betweenness is low. However, although the inspection of a network matrix of edge betweenness scores is feasible with small networks, such tasks become increasingly implausible with large networks. An easier way to examine the network is to visualize it. We begin with a simple example and then move to a more complex one.[3]

Figure 7.6 presents the Koschade Bali I network (created in igraph), where the width of the edges reflects edge betweenness. To interpret the visualization in terms of brokerage, the thicker the line the more likely that a tie/edge functions as a bridge within the network. There is a fairly clear pattern of most of the thick lines—those with greatest edge betweenness—emanating from Samudra. This pattern is unsurprising since, as noted above (Figure 7.1), Samudra is a cutpoint. Most networks, however, will not exhibit such starkly obvious patterns. For an example of what a somewhat more elaborately structured network, consider the patterns that edge betweenness analysis reveals in the Noordin Top Trust Network, as visualized in NetDraw (Figure 7.7). Again, treat the thickness of edges/ties as indicating bridging ties, with thicker edges indicating bridges or potential bridges. Although the bridges identified using this method bear some strong similarities with the bridge analysis depicted in Figure 7.2, there are some notable differences. The edge betweenness approach also identifies ties that are potential bridges

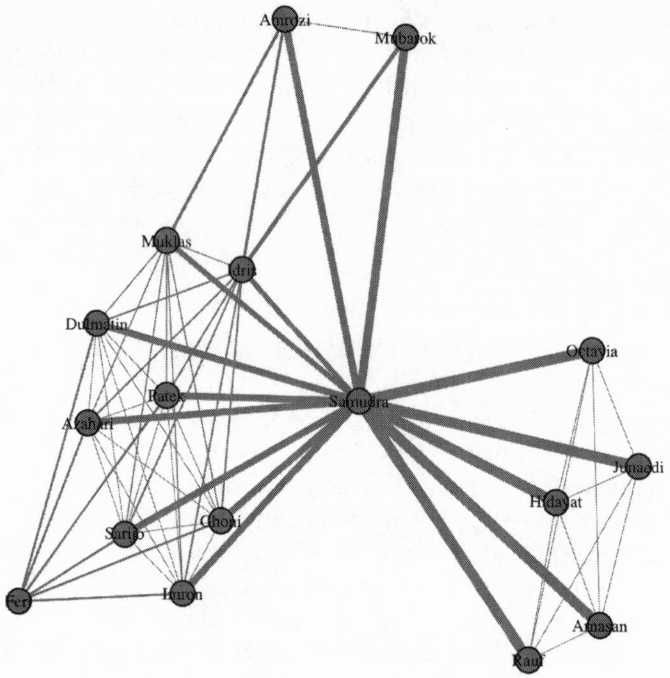

Figure 7.6 Edge Betweenness, Koschade Bali I Network

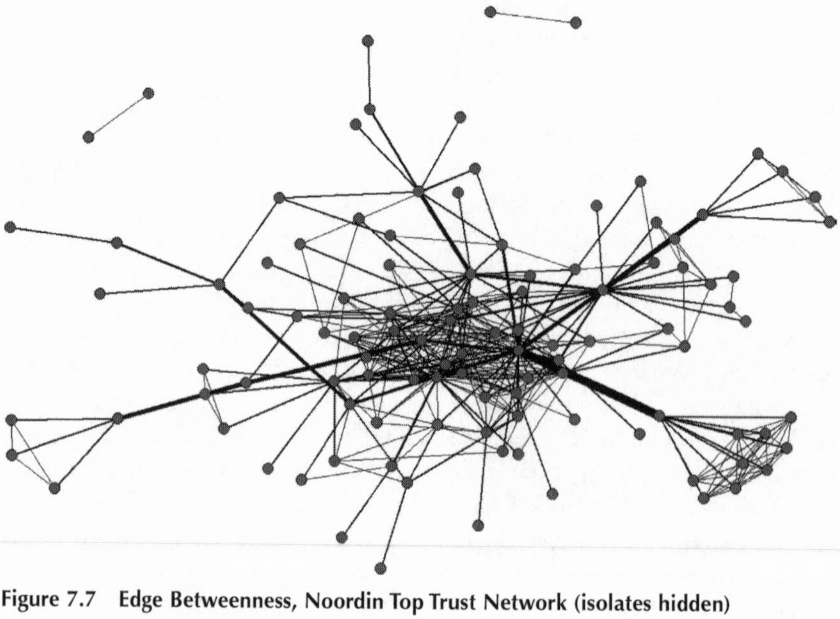

Figure 7.7 Edge Betweenness, Noordin Top Trust Network (isolates hidden)

but would not necessarily disconnect the network if removed. Therefore, a much more detailed pattern of brokerage emerges within the system of ties, but in this case, it is in reference to particular ties that actors hold rather than the actors themselves. Such a shift in attention from actors to their individual relationships can inform more nuanced strategies to influence or compromise individual relationships, without necessarily having to deal directly with the actors themselves.

7.5 STRUCTURAL HOLES

The related concepts of bridging ties and structural holes present the opportunity to accomplish many of the same research goals, while shifting attention away from individuals or groups to instead focus on the relationships that join them. Such a shift can, at times, add nuance and shifts in perspective that can sometimes change the nature and context of potential responses or interventions. To better understand the perspective that these concepts offer to the analyst, it may be meaningful to revisit the background and implications upon which they rest.

The idea of focusing upon ties as an indication of brokerage potential first found popular application through Mark Granovetter's (1973, 1983) work on "weak ties," which found that people were more likely to find jobs through weak rather than strong ties because the former functioned as bridges that tied densely knit clusters of people together. More precisely, Granovetter argued that, while not all weak ties are necessarily bridges, all bridges are weak ties, or at least are far more likely to be weak ties. Ron Burt (1992b) later expanded Granovetter's argument. He agreed that weak ties are more likely to be bridges but argued that occasionally strong ties will also function as bridges. This led Burt to deemphasize the type of tie and focus instead on the gaps in networks, which he calls "structural holes." Burt believes that actors whose ties span these gaps enjoy a competitive advantage over those who do not because bridging ties provide them with an opportunity to broker the flow of various resources that pass through a network. In constructing his structural holes measure, Burt focused on each actor's ego networks (i.e., the actor, their neighbors, and the ties between them) and the triads in which they are embedded.

To illustrate this, consider the following four triads (Figure 7.8). Each consists of a different pattern of ties between the same three actors—Barry, Joseph, and Hillary. One of the triads (1) is complete (aka, closed), and each of the rest is missing one if its three potential ties. As a complete triad, the first of the four triads is thought of as indicating a tight group that shares some degree of culture in the form of norms, trust, and conflict mitigation (Simmel 1950c).

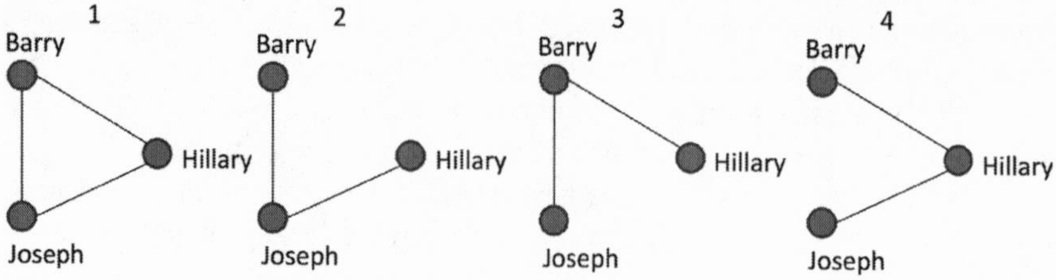

Figure 7.8 Four Types of Triads

But the triads that are of particular interest are the open triads (2–4) because in each case the actor at the center of the triad enjoys a potential advantage since the actor is in a position to broker between each of the other two. This, in turn, implies that none of the actors in the complete triad can break a tie without creating a brokerage position for someone else, thus putting oneself at a disadvantage. For example, in the first triad, "Joseph" has to maintain his tie to "Barry" as well as his tie to "Jake" if he is to prevent either one from gaining a position of brokerage. For instance, if he were to cut his tie to "Hillary" (triad 3), then "Barry" would be in a position of brokerage. Of course, Joseph would benefit (and probably prefer) if Barry cut his tie to Hillary (triad 2), and Hillary undoubtedly feels the same way about Barry's tie to Joseph. Advantage within the triad is in balance only when all ties are maintained.

Clearly, open triads present an opportunity for brokerage that is not present in complete triads. The actors in a complete triad are, on the other hand, constrained by their need to maintain the ties they have. It is this constraint that allows analysts to locate positions of relative advantage and disadvantage. Although it does not directly identify structural holes, Burt's structural holes measure uses constraint as a means of bringing them to light. Burt's measure calculates each actor's constraint based on the various triads in which he or she is involved, weights this by the number of ties in which an actor is involved, and then sums the resulting calculations to arrive at a measure of constraint. A helpful way to think of constraint is that it measures the extent to which an actor (ego) invests his (or her) time and effort in others (alters), who in turn invest in each other (Borgatti, Everett and Johnson 2013:275). There are two approaches for calculating constraint. One follows Burt's original formulation and considers each ego network as if the rest of the network did not exist; thus, only alter-alter ties are taken into account. The other takes into account all of the alters' ties, whether they are tied to ego or not. The former is called the ego network model; the latter, the whole network model (Borgatti, Everett and Freeman 2002b). The same formula is used for both approaches (7.1). The only difference in calculation between the ego network approach and the whole network approach lies in whether we focus upon each triad individually and ignore ties that fall outside the triad (ego network approach), or whether we consider all ties to those in the triad being considered (whole network approach). Constraint is calculated from the perspective of the alters in a triad, as

$$c_i = (p_{ij+} \sum p_{iq} p_{qi})^2, q \neq i, j \quad (7.1)$$

where p_{ij} represents the proportion of *i*'s ties that are shared with alter *j*, and p_{iq} represents the proportion of *i*'s ties that are shared with alter *q*, which is multiplied by p_{qj}, which represents the proportion of *q*'s ties that are shared with alter *j*. Constraint scores range between 0.00 and 1.125, but with the whole network model, they are seldom larger than 1.00.

We can illustrate the two approaches by computing Hillary's level of constraint in the network presented in Figure 7.9. Let's begin with the ego network approach, which ignores Joseph's ties to Liz and Al and focuses only on the Hillary's ego network. The first step is to calculate the various tie proportions—which may also be conceptualized as *dyadic strength, proportional strength,* or *dyadic redundancy*—for the ties of all three actors in the ego network. These proportions are calculated by first dividing each actor's ties by the total number of ties they have in the ego network. Thus, the tie between Hillary and Barry equals 0.50, since that tie is one of her two ties in the ego network. Therefore, Hillary's tie to Joseph also represents half (0.50) of her ties in the ego network. Similarly, Barry's and Joseph's dyadic constraint with each other and with Hillary have a proportion of 0.50. With that information, we can calculate the *dyadic constraint* for each of the ties between actors in the triad. Dyadic constraint—the constraint represented by Hillary's tie to Barry—is $(0.50 + (0.50 \times 0.50))^2 = 0.5625$. Given that the ego network we are using is a complete triad, both Barry's and Joseph's constraint will also be 0.5625. In the final step, we may calculate *aggregate constraint* for each actor by summing the constraint value for each of an actor's ties. Thus, Hillary's aggregate constraint using the ego network approach is (0.5625 + 0.5625) = 1.125, as are the scores of the alters in this case.

Now consider the whole network approach, which takes into account Joseph's ties to Liz and Al. Again, we begin by calculating the proportion

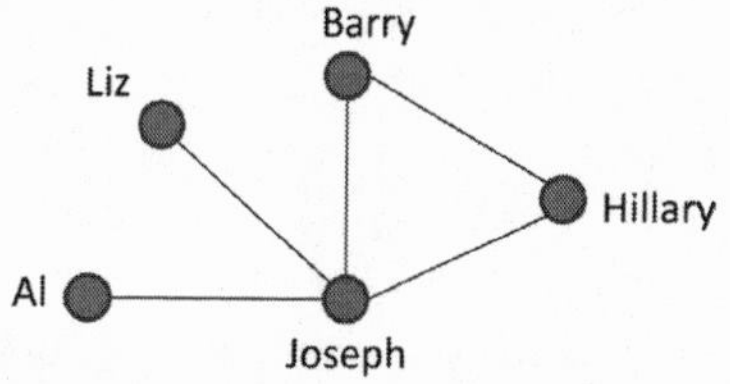

Figure 7.9 Structural Holes, Ego, and Whole Network Approaches

that each tie represents for each of the three actors. Once again, Hillary's tie to Barry and Joseph each represent half of her ties (p_{ij} = 0.50). The same is true for Barry, who also has only two ties in the network. However, given that we are now using the whole network approach, and Joseph has four ties in the network, the proportion of ties that each tie represents *for Joseph* is 0.25. The constraint value for the tie between Hillary and Barry is now calculated using Hillary's tie to Barry (p_{ij} = 0.50), Hillary's tie to Joseph (p_{iq} = 0.50), and Joseph's tie to Barry (p_{qi} = 0.25). The dyadic constraint for the tie between Hillary and Barry is therefore $(0.50 + (0.50 \times 0.25))^2 = 0.3906$. Hillary's tie to Joseph is calculated using her tie to Joseph (p_{ij} = 0.50), Hillary's tie to Barry (p_{iq} = 0.50), and Barry's tie to Joseph (p_{jq} = 0.50), resulting in a constraint of $(0.50 + (0.50 \times 0.50))^2 = 0.5625$. Hillary's aggregate constraint when taking the whole network into account is therefore 0.3906 + 0.5625 = 0.9531.

Constraint is a useful concept for conceptualizing the limitations experienced by each actor in the network, but for a more intuitive visual presentation, the relative *capacities* of the actors in the network are likely to be more useful. It is therefore a good practice to convert actor constraint values to instead reflect their brokerage potential using the additive inverse of the constraint values. The resulting measure—which may be thought of as "autonomy" or "brokerage potential"—is calculated by subtracting each actor's constraint score from 1.125 (its theoretical maximum). The resulting value may then be reflected in the size of actors when visualizing the network. Another thing to keep in mind is that Burt's measure of constraint assigns the lowest possible level of constraint (and thus the highest brokerage potential) to isolated actors. This, of course, is illogical, given that isolated actors are not in a position to broker anything. Consequently, most analysts adjust for this by assigning isolates a maximum constraint score.

Figure 7.10 presents the Noordin Top Trust Network, where actor size reflects the additive inverse of Burt's measure of constraint (i.e., brokerage). We estimated it in UCINET using the whole network model. In the figure, edge size reflects edge betweenness centrality (as in Figure 7.7). As you can see, the brokerage potential of actors is closely associated with the presence of bridges in the network.

What should be clear at this point is the variety of options that the competing perspectives offered by cutpoints/cutsets and bridges bring to bear. By conceptualizing the network's structure in terms of both cutpoints/cutsets, and structural holes, the analyst is able to present a wider range of strategic options for deterring or disrupting dark networks. The nature of an intervention that focuses upon one or more actors will, by necessity, be qualitatively different from an intervention that focuses upon cutting or disrupting the ties between them. Whereas the removal of one or more actors may require either kinetic or multidimensional action, the severance of ties between them may

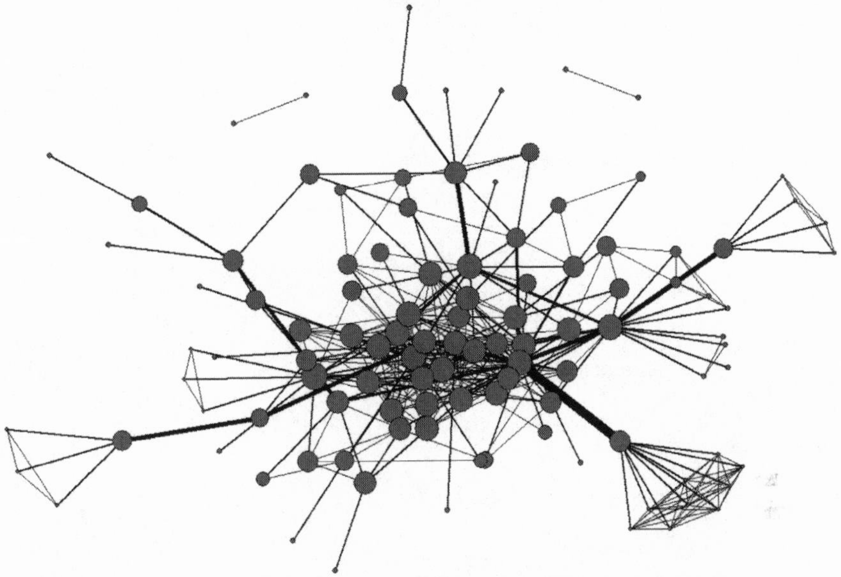

Figure 7.10 Noordin Top Trust Network, Constraint and Edge Betweenness

sometimes be facilitated through a change in the environment or context in which they act. This brings about the possibility of enacting some of the more oblique strategies for foiling dark networks.

7.6 AFFILIATIONS AND BROKERAGE

It is also possible to add additional context and depth to our understanding of brokerage by taking into consideration how each of the actors involved in the act of brokerage is affiliated. Such an approach takes account of constraints as they may apply to identity, loyalty, or other aspirations. Deals brokered between any two competing groups, regardless of the level of competition, must take into account not only the interests and capacities of each of the actors involved, but also the groups with which they are affiliated or with which they identify. To do this, Roger Gould and Roberto Fernandez developed a brokerage roles algorithm (Fernandez and Gould 1994; Gould 1989) that takes into account both tie structure and actor affiliation and calculates a brokerage measure for each of five different brokerage roles they identified: (1) coordinator, (2) itinerant broker/consultant, (3) representative, (4) gatekeeper, and (5) liaison (see Table 7.2 where actor shade indicates group affiliation). The algorithm was developed for use with directed networks, where tie direction distinguishes between the roles of gatekeeper and representative.

Table 7.2 Joe's Brokerage Roles

	Brokerage by Affiliation
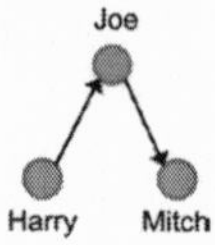	***Coordinator*** Mediation between members of a group in which the mediators are also members of the group
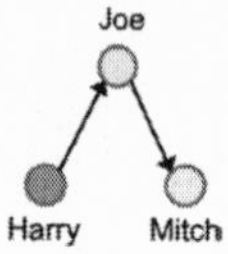	***Gatekeeper*** Mediation between two groups in which the mediators control the flow of information or goods to their group
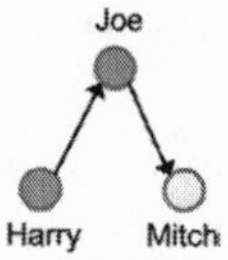	***Representative*** Mediation between two groups in which the mediators control the flow of information or goods from their group
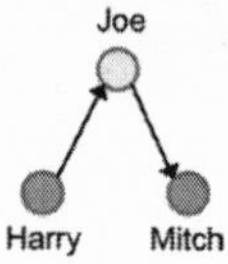	***Itinerant Broker/Consultant*** Mediation between members of one group in which the mediators are members of a different group
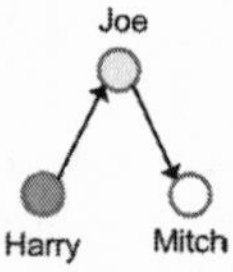	***Liaison*** Mediation between two groups in which the mediators do not belong to either group

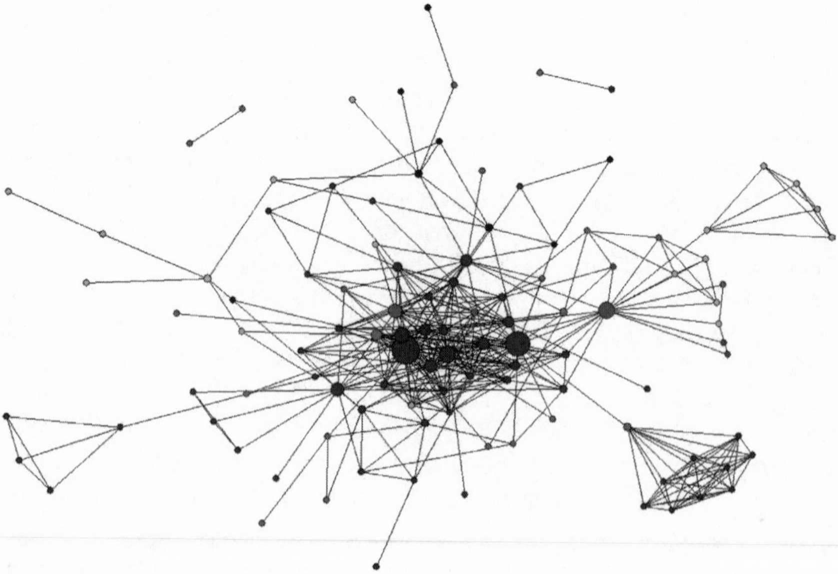

Figure 7.11 Noordin Top Trust Network Total Brokerage Roles

Table 7.3 Noordin Trust Network, Brokerage Roles Scores

	Coordinator	Gatekeeper/ Representative	Consultant	Liaison	Total
Abdullah Sungkar	336	112	20	8	476
Noordin Mohammed Top	162	152	42	46	402
Mohamed Rais	160	46	6	4	216
Iwan Dharmawan	6	44	40	124	214
Abu Bakar Ba'asyir	128	43	6	4	181
Son Hadi	152	13	0	0	165
Fathur Rahman Al-Ghozi	136	23	0	2	161
Tohir	124	24	2	2	152
Jabir	76	46	8	10	140
Ubeid	110	19	0	4	133

Thus, if we apply their brokerage roles algorithm to undirected dark networks, each actor identified as a representative will also be a gatekeeper and vice versa, so their values will be equal.

The brokerage roles algorithm requires network data as well as a partition data that indicates to which groups each actor belongs. To illustrate this approach we estimated brokerage roles based on each actor's primary group affiliation in UCINET (e.g., Ring Banten, Jemaah Islamiyah, KOMPAK). Figure 7.11 presents the results. The shade of actors indicates the different groups in the network, and actor size indicates the total number of brokerage roles for each actor. While visualizations are helpful here, it makes sense to examine each actor's score. Table 7.3 lists the top-ten actors in terms of brokerage role scores. Notice that actors may score highly in some forms of brokerage, but not in others. Abdullah Sunata, for example, ranks the highest in terms of coordinator brokerage roles, but he does not actually make the top ten in terms of itinerant/consultant brokerage roles.[4] Also note the gatekeeper and representative roles are the same given the Trust network is undirected.

7.7 SUMMARY: LESSONS LEARNED

In this chapter we have examined five approaches for identifying brokers and/or bridges in a network. We began with a discussion of bi-component analysis, which helps to identify a network's actors (cutpoints) and bridges (bi-components of size 2) whose removal will disconnect the network. Next, we considered Borgatti's (2006) key player algorithms, which identify optimal sets of actors that can be targeted for either fragmenting the network or for diffusing resources through a network. This approach offers an improvement over bi-component analysis in cases of well-connected networks, where cutpoints often do not exist. In a similar vein, we examined an approach that uses betweenness centrality to identify ties that are more likely to function as bridges in the network. This too provides a resource that transcends the simplified viewpoint of bi-component analysis since, in well-connected networks, locating a bridge that spans what would otherwise constitute two separate components is an unlikely event. We then turned our attention to Burt's (1992b) notion of structural holes, which calculates the level of constraint each actor in a network faces. As we saw, it builds on Mark Granovetter's (1973, 1983) notion of weak ties but takes the position that, when it comes to identifying brokerage potential, it is not the type of tie, but rather the gaps in the social structure that is important. As we saw, there are two approaches to estimating this type of brokerage potential. One is known as the ego network approach, which considers each ego network as if the rest of the network did not exist; the other is known as the whole network approach because it takes into account all of the alters' ties whether they are tied to the ego or not. Finally, we examined the Gould and Fernandez algorithms (Fernandez and Gould 1994; Gould and Fernandez 1989), which assume that brokerage is a function of the different groups with which actors are affiliated; thus, not only does this approach require network data, it also requires attribute data indicating the specific groups to which actors belong. All that being said, the measures described in this chapter are only some of the more commonly used approaches to identify potential brokers.[5]

As with the metrics described in the previous chapters, it is important to understand potential interpretations of the results that these measures produce. An often-overlooked aspect of brokerage, which this chapter attempts to highlight, is that there can be several types of brokers within a dark network. For instance, betweenness centrality can highlight actors that serve as potential brokers within and between clusters, whereas the approach offered by Gould and Fernandez suggests that the specific nature of an actor's brokerage potential is influenced by their affiliations and the affiliations of their neighbors. Table 7.1 summarized some of the potential interpretations for the brokerage measures discussed in this chapter, along with a few other items that network analysts should consider when using these metrics.

Before selecting a particular metric, however, readers should approach the concept of measuring brokerage within dark networks somewhat critically. This is not meant as a critique of the algorithms or the work of the scholars who developed them. It simply means that each measure is only a potential structural indicator of some element of brokerage within a dark network. One reason for this, as alluded to in chapter 3, is that the results of these measures are largely dependent upon the data on which they are applied. For instance, a data set built around a dark network actor of interest (e.g., a high-valued target), meaning collection efforts focused on those individuals, will likely reinforce the notion that such actors are structurally important. A second reason is that just because a dark network actor (or set of actors) appears to

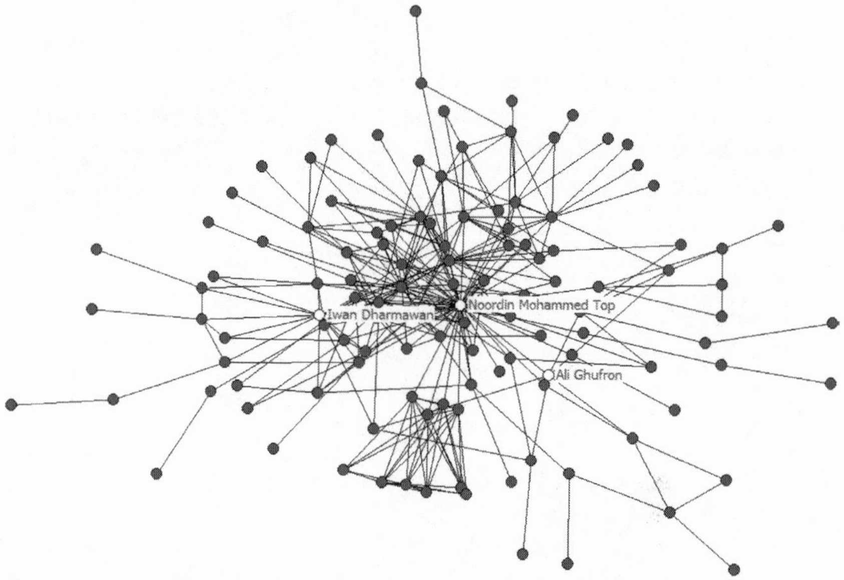

Figure 7.12 Noordin Communication Network, Key Players—Percent Actors Reached

have brokerage potential, as indicated by one or several of these measures, does not mean they will actually act as a broker. Consider Noordin Top's Communication Network in Figure 7.12.

Suppose that an analyst wishes to develop a series of misinformation strategies to sow distrust within this network, which leads the analyst to run the Key Players–Percent Actors Reached measure, and based on available resources, the analyst chooses a set of three actors who can serve as brokers to disseminate the information. The results suggest Iwan Dharmawan, Noordin Top, and Ali Ghufron (i.e., the white actors) make up the optimal set of actors to diffuse the misinformation. As useful as such an analysis is these dark network actors may not realize they are in these favorable locations within the social structure, or once they receive misinformation, they may decide not to pass it along to other actors. Hence, it is more appropriate to say that actors have "brokerage potential," rather than argue that certain actors are "brokers."

7.8 QUESTIONS

1. Which of the following statements is correct?
   a. Weak ties are more likely to be bridges than are strong ties.
   b. Ron Burt structural holes measure is (conceptually) based on Mark Granovetter's strength of weak ties hypothesis.

c. Burt argues that strong ties can also be bridges.
d. There are two approaches for estimating Burt's measure of constraint.
e. All of the above statements are correct.

2. Consider the network graph presented below (it is the same as the one presented in the previous chapter's questions). Which actor do you think is less constrained (i.e., possesses more brokerage potential: two or three?

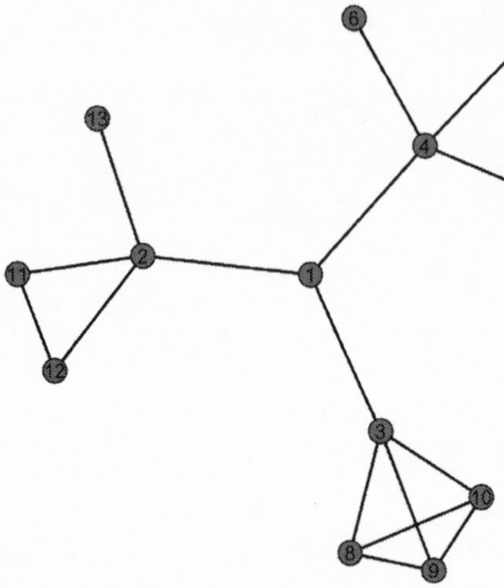

3. Actors, that if removed, disconnect a network are
   a. Bridges.
   b. Structural Holes.
   c. Cutpoints.
   d. Central.
4. Which of the following algorithms identify optimal *sets* of actors to diffuse information?
   a. Key Player–Percent Actors Reached.
   b. Burt Constraint.
   c. Betweenness Centrality.
   d. Key Player–Reach Index
5. Which of the following identifies five types of brokerage based on the triads in which each actor is involved along with their affiliations, and those of their neighbors?
   a. Key Player–Fragmentation
   b. Key Player–Distance-weighted Fragmentation
   c. Brokerage Roles
   d. Edge Betweenness

6. All cutpoints produce the same levels of fragmentation when they are removed.
   a. True.
   b. False.
7. Actors with relatively high levels of brokerage potential can be
   a. Key relationships.
   b. Brokers within clusters.
   c. Brokers between clusters.
   d. Unaware of their position.
8. Which of the following statements about Gould and Fernandez's Brokerage Roles metric is not true?
   a. It identifies five types of brokerage roles with directed network data.
   b. It identifies four types of brokerage roles with undirected network data.
   c. All of the brokerage roles identified by the algorithm are between (rather than within) groups.
   d. It requires the input of two types of data: (1) a network and (2) a partition that assigns each actor to two or more groups.
   e. All of the above statements are true.

7.9 ANSWERS

1. All of the above statements are correct (e).
2. Actor 2 because her alters' are not as interconnected as are actor 3's—see the graph below (Exam Figure 2) where actor size varies in terms of brokerage (i.e., the additive inverse of constraint).

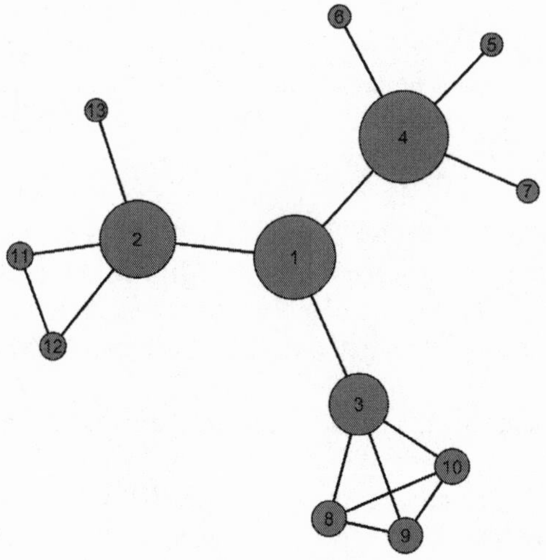

3. Cutpoints (c).
4. Key Player–Percent Actors Reached (a); Key Player–Reach Index (d).
5. Brokerage Roles (c).
6. False.
7. Brokers within clusters (b); Brokers between clusters (c); Unaware of their position (d).
8. All of the brokerage roles identified by the algorithm are between (rather than within) groups (c).

7.10 FURTHER READING

One of the most cited treatments of brokerage is Ron Burt's *Structural Holes: The Social Structure of Competition* (New York and Cambridge: Cambridge University Press, 1992). A shorter and somewhat more accessible account is in his chapter "The Social Structure of Competition," which can be found in *Networks and Organizations: Structure, Form and Action*, edited by Nitin Nohria and Robert G. Eccles (Boston: Harvard University Press, 1992).

Before reading Burt, however, one should first read Mark Granovetter's "The Strength of Weak Ties" (*American Journal of Sociology* 73:1360–1380, 1973), on which, as we noted in the chapter, Burt built his notion of structural holes and the idea of constraint. A decade later, Granovetter followed up his original article with "The Strength of Weak Ties: A Network Theory Revisited" (*Sociological Theory*: 201–33, 1983).

Tests of Granovetter's theory are difficult because it requires whole network data for thousands of actors. Trying to ascertain how many strong and weak ties an actor has from a few questions on a survey is insufficient. Most people have hundreds of friends and acquaintances, and time and resources prevent interviewers from asking each respondent several questions about all of their friends and acquaintances. In 1995, in the afterword to the second edition of his book, *Getting a Job: A Study of Contacts and Career* (Cambridge, MA: Harvard University Press), Granovetter summarizes the results of several studies. Perhaps the most robust test of Granovetter's theory to date is the analysis of Onnela et al. ("Structure and Tie Strengths in Mobile Communication Networks." *Proceedings of the National Academy of Sciences of the USA* 104:7332–36), who, using the communication patterns of millions of mobile phone users, found that weak ties were more likely to form bridges in the network than were strong ties.

Social movement theorists have explored the nature of brokerage in a lot of depth, largely inspired by Doug McAdam, Sidney Tarrow, and Charles Tilly's 2001 book, *Dynamics of Contention* (New York and Cambridge: Cambridge University Press). See for instance the March 2011 issue of

Mobilization, which was co-edited by McAdam and Tarrow (Tilly, unfortunately, had passed away) and featured a series of articles that took up many of the challenges raised by McAdam, Tarrow, and Tilly. In particular, see Ion Bogdon Vasi's "Brokerage, Miscibility, and the Spread of Contention" (*Mobilization: An International Journal* 16:11–24).

Other excellent discussions of brokerage include:

- Wouter de Nooy, Andrej Mrvar, and Vladimir Batagelj. 2011. "Brokers and Bridges." Pp. 159–185 (Chapter 7) in *Exploratory Social Network Analysis with Pajek*.
- Robert R. Faulkner and Eric Cheney. 2014. "Breakdown of Brokerage: Crisis and Collapse in the Watergate Conspiracy." Pp. 263–84 in *Crime and Networks*, edited by Carlo Morselli. New York and London: Routledge.
- Roberto M. Fernandez and Roger V. Gould. 1994. "A Dilemma of State Power: Brokerage and Influence in the National-Health Policy Domain." *American Journal of Sociology* 99:1455–91.
- Roger V. Gould and Roberto M. Fernandez. 1989. "Structures of Mediation: A Formal Approach to Brokerage in Transaction Networks." *Sociological Methodology* 19:89–126.
- Robert A. Hanneman and Mark Riddle. 2005. "Ego Networks" (Chapter 9) in *Introduction to Social Network Methods.* Riverside, CA: University of California, Riverside: http://www.faculty.ucr.edu/~hanneman/nettext/C9_Ego_networks.html
- Carlo Morselli and Julie Roy. 2008. "Brokerage Qualifications in Ringing Operations." *Criminology* 46:71–98.

NOTES

1. Currently, the key player algorithm has been partially implemented in NetDraw and ORA. It has been fully implemented in Borgatti's *Key Player* program (2011), which come with each version of UCINET or can be downloaded for free from the Analytic Technologies website: http://www.analytictech.com/products.htm

2. Both distance-weighted algorithms use average reciprocal distance (ARD) in their calculations rather than the standard measure of closeness since (as we discussed in the previous chapter) the former can be used with disconnected graphs while the latter one cannot.

3. Currently, only UCINET, Gephi, and the igraph R library estimate edge betweenness.

4. Again, these brokerage roles were meant for direct data, which means representative and gatekeeper counts are the same. Consequently, analysts need to pay attention to the output scores to ensure each actor's total score is correct with undirected

data. For instance, an actor in an undirected network with a very high representative score, and therefore a gatekeeper score as well, may rank relatively highly because that score will be counted twice.

5. For instance, UCINET offers users the ability to run attribute-weighted betweenness centrality, which allows users to weight node betweenness by the importance of the actors it brokers.

Chapter 8

Positional Approaches to Analyzing Networks

Up to this point, we have highlighted various methods for examining network topography, detecting cohesive subgroups, identifying brokers and bridges between such groups, and determining which actors are central. These are sometimes referred to as relational approaches to network data (Emirbayer and Goodwin 1994) because they focus on how direct and indirect ties between actors affect actor behavior. In this chapter we will consider what are referred to as positional approaches for analyzing network data. These differ from relational approaches in that rather than focusing on the ties between actors, they seek to identify actors who hold similar structural positions—or simply positions—within a network. These positions are seen as important because they are typically connected with a role or set of roles and actors occupying similar positions will hold similar responsibilities or exhibit similar types of behavior. For example, narcotics traffickers are often located in similar structural positions, and maintain ties to similar other actors within and across dark networks. In fact, some social network theorists argue that actors' positions are more important for explaining their behavior than their ties to others.[1]

The concept of structural equivalence is deceptively simple but can be very useful when it is estimated correctly. In essence, structurally equivalent actors are those who hold similar positions within a network, which also suggests that they are similar in terms of their function within the network. Actors who are structurally equivalent are said to share a position or a "block," and one of the processes by which they are identified is referred to as blockmodeling (White, Boorman and Breiger 1976). Once the blocks of a network have been identified, we can use this information in different ways, such as collapsing a network based on blocks in order to identify patterns among sets of actors that are not obvious using standard relational approaches.[2] The terminology associated with blockmodeling can be confusing for those new to network analysis. A major reason for this is that the algorithms that analysts use to identify structurally equivalent actors vary in their names and assumptions. For example, equivalencies between actors may be established by using algorithms that employ structural, automorphic, isomorphic, or regular equivalence as a mechanism, and each mechanism represents a different definition of equivalence. In other words, regular equivalence methods will also seek to determine which actors are structurally equivalent, but the answers they yield will often differ from those produced by structural equivalence methods. We now turn to a discussion and illustration of the three types of equivalence, beginning with structural equivalence.

8.1 ESTABLISHING ROLES THROUGH STRUCTURAL EQUIVALENCE

For the analyst, the search for equivalencies in the network is, and should be, an exercise that is conceptually different from detecting subgroups in the network. Equivalent actors are those who bear a lot of similarities in terms of their structure in the network. This, however, does not mean that they should necessarily be considered members of a cohesive group. Quite the contrary, structurally equivalent actors are those whose relative positions in the network indicate that they are at least somewhat redundant to one another—like two different managers of the same working crew. Ultimately, such redundancies tend to indicate that two actors are, more or less, interchangeable or at least operating at the same level. As such, structural equivalence frequently translates better as an indication of competition than of solidarity.

One of the more notable differences between locating subgroups and locating equivalent positions is in the mode of visualization. Whereas cohesive subgroups will often be at least somewhat discernible in a network visualization (i.e., a sociogram), such as the one in Figure 8.1, it is much more difficult to use such depictions to visually assess equivalencies in a network. As a result, most analysts favor visualizations that are capable of demonstrating structural regularities on a different dimension, such as matrices, blockmodels, and block matrices, as depicted in Figures 8.2 to 8.4. For some, getting used to reading blockmodels and matrices can offer a somewhat confusing shift in perspective. But these visualization tools can be invaluable for their capacity to demonstrate regularities that will not be apparent in other ways.

Ultimately, however, it is likely that most analysts will discover that the most important factor in making sense of a network in terms of roles and positions is preparation. Without proper background knowledge in the group or the environment in which it operates, much of the information derived from these techniques is likely to be of limited value. It is of little use to state that actor X is structurally equivalent to actor Y if the analyst has little idea of who either of them are.

A much better practice is to develop knowledge about a set of actors in advance and then establish a set of questions relative to their positions in the network. The background knowledge will aid in the interpretation, and provide leads for follow up on the equivalent actors identified or the context of their role in the network. Table 8.1 lists a variety of methods available for actually investigating structural equivalence in a network. Results will vary by method, and depth of knowledge in the topic can make a great deal of difference between a spurious finding and an important discovery.

The next key to success is familiarity with the techniques and algorithms themselves. We strongly recommend experimenting with each of the techniques listed below. We present multiple variations of each of the three forms of equivalence—structural, automorphic, and regular. Some will resonate with particular analysts more than others. It is good to become familiar enough to use a few well and comfortably. Nine different methods are covered in more depth below. Each will provide a somewhat different perspective from the others. As with most other analyses, however, the best tool for the job will likely be the one that best suits the data at hand.

8.2 STRUCTURAL EQUIVALENCE

For two actors to be considered structurally equivalent, they must be exactly substitutable for one another (Hanneman and Riddle 2005). The criteria of being "exactly substitutable" indicate that actors must "have identical ties to and from identical other actors" (Wasserman and Faust 1994:468), such as two or more managers who are in charge of the same group, or several field agents under the same coordinator. Because they share an identical set of ties to exactly the same other actors, they will also score identically in terms of centrality, prestige, and all other social network metrics (Borgatti and Everett 1992:7).[3] Hence, one reason structural equivalence can be helpful to dark network analysts is by helping analysts to identify actors who are equivalent to known, "important" actors of interest in terms of their position. Many leaders of dark networks, for example, are well known to the authorities. Most dark network leaders, however, are also inaccessible, and strategies focused solely on them can be costly in terms of available time and resources. The identification of actors who are structurally equivalent to such leaders therefore may highlight alternative actors on which to collect information.

By far, structural equivalence is the most restrictive understanding of equivalence. In practice, it is generally unreasonable to expect that two or

Table 8.1 Summary of Blockmodeling Approaches

Type of Structural Equivalence	*Formal Explanation*	*Possible Interpretation(s)*	*Caveat(s)*
Structural Equivalence	Two actors are considered "equivalent" if they have ties to the same exact alters. This is the strictest form of equivalence.	Structurally equivalent actors are structurally substitutable for one another.	Real-world actors rarely have identical ties with one another.
Euclidean Distance	Identifies "equivalent" actors based on the most direct route between actors in *n*-dimensional space. For further description, see "Euclidian Distance under Automorphic Equivalence.	Same as "Structural Equivalence."	Same as "Structural Equivalence." Also, not available in some social network analysis programs.
CONCOR	Iterated correlations between actors are used to split a network into groups until it runs out of splits or arrives at the number of "splits" dictated by analysts.	Same as "Structural Equivalence."	Same as "Structural Equivalence." Available in many, but not all, social network analysis programs. Several forms of CONCOR exist (e.g., standard and iterative).
Optimization	Randomly sorts actors into an analyst-specified number of blocks and calculates an initial badness of fit score. It continues to sort actors into blocks until it finds a partition of actors that minimizes the badness of fit score that compares the final model with an ideal model.	Same as "Structural Equivalence."	Same as "Structural Equivalence." Not available in most social network analysis programs.
Automorphic Equivalence	Automorphically equivalent actors are connected to the same number of actors and those actors (i.e., the neighbors) are in identical structural positions within the same network.	Actors are considered automorphically equivalent if they can be mapped on to one another. They occupy indistinguishable positions.	Actors only can be automorphically equivalent only if they are within the same network. Not available in most social network analysis programs.
All Permutations	Compares every possible swapping of actors in search for automorphically equivalent actors.	Same as "Automorphic Equivalence."	Computationally intensive, so better for small networks. Also see caveats for "Automorphic Equivalence."
Optimization	Similar to structural equivalence optimization option. After analysts indicate the number of blocks, the algorithm sorts actors into blocks until it finds a partition that minimizes the badness of fit score.	Same as "Automorphic Equivalence."	Same as "Automorphic Equivalence."

Table 8.1 (cont. . .)

Euclidean Distance	Begins with a (reciprocal of) distance (for binary data) or strength of tie matrix (for valued data), then calculates the distance between all pairs of actors, and regards actors that have similar distance profiles as being more automorphically equivalent.	Same as "Automorphic Equivalence."	Same as "Automorphic Equivalence." Same as with structural equivalence, though the criteria for similarity are relaxed.
Regular Equivalence	Actors who have identical ties to and from regularly equivalent actors (i.e., actors within the same classes).	Actors who are connected to actors in the same classes.	Not available in most social network analysis packages.
Regular Equivalence (REGE)	Using iterative optimization, REGE first measures similarities between actor pairs according to similarities in their local structure (in terms of the absolute difference of the magnitude of their ties) and weights the score according to the prior iteration—if applicable—and optimizes according to the match score. The weighted optimized measure is then summed for each actor's neighborhood and normalized. The entire process is then repeated for all actor pairs for an analyst-specified number of iterations.	Same as "Regular Equivalence."	The original algorithm is best for continuous data. Also see caveats for "Automorphic Equivalence."
Categorical Regular Equivalence (CATREGE)	Using iterative optimization, the algorithm first assigns actors into one of three classifications (sinks, sources, or repeaters), and then classifies actors according to the mix of actor types in their neighborhoods. The entire process repeats using the prior iteration's as a starting point for actor classification. Ideally, iterations continue to convergence.	Same as "Regular Equivalence."	CATREGE works best with binary or nominal data. To use the algorithm with undirected data, one must provide either a starting partition (seed partition), or use a distance matrix of the network. Also see caveats for "Automorphic Equivalence."
Regular Equivalence Optimization	Similar to other optimization options. Analysts first select a number of blocks. It then randomly sorts actors into blocks, calculates an initial badness of fit measure, and continues to sort until it finds a partition that minimizes the badness of fit score.	Same as "Regular Equivalence."	Same as "Regular Equivalence" caveats.

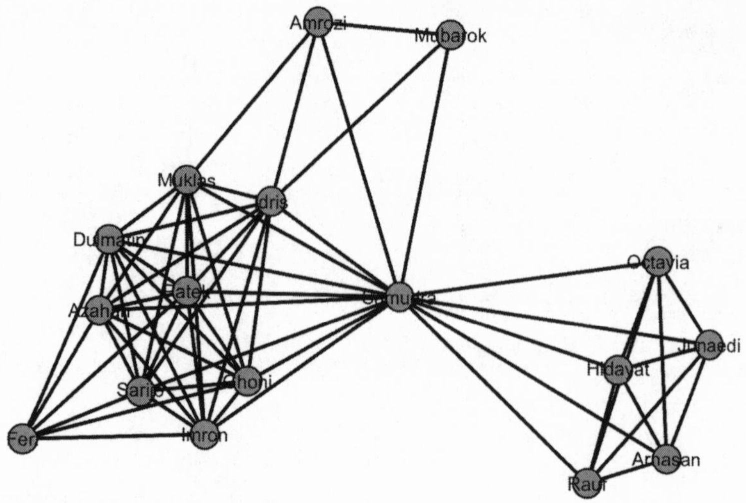

Figure 8.1 Koschade Bali I Network

more actors will have exactly the same relationships to all other actors in order for them to be assigned to the same equivalence class. Dark networks are no exception. It is therefore common practice to use a cutoff value for determining who is assigned to what equivalence class and the ties that exist between equivalence classes. Here, we will consider three approaches for identifying structurally equivalent actors: Euclidian distance, CONCOR, and Optimization, all of which are available in UCINET. Not all of these, however, are available in all of the other programs discussed in this book. We will illustrate them using the Koschade Bali I network (Figure 8.1), which we have used in previous chapters.

Euclidean Distance

A common approach for identifying structurally equivalent actors is to compare them in terms of Euclidian distance. This approach calculates a set of points for each actor in a network in *n*-dimensional space, so that the distances between actors correspond as closely as possible to the input proximities. Euclidean distance is actually a measure of dissimilarity between two actors, and it differs from path distance, in that the distance between two actors is the most direct route between them (i.e., as the crow flies), rather than the number of edges between them. The first step is to use Euclidean distance to estimate a structural equivalence matrix and a corresponding structural equivalence partition. Figure 8.2 presents the structural equivalence matrix of the Koschade Bali I network (estimated by UCINET). Given that this is a

Structural Equivalence Matrix

		1 Mukla	2 Amroz	3 Imron	4 Samud	5 Dulma	6 Idris	7 Mubar	8 Azaha	9 Ghoni	10 Arnas	11 Rauf	12 Octav	13 Hiday	14 Junae	15 Patek	16 Feri	17 Sarij
1	Muklas	0.00	3.74	2.00	3.46	2.24	1.41	3.46	2.00	2.24	4.90	4.90	4.90	4.90	4.90	2.24	2.65	2.00
2	Amrozi	3.74	0.00	3.74	4.69	3.32	3.46	1.41	3.74	3.61	3.74	3.74	3.74	3.74	3.74	3.61	4.36	3.74
3	Imron	2.00	3.74	0.00	4.00	1.73	2.45	4.00	0.00	1.00	4.90	4.90	4.90	4.90	4.90	1.00	2.65	0.00
4	Samudra	3.46	4.69	4.00	0.00	4.12	3.16	4.90	4.00	4.12	4.47	4.47	4.47	4.47	4.47	4.12	4.36	4.00
5	Dulmatin	2.24	3.32	1.73	4.12	0.00	2.65	3.61	1.73	1.41	4.58	4.58	4.58	4.58	4.58	1.41	2.83	1.73
6	Idris	1.41	3.46	2.45	3.16	2.65	0.00	3.74	2.45	2.65	5.10	5.10	5.10	5.10	5.10	2.65	3.00	2.45
7	Mubarok	3.46	1.41	4.00	4.90	3.61	3.74	0.00	4.00	3.87	3.46	3.46	3.46	3.46	3.46	3.87	4.12	4.00
8	Azahari	2.00	3.74	0.00	4.00	1.73	2.45	4.00	0.00	1.00	4.90	4.90	4.90	4.90	4.90	1.00	2.65	0.00
9	Ghoni	2.24	3.61	1.00	4.12	1.41	2.65	3.87	1.00	0.00	4.80	4.80	4.80	4.80	4.80	0.00	2.45	1.00
10	Arnasan	4.90	3.74	4.90	4.47	4.58	5.10	3.46	4.90	4.80	0.00	0.00	0.00	0.00	0.00	4.80	4.58	4.90
11	Rauf	4.90	3.74	4.90	4.47	4.58	5.10	3.46	4.90	4.80	0.00	0.00	0.00	0.00	0.00	4.80	4.58	4.90
12	Octavia	4.90	3.74	4.90	4.47	4.58	5.10	3.46	4.90	4.80	0.00	0.00	0.00	0.00	0.00	4.80	4.58	4.90
13	Hidayat	4.90	3.74	4.90	4.47	4.58	5.10	3.46	4.90	4.80	0.00	0.00	0.00	0.00	0.00	4.80	4.58	4.90
14	Junaedi	4.90	3.74	4.90	4.47	4.58	5.10	3.46	4.90	4.80	0.00	0.00	0.00	0.00	0.00	4.80	4.58	4.90
15	Patek	2.24	3.61	1.00	4.12	1.41	2.65	3.87	1.00	0.00	4.80	4.80	4.80	4.80	4.80	0.00	2.45	1.00
16	Feri	2.65	4.36	2.65	4.36	2.83	3.00	4.12	2.65	2.45	4.58	4.58	4.58	4.58	4.58	2.45	0.00	2.65
17	Sarijo	2.00	3.74	0.00	4.00	1.73	2.45	4.00	0.00	1.00	4.90	4.90	4.90	4.90	4.90	1.00	2.65	0.00

Figure 8.2 Koschade Bali I Structural Equivalence Matrix

measure of dissimilarity, smaller values are preferred. Therefore, the smaller the number in the corresponding cell of two actors, the more similar the two actors are. A score of 0.00 indicates that two actors share an identical pattern of ties and are thus perfectly similar (i.e., equivalent). Looking at the matrix, we can see that although most of the actors in the network are not structurally equivalent, five are: Arnasan, Rauf, Octavia, Hidayat, and Junaedi.[4]

The next step is to permute the original network so that the actors who are assigned to the same block occupy adjacent columns and rows. To this we need to first examine the structural equivalence partition (Figure 8.3).

As you can see, the structural equivalence partition actually includes nine subsets (i.e., the columns): one at similarity 0.00 (column one—highest level of similarity), one at similarity level 1.00 (column two—second highest level of similarity), one at similarity level 1.40 (column three—third highest level of similarity), and so on, until the ninth partition with a similarity level of 4.60, which with this network is the lowest level of similarity. If we choose to use perfect similarity as our criterion for assigning actors to blocks, then we would use the first partition (or column at 1.00); each actor would be assigned to separate (and individual) blocks, except actors 10–14 (Arnasan, Rauf, Octavia, Hidayat, and Junaedi), all of whom are assigned to Block 14. Note that these actors (along with Sumadra) were a part of the same operational cell during the Bali operation. It is therefore not unexpected that they would be structurally equivalent (Koschade 2006).

Partition Indicator Matrix

		1 0. 00 0	2 1. 00 0	3 1. 40 0	4 1. 60 0	5 2. 40 0	6 2. 70 0	7 3. 60 0	8 3. 90 0	9 4. 60 0
1	Muklas	1	1	6	6	17	17	17	17	17
2	Amrozi	2	2	7	7	7	7	14	14	17
3	Imron	17	17	17	17	17	17	17	17	17
4	Samudra	4	4	4	4	4	4	4	17	17
5	Dulmatin	5	5	5	17	17	17	17	17	17
6	Idris	6	6	6	6	17	17	17	17	17
7	Mubarok	7	7	7	7	7	7	14	14	17
8	Azahari	17	17	17	17	17	17	17	17	17
9	Ghoni	15	17	17	17	17	17	17	17	17
10	Arnasan	14	14	14	14	14	14	14	14	17
11	Rauf	14	14	14	14	14	14	14	14	17
12	Octavia	14	14	14	14	14	14	14	14	17
13	Hidayat	14	14	14	14	14	14	14	14	17
14	Junaedi	14	14	14	14	14	14	14	14	17
15	Patek	15	17	17	17	17	17	17	17	17
16	Feri	16	16	16	16	16	17	17	17	17
17	Sarijo	17	17	17	17	17	17	17	17	17

Figure 8.3 Koschade Bali I Structural Equivalence Partition

By contrast, if we choose to assign actors to blocks based on the lowest level of similarity, we would select the last (i.e., ninth) partition (i.e., column). This would result in all of the actors being assigned to the same (and only) block, which is unhelpful. Generally, we want a partition somewhere in between the two extremes. Here, since we are engaging in more of an exploratory analysis of the network, rather than operating with a theory as to how many blocks of actors there should be in the network or based on our interest in a specific actor and identifying similar other actors, we have selected the partition in the middle (fifth). This assigns Samudra to a block of his own, which, given his somewhat unique position within the network (see Figure 8.1), this seems like a reasonable place to start.

Figure 8.4 presents original network with the rows and columns permuted (rearranged) so that the actors assigned to the same block occupy adjacent rows and columns. The “1s” represent ties between the actors, and therefore, the blocks. It is clear that Samudra has been assigned to a block of his own,

```
                                1 1 1 1 1   1               1   1
                4   7 2         3 1 4 2 0   6   1 9 3 5 6 5 8 7
                S   M A         H R J O A   F   M G I D I P A S
              ---------------------------------------------------
 4    Samudra |   | 1 1 | 1 1 1 1 1 |   | 1 1 1 1 1 1 1 1 |
              ---------------------------------------------------
 7    Mubarok | 1 |   1 |           |   |         1       |
 2     Amrozi | 1 | 1   |           |   | 1       1       |
              ---------------------------------------------------
13    Hidayat | 1 |     |   1 1 1 1 |   |                 |
11       Rauf | 1 |     | 1   1 1 1 |   |                 |
14    Junaedi | 1 |     | 1 1   1 1 |   |                 |
12    Octavia | 1 |     | 1 1 1   1 |   |                 |
10    Arnasan | 1 |     | 1 1 1 1   |   |                 |
              ---------------------------------------------------
16       Feri |   |     |           |   |   1 1 1   1 1 1 |
              ---------------------------------------------------
 1     Muklas | 1 |   1 |           |   |   1 1 1 1 1 1 1 |
 9      Ghoni | 1 |     |           | 1 | 1   1 1 1 1 1 1 |
 3      Imron | 1 |     |           | 1 | 1 1   1 1 1 1 1 |
 5   Dulmatin | 1 |     |           |   | 1   1   1   1 1 |
 6      Idris | 1 | 1 1 |           |   | 1 1 1 1   1 1 1 |
15      Patek | 1 |     |           | 1 | 1 1 1 1 1   1 1 |
 8    Azahari | 1 |     |           | 1 | 1 1 1 1 1 1   1 |
17     Sarijo | 1 |     |           | 1 | 1 1 1 1 1 1 1   |
              ---------------------------------------------------
```

Reduced BlockMatrix

	1	2	3	4	5
1		1.000	1.000	0.000	1.000
2	1.000	1.000	0.000	0.000	0.188
3	1.000	0.000	1.000	0.000	0.000
4	0.000	0.000	0.000		0.750
5	1.000	0.188	0.000	0.625	0.964

Figure 8.4 Block Matrix and Permuted Koschade Bali I Network (Euclidean Distance)

but so has Feri. As noted above, Samudra makes sense, but what about Feri? Feri is attached to the cluster on the left (see Figure 8.1), but he is somewhat removed from them. This may be because he was one of the suicide bombers, so it is not unreasonable that he is assigned to his own block. Below the permuted matrix in Figure 8.4 is a reduced blockmatrix, which collapses each block of the permuted matrix into a single actor where the number in the cell indicates the density of ties between the actors of those two blocks. A cell with a density level of 1.00 indicates that all of the actors in the two blocks have ties with each other. In other words, according to the results presented in Figure 8.4, the actors in blocks 1 and 2 all have ties with one another as do the actors in blocks 1 and 3. By contrast, a cell with a density level of 0.00 indicates that the actors in the two blocks have no ties with one another. In other words, there are no ties between the actors assigned to blocks 2 and 3.

The next step in the blockmodeling process is to determine which blocks (or sets of actors) are tied with one another. Generally, when the density in the common cell in the blockmatrix equals 1.00, analysts assume there is a tie between the two blocks, and when the density in the blockmatrix equals 0.00, analysts assume there is not a tie between the two blocks. It gets tricky, though, when the density lies somewhere between 0.00 and 1.00. At what point (i.e., at what density level) do we consider that two blocks share a tie? There are a number of different approaches for doing so. The zero-block or lean-fit approach (Wasserman and Faust 1994:399) only classifies a block as null if its density equals 0.00 (i.e., if there is a complete absence of ties) and then treats the remaining blocks as one or complete blocks. If we apply this approach to the Koschade Bali I network, the final image matrix (i.e., blockmodel) would look like Figure 8.5. As you can see, this produces numerous cells containing "1s."

An alternative approach is the one-block method (Wasserman and Faust 1994:400), which only classifies a block as complete if its density equals 1.00. If we applied this approach to the Koschade Bali I network, the final image matrix would look like Figure 8.6. Note how this approach produces numerous zero cells.

	1	**2**	**3**	**4**	**5**
1	0	1	1	0	1
2	1	1	0	0	1
3	1	0	1	0	0
4	0	0	0	0	1
5	1	1	0	1	1

Figure 8.5 Reduced Zero-Block Matrix

	1	2	3	4	5
1	0	1	1	0	1
2	1	0	0	0	0
3	1	0	0	0	0
4	0	0	0	0	0
5	1	0	0	0	0

Figure 8.6 Reduced One-Block Matrix

	1	2	3	4	5
1	0	1	1	0	1
2	1	0	0	0	0
3	1	0	0	0	0
4	0	0	0	0	1
5	1	0	0	1	0

Figure 8.7 Final Image Matrix

Probably the most common approach for distinguishing complete from null blocks is to set a cutoff, such that if a particular block's density is greater than or equal to that cutoff, it is classified as a complete block, and if it is not, it is classified as a null block (Wasserman and Faust 1994:400–401). It is often prudent to set the cutoff equal to the overall density of the network (although other values can be used). If we use the overall density of the Koschade Bali I network, which equals 0.452, we end up with the final image matrix presented in Figure 8.7 and a graph of the final image matrix presented in Figure 8.8.

What do they suggest? For one thing they indicate that the first block (which only consists of Samudra) functions as a broker between blocks 2 (Amrozi and Mubarok), 3 (Arnasan, Rauf, Octavia, Hidayat, Jenaedi), and 5 (Muklas, Imron, Dulmatin, Idris, Azahari, Ghoni, Patek, and Sarijo), while Feri (block 4) is only connected to the group through block 5. It also suggests there are five sets of actors who, within their respective blocks, are potentially substitutable for one another. Such a conclusion is tentative, of course, since at this point we are only engaging in exploratory analysis. We will reconsider these findings as we explore the other structural equivalence algorithms below. For now, however, this strikes us as a reasonable interpretation of the network.

CONCOR

CONCOR, which was one of the earliest approaches to identifying structurally equivalent actors, stands for "CONvergence of iterated CORrelations."

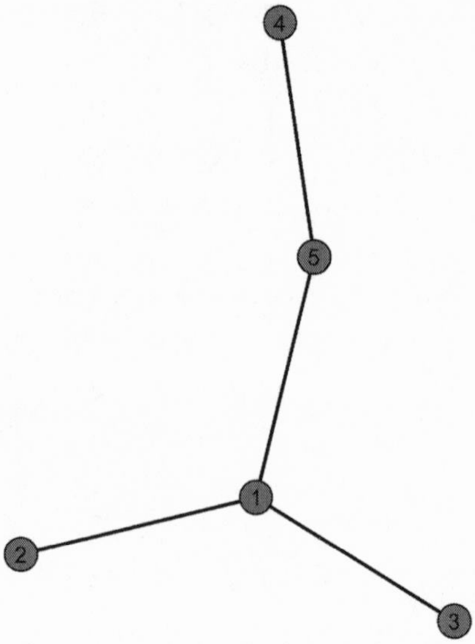

Figure 8.8 Graph of Final Image Matrix (Euclidean Distance)

It is found in most SNA programs and is based on the discovery that repeated calculation of correlations between a matrix's rows (or columns) eventually results in correlation matrix consisting of only +1.00s and −1.00s (Wasserman and Faust 1994:376).[5] The algorithm begins by correlating each pair of actors, and then each row of the resulting actor-by-actor correlation matrix is then extracted and correlated with every other row. This process is repeated until all of the coefficients approach +1.00 or −1.00. CONCOR then splits the data into two sets (i.e., the +1.00 set and the −1.00 set), and the process is repeated for each of the sets—or at least those sets with two or more actors—until it runs out of actors to split or arrives at the number of "splits" dictated by analysts for theoretical or strategic reasons. In practical terms, network analysts who would like to partition a dark network into two sets will have the data split one time, while those who want four sets of actors will have their data split twice, and so on. Each of these sets will contain a different threshold of structurally equivalent actors.

UCINET currently includes two CONCOR algorithms: (1) the classic approach, where analysts indicate the number of splits and (2) an interactive version, where analysts can exert some control over how many splits there should be and where they should occur. Both algorithms provide a measure of fit (R^2) that compares the densities of the partitioned data matrix with an ideally structured one (where cell densities equal block means) that contains the same number of blocks.[6] In general, a higher R^2 indicates a better fit.

However, after every split, the R^2 almost invariably becomes higher. Thus, while it can serve as a guide for determining how many blocks we should partition the network into, we should also be guided by theory and strategic concerns. In other words, if the CONCOR produced its highest R^2 when the network was split into 17 blocks (i.e., the number of actors in the network), that would not be terribly helpful, and we would probably want to rely on another "metric" for determining the ideal number of blocks.

Using the interactive CONCOR algorithm, we once again partitioned the network into five blocks, but as Figure 8.9 indicates, block membership differs somewhat from that identified using Euclidean distance. Samudra is still the only member of his block, but Feri is now assigned to the same block as Muklas and Idris, who previously had been assigned to the block that includes Imron, Dulmatin, Azahari, Patek, Ghoni, and Sarijo. Figure 8.10 presents a slightly different story from the one presented in Figure 8.8. Once again, Samudra (this time assigned to the fourth block) is in a position of brokerage, but the brokerage is now between members of block 5 (Arnasan, Rauf, Octavia, Hidayat, Jenaedi) and the other three blocks. The primary difference lies in the fact that Samudra no longer is the sole broker between blocks 1, 2, and 3. All three possess alternative pathways to deal directly with one another. In other words, while the earlier Euclidean distance analysis suggested that

		1 M	6 I	16 F	3 I	5 D	8 A	15 P	9 G	17 S	2 A	7 M	4 S	10 A	14 J	11 R	12 O	13 H
1	Muklas		1		1	1	1	1	1	1	1		1					
6	Idris	1			1	1	1	1	1	1	1	1	1					
16	Feri				1	1	1	1	1	1								
3	Imron	1	1	1		1	1	1	1	1			1					
5	Dulmatin	1	1		1		1			1			1					
8	Azahari	1	1	1	1	1		1	1	1			1					
15	Patek	1	1	1	1	1	1		1	1			1					
9	Ghoni	1	1	1	1	1	1	1		1			1					
17	Sarijo	1	1	1	1	1	1	1	1				1					
2	Amrozi	1	1									1	1					
7	Mubarok		1								1		1					
4	Samudra	1	1		1	1	1	1	1	1	1	1		1	1	1	1	1
10	Arnasan												1		1	1	1	1
14	Junaedi												1	1		1	1	1
11	Rauf												1	1	1		1	1
12	Octavia												1	1	1	1		1
13	Hidayat												1	1	1	1	1	

Figure 8.9 Permuted Koschade Bali I Network (CONCOR)

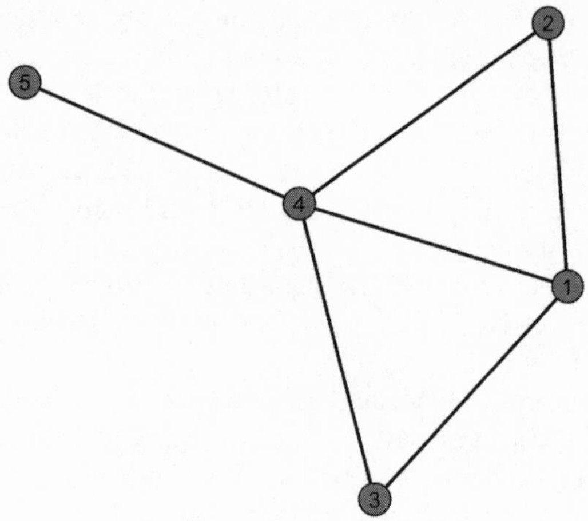

Figure 8.10 Graph of Final Image Matrix (CONCOR)

Samudra was the broker between all groups within the network, the CONCOR algorithm suggests that his brokerage potential is more limited.

Optimization

In network optimization, analysts indicate the number of blocks into which they wish to assign the network's actors. Next, the optimization algorithm randomly sorts actors into blocks and calculates an initial badness of fit score that is based on a comparison between the current model and an ideal model. The algorithm continues to sort actors into blocks until it determines a partition of actors that minimizes the badness of fit score.[7] As the name indicates, the lower the badness of fit score, the better. Recall that in the ideal example of structural equivalence, all possible ties are expected to be present in complete blocks and no ties should be present in a null block. Consequently, with this approach, an error is considered to occur when a tie is present in a null block or one is missing tie in a complete block.

Optimization, like the other equivalence algorithms, indicates the blocks to which each actor is assigned, it provides a permuted adjacency matrix, and it displays a density table. It also generates a partition that allows for the blockmodel visualization of a permuted network (Figure 8.11), a final image matrix (not shown), and a graph of the final image matrix (Figure 8.12). Using the optimization algorithm, we identified six (rather than five) blocks in the Koschade Bali I network. Seven blocks actually yielded a slightly lower error score (from 5 to 4), but it also detached Dulmatin from the group that includes Ghoni, Azahari, Imron, Sarijo, and Patek for the simple reason that Dulmatin

		4 S	7 M	2 A	9 G	5 D	8 A	3 I	17 S	15 P	6 I	1 M	16 F	10 A	14 J	11 R	12 O	13 H
4	Samudra		1	1	1	1	1	1	1	1	1	1		1	1	1	1	1
7	Mubarok	1		1							1							
2	Amrozi	1	1								1	1						
9	Ghoni	1				1	1	1	1	1	1	1	1					
5	Dulmatin	1					1	1	1		1	1						
8	Azahari	1			1	1		1	1	1	1	1	1					
3	Imron	1			1	1	1		1	1	1	1	1					
17	Sarijo	1			1	1	1	1		1	1	1	1					
15	Patek	1			1	1	1	1	1		1	1	1					
6	Idris	1	1	1	1	1	1	1	1	1		1						
1	Muklas	1		1	1	1	1	1	1	1	1							
16	Feri				1	1	1	1	1	1								
10	Arnasan	1													1	1	1	1
14	Junaedi	1												1		1	1	1
11	Rauf	1												1	1		1	1
12	Octavia	1												1	1	1		1
13	Hidayat	1												1	1	1	1	

Figure 8.11 Permuted Koschade Bali I Network (Optimization)

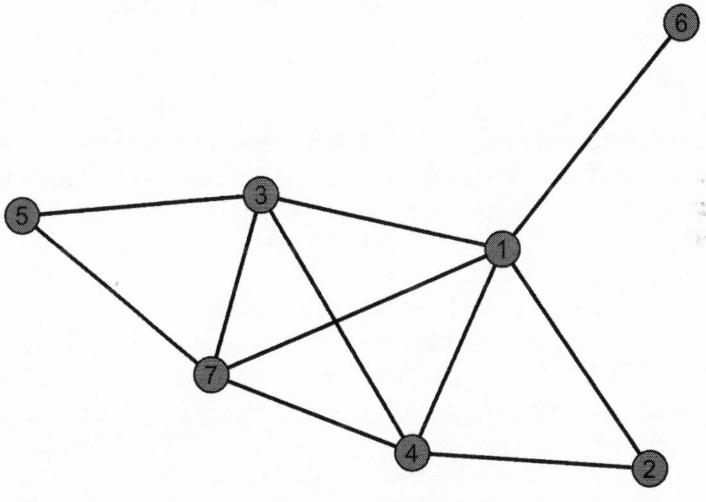

Figure 8.12 Graph of Final Image Matrix (Optimization)

does not have a tie with Patek. Thus, we decided that six blocks made more sense than seven (and the error score of six improved substantially on the error score for five—from 11 to 5).

The graph derived from the final image matrix (Figure 8.12) tells a somewhat more complicated story than the graph in Figure 8.10. Samudra (Block 1 here Figure 8.11) is still in a position of brokerage, but now there appears to be a core set of blocks (3, 4, and 7) that are tied with Samudra and each other, while two other blocks (block 2, which includes Mubarok and Amrozi, and block 5, which only includes Feri) are presented as being somewhat on the margins.

While it can be very difficult to judge which blockmodel is ideal for this network, it is safe to conclude that Arnasan, Junaedi, Rauf, Octavia, and Hidayat together constitute a block, and Samudra functions as broker between their block and the rest of the group. The Euclidean distance and optimization algorithms suggest that Feri lies on the margins of the network, while the CONCOR and optimization algorithms suggest the same of Mubarok and Amrozi. Thus, perhaps we can tentatively conclude that Samudra lies between two main groups: (1) Arnasan, Junaedi, Rauf, Octavia, and Hidayat, on the one hand, and (2) Ghoni, Dulmatin, Azahari, Imron, Sarijo, Patek, Idris, and Muklas, on the other, while (3) Feri, Mubarok, and Amrozi lie on the network's margins, albeit on opposite sides.

Summary

Thus far, we have illustrated three different structural equivalence algorithms along with the corresponding methods for permuting the original network as per a structurally equivalent partition, creating a final image matrix, and a graph of a final image matrix. Generally speaking, the three approaches produced similar results in regard to Koschade's Bali I network. All three suggest Samudra is a somewhat unique actor in the network, and we also saw that certain sets of actors, such as Arnasan, Junaedi, Rauf, Octavia, and Hidayat, were consistently members of the same block, and therefore are substitutable for one another. These results should ease the minds of those new to this topic and those who feel somewhat overwhelmed by the process of selecting a method for identifying structurally equivalent actors.

As we saw, structural equivalence is the most restrictive approach to identifying equivalent actors, which is why we used overall network density for identifying one (complete) and zero blocks. Although structural equivalence is technically a positional approach, the results it produced are not too terribly different from some of the clustering algorithms we employed in chapter 5. Indeed, Borgatti and Everett (1992) have argued that structural equivalence is really another form of clustering (i.e., subgroup analysis) based on position rather than cohesion. They note that structurally equivalent actors are always completely contained within the same component and are never more than two ties apart. As a consequence, they and others have argued on behalf of more relaxed definitions of equivalence, which they believe possess somewhat more realistic measures of what it means for two actors to be regarded as "equivalent" or "structurally similar" (see e.g., Borgatti and Everett 1992;

Faust 1988; Wasserman and Faust 1994). Automorphic equivalence is one such approach; regular equivalence is another. We begin with the former before moving to the latter.

8.3 AUTOMORPHIC EQUIVALENCE

To illustrate automorphic equivalence (and regular equivalence after it), we turn to a more complicated network: the 91 Afghan tribes connected by their kinship ties (Figure 8.13). Unlike the previous section, we will not illustrate every different type of automorphic equivalence algorithm. This is not because we think structural equivalence superior to automorphic equivalence. Quite the contrary, it is because the process of identifying equivalent actors using automorphic equivalence algorithms is similar to that of structural equivalence algorithms. Thus, to illustrate each one is not only unnecessary but also potentially tedious. We will exercise the same restraint when illustrating regular equivalence in the section below.

Automorphic equivalence is essentially a relaxation of the approach used in structural equivalence. Rather than require that equivalent actors possess identical ties to identical alters, equivalencies (roles) are instead based on

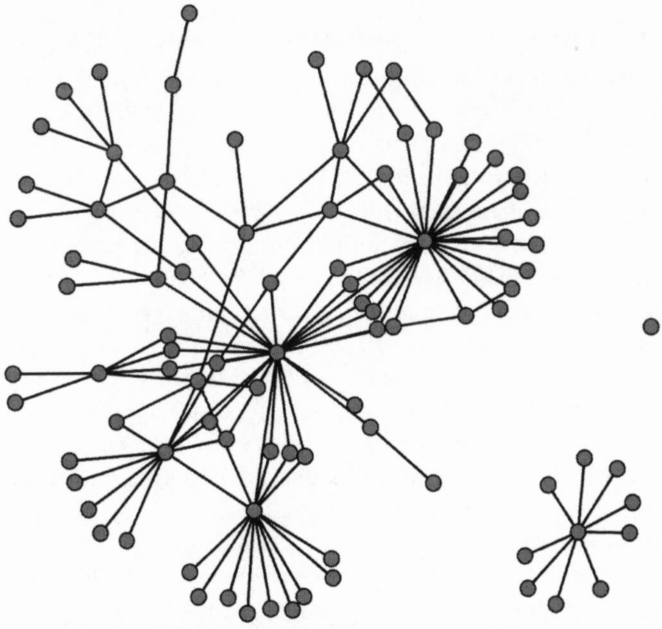

Figure 8.13 Afghan Tribes Kinship Network

that idea that identical patterns may be used to identify equivalent roles. The name of the approach comes from the idea of isomorphism, which in graph theory refers to a one-to-one mapping of one set of objects on to another such that the relationships between the objects are preserved (Borgatti and Everett 1992:11). Networks that are isomorphic are identical across all of their graph theoretic attributes (e.g., density, centralization, and number of cliques) and they only differ in terms of actor and edge labels. Automorphism, on the other hand, refers to the mapping of a graph onto itself. Actors and actor sets are, therefore, considered to be automorphically equivalent if they occupy indistinguishable positions within the same network. For example, two insurgent subcommanders are automorphically equivalent if they command the same number of guerrillas—although not necessarily the same individuals—and are in turn commanded by the same number of people—although, again, not necessarily the same people—in identical structural positions.

UCINET implements three automorphic equivalence algorithms. One (all permutations) literally compares every possible swapping of actors (i.e., all permutations) in its search for automorphisms. Doing so, however, is computationally intense, making this approach practical only when used with small networks, so we will not use it here. A second option is an automorphic optimization algorithm similar to the one we used for structural equivalence above. After analysts indicate the number of blocks or classes into which they want to partition the network, the algorithm randomly sorts actors into blocks until it finds a partition that minimizes the badness of fit score. Like factional analysis, analysts will generally need to examine a range of possible block sets—unless one has information or a prior theory in mind to dictate such a number—to determine which provides the best measure of fit. It may be apparent that, with a relatively large network, this can become a time-consuming process, which is why it is best to be guided by an a priori understanding of approximately how many blocks there should be. When we applied this algorithm to the kinship network, it consistently sorted most of the tribes to a single block (including those that were disconnected from the main component), and then, depending on how many blocks were sought, it sorted the remaining tribes to separate blocks consisting of single tribes. In other words, when we specified two blocks, the automorphic optimization algorithm assigned 90 tribes to a single block and the remaining tribe to its own block; when we specified three blocks, it assigned 89 tribes to a single block and the remaining two tribes to two separate blocks; and so on. Thus, optimization does not appear to work well with the kinship network.

Another option to consider is using the Euclidean distance between actors to estimate the degree of automorphic equivalence for each pair of actors. The Euclidean distance approach begins with a reciprocal distance matrix for binary data, or a tie strength matrix for valued data, and calculates the distance between all pairs of actors. Actors with similar distance profiles are treated as possessing greater automorphic equivalence. Like the structural equivalence version, Euclidean distance generates an equivalence (distance) matrix and an equivalence partition. When applied to the Afghan Tribal Kinship network, it identified 37 potential partition structures for the network, ranging from perfect automorphic equivalence to a partition in which each tribe has its own partition. Since we are not guided by a theory at this point, we choose the middle partition in order to create the final image matrix (blockmodel). It consists of 19 blocks of tribes, most of which are tied directly or indirectly to one another. Figure 8.14 presents the graph of the final image matrix of the Afghan Tribes Kinship network. Note that the tribal network appears to be split into two or three clusters of blocks with blocks 19 and 4 acting as brokers between them. In both cases, the blocks consist of a single tribe: Zirak (block 19) and Durrani (block 4).

On a technical note, analysts should resist the urge to refer to actors from different networks as being automorphically equivalent. The term "automorphic equivalence" is reserved only for use with equivalence that is present

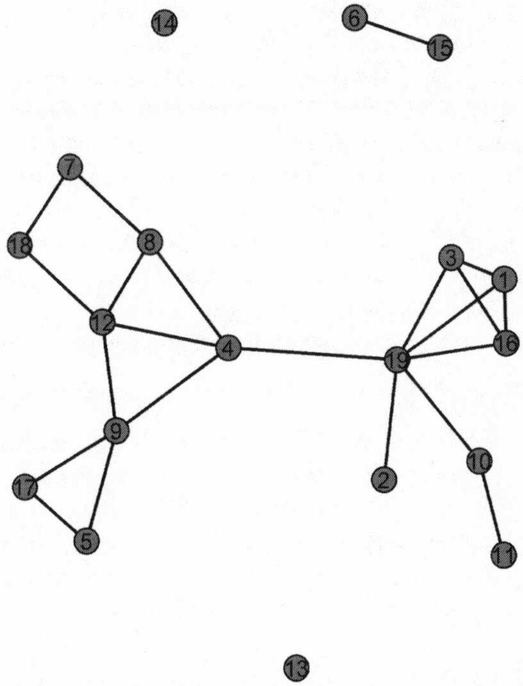

Figure 8.14 Afghan Tribes Kinship Network (Automorphic Equivalence)

within a network. Although it is possible for actors from different networks to occupy indistinguishable positions that form of equivalence is more properly referred to as *isomorphic equivalence*. Consider, for example, the network of relations in the Afghan Taliban as distinct from the Pakistani Taliban, then you would say commanders in the two organizations were isomorphically equivalent if they commanded the same number of fighters, were commanded by the same number of people, and have the same number of colleagues (i.e., other commanders).

8.4 REGULAR EQUIVALENCE

Conceptualizing equivalence in terms of regularity in patterns of ties provides that broadest and most forgiving of the three definitions. In practice, this approach may produce many more partitions that either structural or automorphic equivalencies will tend to reveal. For this reason, when using regular equivalence to determine equivalencies between actors in a network, it is good practice to select the partition that assigns actors into the fewest number of meaningful equivalence classes. This practice is referred to as seeking maximal regular equivalence. For a class of actors to be considered regular, the actors within the class must have identical ties to and from other regularly equivalent actors (Borgatti and Everett 1989; White and Reitz 1983).

The original regular equivalence algorithm (REGE) was developed by Douglas White and Karl Reitz (White 1985; White and Reitz 1983) for use with valued continuous data. REGE uses an iterative optimization approach to first measure similarities between actor pairs according to similarities in the value of their ties to their alters (in terms of the absolute difference of the magnitude of their ties). The network is then optimized according to the match score and the weighted optimized measure is then summed for each actor's neighborhood and normalized. The entire process is then repeated for all actor pairs for a given number of iterations, with successive similarity scores being weighted according to the results of prior iterations (Borgatti, Everett, and Freeman 2002a).

Because REGE was designed only for use with valued data, a generalized version of the algorithm was developed for use with binary data (Borgatti and Everett 1989; Borgatti and Everett 1993). The categorical REGE (CATREGE) algorithm is recommended. It also uses an iterative optimization approach, but in a manner that is more suitable to undirected data. The algorithm first assigns actors into one of three classifications—sinks, sources, or repeaters. Next, actor classifications are adjusted according to whether their neighborhoods match. In the case of neighborhoods, differences are measured in terms of how many of each actor type are present. The entire process repeats, with actor classifications being based upon the results of the prior iteration, and terminates once a stable solution is reached (Borgatti, Everett and Freeman 2002a).

The problem that remains for dark network analysts is that the CATREGE algorithm is not well suited for undirected data. When analyzing undirected networks, maximal regular equivalence results in a single block—not including disconnected clusters and isolates—that includes all actors (Borgatti 1988; Doreian 1987; Wasserman and Faust 1994). This is due to the fact that, in undirected networks, all actors are tied to some other actor that is also in the same equivalence class. This has led analysts to think in terms of "neighborhoods" to develop methods for identifying meaningful classes of regularly equivalent actors (Everett, Boyd and Borgatti 1990). The solution, in practice, is for the network data either to be first converted to geodesic distances (Borgatti, Everett and Freeman 2002a) or to create a seed partition (Butts 2014, 2015) for undirected data to be analyzed with CATREGE. This latter approach is similarly replicated in the "regular equivalence optimization" approach to assigning actors to equivalence groups. The optimization algorithm operates in a manner similar to the structural and automorphic equivalence optimization algorithms. It requires the analyst to specify the number of desired equivalency groups, and then randomly assigns actors in a network to the groups before sorting them into an optimal representation. Regularity within a group is determined as there being at least one "1" in either every column, or in every row within a block. Ideally, blocks should be either regular, or zero blocks and optimization will continue until a parsimonious solution is achieved for the data provided.

For an example of regular equivalence, consider again the Afghan Tribal Kinship network. After extracting the main component, UCINET's categorical regular equivalence algorithm (CATREGE) identified eight partitions of regularly equivalent actors in the kinship network. Here we chose a partition that resulted in the fewest number of blocks but still assigned the Durrani and Zirak tribes to separate (and individual) blocks. Figure 8.15 presents the graph of the final image matrix of the Afghan Tribes Kinship network using regular equivalence. The regular equivalencies derived through the CATREGE algorithm present a very different conceptualization of the relationships between the various blocks of tribes. Neither the Durrani (block 8) nor the Zirak (block 15) tribes appear to be in positions of brokerage, at least not to the extent that was apparent in the analysis using automorphic equivalence. Instead, it is the Ghilzai tribe (block 9) that appears to enjoy brokerage potential. So, what can we conclude? At this point, it is difficult to draw any definitive conclusion. It would not be surprising to learn that the Durrani, Zirak, and Ghilzai all possess brokerage power within the Afghan Tribal network. But the suspicion should be confirmed.

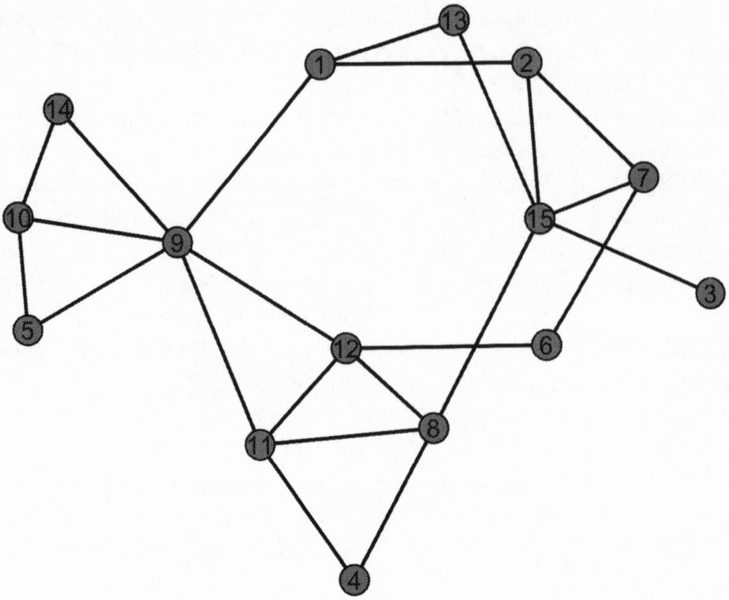

Figure 8.15 Graph of Final Image Matrix, Afghan Tribes Kinship Network (Regular Equivalence)

It should be apparent at this point that prior information is critical to performing analysis in terms of actor equivalencies. Ultimately, what analysts need to bring to the table when using techniques such as blockmodeling are hypotheses about how many blocks there are and what types of blockmodels best capture the network under examination. This is especially true when using blockmodeling techniques with large networks. Otherwise, you can end up simply trying one partition after another until one "appears" to fit better than the others.

8.5 SUMMARY: LESSONS LEARNED

In this chapter we have explored three conceptualizations that may be applied for identifying actors holding similar positions in a network and sorting them into distinct classes or blocks: structural, automorphic (isomorphic), and regular equivalence. As we saw, structural equivalence is a very restrictive understanding of equivalence, but it is often the easiest for new network analysts to internalize. Actors who are tied to the same exact actors are substitutable for one another. The three methods discussed in this chapter to identify this type of equivalent actors were Euclidian distance, CONCOR, and Optimization. Seldom do two or more actors have exactly the same relationships to all other actors, however, which is why many analysts use a threshold or cutoff to determine the blocks to which each actor belongs and the ties that exist between them.

Several researchers have argued on behalf of more generalized or relaxed definitions of equivalence, in particular, automorphic and regular equivalence. With automorphic equivalence, actors are considered equivalent if they can be mapped on to one another, meaning that they are connected to the same number of actors and those actors are in identical structural positions within the same network. Network analysts can draw from the All Permutations, the Optimization, and the Euclidean distance options to group automorphic equivalent actors. With regular equivalence, actors are considered to be equivalent if they are connected to actors in the same classes. Analysts can use methods, such as the REGE, CATREGE, and regular equivalency optimization procedures, to identify regularly equivalent actors. Table 8.1 summarize the approaches discussed in this chapter.

The three broader approaches are nested within one another in terms of strictness. That is, structurally equivalent actors (i.e., actors with ties to the same exact other actors) are also automorphically (i.e., mappable onto one another) and regularly (i.e., connected to actors in same class) equivalent with one another, and automorphically equivalent actors are also regularly equivalent with one another. The reverse is not true, however. Regular equivalent actors are not necessarily automorphically or structurally equivalent with one another, and automorphically equivalent actors are not necessarily structurally equivalent with one another. One approach to blockmodeling that we have not considered in this chapter is generalized blockmodeling, as developed by Patrick Doreian, Vladimir Batagelj, and Anuska Ferligoj. It allows analysts to specify a specific combination of block types for a given network and use either optimization, or random ordering to fit actors to the blocks (see de Nooy, Mrvar and Batagelj 2011; Doreian, Batagelj and Ferligoj 2005). Generalized blockmodeling, which is likely to prove useful for analysts looking at dark networks, is not discussed here because the basics of the positional approach are intensive and they have yet to be adopted by many analysts in the area of dark networks.

What should be clear is that, in many ways, blockmodeling is more art than science. As we saw, the various algorithms, even within a particular type of equivalence, can produce very different results. Thus, we strongly recommend that analysts operate with some sort of theory or hypothesis in mind as to how many blocks there are and what types of equivalence best captures the network under examination. Alternatively, analysts may begin with an actor or set of actors of interest about whom they want to identify similar, or substitutable, actors within the bounds of a strategic approach.

Still others may want to see how blocks of actors are tied to one another to get a different view of the network.[8] Regardless of the approach, positional approaches can provide unique views into dark networks that cannot be seen using relational approaches. Ultimately, however, they are most valuable when used in conjunction with prior research and knowledge in and of the network.

8.6 QUESTIONS

1. Positional approaches differ from relational approaches in that rather than focusing on the ties between actors, they seek to identify actors who hold similar structural positions—or simply positions—within a network.
   a. True.
   b. False.
2. Structurally equivalent actors are actors that hold similar positions within a network.
   a. True.
   b. False.
3. Which of the following are types of equivalent actors?
   a. Automorphic.
   b. Topographic.
   c. Regular.
   d. Structural.
4. Which is the most restrictive approach to understanding equivalence?
   a. Automorphic.
   b. Structural.
   c. Regular.
   d. Euclidean Distance.
5. REGE and CATREGE are examples of which type of equivalence approach?
   a. Automorphic.
   b. Structural.
   c. Isomorphic.
   d. Regular.
6. Structurally equivalent actors (i.e., actors with ties to the same exact other actors) are also automorphically (i.e., mappable onto one another) and regularly (i.e., connected to actors in same class) equivalent with one another.
   a. True.
   b. False.

8.7 ANSWERS

1. True.
2. True.
3. Automorphic (a); Regular (c); Structural (d).
4. Structural (b).
5. Regular (d).
6. True.

8.8 FURTHER READING

The classic article on blockmodeling is Harrison C. White, Scott A. Boorman, and Ronald Breiger's 1976 article "Social Structure from Multiple Networks I: Blockmodels of Roles and Positions" (*American Journal of Sociology* 81: 730–80). It is long and dense but worth it. Wasserman and Faust provide an excellent introduction in Chapters 9, 10, and 12 in their book *Social Network Analysis: Methods and Applications* (Cambridge, UK: Cambridge University Press, 1994). The discussion by Borgatti et al. in Chapter 12 in their book *Analyzing Social Networks* (Thousand Oaks, CA: SAGE Publishing, 2013) is also quite helpful.

As noted above, we did not explore the generalized blockmodeling approach advocated by Patrick Doreian, Vladimir Batagelj, and Anuska Ferligoj in *Generalized Blockmodeling* (New York and Cambridge: Cambridge University Press, 2005), which allows analysts to specify a specific combination of block types for a given network and use either optimization, or random ordering to fit actors to the blocks. Before jumping into this book, however, readers may first want to read the overview of generalized blockmodeling found on pp. 324–25 (Chapter 12) of Wouter de Nooy, Wouter, Andrej Mrvar, and Vladimir Batagelj, *Exploratory Social Network Analysis with Pajek* (Cambridge, UK: Cambridge University Press, 2011). Finally, readers may want to consider the following readings:

- Vladimir Batagelj. 1997. "Notes on Blockmodeling." *Social Networks* 19:143–55.
- Stephen P. Borgatti and Martin G. Everett. 1989. "The Class of All Regular Equivalences: Algebraic Structure and Computation." *Social Networks* 11:65–88.
- Anuska Ferligoj, Patrick Doreian, and Vladimir Batagelj. 2011. "Positions and Roles." Pp. 434–46 in *The SAGE Handbook of Social Network Analysis*, edited by John Scott and Peter J. Carrington. Los Angeles and London: SAGE Publications.

- Christina Prell. 2011. Pp. 175–96 (Chapter 9) in *Social Network Analysis: History, Theory & Methodology*. London and Thousand Oaks, CA: SAGE Publications.
- John Scott. 2013. Pp. 99–120 (Chapter 7) in *Social Network Analysis*. London and Thousand Oaks, CA: SAGE Publication.

NOTES

1. Of course, positional approaches are still relational, in that an actor's position in a network is a function of the network's patterns of ties, but here the emphasis is more on network position, what we earlier referred to as structural location, than to which actors a particular actor is tied.

2. We saw how to collapse networks back in chapter 3 (section 3.9). There we collapsed the network based on shared attribute (logistical function). Here, we would collapse the network based on shared block assignment. Another approach is to use various regression techniques (see next chapter) to test whether membership in one block leads to better outcomes than membership in another.

3. The reverse is not true, however. "Actors who are indistinguishable on absolutely all graph-theoretic attributes are not necessarily structurally equivalent" (Borgatti and Everett 1992:7).

4. Close observers will note that along the diagonal the similarity scores are also 0.00, which makes complete sense since actors are always perfectly similar with themselves.

5. Recall that correlation coefficients range from −1.00 to 1.00, where −1.00 indicates perfect negative correlation and 1.00 indicates perfect positive correlation. If two actors share an identical pattern of ties (i.e., they are tied to the same actors), their correlation will be 1.00; if two actors have exactly opposite ties to other actors, their correlation will be −1.00; and if two actors' ties indicate neither a positive nor a negative association, their correlation will be 0.00.

6. R^2 is shorthand for the "coefficient of determination." It is an estimation of the extent to which a model's variables account for the variation in the dependent variable.

7. This approach provides the analyst with an option of using either valued or binary data. We will continue to use binary data here so that the results are comparable to the results we got above.

8. Unfortunately, most of these algorithms are not available in many of the more commonly used programs, which means the choice of an approach will be often driven by an analyst's choice of an analytic program.

Part III

CONFIRMATORY SOCIAL NETWORK ANALYSIS

Chapter 9

Digging Deeper and Testing Hypotheses

Statistical techniques hold the potential to greatly enhance the depth and validity of analytic work. Thus far, we have focused on using network analysis for the purpose of discovery. In so doing, we have covered techniques to describe networks, to break them down into separate communities and role sets, and to identify key actors. All of these techniques hold strong potential to uncover facets of a network that may be important or at least useful to a larger intervention, disruption, or information collection process. But despite the rigor and focus on validity upon which many of these procedures are based, it is still very important to seek an unbiased assessment and reduce the effect of our own biases. It can also be very helpful to have a tool that helps to complete a story, test suspicions, make predictions, or explain outcomes. Given the various advantages that statistical techniques offer, it is surprising that people are often hesitant to apply them. This chapter, along with the next two, introduces statistical tools that analysts working in the area of dark networks should strongly consider.

A major factor that brings new analysts to network analysis is the intuitive nature of networks themselves. Everyone has had experience with networks in one form or another. Networks, and social networks in particular, are concepts that have entered the public consciousness across the globe and many experience the concepts around interconnectedness and how networks function on an intuitive level. However, it is this sense of familiarity and intuition that can be a source of some notably problematic tendencies for social network analysts. Humans are incredibly well equipped to detect patterns, oftentimes where none even exist (Shermer 2008). Although this pattern-matching skill serves us well in hostile environments, where quick decisions are necessary, it can be somewhat less helpful when it clouds an analysis. When we begin to suspect that a relationship exists between two events or other factors, we will frequently rationalize or search out more information to bolster that belief, rather than investigate how plausible the relationship actually is (Stanovich 2007). Without some method of verification, such as statistical tests, there is little to prevent analysts from uncritically accepting what, at first blush, may appear to be genuine patterns.

An additional complication for conducting statistical analyses of networks is the difficulty inherent in establishing how the various factors—structure, substructures, social pressures, actor attributes—relate to one another or to the creation of ties within a network. As with any other artifact of human interaction, networks are the product of complex interrelations that, in turn, merit further investigation. While it is often possible to find evidence in support of a suspicion or theory, we should verify the evidence as well. We, therefore, *very strongly suggest* that analysts test such suspicions, theories, measures, or apparent associations in order to discover whether their evidence constitutes a (statistically) significant finding, or a spurious result (i.e., it is something that could just as easily have happened at random in a similar network). Although statistical tools themselves are fallible, they do a much better job of unbiased estimation than we can manage on our own. Their power resides in the process of falsification through hypothesis testing. Hypothesis testing, and the methods outlined below, allows network analysts to produce stronger work and help them to convince others through the increased plausibility that these tests tend to imply.

With that in mind, this chapter discusses some basics of hypothesis testing and sets the groundwork for several types of explanatory analyses that will be discussed in subsequent chapters. It begins with a general explanation about what hypothesis testing is and what it does. It then provides some general guidelines for developing hypotheses to examine dark networks, including considerations regarding cause-and-effect relationships. This chapter then illustrates two broad approaches for testing hypotheses, namely, Quadratic Assignment Procedure (QAP) and Conditional Uniform Graphs (CUGs). Overall, this chapter is relatively nontechnical and focuses instead on the concept of hypothesis testing, its role in dark network analysis, and some information regarding how it may be applied.

9.1 DEVELOPING AND TESTING WORKING HYPOTHESES

Theoretical considerations should drive the development of research questions that lead to hypotheses (see chapter 2). The manner in which one develops these expectations, however, will likely depend on the nature of their work. Researchers and academics typically develop them through the process of conducting thorough reviews of available literature to leverage theories and background information about dark networks, similar situations, and any other pertinent factors. Practitioners, on the other hand, will often rely on different approaches, given the constraints they face (e.g., the time to conduct an analysis).[1] The previous eight chapters have described several techniques to explore, and subsequently describe, dark networks of interest. These approaches, however useful they may be, are limited in at least two important ways. First, they cannot establish *causal* relationships among variables of interest when using descriptive techniques alone (see section 9.4). For example, social network analysts cannot (and should not) state that certain relationships (e.g., communication and kinship) predict others (e.g., trust relations) without testing their hypothesis. Second, additional relational and nonrelational (i.e., attributes) factors may be at play for which analysts need to account. In other words, analysts should consider and simultaneously test several plausible effects to better understand network phenomena. That being said, a combination of these two approaches can be ideal for the opportunity that multiple viewpoints provide to account for a range of theories, and different points of view.

The Importance of Hypotheses

Dark network analysts should make hypothesis testing a consistent element of their analytic practice for several reasons. The first is that hypothesis testing allows us to simultaneously test several theories regarding dark network structures and outcomes. Several scholars, for example, have tested hypotheses regarding tie formation in dark networks using methods discussed in subsequent chapters. One example is Papachristos, Hureau, and Braga's (2013) study that utilized exponential random graph models (ERGMs) to test several potential influences regarding gun violence among gangs in Boston and Chicago. These researchers found that while spatial proximity is a predictor of shootings among gangs, prior network connections defined by intergang conflict have a larger effect on the probability of a shooting. Cunningham, Everton, and Murphy's (2015) study used a different approach, namely, stochastic actor-oriented models (SAOMs), to examine stochastic processes that led to tie formation in Noordin Top's network. The study, which tested a handful of hypotheses regarding tie formation in dark networks, found that, among other things, strong ties and certain inter- and intra-organizational dynamics played important roles in tie formation among the network's actors. The important thing to note here is that in both studies—and there are certainly many more examples—the authors drew from a range of theories about tie formation in dark networks. The next two chapters will discuss these explanatory methods in detail.

A second reason for adopting of hypothesis testing is because it allows us to test our assumptions about the nature of dark networks. For example, suppose for a moment that evidence that we accumulate during the process of exploratory analyses leads us to expect that central actors in a dark network appear to have higher levels of education, and subsequent investigation reveals no other alternative explanations. In such a situation, however, we should not stop there. We should instead use a different set of analytic tools—such as statistical tests—to explore whether other characteristics, such as military training in a foreign country or an actor's nationality, may also account for actors' centrality in the network. Or, using some of the techniques discussed in chapter 5, we may observe what appears to be clustering in a network. We do not know, however, whether the pattern that the clustering techniques identified could just be spurious—that is, the pattern may just as well have appeared by random chance—rather than through the interactions of that particular group. Just as with people and patterns, the algorithms designed to detect subgroups will find clusters most of the time, even when they do not exist. It is therefore important to rule out whether we consider the identified clusters to be meaningful.

A third reason is that the results from testing hypotheses are more likely to convince others and lend credence to what one is presenting. Statistical testing permits analysts to have greater confidence in their results. The processes—and even the conceptualizations—involved in the "testing" paradigm may also help to reduce analysts' tendency to seek out results that support their established views about a network (i.e., confirmation bias), compelling them instead to consider other factors and points of view regarding the topic at hand. By no means is this to suggest that results derived from statistical analyses produce objective "truth." We need to remember that algorithms, even SNA algorithms, are not entirely objective (i.e., someone, after all, had to develop them), and we can still derive inappropriate or biased conclusions during the interpretation phase of our analysis. That being said, hypothesis testing is simply a more critical approach than relying solely on the exploratory measures discussed in the first eight chapters. Hypothesis tests can bolster analysts' claims to validity, help them to rule out the possibility that their findings are more due to chance than structure, and help them to more deeply explore what makes a particular network take the form that it does.

Constructing Hypotheses

Hypotheses are explicit, falsifiable statements about relationships between variables (Kerlinger and Lee 2000). When used well, they can help to clarify research aims and drive further work. The explicit nature of hypothesis statements forces us to consider precisely what we are seeking to discover. The logic behind what makes hypotheses powerful, however, is the concept of falsifiability. Whereas most of this book has been concerned with describing networks and building a body of proof for further conjecture, hypothesis testing takes the opposite tack. It requires that analysts *attempt to disprove* what they have found. If they fail in their attempt, then they can have far more confidence when presenting their claim. This is the essential mechanism that makes statistical techniques powerful: By failing to disprove a hypothesis, then supporting or drawing inference from it becomes a much more straightforward task.

The way in which one presents hypotheses can take several forms, depending on the nature of the researcher's prediction. Researchers can develop alternative—directional or nondirectional—hypotheses or they can state a null hypothesis (Creswell 2014). For the sake of simplicity, we will forego a deep discussion on the nature and variety of directional hypotheses. However, analysts who are unfamiliar with such ideas are encouraged to explore their options further, as they continue to employ statistical methods in their work. Most any introductory statistics text or website should provide fair coverage of directional hypotheses. Without experience in using hypothesis tests, it is often better to begin by simply employing nondirectional hypotheses. Nondirectional hypotheses simply predict the presence of a relationship among variables but with no assumption of the *direction* that such a relationship between variables may take. So, while we may hypothesize about the presence of a relationship, we do not include the expectation of how the relationship functions as a part of that hypothesis. The manner in which the relationship functions will be available in the test output in any case, and should be included in the interpretation if it is not in the hypothesis itself.

The *null hypothesis* is often implicit in a hypothesis statement, though it is *the version of a hypothesis statement that is actually tested* when conducting a statistical test. The null hypothesis—or just "null"—is essentially a claim that no relationship exists between the variables of interest. Think of the null as a naysayer. Any statistical test will be conducted with the sole purpose of testing the null, rather than the hypothesis itself. In other words, we test whether the evidence at hand is sufficient to silence the naysayer. If the test results *fail to reject* the null, then we do not possess sufficient evidence to conclude that a relationship exists. On the other hand, if the test results do reject the null, then we are free to conclude that the evidence supports the actual hypothesis. We can then use the test output and descriptive information about the variables to expound on the direction, magnitude, or implications of the finding. Some advanced analysts may not formally state their hypotheses, but they are using them nonetheless. Statistical tests and hypotheses are simply indivisible.

Consider, for example, a team of analysts that has an interest in identifying factors that lead individuals to join terrorist groups in a certain region, Region X. Say, after consulting existing literature on the subject and consulting with subject matter experts, the team believes there is a higher probability that individuals with few economic opportunities (i.e., predictor or independent variable) will join a terrorist group (i.e., outcome or dependent variable) in that region than those with many opportunities. The examples below illustrate how the research team can state their hypothesis using the forms described above (adapted from Creswell 2014).

Hypothesis Example:

(Null hypothesis): An individual's economic opportunities in Region X are unrelated to the probability of them joining a terrorist group.

(Alternative—nondirectional hypothesis): An individual's economic opportunities in Region X are related to the probability of him or her joining a terrorist group.

Due to the inherent succinctness of hypothesis statements, the process of constructing them requires analysts to essentially deconstruct longer, more complex arguments into smaller, testable statements that address only one relationship at a time. This is an important time in which analysts must decide whether to include several other variables (i.e., additional hypotheses or control variables) to account for a wider set of possible explanations regarding the outcome (i.e., dependent) variable. Again, consider the example of economic opportunity and terrorism recruitment in Region X. Existing information about the topic could also suggest that individuals who received little education and grew up in religiously devoted households during their youth are more likely to join a terrorist group than those without such characteristics. In order to control for the possibility of these two additional factors, analysts investigating this scenario should construct two additional hypotheses: one regarding a possible relationship that might exist between education and joining terrorist groups, and one regarding the possible relationship that might exist between religious devotion and joining terrorist groups. Multiple hypotheses may dictate either multiple statistical tests or a more detailed multivariable model.

Testing Hypotheses

Once constructed, the hypotheses should serve as a guide for either collecting or assembling data appropriate to the tests that the statements imply. In the case of a researcher analyzing networks, those data will take the form of at least one network and data regarding the attributes of the actors in the network(s). Ultimately, the data chosen will depend largely upon the statistical test that analysts hope to conduct. But at minimum, analysts will require an independent (i.e., explanatory, predictor) and a dependent (i.e., outcome) variable. An independent variable is essentially information that is hypothesized to explain or predict changes in some outcome, and, correspondingly, a dependent variable is information that describes the outcome of interest. Networks can serve as independent, dependent, or in some cases, both (such as correlation tests and regressions). Attributes can be either converted into networks or used as independent variables in regressions or ANOVA models.

Although there are some special considerations and tools for running statistical models with network data, the general process is analogous to that of using classical statistics. As mentioned above, all statistical tests focus on whether there is sufficient evidence to reject the null hypothesis. Alternatively, if there is no sufficient evidence to *reject* the null, then analysts are obliged to *fail to reject* the null. The evidence that is most commonly used to test the null is referred to as the *p-value*. Although there are numerous alternative methods for conveying the same information, the *p*-value is one of the most intuitive. Some form of *p*-value is therefore produced for most statistical tests. For ease of interpretation, p-values can generally be thought of as *the probability that the null hypothesis is true*.[2] Most analysts will reject the null hypothesis if, and only if, the probability that it is true is exceptionally small. A probability (*p*-value) of 0.05 or less is conventionally used to indicate a sufficiently unlikely event as to justify rejecting the null.[3] And while there may be some contention around whether 0.05 is a valid cutoff (Ziliak and McCloskey 2008), it is the conventionally accepted criterion and thereby serves as a fair place to start for most analysts.

If the null is rejected, then analysts are free to accept the alternative (i.e., actual) hypothesis. They are also encouraged to interpret and discuss the meaningfulness of the output and its implications for the analysis, or for the network in general. Again, the interpretation of most statistical techniques for network analysis is not substantially different from what analysts may have experienced in using classical statistical techniques. Correlations and differences are interpreted as usual, and regression and logistic regression output are interpreted in much the same manner as with conventional parametric statistics, with the exception that their interpretation relates to network structure or formation. Where statistical testing for networks most profoundly diverges from classical techniques is in the assumptions that underlie how they are performed.

Classical parametric statistics are simply not valid for network data. Whereas parametric statistics are designed to use a relatively small, random sample of independent individuals to make a generalized inference about a population, network analysis is based on complete samples of interdependent actors, and network statistics can be generalized only to the network itself. Networks, by their nature, are comprised of interdependent, not independent actors. In network analysis terms, interdependencies are a feature, not a problem, and they are employed to capture the richness of how social interactions and interdependencies profoundly impact actor behavior. Additionally, the lack of independent observations constitutes an additional serious violation of parametric assumptions, although it is a moot point since there is no larger population to which we may generalize our findings. The benefit of working with a complete population generally means that statistics are not necessary for estimating the population's values on various network measures. The need for statistical models arises from the desire to investigate relationships in a network, or to rule out whether certain features of a network may just as easily have occurred in a network of similar structure or size.

Given that social network data are ill suited to standard parametric statistics, standard statistical models are not valid for testing hypotheses in networks. However, the need for statistical models remains. To overcome this limitation, statistical procedures have been developed to specifically account for the interdependencies of social network data and allow for statistical inference, namely permutation (or randomization) and simulation tests, which we will discuss in further detail in sections 9.2 and 9.3 when we discuss QAP and CUG techniques.

9.2 QUADRATIC ASSIGNMENT PROCEDURE (QAP)

As we stated above, the analysis of social network data differs from standard statistical models in several important ways. Thus, social network analysts cannot use standard approaches for testing hypotheses when analyzing social network data. One approach, known as the quadratic assignment procedure or QAP (Hubert and Schultz 1976; Krackhardt 1987b, 1988; Mantel 1967), was designed to overcome this limitation. The technique is similar to bootstrapping, in that it essentially builds its own distribution using network simulations that are based on the network being estimated. This particular simulation process is referred to as a permutation test, and it is designed to mimic all of the scenarios that would be possible if everyone were able to switch places in the social order. In other words, the names (and all their corresponding attributes) are shuffled randomly around the network without disturbing the underlying structure (See Figure 9.1 for an example of a permuted network). This random rearrangement is repeated to create thousands of simulated networks, which are then analyzed in the same manner as the original network in order to calculate a sampling distribution of statistical measures that can then be compared to the measures calculated for the observed (i.e., actual) network. The proportions of measures in the distribution that are greater than and less than the measure taken from the original network are then produced to give the "*p*-value"-type information. If the observed measure occurs

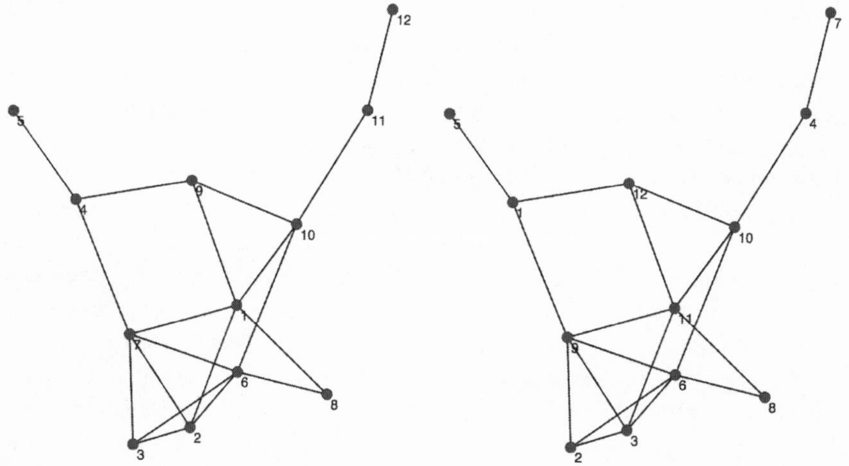

Figure 9.1 Two Permutations of the Same Network

sufficiently rarely ($p \leq 0.05$) within the distribution of simulated networks, then we can reject the null and conclude that the observed statistics are not likely to have occurred by random chance.

For example, when calculating the level of correlation between two networks, the first step is to compute the correlation coefficient between corresponding cells. Next, one of the networks is randomly permuted and the correlation is recalculated. This step is carried out hundreds or thousands of times in order to compute the proportion of times that a random measure is larger than or equal to the observed measure calculated in the first step. A low proportion suggests that a correlation between networks is unlikely to have occurred by chance and thus considered statistically significant.[4]

Take, for example, the Afghan Tribe Kinship network that we examined in the previous chapter. We first created two new networks, one based on whether two tribes shared the same ethnicity and the other on whether two tribes were members of the same block (we used the 19 block partition in the previous chapter that we created when investigating automorphic equivalence). The correlation between the two networks is positive (0.15) and statistically significant ($p < 0.001$), which suggests that the association between the two is unlikely to have occurred by random chance. However, since the correlation is not overwhelming (remember, correlation coefficients range between –1.00 and 1.00), our blockmodeling of the network in the previous chapter may need to be revisited, assuming, of course, that we believe that ethnicity is a factor in determining which tribes in the network are structurally equivalent.

A similar approach is used when regressing a dependent network on a series of independent networks. First, using standard multivariate regression techniques, the coefficients are estimated across the corresponding cells of the dependent and independent networks. Then, the dependent network is randomly permuted over thousands of iterations; and the regression coefficients are reestimated each time. As before, the proportion of estimates that are either greater than, or less than those generated in the first step are calculated. Once again, a if very low proportion (≤ 0.05) of estimates from the permutations are either greater or less than the original estimate, then the estimate is interpreted to be "significant" (e.g., not likely to have occurred by random chance). Finally, the same approach is used when calculating the correlation or regression of attribute data (e.g., centrality and education level). In the first step, a correlation or standard multivariate regression is estimated across corresponding values of the dependent and independent attributes; in the second, the elements of the dependent attribute data are randomly permuted numerous times, and the distribution of randomly generated results is compared to the actual results to see if the latter is likely to have occurred by random chance.[5]

For an illustration, consider the Noordin network. Assume that we want to determine whether certain types of network ties are good predictors of who participated in operations together. Also assume our contextual understanding of the network, based on qualitative analysis along with our intuition, suggests several types of ties appear to have led actors to form operational ties. To test this, we regress the shared operations network on nine different networks, the results of which are presented in Table 9.1 (Full Model). The results indicate that only four types of network ties had a positive and statistically significant effect on whether two individuals participated in the same operation: classmate, friendship, organizational, and training ties. In other words, we can conclude that these four relationships provide a better explanation of the formation of operational ties, as opposed to random chance alone. Of these four, however, only two—classmates and friendship ties—had a substantially large effect. This may help explain why the coefficient of determination (i.e., adjusted R^2) is only equal to 0.097 (remember, the higher the better), which indicates that the types of networks included in the model only account for approximately 10 percent of the variation present in the operations network.[6] Put rather bluntly, our models do not account for many factors (e.g., other relationships) that lead to operational ties.

Analysts will often compare several models during hypothesis testing. The use of multiple models, all of which should fit within the bounds of theories and contextual knowledge about the network at hand, allow analysts to develop better models, and examine the effects of removing individual independent variables from certain models. For instance, the reduced model presented in the table removes all of the statistically nonsignificant networks from the regression model. After doing so, the coefficients of the four remaining networks are virtually unchanged. Perhaps even more striking is how

Table 9.1 Estimated QAP Regression Coefficients Predicting Shared Operation

	Estimate (SE)		
	Full Model	*Reduced Model*	*Final Model*
Business and Finance	−0.073		
	(0.046)		
Classmates	0.182***	0.186***	0.195***
	(0.026)	(0.027)	(0.028)
Friendship	0.481***	0.481***	0.497***
	(0.025)	(0.025)	(0.025)
Kinship	0.011		
	(0.035)		
Logistics	−0.158		
	(0.048)		
Meetings	0.051		
	(0.026)		
Organizations	0.044**	0.041**	
	(0.014)	(0.013)	
Trainings	0.046*	0.048*	
	(0.019)	(0.019)	
Soulmates	0.039		
	(0.064)		
Intercept	0.034***	0.034***	0.040***
	(0.000)		(0.000)
Adjusted R^2	0.097	0.095	0.090

Note: * = $p < 0.05$, ** = $p < 0.01$, *** = $p < 0.001$; standard errors in parentheses.

little the adjusted R^2 changed, illustrating how little the other networks mattered to the formation of the operational network.

The final model drops the two networks (shared organizational affiliation and trainings) that, while statistically significant, are arguably not substantively significant.[7] That is, they do not appear to have had a substantial effect on which individuals participated in operations together. This appears to be confirmed in the final model. As you can see, the removal of the two networks had little effect on the model's predictive ability; the adjusted R^2 is slightly lower but just barely, and the coefficients for the two networks remaining in the model are only marginally larger. Thus, we can tentatively conclude that classmate and friendship ties were the most important factors in determining which pairs of actors participated in operations together. Had this been an active network, the development of strategic options to counter the network should account for the role of friendship and classmate ties in the formation of operational relationships. Moreover, this approach is certainly more helpful than devising strategies based on our preliminary research and intuition alone, which do not allow us to test the relative importance of our initial nine networks in the formation of operational ties. All of that being said, let's not forget that the adjusted R^2 in all of these models is less than 0.10, so the majority of what caused people to participate in operations together is not being captured by this model. In other words, just because we have a couple of statistically and substantively significant variables, we should not get too excited. There is still a lot going on that we have not captured.

The same approach is used when calculating the correlation or regression of attribute data (e.g., centrality and education level). In the first step, a correlation or standard multivariate regression is estimated across corresponding values of the dependent and independent attributes; in the second, the elements of the dependent attribute data are randomly permuted numerous times, and the distribution of randomly generated results is compared to the actual results to see if the latter is just as likely to have occurred by random chance.

Suppose we are wondering what factors contributed to how central actors are in the Noordin network. Again, we can develop several hypotheses given our preliminary research and contextual knowledge about the network. For example, we may want to test, among other things, whether prior training experience—specifically training in Pakistan and Afghanistan in the late 1980s and/or early- to mid-1990s—provided those actors with relatively higher levels of status (as indicated by actor centrality) among other militants once they returned to Southeast Asia. To test this, we regressed the four primary centrality measures (i.e., dependent variables) discussed in chapter 6 on four potential factors (i.e., independent variables): education level, contact with individuals in Afghanistan or Pakistan, military training in Afghanistan or Pakistan, and whether or not an individual is Indonesian.

The results are presented in Table 9.2. As you can see, education level is the only consistent predictor of network centrality. It exerts a positive and statistically significant effect on degree, betweenness, and eigenvector centrality. In other words, actors with higher levels of education are more

Table 9.2 Estimated Effect of Select Variables on Network Centrality

Variable	*Degree*	*Closeness (ARD)*	*Betweenness*	*Eigenvector*
Education Level	0.018**	0.002	0.004*	0.015**
	(0.005)	(0.008)	(0.001)	(0.004)
Afghan/Pakistan Contact	0.041	0.034	0.025*	0.019
	(0.034)	(0.053)	(0.010)	(0.030)
Afghan/Pakistan Military Training	−0.032	0.001	−0.023	−0.020
	(0.045)	(0.069)	(0.012)	(0.039)
Indonesian	0.0002	0.088	−0.014	0.007
	(0.029)	(0.044)	(0.008)	(0.025)
Intercept	0.083	0.349	0.014	0.062
	(0.022)	(0.034)	(0.006)	(0.020)
Adjusted R^2	0.117	0.009	0.220	0.087

Note: * = $p < 0.05$, ** = $p < 0.01$; standard errors in parentheses.

central in terms of those three measures of structural power. Contact with individuals in Afghanistan or Pakistan has a positive and statistically significant effect on betweenness centrality, but that is it. Looking at the adjusted R^2 scores for the four models, we can see that the model predicting betweenness centrality does a better job than the other three models. The worst is the model predicting closeness centrality, which is not surprising since none of the variables included in the model are large or statistically significant. Still, all of the models leave at least 80 percent of the variance in centrality scores unexplained, so once again there is a lot going on that we have not captured. We can, however, say with some confidence that higher levels of education contributed to the centrality of actors in the Noordin network.

9.3 CONDITIONAL UNIFORM GRAPHS (CUGs)

Matrix permutations are not the only simulation method available to network analysts. Sometimes, an analyst may wish to test whether the network structure itself is unlikely or biased in some manner. Conditional uniform graphs (CUGs) offer an alternative to QAP that allows the structure of simulated networks to vary, while still retaining some fundamental properties of the original—tested—network. A Conditional Uniform Graph (CUG) test (Katz and Powell 1957) is fairly similar to a QAP test, and actually predates QAP in its creation. The use of CUG tests, however, had not seen wide application (Butts 2011; Robins 2013) until only fairly recently (see, e.g., Butts 2011; Kolaczyk and Csardi 2014). The two approaches mainly differ in the distribution used for comparison. Whereas QAP builds a distribution from a large number of permuted networks, the CUG procedure generates a large number of randomly generated networks. When a network is permuted, the structure remains the same. So QAP is not useful for testing whether the structure is uniquely displaying a particular feature since the structure will not vary between the original network and the permuted comparisons. CUG presents the opportunity to test some structural characteristic of a network due to the fact that the structures of the randomly generated networks will vary randomly. The parameters used to generate conditional uniform graphs are *conditional* on some specified aspect of the network being tested, such as—in the case of the R package "sna"—degree distribution, the number of nodes in the network (i.e., the order of the graph), or dyad census.

Although few social network analysis programs explicitly offer CUG tests as an option, provided the program has the capacity to generate random networks, it can perform a CUG test. The basic process is conceptually simple. First, calculate the parameter (e.g., density, average degree, or dyad census) upon which to base the simulated networks. Next, generate a large number

($n \geq 1000$) of random networks that are based upon the chosen parameter. Finally, calculate a global measure (e.g., transitivity, centralization, number of subgroups) of the network being analyzed, and then repeat for all simulated networks. Compare the measure of the network being analyzed with the distribution of measures from the simulated networks. As with QAP tests, calculating the proportion of simulated measures that are greater than that of the original network and the proportion that fall below the original network's measure will provide something similar to a *p*-value. Alternatively, the distribution may be graphed to compare with the measure for the original network.

Analysts using a CUG test are simply testing some measure of a given network against that same measure in a series of randomly generated networks that share some substantive property in common with the original. This process is suited to univariate graph-level measurements, such as those covered in chapter 4. The null hypothesis for this test states that there is no difference between the measure taken on the original network and the distribution of measures from the simulated networks. In comparing the network measure with the distribution of measures, the analyst is checking to see whether the network measure is different from all but just a few of the measures in the distribution. Provided the measure falls on one of the extreme ends of the distribution—meaning that no more than 5 percent (0.05) of the distribution is greater than that value, or no more than 5 percent of the distribution is less than that value—then the analyst may consider the difference to be significant, rejecting the null. The inference that the analyst may draw from rejecting the null in a CUG test is that the measure cannot be explained by whatever property was employed to create the simulations—given that the property could only rarely replicate a value as extreme as the one calculated in the original network. So, if the simulations were created according to the size of the original network and there is a significant difference, then the analyst may conclude that the size of the network does not explain why the measure is as extreme as it is (Robins 2013).

As an example, consider once again the Koschade network (Figure 9.2). As mentioned in chapter 7, Samudra (white node) is clearly dominating the network in terms of brokerage potential. Put another way, the Koschade network also provides a clear example of centralization, as covered in chapter 4. Centralization reveals the extent to which a single actor dominates a network. But in a network this size, it should not be too surprising that any one actor may have ties to all others. How odd can this situation really be, given that it is such a small, dense network?

We can also calculate a centralization value for a network and report whether we feel it to be fairly high, given what we usually expect to see. But that is bound to impress the listener as arbitrary. It can be much more valuable to put that value into perspective by testing to see whether a network's

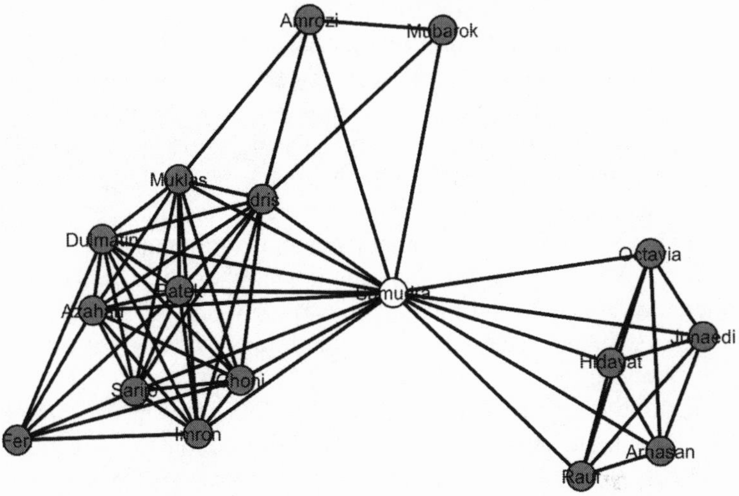

Figure 9.2 Koschade Network

Table 9.3 Conditional Uniform Graph Test Output

	Centralization Value	*Conditioning Parameter*	*Proportion Greater Pr(X >= Obs)*	*Proportion Less Pr(X <= Obs)*
Closeness	0.65	Edges	0	1
		Graph Size	0	1
Degree	0.55	Edges	0	1
		Graph Size	0	1
Betweenness	0.50	Edges	0	1
		Graph Size	0	1
Eigenvector	0.24	Edges	0.04	0.96
		Graph Size	0.01	0.99

centralization differs from what we should ordinarily expect (by chance alone) from a network of this size. We may also compare centralization measures to networks that have been simulated based upon the number of edges in the Koschade network or the dyad distribution.

We calculated four centralization measures that we tested using the CUG test available in the R package "sna." The object was to test whether the centralization observed in the Koschade network is greater than would be expected, given either the size, or the edge distribution of the network. We, therefore, ran a CUG test on four measures of centralization—closeness, degree, betweenness, and eigenvector—each compared with a null distribution conditioned on (i.e., from networks that are simulated based upon) edges and another conditioned on size. The results of the CUG tests performed on the Koschade network are provided in Table 9.3.

Conditioning the simulated networks alternatively on edges and network size produced a somewhat different distribution of values within each of the centralization measures, but those differences are not strongly apparent, given how unique the Koschade network appears to be when compared with the simulations. The proportion of simulated networks with centralization values greater than that observed in the Koschade network was zero in three out of four measures, and the fourth, eigenvector centralization, has only a very small proportion of values that are greater in the simulated null distribution (<0.05). We may treat the proportions as we would *p*-values, with the exception that it is not technically possible to derive a *p*-value of zero or one. So any reports should refer to the zero proportions by using some arbitrarily small *p*-value (e.g., $p < 0.00001$).

For an intuitive version of the CUG test, consider the eigenvector centralization distributions provided in Figure 9.3. Distributions were produced for all of the tests listed in Table 9.3. These two are presented for the purpose of comparison and example. The distribution on the left was conditioned using the edge distribution from the Koschade network. The distribution on the right was conditioned only according to the size of the Koschade network. In each case, the actual value of eigenvector centralization in the Koschade network is represented by the vertical line that intersects the *x*-axis at the 0.24 level. It is apparent that the number of simulations that exceed this value is very small. The table lists the proportions as 0.04 and 0.01, respectively. In both cases, we consider these to be significantly different from the sample (null) distributions, even though the network's actual value does not

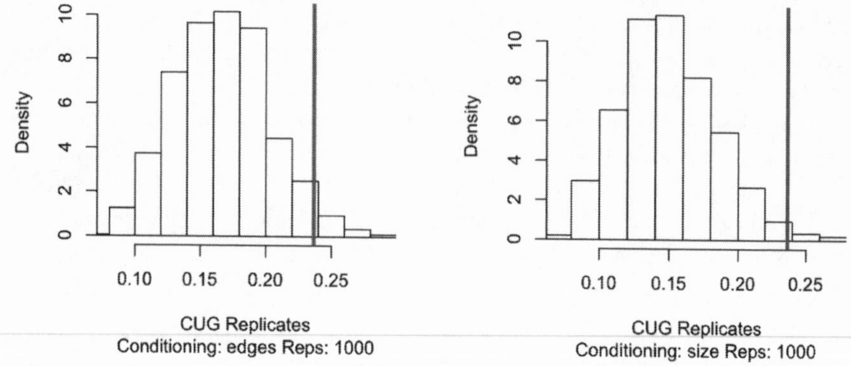

Figure 9.3 Comparison of CUG Distributions of Eigenvector Centralization by Method of Conditioning

fall entirely outside of the null distribution. This is because the distribution represents a sample of what is possible for networks with the same edge distribution or size. The amount of simulated values that are greater than the actual network's measure is sufficiently small as to constitute a relatively rare occurrence.

This example tested whether the centralization measures for the Koschade were large enough to be considered significant—meaning that they are significantly greater than we would expect by random chance alone. We were obliged to reject the null hypothesis in each of the tested measures, and we may therefore conclude that the centralization that is apparent in the Koschade network is significantly—and substantially—greater than could be expected by chance alone. Such a level of dominance by one central actor is not something that can be explained in light of the size of the network, or the manner in which edges are distributed in the network.

9.4 A NOTE ON INTERPRETATION: CAUSALITY IN NETWORKS

Whenever employing statistical techniques—or any of the other techniques mentioned in this book—to draw inference about the mechanisms that appear to drive the network in some fashion, it is best to conclude that the tested theory "explains," "predicts," "is consistent with," or "describes" such processes, or that they fail to do so. Be very careful when making statements about "causes," whether or not the interaction, correlation, or other feature has been statistically verified. Generally, what any analyst should keep in mind when working with dark networks is that actual *causes* are difficult, at best, to demonstrate (Doreian 2001). But, if causes truly are what the analyst is pursuing in their work, a few words of guidance may help.

Strong analyses are built from a strong command of the context, culture, and actors being analyzed. Background research is the worst topic on which to cut corners when analyzing dark networks. Preparation in terms of learning about the network will pay dividends when it comes time to interpret the results of any test or measure conducted on a network. Similarly, preparation in terms of being conversant with theories developed by others in their work with similar networks will help to set up expectations and should alert analysts to situations that are surprising for their deviation from the norm. It is always helpful to know when something unexpected is taking place, and one generally will not recognize such things in the absence of background research. Keep in mind, however, that background research functions primarily as a filter through which to interpret analyses. It does not establish causal mechanisms. In order to do this, four essential factors must be in place (adapted from Shadish, Cook, and Campbell 2002):

- A plausible argument
- Correlated predictor and outcome
- Temporal precedence
- Account for/rule out alternate explanations

The first item is relatively straightforward. The argument that sets out the causal chain should be logically consistent and hold true to the facts concerning the background and actors involved in the network. Next, there must be some relationship between the variables implied by the argument. This is where statistics become more important. For there to be a relationship between the assumed cause and its effect, there must be some measureable relationship, such as a correlation. Correlations, however, are necessary but not sufficient grounds for establishing a *causal* relationship. The next hurdle is to establish temporal precedence. The cause must precede the effect and that precedence must be demonstrable. The last criterion on this list is likely to be the most difficult. For a relationship to be considered causal, it is important to account for all of the other possible causes of the outcome in question. That is not to say that analysts will be forced to counter every absurd claim that they can invent, only that they should consider *all plausible* explanations and rule them out if possible. If alternative explanations cannot be ruled out, then they will remain a caveat whenever making conjecture as to the causes of the outcome. If, and only if, all of the above conditions are satisfied, can analysts feel somewhat justified in making a claim concerning actual causation. However, one should always keep in mind that there will always remain some possibility—however small—of having made the wrong call. Preparation and rigor decrease those chances considerably. But they will never disappear.

9.5 SUMMARY: LESSONS LEARNED

In this chapter we provided a basic introduction to testing hypotheses about dark networks. We began by explaining what hypothesis testing is and how it works. We illustrated it using two statistical models for social network data that can help us disentangle genuine from spurious effects. As we saw QAP correlation and multivariate regression models are invaluable to researchers when confronted with the problem of too many variables; that is, when they have identified several factors that could be associated with a particular outcome, but it is impossible to distinguish which factors truly are associated from those that only appear to be associated.

QAP and CUG models are not the only statistical model available to test hypotheses. As previously mentioned, analysts can also leverage many other techniques such as exponential random graph models (ERGMs) and stochastic actor-oriented models (SAOMs) to develop and test hypotheses regarding tie formation in dark networks. The former provide analysts with a way to examine the endogenous and exogenous social processes that give rise to a network's observed patterns at the macro level. They assume that observed social networks are built upon local patterns of ties, sometimes called micro-configurations, which are a function of local social processes (Lusher, Koskinen and Robins 2013). SAOMs are similar to ERGMs, in that they assume that observed social networks are built upon local patterns of ties, which are a function of local social processes. However, they differ from ERGMs in that they are designed for longitudinal social network data and assume that tie formation reflects the choices of actors who seek to form ties with other actors in a network (Snijders, Bunt and Steglich 2010; Snijders and Koskinen 2013). We consider ERGMs in chapter 10 and SAOMs in chapter 11.

Readers should take away (and keep in mind) several important points about hypothesis testing and dark networks. The first is that hypotheses require more thought than exploratory questions because analysts must explicitly state their independent and dependent variables and the possible relationships between them. The choice of variables should be based on theoretical considerations from existing literature, subject matter expertise, and/or exploratory analyses. Analysts should consider several different theoretical points of view when developing hypotheses, and avoid using hypothesis testing in an exploratory fashion. Readers will recognize this immediately as they begin to understand ERGMs and SAOMs. The second is that hypothesis testing can provide greater insight into many important factors and processes related to dark networks, such as tie formation, that cannot be found using exploratory approaches. At the same time, social network analysts still must be careful about claiming objective "truth" as a result of their hypothesis testing. They simply should be more confident about certain dynamics regarding dark networks. Finally, social network analysts should consider hypothesis testing as an investment of their time as opposed to an overly "academic" approach. On the one hand, investigations that lead to well-thought-out hypotheses can take more time than basic exploratory approaches. On the other hand, the more advanced methods described in the present and the next two chapters can prevent many of the errors that can arise from purely descriptive approaches by forcing analysts to consider alternative explanations and challenge their intuition.

9.6 QUESTIONS

1. Theoretical considerations should drive the development of hypotheses.
   a. True.
   b. False.

2. Hypotheses are
   a. Explicit and falsifiable.
   b. Facts.
   c. Never correct.
   d. Always correct.
3. Hypotheses are always directional statements.
   a. True.
   b. False.
4. Networks can only serve as dependent variables using QAP techniques.
   a. True.
   b. False.
5. Given that social network data are not well suited to standard parametric statistics, standard statistical models are not valid for testing hypotheses in networks.
   a. True.
   b. False.
6. Which of the following are essential factors that must be in place to establish causality when examining dark networks?
   a. A plausible argument.
   b. Correlated predictor and outcome.
   c. Temporal precedence.
   d. Account for/rule out alternate explanations.
   e. All the above.

9.7 ANSWERS

1. True.
2. Explicit and falsifiable (a).
3. False.
4. False.
5. True.
6. All the above (e).

9.8 FURTHER READING

There are numerous texts that contain excellent discussions of hypothesis testing. As a general introduction see Fred Kerlinger and Howard B. Lee's *Foundations of Behavioral Research* (Orlando, FL: Harcourt Inc., 2000), especially Chapter 2. With regard to causality, see Patrick Doreian's 2001 article, "Causality in Social Network Analysis." Pp. 81–114 in *Sociological*

Methods and Research. Two excellent treatments of the use of statistical methods with social network data, see Garry L. Robins "A Tutorial on Methods of the Modeling and Analysis of Social Network Data." Pp. 261–74 in *Journal of Mathematical Psychology* (2013) and Eric D. Kolaczyk and Gabor Csardi's *Statistical Analysis of Network Data* (New York, NY: Springer, 2014). Additional resources include:

- Brigham S. Anderson, Carter Butts, and Kathleen M. Carley. 1999. "The Interaction of Size and Density with Graph-Level Indices." *Social Networks* 21:239–67.
- Stephen P. Borgatti, Martin G. Everett, and Jeffrey C. Johnson. 2013. Pp. 89–99, 125–148 (Chapters 6 and 8) in *Analyzing Social Networks*. Thousand Oaks, CA: SAGE Publications.
- Carter Butts. 2011. "Bayesian Meta-analysis of Social Network Data via Conditional Uniform Graph Quantiles." *Sociological Methodology* 41:257–98.
- David Dekker, David Krackhardt, and Tom Snijders. 2007. "Sensitivity of MRQAP Tests to Collinearity and Autocorrelation Conditions." *Psychometrika* 72:563–81.
- David Krackhardt. 1987. "QAP Partialling as a Test of Spuriousness." *Social Networks* 9:171–86.
- Marijtje A. van Duijn and Mark Huisman. 2011. "Statistical Models for Ties and Actors." Pp. 459–83 in *The SAGE Handbook of Social Network Analysis*, edited by John Scott and Peter J. Carrington. Los Angeles and London: SAGE Publications.

NOTES

1. Of course, researchers and academics may also work with experts, other researchers, and those in the field. Practitioners may consult existing literature; however, we recognize that practitioners will likely approach hypothesis development differently than researchers and academics due to the unique contexts in which practitioners work.

2. Also referred to as the *observed significance level*, the *p*-value is more correctly defined as "the probability of observing the test statistic as extreme as or more extreme than that observed. By *extreme* we mean 'far from what we would expect to observe if the null hypothesis were true'" (Weiss 2008:438).

3. Keep in mind that probabilities only range from zero (0) to one (1). So a probability of 0.05 (one chance in 20) does constitute a relatively unlikely event.

4. More precisely, if an estimated coefficient differs from the mean of the randomly generated distribution by 1.96 standard deviations, there is only 5 percent chance that the estimated coefficient could have occurred randomly. Put in the language of statistical significance, $p < 0.05$.

5. For an excellent discussion of testing hypotheses using permutation methods, see Borgatti et al. (2013:125–138).

6. If you recall R^2 estimates the extent to which a model's variables account for the variance in the dependent variable. Adjusted R^2 takes into account how many independent variables are included in the model.

7. Social scientists routinely conflate statistical and substantive significance. Variables (or in this case, networks) can be statistically significant but have not substantive effect on the outcome (i.e., dependent) variable. For an excellent discussion of this see the work of Deirdre McCloskey (and her colleague Stephen Ziliak) (1995, 1985, 2008).

Chapter 10

More Hypothesis Testing

Using Exponential Random Graph Models (ERGMs) to Explain Tie Formation

The preceding chapter explored methods for testing whether relationships and/or attributes predict or explain the resulting network. Such global tests are useful for understanding how various aspects relate to the formation of the overall network, but it is also valuable to understand what drives tie formation within a network at a more micro level. This is the logic underlying the development of exponential random graph models (ERGMs, also referred to as p* models), which provide analysts with a method for examining the internal (endogenous) and external (exogenous) social processes that give rise to a network's observed patterns at the macro level (Harris 2014; Lusher, Koskinen and Robins 2013; Robins et al. 2007). Every network constitutes a complex environment with a particular mix of attributes and social or other relationships. We may, therefore, assume that actors within the network monitor and respond to their environment: taking advantage of opportunities to connect with others, forming ties with similar alters, or may be simply sharing too many commonalities not to have a tie with certain others. Dark networks are no exception. The opportunity to test whether—or to what degree—any or all of the various relations or attributes present in a network influence tie formation can therefore be valuable to creating a better understanding of what predicts growth within a given dark network. This understanding of micro processes, in turn, can inform the development of strategies to counter dark networks.

This chapter builds upon the last by extending the idea of hypothesis testing to how analysts can use ERGMs to test whether various relationships between actors and/or their attributes help explain tie formation. It is important to keep in mind that ERGMs allow analysts to test one or more hypotheses regarding how a particular network is formed or what would cause it to grow. Again, ERGMs are used to *test*—not to *prove*—a hypothesis. They are, therefore, generally most valuable after having carried out the discovery phase—exploratory network analysis—and a review of the information you have about the network. This provides analysts with an opportunity to form expectations about what drives tie formation. For instance, after exploring data about an insurgent network, analysts may hypothesize that homophily-based processes lie behind tie formation. Similarly, practitioners in the field who have collected the data may also develop their own suspicions or expectations. Such hypotheses are generally testable, provided that we have collected the appropriate network and attribute data. As is generally the case in researching dark networks, the greatest limitation is generally the type and quality of data available. When analysts believe they have a good "feel" for the network and the relationships it represents, they can begin building a model, which is simply a mix of micro-configurations and attributes that explain a network's observed pattern of ties. This process is by no means trivial. Rather, they will engage in a series of steps, repeating some as necessary. For best results, analysts will:

1. Review the context and what is known about the network
   - Consult various theories about tie formation within that given context
   - Conduct exploratory analysis using visualizations and/or descriptive measures
2. Construct the model to be tested
   - Develop hypotheses based on context and/or exploratory analysis
   - Identify and prepare attribute variables of interest
   - Evaluate the network structure for motifs, or structural configurations, to be included in the model
     - Consider including structures that best characterize the network
     - At minimum include, the "edge" variable
3. Refine or augment the model
4. Evaluate the final model's goodness of fit
5. Interpret and report the output

As with other analytic topics, the steps listed above are a general guide and should not be seen as written in stone. There is always room for variation, which is largely what makes ERGMs so challenging. Indeed, Borgatti, Everett, and Johnson (2013:142) note that building a model is a "challenging and time-consuming process and is more of an art than a science." Nevertheless, these are the basic building blocks for constructing an ERGM; following them will help reduce the frustration of heading down the wrong path or trying to do too much all at once.

In this chapter we provide an introduction to ERGMs and their intended function, followed by an example of how to run and report the results of one.

We begin with an overview of the theory underlying ERGMs, as well as an overview of how they work. This is followed by a technical overview of their mathematical underpinnings. The technical portion is provided for those who are interested in such matters, but those who are not can likely skip it without any deleterious effects. We then turn to a step-by-step example of how to estimate an ERGM. As with many statistical models, ERGMs make a lot more sense when they are illustrated.

10.1 EXPONENTIAL RANDOM GRAPH MODELS

ERGMs can help us discover what internal and external factors drive the growth of ties within the network. They "are designed to predict the probability of tie formation in an observed network, while incorporating properties of the network itself as well as an array of covariates pertaining to the network actors and sets of ties among them" (Papachristos, Hureau and Braga 2013:427). They assume that observed social networks are built upon local patterns of ties, often called micro-configurations, that are a function of social processes, such that "actors in the network form connections in response to other ties in their social environment" (Lusher, Koskinen and Robins 2013:1). They are similar to the general linear models (in particular, logistic regression models), except that they include important modifications in order to account for the dependencies between observations (Harris 2014; Lusher, Koskinen and Robins 2013; Robins et al. 2007). Each process is compared to similar, randomly generated networks in order to test whether they are likely to be what is driving tie formation or whether the observed network could have occurred by chance alone. In other words, in an ERGM the network itself is the dependent variable, while structural parameters and attributes, or some combination of them, are the predictors or independent variables.

In general, ERGMs help to test or explain what drives a particular network to be the way it is. Some such investigations may only consider the internal forces—described here as structural attributes (or micro-configurations, such as open and closed triads)—that are present within the network to evaluate whether they occur more commonly within the network than what may be expected by chance. For example, analysts may wish to evaluate whether a particular network is best described as an assemblage of highly connected cells (cliques), or whether the cliques could just as easily occur by chance alone in a similarly sized network. Even when we are only interested in testing one particular factor, we still need to take into account (i.e., control for) other structures or attributes that may explain tie formation. This is because several underlying processes can be active simultaneously. For instance, it is possible that processes related to preferential attachment and social selection (e.g., homophily) are both at work in a given network, not just one or the other.

The advantage of using ERGMs lies in how well they capture complex environments. Using them, analysts can construct (or test) a more complete story by including a wide selection of parameters that take into account the attributes that may commonly appear in statistical analysis, as well as the structure of the network itself to reflect the social and similar forces that act upon each actor in the network. After all, given the many complex forces that make up everyday life, it is unlikely that just one or two factors—social or otherwise—sufficiently explain what makes a particular network the way it is. For this reason, most ERGMs incorporate many other potential structural attributes that, *in aggregate*, may explain how ties form within a particular network. Specifically, ERGMs are designed to calculate the likelihood of a tie being formed, depending on a particular predictor, or a set of predictors.

Unfortunately, ERGMs can be quite challenging to analysts new to network analysis. They often require patience, along with a strong grasp of basic network theory and a statistical background. One important aspect of ERGMs, which is related to what we discussed in chapter 3, is that analysts must be confident in their data. ERGMs operate under the assumption that if the model adequately captures a network, as indicated by its goodness of fit (GOF), then it can be used to describe the processes that underlie the network's observed features. It is, however, possible to include parameters that have nothing to do with a particular network's tie formation but produce a good fit nonetheless. It is also possible that the data collected do not reflect the actual network (e.g., poor data collection, speculation is used in lieu of empirical evidence, and inappropriate choice of relationships in the network). It is for these reasons that it is imperative that analysts select the network and attribute data with care and only choose attributes that are appropriate for that particular network and set of relational ties.

One of the larger barriers for building an ERGM is the bewildering array of structural variables that may be included in a model. Micro-configurations, such as star patterns, triangles, and actor pairs (see Table 10.1), are some of the more intuitive structural variables available. However, with multiple options to account for those micro-configurations (e.g., statnet includes at minimum ten options for incorporating triangles), it is incumbent upon analysts to thoroughly investigate the options they select. Dark network data are generally undirected, which reduces the number of possible options a great deal; on the other hand, it limits the analyst's ability to explore several important micro processes, such as "sender" and "receiver" effects.[1] Also, many of the options will not apply to a particular network. This is especially true of smaller networks, which are frequently the subject of dark network analysis.

It is unlikely that medium-to-small networks will contain all possible micro-structures. Thus, it is important early in the model specification process to rule out structures that are not present in order to avoid false trails and to focus upon those aspects of the network that may be meaningful. Another difficulty is software selection. The two current options are the PNet suite of programs and the R statnet package. They are similar in terms of quality but differences in terminology and output can make it difficult to switch from one program to the other. For instance, the steps for running GOF statistics, along with its actual outputs, differ between the programs. The two appear to be slowly becoming standardized, but at the time of this writing the differences should be noted.

Be that as it may, the *payoff* for learning ERGMs can be huge. ERGMs (and the stochastic actor-oriented models we will explore in the next chapter) can reveal processes that are not readily apparent when employing standard measures or visualizations. Their allowance for complexity provides analysts with the opportunity to view each process as a part of a larger system and evaluate its contribution in that light. For instance, analysts examining a dark network in an area of operation may find that it is relatively centralized compared to other networks, and their exploratory analysis suggests that many of the actors (but not all) who score high in terms of degree centrality possess certain characteristics, in particular, college degrees. Taken together, this could lead them to recommend the monitoring of college students, but if they are wrong, it would result in the misuse of valuable resources. A better approach would be to develop hypotheses that test whether such an effect actually impacts tie formation and not some other factor, such as those related to preferential attachment. In fact, a better understanding of the generative factors that gave rise to the network will likely help analysts make better recommendations about the allocation of (often scarce) resources or to redirect investigations in new directions.

10.2 HOW ERGMs WORK (A NONTECHNICAL OVERVIEW)

The construction of an ERGM is a logical process of accounting for the various network features that are expected to explain the formation of ties in a network. Once analysts have specified a model, the model is then estimated to assess how well it fits (i.e., accounts for) the data and the impact that each of the specified variables plays in tie creation. The computational process of fitting an ERGM is far more complex and challenging than estimating the QAP regression model covered in the previous or the longitudinal model (SAOM) we discuss in the next. ERGMs are designed to calculate the odds of a tie forming between one or more actors, taking into account relatively complex set of circumstances with a limited amount of data from which to make such estimations.

The ties that a given actor has with other actors in the network essentially depend upon all other factors or processes at work in the network. These processes take two general forms in an ERGM: endogenous and exogenous. *Endogenous factors*—those formed by forces from within a network—account for the social and similar pressures that arise from how actors (e.g., people, organizations) can and do influence one another. For example, as with spatial data analysis, we generally assume that actors are influenced more by actors that are nearby than those that are distant. We also assume that the way that actors are tied to one another greatly influences their behavior; actors that are either isolates or on the network's periphery may be less likely to form ties than those that with numerous ties or located in the center of the network. And we usually expect that two actors that are tied to many of the same other actors are likely to form a tie between them. *Exogenous factors*—factors from outside of the network, such as the attributes of actors and the environment in which they operate—can also influence tie formation. These can help account for tendencies toward homophily, heterophily, or the general attractiveness of some actors because they are affiliated with a particular group, occupy some role or position, or possess a particular characteristic such as a college degree. Because they are independent of how actors are tied with one another, they are treated as factors that actors bring with them to the network. In other words, endogenous and exogenous factors account for somewhat different aspects of tie formation. The former govern how ties are created and reinforced through social (and similar) forces, while the latter operate independently of an actor's position in the network, and ERGMs account for both.

ERGMS also control for the effect of processes that we may fail to include in our models, as well as the randomness of everyday life. When we estimate an ERGM, we (i.e., our computers) generate thousands, sometimes millions, of simulated networks that predict what a network of the same size would look like, given the endogenous and exogenous factors specified in the model, along with a few stochastic (i.e., random) adjustments for each simulation. These "random" adjustments are modeled with Markov chain Monte Carlo (MCMC) methods that vary the parameters during the simulation phase. The resulting simulations are then compared with the original network to determine whether the model generated reliable estimates for that particular network, a process that is referred to as checking for convergence. The means by which convergence is checked varies according to the software one uses. An important limitation of convergence checks is that they only concern the *reliability* of the estimates. They do not tell us whether the model provides a good representation of the network. To assess this, we must estimate the model's GOF. A model is considered a good fit if it can be used like a blueprint to guide simulations in essentially growing networks with structural characteristics that are similar to those of the observed network. In particular, a good model should be able to generate not only the structures specified in the model but also, at least to some extent, the unspecified structures (Hunter, Goodreau and Handcock 2008; Lusher, Koskinen and Robins 2013).

Keep in mind that the objective is to measure "goodness" of fit, not "perfection" of fit. It is not necessary or even expected that the model will perfectly reproduce the original network. Rather, the simulations it generates should be relatively similar and, on average, not differ significantly from the original network. When they do, it is incumbent upon analysts to adjust the model in order to improve its fit to the best possible extent. It is also possible that the process of fitting and refitting models may yield equally plausible models that all converge and fit the data well. In such cases, the analyst may fall back on their background knowledge about the network, the environment in which it is embedded, and their original hypotheses about the network's underlying processes. Model assessment measures, such as Mahalanobis distance (Wang et al. 2014:24), Akaike Inference Criterion (AIC) (Akaike 1974), and Bayesian Inference Criterion (BIC) (Raftery 1995), can provide a general comparison between models, although they offer no indication of model reliability or fit. As a general rule, the best practice is to stick to the original hypothesis, accounting for other potential explanations of tie formation *in the same model* when possible. This implies attempting to strike a balance between fitting additional variables that plausibly reflect processes at work in the network and developing an elegant (i.e., simple and parsimonious) model that converges and fit the network well.

This can be frustrating, and it is not uncommon for the whole process of model specification, estimation, convergence checks, and GOF checks to require analysts to revisit the model specification phase over multiple iterations. This is largely why many practitioners have been slow to adopt ERGMs as a standard practice. When done correctly, however, the results can be rewarding for the unique insight that they provide into what predicts or explains how a particular network has developed. We now turn to a brief technical overview of ERGMs. As noted above, some readers may want to skip to the step-by-step example in the next section.

10.3 HOW ERGMs WORK (A TECHNICAL OVERVIEW)

The basic form of the ERGM model, as defined in Lusher et al. (2013), is

$$P(X = x|\theta) \equiv P_\theta(x) = \exp[\theta_1 z_1(x) + \theta_2 z_2(x) + \cdots + \theta_p z_p(x)] / K(\theta) \qquad (10.1)$$

In essence, this is a modification of a logistic regression model to predict the probability of a tie, conditional upon a set of p factors, with additional parameters to make it relevant for use with networks. The equation states that the probability that the network (X) consists of a particular set of ties (x) is conditional upon a vector attributes (θ). On the right side of the equation, the $z_k(x)$ functions are counts of the number of times particular parameters (such as edges, triangles, or isolates) appear in the network, with θ functioning as the estimate/coefficient for that particular parameter. The normalizing term ($K(\theta)$) ensures that the probability mass function ($P_\theta(x)$) over all networks sums to one. It is defined as

$$K(\theta) = \sum_{y \in X} \exp[\theta_1 z_1(y) + \theta_2 z_2(y) + \cdots + \theta_p z_p(y)] \qquad (10.2)$$

Those familiar with multivariate regression may recognize the similarity between the attribute counts and coefficients in this model $(\theta_1 z_1(x)) + \theta_2 z_2(x))$ $+ \cdots + \theta_p z_p(x))$ and those of a standard regression model:

$$Y = \alpha + \beta_1 x_1 + \beta_2 x_2 + \cdots + \beta_p x_p \qquad (10.3)$$

However, in an ERGM, the intercept (α) is nearly always a coefficient of the density of the network, as represented by the number of ties present within the network ($\theta_{edges} z_{edges}(x)$). So an ERGM that employs only edges and isolates as predictors would have the following form:

$$P(X = x|\theta) \equiv P_\theta(x) = \exp[\theta_{edge} z_{edge}(x) + \theta_{isolate} z_{isolate}(x)] / K(\theta) \qquad (10.4)$$

The $z_{edges}(x)$ function is calculated according to a simple count of the number of edges in the network, and the coefficient associated with the edge attribute is represented by θ_{edges}. Similarly, the $z_{isolate}(x)$ function is based upon a count of the number of isolates in the network, and the coefficient associated with the isolate attribute is represented by $\theta_{isolate}$, and so on.

Parameter estimates are iteratively fit using maximum likelihood estimation (MLE). Because the MLE process is frequently unsuccessful, checking for whether the estimates were successfully produced (converged) is an important step in estimating an ERGM. Convergence is determined by comparing the parameter estimate with the observed network. In a converged model, the estimated parameters are very nearly equal to the corresponding parameters in the observed network. Such similarities—or differences—are assessed using t-statistics or a combination of p-values and graphic representations of each of the parameters in the model, depending on which software suite one uses. Relatively small t-values ($|t| \leq 0.1$) in PNet, or relatively large p-values (minimally, $p > 0.05$) in statnet, indicate that the estimate has converged with the observed parameter. T-values with an absolute value greater than 0.1 or *p*-values less than 0.05 indicate a failure to converge. Models with one or more parameters that have not converged are considered to be degenerate and cannot (or at least should not) be interpreted. If, and only if, all parameter estimates converge, should a model's estimates be checked for GOF, which is determined by using the model's parameters to simulate a distribution of networks. The averages of the aggregated measures are then compared with those of the original model. If they are very close to the structural variables specified in the model and do not differ significantly from those that were not, then the model is considered to be a good fit, and its coefficients are considered to be a meaningful representation of that network.

Estimated coefficients indicate the tendency for each of the variables in the model to predict or explain the formation of a new tie. Initial inspection of the coefficients provides a general idea of how each specified factor predicts or explains the tie formation. Negative estimates indicate that the factors are associated with a lower likelihood of a tie forming between two actors, and positive estimates are associated with a greater likelihood of a tie forming between two actors. The likelihood that a tie will form can be more intuitively interpreted as an odds ratio, which is the exponential function of the coefficient. For example, if the estimated coefficient of a particular factor equals 1.10, then the odds of a tie forming, given that factor (and holding all other factors constant), is approximately three to one (exp[1.10] = 3.004). Put somewhat differently, a tie is a little more than three times likely to form in the presence of that particular factor than if it is not present. An odds ratio can also be converted to a probability by dividing the odds of a tie forming by one plus the odds of a tie forming,[2] which, using the above example works out as: 0.75 = (3.004/[1 + 3.004]). That is, 75 times out of 100 a tie would form in the presence of that factor, holding all other factors constant. Whether analysts choose to present the estimated coefficients, the odds ratios, or the probabilities is up to their discretion and requirements.

10.4 MODELING, EVALUATING, AND INTERPRETING AN EGRM: A STEP-BY-STEP EXAMPLE

To illustrate estimating an ERGM we will examine the network of sentiments between several Afghan tribes.[3] In this scenario, we will consider a hypothetical situation where analysts are assessing the enmities between tribes for the purpose of improving stability and reducing the Taliban's influence. The process of *mapping* the various tribes and how they are allied or opposed to one another is a relatively straightforward task. In this example, however, analysts may want to dig deeper into the reasons *why* such adversarial ties form between tribes. ERGMs provide a relatively efficient means for testing theories about why ties form, whether those ties represent positive or negative sentiment.

Step 1: Review the context and what is known about the network

The Afghan tribal sentiment network includes both positive (allies) and negative ties (adversaries). After recoding the network to include only adversarial ties, we should first represent the network of tribal adversaries (Figure 10.1) before considering possible reasons (i.e., hypotheses) why Afghan tribes become enemies with one another. If this were an actual scenario, this would entail a thorough review of what others have already discovered about the history of Afghan tribal relations. Prior knowledge will almost certainly be available in a range of formats, and analysts should investigate as many as reasonably possible before proceeding further. In fact, it is likely that other analysts or researchers have investigated similar or analogous scenarios. These studies are an important first step in developing hypotheses. The people

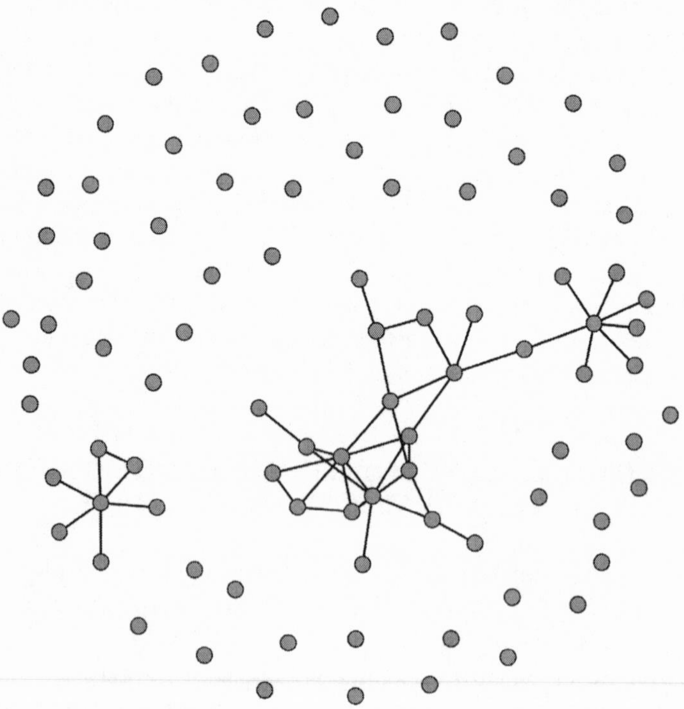

Figure 10.1 Afghan Tribal Adversaries

who collected the original data would also be a good source of potential ideas on how the network formed and grew. In most cases, those nearest to the raw data will have developed ideas about what drives the network. One last source for developing hypotheses is our own suspicions, based upon a gestalt of the information that has been collected and synthesized.

We cannot overemphasize the importance of conducting such a review and resisting the temptation to skip this step and "get on with the analysis." Skipping or skimping on this stage is almost always a mistake. Ultimately, drawing on the wisdom of other people's research pays off in terms of avoiding the dead ends and pitfalls they may have encountered. It is best to think of this step as a shortcut although it may not seem like one at the time. Even if one is an expert in an area, there is always room for entertaining other points of view—if for no other reason than to anticipate what others may look for when they vet your work. At best, this stage will streamline data collection and speed up the rest of the analysis.

For purpose of this illustration, we will assume that the background research discovered that much of the intertribal violence and enmity is likely to be left over from the independence and interdependencies formed over more than two decades of almost constant war and the excesses of the Sunni Taliban. As a consequence, we want to use our model to test whether the animosity arises from religious differences, while taking other possible factors into account. For these reasons, we will include in our model the *religious affiliation* of each tribe. We will also control for (i.e., take into account) *intertribal relationships* (kinship between tribes), whether each tribe was *neutral, for, or against the Taliban*, and whether each tribe is currently *neutral, pro-, or anti-government.* These are included for two reasons. One is that they help to account for important aspects of tribal relations. The other is that they hold the potential to help describe the structure of the tribal adversary network. In effect, we are testing the effect that four factors have on tie formation, but our particular interest here is in testing the hypothesis that *religion is ultimately what is driving animosities between tribes in Afghanistan.*

Tribal religious affiliation and attitudes toward the Taliban and the Afghan government are attributes of the tribes (i.e., they are nonrelational), while the kinship network constitutes a dyadic relationship and is included in the model as a network. All four of these variables (i.e., covariates) are considered exogenous because they are determined by something other than the pattern of ties in the adversarial network. They can be included in the model to capture homophily effects (actormatch/Matching), heterophily effects (actormix/Mismatch), or for their popularity (actorfactor/Attribute-based Activity),[4] depending on our hypotheses (see Table 10.1). The results can also be compared during model fitting and refinement. Visualizing a network's attributes (Figure 10.2) can often be helpful at this stage for assessing the exogenous variables. The religion in the Afghan adversaries' network does not appear at first glance to be a determinant of tribal enmity; as Figure 10.2 indicates there are numerous adversarial ties between Sunni tribes. This, however, could indicate some sort of homophilous process at work and, as such, be included in our model. Sentiment toward the government does appear to be driving some of the enmity, given that there are adversarial ties linking a variety of different sentiments. Similarly, adversarial ties in the network appear to be linking dissimilar affinities for the Taliban, suggest that we may wish to model the effect of tribes taking a pro- or anti-Taliban stance.

Step 2: Construct the model to be tested

Once we have identified possible exogenous factors, it is time to specify the rest of the model. As noted above, ERGMs allow for the inclusion of a wide variety of endogenous variables (i.e., structural effects and micro-configurations) in addition to exogenous ones. A little time spent assessing which structures are prevalent in a network can save a lot of time later. Including numerous configurations in our models just to see if they work is

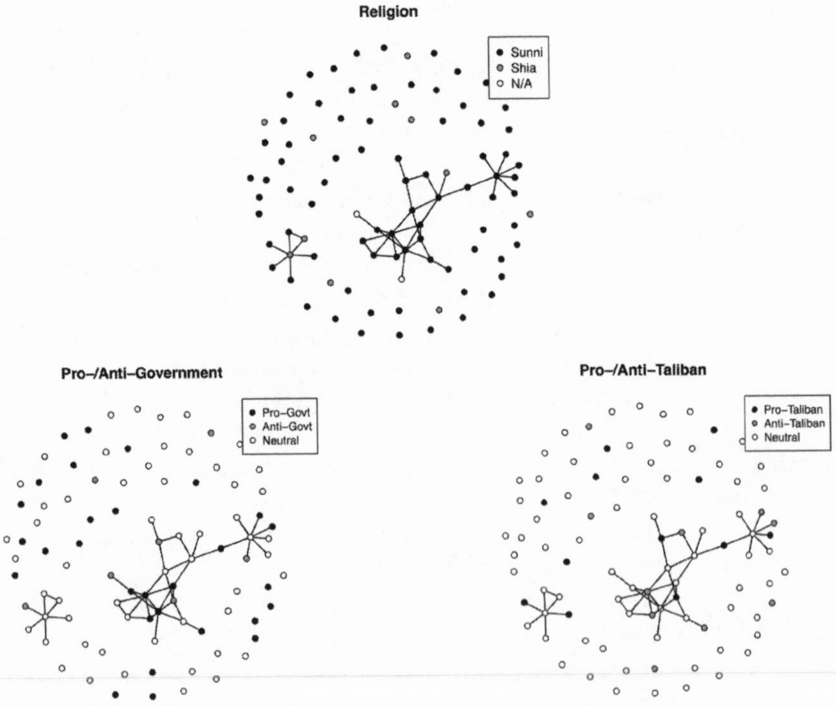

Figure 10.2 Afghan Tribal Adversaries, Shaded by Attribute

a tempting but poor practice and can be extremely time consuming. Rather, we should only add micro-configurations in our models if their inclusion is logically consistent with what we know about the network. At a minimum, most ERGMs of undirected networks will include "edges" as a covariate.[5] It functions in a manner similar to the intercept in a logistic regression model, and its estimated coefficient can be interpreted as the likelihood of a tie forming if all other variables remain constant. Other structural effects that often play a role in tie formation in undirected networks include "alternating independent two-paths" (i.e., when two unconnected actors share many of the same alters), "alternating k-triangles" (i.e., when two connected actors share the same alters), and "geometrically weighted degree" or "alternating k-stars" (i.e., when actors have numerous ties, which is often interpreted as a sign of popularity) should generally be included in the initial model (Snijders 2002; Snijders et al. 2006). In both PNet and statnet they can be modeled in order to account for how the magnitudes of each effect are distributed within the network. For example, rather than including a unique covariate for each magnitude of the *k*-star parameter (2-stars, 3-stars, 4-stars, and so on), a single geometrically weighted degree effect is specified, along with a dampening parameter that captures how the magnitudes are distributed. In general, the dampening parameter should correspond with where the bulk of observations of the modeled effect appear in the distribution. In other words, a *k*-star distribution concentrated in the 2-, 3-, and 4-star range would be more adequately captured with smaller values for the dampening parameter in order to emphasize only those first few levels. Conversely, a *k*-star distribution that has a wide range of larger magnitude stars would be better modeled using larger values of the dampening parameter in order for the emphasis to be shared among higher magnitudes as well (Hunter and Handcock 2006).

Both statnet and PNet include functions for assessing the basic structure of the network and revealing the relative frequency with which various configurations appear in a network. Analysts can (and should) produce these summaries because they can help identify possible structural effects to include in the model. Alternatively, if a configuration is not present or only appears a few times, then it will perform poorly in the model and should not be included. Because dark network data tend to be undirected, the list of potential endogenous effects is somewhat shorter than it would be for a directed network. Table 10.1 contains a short list of some common structural effects that should be considered for undirected networks. Not all of these will work in every model, but they are a good place to start. Because there are many more possible effects that may be included in any given model, we strongly recommend that analysts consult other sources such as the interactive searching page for statnet[6] or Appendix B of the PNet manual (Wang et al. 2014), where they can find a relatively up-to-date list of effects.

Analysts should conclude this step by writing down an initial model. In this case, given that the Afghan tribal adversaries' network contains isolates (see Figure 10.1), our initial model took the following form:

Adversaries = Edges + Isolates + Alt-Triangle + Alt-2-Path + Alt-Star
+ Religion + Taliban Sentiment + Government Sentiment
+ Tribal Relationships

Steps 3 and 4: Refine and augment the model, and evaluate Goodness of Fit

This part of model fitting is often the longest and most tedious. At this point, the analyst specifies and estimates the model. In cases on nonconvergence, the model will need to be modified and reestimated until convergence checks reveal that the model can produce reliable estimates. The trial and error involved in the model fitting process is presented here in a very general manner to provide a gentle introduction to fitting a set of ERGMs in the interest of exploring a particular hypothesis.

Keeping in mind that the analyst in this example set out to test the hypothesis that religion lies at the core of tribal animosities, our initial model included religious affiliation as the main effect—operationalized as "actor-factor" in statnet, and "activity" in PNet. In particular, it captures the effect of a Shia tribe (as opposed to a Sunni tribe) becoming an enemy. The other three variables—a tribe's stance on government, a tribe's stance or affiliation with the Taliban, and tribal interrelationships—are included in the model as main effects as well. Interestingly, but perhaps unsurprisingly, our initial model failed to converge. It did converge, however, after we removed the Alt 2-Path (gwdegree) from the model.[7] The variables remaining in the model (see Table 10.2) are therefore interpretable.

The estimated parameters for Model 1[8] are presented in Table 10.3. Because there are some important differences between the statnet and PNet, analysts should consult the manual and tutorials available for their software of choice. Here, we present the output in a more generic format in order to focus upon the process rather than the specific software involved.[9] The estimates for Model 1 suggest that the main effect of a tribe adhering to the Shia branch of Islam is not a statistically significant factor. That is, holding other factors constant, being a Shia tribe does not appear to explain the formation of adversarial ties any more than being a Sunni tribe.

This suggests that religion may not play a role in the formation of adversarial ties between tribes in Afghanistan. This led us to estimate additional models to explore whether the lack of statistical significance was due to how religion was incorporated into the model or whether that it is the effect of the variable in general. In the visualization of how Shia and Sunni tribes are

Table 10.1 Selection of Structural Effects

Suggested Initial Structural Parameters (Undirected Network)			
PNet	*Statnet's ERGM*	*Graphic*	*Indicates/Suggests*
Structurally Based Parameters			
Edge	edges		Overall propensity to create a new tie within the network
Alt-Star (AS)	gwdegree (geometrically weighted degree) (see also: *k*-star)	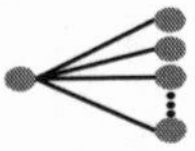	*Popularity, preferential attachment, etc.
Alt-Triangle (AT)	gwesp (geometrically weighted edgewise shared partner distribution) (see also: esp)	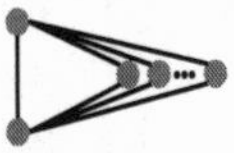	*A tendency toward transitive closure or clique formation, friends meeting through friends, etc.
Alt-2-Path (A2P)	gwdsp (geometrically weighted dyadwise shared partner distribution) (see also: dsp)	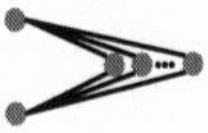	*A tendency away from transitive closure and toward bridging structural holes
Isolate	Isolates		Actors devoid of ties to others in the network
Attribute-Based Parameters			
Matching	actormatch		*Homophily*: Tendency for actors belonging to the *same* category to form ties
Mismatch	actormix		*Heterophily*: Tendency for actors belonging to *different* categories to form ties
Sum	absdiff (negative values indicate homophily)		Tendency for actors to be *similar* in some continuous attribute measure
Difference	absdiff (positive values indicate heterophily)		Tendency for actors to be *different* in some continuous attribute measure
Attribute-based Activity (binary)	actorfactor		*Main effect* of a particular attribute on tie formation
Dyadic Attributes	dyadcov		Dyadic relationships of some other sort as a predictor

*These parameters should be considered analogous between PNet and statnet, given that their calculations and the assumptions behind them differ in some important ways. For more, see Lusher et al. (2013).

Table 10.2 Variables included in Model 1

Endogenous Effects	*Exogenous Effects*
Edges	Main effect: Religion (reference group: Sunni)
Isolates	Main effect: Stance on Government (reference group: Neutral)
GWDSP	Main effect: Stance on Taliban (reference group: Neutral)
GWESP	Dyadic covariate: Afghan Tribal Relationships

present within the adversarial network (Figure 10.2), there are a number of adversarial ties between tribes that share religious affiliation. Thus, in order to account for the possibility of internecine rivalries, we altered the manner in which we included religion in the model from a main effect to one of homophily. In other words, in Model 2, the estimated parameter for religion indicates the effect that two tribes sharing the same faith has on the formation of adversarial ties. As we can see, the effect is not statistically significant. This result led us to estimate a third model in which we dropped religion altogether in order to see if its removal has a strong effect (a 10 percent difference) on the parameter estimates of other variables. This was to test whether religion plays a confounding role; that is, whether it affects the other parameters, regardless of whether it is statistically significant itself. As we will see, it did not. Looking at the other parameter estimates, we can see that a tribe's stance on government is not statistically significant, as neither are dyadwise nor edgewise shared partners. We could have estimated additional models in order to determine whether these variables should remain in the models or be discarded, but since here we are primarily concerned with religion's effect on adversarial tie formation.

We also evaluated the GOF for each of the models. In each case, the models generated graphs that did not significantly vary from the original network in terms of the distribution of degree, edgewise shared partners, or other measures—some of which, such as geodesic distance, were not specified in the model.[10] The models are therefore considered to provide a reasonable fit for the data. That is to say, they describe the data well.

Step 5: Interpreting ERGM output

As we noted above, because religion was not a statistically significant predictor of adversarial tie formation in the first two models, we estimated a third model without religion as a variable in order to see whether it plays a confounding role. Because the values of none of the variable estimates changed by more than 10 percent, we can conclude that religion is not a confounder and therefore unimportant in terms of fitting a model.[11] This point was reinforced by the fact that according to the GOF tests Model 3 proved to be a good fit for the data. We can also use the AIC and BIC measures to compare

Table 10.3 Output from models 1, 2, and 3

		Estimate (SE)		
		Model 1	*Model 2*	*Model 3*
Endogenous (Structural) Effects				
Edges (intercept)		−3.44***	−3.39***	−3.52***
		(0.66)	(0.64)	(0.68)
Isolates		1.98***	1.94***	1.89***
		(0.56)	(0.53)	(0.58)
GWDSP		−0.11	−0.08	−0.08
		(0.15)	(0.17)	(0.23)
(GWDSP alpha)		−1.13	−1.25	−1.35
		(2.87)	(3.95)	(5.31)
GWESP (fixed, 0)		0.40	0.38	0.37
		(0.25)	(0.25)	(0.26)
Exogenous Effects				
Homophily				
Religion			−0.12	
			(0.31)	
Main effects				
Religion=Shia	(Reference=Sunni)	0.12		
		(0.27)		
Anti-government	(Reference=neutral)	−0.11	−0.12	−0.10
		(0.34)	(0.33)	(0.33)
Pro-government	(Reference=neutral)	−0.37	−0.34	−0.38
		(0.25)	(0.25)	(0.27)
Anti-Taliban	(Reference=neutral)	1.21***	1.17***	1.19***
		(0.27)	(0.29)	(0.31)
Pro-Taliban	(Reference=neutral)	0.46+	0.44+	0.43
		(0.26)	(0.26)	(0.25)
Dyadic covariates				
Afghan tribal interrelations		−0.44	−0.31	−0.18
		(1.09)	(1.01)	(1.02)
AIC		402.5	402.8	401.3
BIC		472.0	472.3	464.5

+ Statistically significant at the 0.10 probability level.
*** Statistically significant at the 0.001 probability level.

the models.[12] These are global measures and should not be used to infer a model's actual fit. Instead, they are intended to compare the models in terms of their relative efficiency in describing the network, given the number of variables in the model. For both, lower values are considered to be better, more efficient models. As we can see the smaller AIC and BIC scores suggest that Model 3 is better than the other two models but not to any great extent.

What remains to be done is describe what may still be ascertained from the model in the absence of the religious explanation. Focusing on Model 3, it is apparent that neither sentiment for government, nor dyadwise shared partners, nor edgewise shared partners, nor intertribal relationships are significant. We interpret this to mean that the likelihood of creating an adversarial tie, given any one of them, is not meaningfully different from random chance (probability = 0.5, or the same as a coin flip). Interestingly, while pro-Taliban tribes are no more likely than unlikely to form an adversarial tie, anti-Taliban ties are. The estimated anti-Taliban coefficient is both positive and statistically significant, indicating that negative sentiment toward the Taliban predicts (or explains) an *increase* in the chance of an adversarial tie forming, holding all other variables constant. Put somewhat more simply, all things equal, anti-Taliban tribes are more likely to make enemies. In terms of odds ratios we can conclude that anti-Taliban tribes are a little more than three times as likely (exp[1.19] = 3.29) to make an enemy than are other tribes. In terms of probability, we can say that anti-Taliban tribes have a 0.77 probability of forming an adversarial tie (3.29/[1 + 3.29] = 0.77).

Both the edges and isolates parameter estimates are statistically significant. The edges coefficient indicates that there is an overall negative tendency (i.e., tendency away) to forming adversarial ties, holding all other variables constant. The positive parameter for isolates is somewhat counterintuitive. By definition, isolated tribes have no ties, so how can being an isolated tribe increase the likelihood of forming an adversarial tie? The answer lies in recognizing that this is in comparison to tribes that do have adversarial ties. What the positive parameter may suggest is that tribes can only have so many enemies, and having too many enemies is a form of constraint.[13]

10.5 SUMMARY: LESSONS LEARNED

This chapter has shown how exponential random graph models can test hypotheses regarding the generative processes of tie formation. In these models, an observed dark network is the dependent variable, whereas a series of structural effects (micro-configurations) and attributes are the independent variables that explain the network. To illustrate how to estimate an ERGM, we modeled the formation of negative ties among Afghan tribes to inform hypothetical strategies regarding intertribal contention. This allowed us to rule out religion as a primary cause of intertribal feuds even though its role was unclear during our initial exploratory analysis. This example is somewhat out of the ordinary because it is more common to model positive ties between actors,[14] but the process is identical. In terms of actually estimating a model, the structure of ties is generally more important than the nature of the ties. In setting up the model, however, the nature of the ties—and what the analyst knows about how they are formed—can be deeply important.

This chapter also outlined a process for building ERGMs to understand tie formation in observed dark networks. We recommend that network analysts begin by reviewing what they know about the dark networks they are analyzing. This is largely accomplished using traditional research methods, discussions with experts, and exploratory analysis. Once this is done, they can develop hypotheses regarding tie formation, which will result in the selection of configurations and attributes to include in a model. The next step (i.e., refining or augmenting a model) can be quite tedious and time consuming. It is unlikely that analysts will get their model to converge and pass the GOF test in their first try. It is important not to get too discouraged at this point; building an ERGM is an iterative process. The final step is to interpret and report the output, which can be unintuitive at first. Fortunately, ERGMs are becoming more common, and several excellent examples exist that one can consult, such as Papachristos, Hureau, and Braga's (2013) analysis of gun violence among gangs, and Gondal and McClean's (2013a, 2013b) examination of lending patterns among Florentine families. To be sure, time is an issue when it comes to estimating ERGMs. However, the time involved should be seen as an investment that can help analysts illuminate processes that underlie the formation of dark networks.

10.6 QUESTIONS

1. ERGMs, unlike QAP and CUG, attempt to explain internal and external factors that give rise to a network's patterns at the local or micro level.
   a. True.
   b. False.
2. In ERGMs, the observed network serves as the dependent variable.
   a. True.
   b. False.
3. Factors that arise or are formed within a network that can be used to help explain an observed network are
   a. Endogenous.
   b. Exogenous.
   c. Both endogenous and exogenous.
   d. Unimportant.
4. Factors from outside of a network that can be used to help explain an observed network are
   a. Endogenous.
   b. Exogenous.
   c. Both endogenous and exogenous.
   d. Unimportant.

5. Which of the following are examples of exogenous factors?
   a. Actor nationality.
   b. Actor area of operation.
   c. Actor gender.
   d. All of the above.
6. The objective of a goodness of fit is to measure a goodness of fit, not a "perfection" of fit.
   a. True.
   b. False.
7. Mahalanobis distance, Akaike Inference Criterion (AIC), and Bayesian Inference Criterion (BIC) are examples of
   a. Model assessment measures.
   b. ERGMs.
   c. Endogenous factors.
   d. Exogenous factors.

10.7 ANSWERS

1. True.
2. True.
3. Endogenous (a).
4. Exogenous (b).
5. All of the above (d).
6. True.
7. Model assessment measures (a).

10.8 FURTHER READING

Two books are essential for learning more about ERGMs. Jenine Harris's *An Introduction to Exponential Random Graph Modeling* (Los Angeles and London: Sage Publications, 2014) and Dean Lusher, Johan H. Koskinen, and Garry L. Robins' (eds.) *Exponential Random Graph Models for Social Networks* (New York and Cambridge: Cambridge University Press, 2013). The former uses the R statnet package, while the latter uses the PNet suite of programs. Regardless of whether you use statnet or PNet, both books provide excellent introductions to ERGMs. In addition, analysts may want to consider the following:

- Stephen P. Borgatti, Martin G. Everett, and Jeffrey C. Johnson. 2013. Pp. 139–45 (Chapter 8) in *Analyzing Social Networks*. Thousand Oaks, CA: SAGE Publications.

- Christina Prell. 2011. Pp. 238–48 (Appendix 2) in *Social Network Analysis: History, Theory & Methodology*. London and Thousand Oaks, CA: SAGE Publications.
- Garry L. Robins. 2011. "Exponential Random Graph Models for Social Networks." Pp. 484–500 in *The SAGE Handbook of Social Network Analysis*, edited by John Scott and Peter J. Carrington. Los Angeles and London: SAGE Publications.

NOTES

1. Analysts can capture "sender" and "receiver" effects when they work with both directed networks and attribute data. For example, one could observe a "sender" effect when central actors send a lot of ties to others because of their attributes, which could also reflect processes related to homophily when actors choose their neighbors based on shared attributes.

2. This can be expressed as exp(estimate) / [1+exp(estimate)] = probability.

3. We use statnet in this example, but the following process is transferrable to the Windows program PNet.

4. The terms "actormatch/Matching," "actormix/Mismatch," and "actorfactor/Attribute-based Activity" are used by statnet and PNet, respectively.

5. Analysts can also use options to fix the graph density, which can help models converge.

6. https://cran.r-project.org/web/packages/ergm/vignettes/ergm-term-crossRef.html.

7. In such cases, it is an acceptable practice to experiment with removing any variables that appear problematic.

8. Estimated in statnet.

9. Consult the book's website for more detailed treatment of how to process these data in each program.

10. For details on how this was done, see the book's website.

11. The benchmark used here—a change in the estimates of 10 percent or more—is somewhat arbitrary. In practice, an analyst will generally not have such a clear-cut delineation. Hosmer and Lemeshow (1989:66) recommend that the any "important" changes in the estimates for any variable of particular interest to the analyst be treated as a confounder and retained within the model, regardless of the significance of the confounding variable. In this case, religion was the variable of interest, and its inclusion and exclusion appeared to have no substantial effect on any of the other variables.

12. The Mahalanobis distance is an overall measure of model GOF used by the PNet suite of programs, which takes into account the covariance of the included statistics (Wang, Robins and Pattison 2009). Smaller Mahalanobis distances indicate a better fit of the data (Wang et al. 2014:24).

13. One last item of note concerns the values of GWDSP, GWDSP alpha, and GWESP. These models were run in statnet, which offers the analyst the option of having the program calculate the alpha value for them. That function was not implemented

in PNet at the time of this writing, and no plans have yet been announced to add the capability. Rather, PNet offers the equivalent function of statnet's GWDSP (fixed) where the user must input an alpha level. It is recommended that the alpha value (or lambda value in PNet) is incrementally raised for each successive iteration of the model until its estimates cease to improve (Goodreau et al. 2008). Keep in mind that the conversion between alpha in statnet and lambda in PNet is alpha = ln(lambda), so an alpha value of 0.2 in statnet would correspond to a lambda value of ln(0.2) = 1.22 in PNet.

14. However, Papachristos et al. (2013) use ERGMs to estimate the probability of gang-on-gang violence.

Chapter 11

Longitudinal Analyses of Dark Networks

Although the use of social network analysis (SNA) to study of dark networks has grown dramatically in recent years, most analyses have used data that provided only snapshots at a single point in time. Seldom have they drawn on longitudinal network data that capture how groups have changed and adapted, making it difficult to explore the possible causes and consequences of such changes. In part, this has been because longitudinal network data have been difficult to come by and the methods for examining them underdeveloped. For instance, Wasserman and Faust (1994) make little mention of longitudinal networks in their canonical SNA text. Only in the final chapter do they note the importance of developing good and easy-to-use methods for examining longitudinal network data (Wasserman and Faust 1994:730–31). In recent years, this situation has begun to change among researchers and scholars. Longitudinal network data and methods for their analysis are becoming more common. Early studies have been largely descriptive in nature, but they are increasingly becoming more sophisticated, employing various methods that seek to identify the causes and consequences of network change (Breiger, Carley and Pattison 2003a; de Nooy 2011; Doreian and Stockman 1997; McCulloh and Carley 2011; Snijders 2005; Snijders, Bunt and Steglich 2010; Steglich, Snijders and Pearson 2010).

To date, most of these studies have focused on "bright" or "light" networks. Only a handful have examined dark networks longitudinally. One example is Xu, Hu, and Chen's (2009) analysis of the global Salafi jihad, which found that it not only evolved into a scale-free network but also appeared to have passed through three distinct phases. Another (Hu, Kaza, and Chen 2009), which studied a co-offending network, found that acquaintances and shared vehicle affiliations served as key facilitators of tie formation, while age, race, and gender did not. More recently, Everton and Cunningham (2014,

2015) have examined a terrorist network that adapted itself to a changing and increasingly hostile environment. Perhaps the greatest amount of work on longitudinal dark networks belongs to Kathleen Carley and her colleagues (Carley 2003, 2006; Carley et al. 2003; Carley, Lee and Krackhardt 2002) whose dynamic dark network modeling have contributed greatly to the field. For instance, McCulloh and Carley (2011) modeled a series of longitudinal networks using the social network change detection (SNCD) method and found that the al-Qaeda communication network underwent a statistically significant change in 1997, which may explain a series of events that helped unite Islamic militants and organize al-Qaeda for terrorist attacks aimed at the United States. Everton and Cunningham (2012) also used this method to detect significant changes and identify possible causes of changes in the topography of the Noordin Top network.

The most recent, and perhaps the most fruitful progress in modeling longitudinal network data is the actor-oriented models (SAOMs) developed by Tom Snijders and his colleagues (Snijders 2005; Snijders, Bunt and Steglich 2010; Van de Bunt, Van Duijin and Snijders 1999), which can model the mechanisms underlying a network's structural evolution. SAOMs are just beginning to be used for analyzing dark networks (Cunningham, Everton and Murphy 2015). In this chapter, we explore the how-to of these models, using longitudinal data on a sixteenth-century Anabaptist Leadership Network. As we noted back in the preface, the term dark network is typically reserved for groups such as terrorists, gangs, drug traffickers, criminal organizations, white collar conspiracies, and the like. However, it can refer to groups that history considers "good," and history generally considers most sixteenth-century Anabaptists to be good. They were, after all, the forerunners of contemporary religious groups such as the Mennonites, Amish, Hutterites, and Bruderhof. However, in the sixteenth century, they almost certainly were a dark network. In their quest to practice adult baptism (Anabaptist means "rebaptizer"), they endured relentless persecution at the hands of Roman Catholic and Protestant authorities. Indeed, of the 55 individuals in the network we will examine who were Anabaptists, 26 were either executed or killed in battles. Moreover, one Anabaptist group briefly established a theocracy in Münster, Westphalia, where torture and mass executions became commonplace.

In this chapter, we will draw on SAOMs in order to tease out some of the potential mechanisms behind the radicalization that led to the Münster Rebellion of 1534–1535. As we stated in chapter 9, the manner in which social network analysts develop models largely depends on how they draw from theory. This chapter, which in slight contrast to the exponential random graph model (ERGM) chapter that drew more from exploratory analysis, develops models based on theories regarding social networks and radicalization. We begin with an introduction to SAOMs. As we will see, they share similarities with the ERGMs examined in the previous chapter. Next we turn to a brief history of the Münster Rebellion. This will not, of course, be exhaustive; only enough is provided in order to set the stage for the subsequent analysis. Next, we turn our attention to the interplay of social networks and religious radicalization to illustrate the applicability of these models.

11.1 STOCHASTIC ACTOR-ORIENTED MODELS

SAOMs seek to represent network dynamics on the basis of observed longitudinal network data and evaluate these according to the paradigm of statistical inference. They are similar to ERGMs (Harris 2014; Lusher, Koskinen and Robins 2013; Robins et al. 2007), in that they assume that the observed network structure is, in part, a function of local patterns of ties, sometimes called micro-configurations (e.g., closed triads), that reflect endogenous social processes (e.g., network closure). Like ERGMs, they test whether a particular configuration occurs more frequently than one would expect given the other configurations included in the model. They differ in that they are designed for longitudinal social network data and explicitly model the choices of actors, who "are assumed to control their outgoing ties and to make changes in these ties according to short-term goals and restrictions" (Snijders and Koskinen 2013:138). Despite this difference, analyst can develop and apply SAOMs in a similar fashion as ERGMs. Readers will recognize many of the similarities outlined below to a proposed set of guidelines in the previous chapter.

1. Review the context and what is known about the network
   - Consult various theories about the processes behind tie formation
   - Conduct exploratory analysis using visualizations and/or descriptive measures, such as network interconnectedness and centralization
2. Construct the model to be tested
   - Develop hypotheses based on previous research and/or exploratory analysis
   - Identify variables of interest
   - Evaluate the network structure for micro-configurations to be included in the model
3. Check initial model for convergence and evaluate goodness of fit (GOF)
4. Refine the model
5. Evaluate the GOF for the final model
6. Interpret output

When one considers the structure of ties between actors in a network at some initial point $X(t_0)$ and then revisits the structure of ties between the same actors at a later time $X(t_1)$, it is expected that there may be some differences in the network's structure between $X(t_0)$ and $X(t_1)$. Observations of the same set, or panel, of actors may be taken at numerous points in time $X(t_0)$, $X(t_1)$, ..., $X(t_{M-1})$, where M is the number of time points, or observation moments. SAOMs make use of the structural variations observed within the network over two or more points in time. Beginning with a network's initial state $X(t_0)$, SAOMs model the changes in ties between each time point to estimate how ties within the network grow and change over time. Changes in network structures over time are, in most cases, not arbitrary. Some ties will be particularly resilient, making them resistant to change over the course of repeated observations. However, new ties will almost certainly form and others will probably dissolve. There is also the possibility, particularly in dark networks, for some actors to drop out of the network.

We may therefore use the network's structure at the initial and subsequent observations to infer about whether particular endogenous forces, starting with the network's structure at $X(t_0)$, explain the changes in ties within a particular network. In SAOMs, *endogenous effects* are structural characteristics that may predict a change in state such as an added or dissolved tie. Such effects include commonly noted social processes such as popularity (measured as the degree of actor), when an actor acts as an intermediary (measured as betweenness), and the tendency for a friend of a friend to become a friend (measured as triadic closure) (Ripley et al. 2015). In most social situations, however, endogenous factors are insufficient for predicting or explaining how ties form or break within a network (Scott 2011). SAOMs, therefore, also incorporate the option of modeling *exogenous effects* in the form of actor and dyadic covariates. Attributes such as age, affiliation, or experience can be tested for their power to explain changes in ties between time points. Covariates may be incorporated in terms of attribute similarity or in terms such as homophily/heterophily, that is, the tendency for actors to form ties with alters who are similar/dissimilar in regard to some attribute (e.g., age, race, gender, and religion) (Ripley et al. 2015).

In order to test whether, and to what extent, various effects predict changes in the network, SAOMs model tie changes between time points as a continuous time Markov chain, in which a finite number of actors have an opportunity to change a tie. Tie changes in the network are, therefore, estimated in a manner analogous to that of agent-based simulation models (Snijders, Bunt and Steglich 2010), and the resulting models can be expressed in a manner similar to generalized linear models where the probability that an actor will change a tie is expressed as a linear combination of effects (Snijders, Bunt and Steglich 2010):

$$f_i(\beta, x) = \sum_k \beta_k s_{ki}(x) \qquad (11.1)$$

The objective function $f_i(b, x)$ represents the probability of actor i changing a tie, given the opportunity. The probability of a tie change is calculated as the sum of a set of effects $s_{ki}(x)$, each with a corresponding weight β_k. The effects may be endogenous, exogenous, or a combination of both.[1]

Although the stochastic actor-based approach has seen substantial use in the study of directed networks, the clandestine nature of dark networks poses a substantial limit on inferring tie direction or dissolution. For this reason, dark network data make it necessary to model only the establishment of edges (mutual ties), with the assumption that—in a network where trust is equated with survival—ties, once formed, are mutual and persistent. In many instances ties may both form and dissolve, all in the unobserved space between observations. All the observer will generally know is the start and end states of the network. When tracking dark networks, as a rule, it is much easier to detect the formation of a tie than its dissolution (except, of course, when one or both actors are removed or remove themselves).

The limitations of data collection in dark network models typically limit analysts to testing factors involved in the *establishment or growth of connections* within this network. An effective means for estimating such factors under these conditions is to use the *unilateral initiative and reciprocal confirmation* (UIRC) *model*, which assumes that undirected ties are established when one actor will unilaterally propose a tie, and the tie is created only if the alter agrees (Ripley et al. 2015:47).[2] SAOMs implicitly assume that all actors in the network are aware of one another and therefore possess the potential to form a mutual tie (Snijders, Bunt and Steglich 2010:49). This is an important consideration and may in some cases make it necessary for an analyst to subset the network accordingly. For instance, social network analysts may want to extract a network's largest component before developing an SAOM. Such subsetting, however, is left to analysts' discretion and should be based on factors that may reasonably be construed as either inhibiting or facilitating mutual access between actors. Finally, because SAOMs use panel data, each network must include the same number and set of actors. However, since actors often drop out of dark networks because members are killed, we often have to introduce structural zeroes in order to indicate that it was no longer possible to form or maintain ties with those actors.[3]

11.2 A STUDY IN RADICALIZATION: SIXTEENTH-CENTURY ANABAPTISTS AND THE MÜNSTER REBELLION

Anabaptists trace their beginnings to Zurich in 1524, with a small group known as the Zwingli Radicals, who later became known as the Swiss Brethren (Williams 1975). They originally followed the teachings of the

Protestant Reformer, Ulrich Zwingli, but after they began practicing adult (i.e., believer's) baptism, the ruling authorities (both magisterial and religious) quickly outlawed the practice and made it punishable by death (McDaniel 2007). Although in today's world, most Christians regard adult baptism as a legitimate practice, in the sixteenth century most did not. It was seen as a form of revolt. Infant baptism not only marked individuals as Christians, but it also marked them as citizens of the state. Thus, authorities sought to repress it, and religious groups, such as the Anabaptists, did not adopt the practice lightly.

Although we generally associate Anabaptists with pacifism, a small group of violent Anabaptists seized control of Münster, Westphalia (present-day Germany) from 1534 to 1535 and attempted to install a theocracy. The group was indirectly influenced by Melchior Hoffman, an Anabaptist leader with ties to the Netherlands and the Lower Rhine region (Williams 1975). Hoffman converted to Lutheranism in 1522 and immediately entered into the ministry, although in 1525 he traveled to Wittenberg in order to receive Luther's blessing of his preaching (Neff and Packull 1987). He traveled extensively through Europe preaching the virtues of Lutheranism, but over time his teachings increasingly incorporated apocalyptic beliefs about the end times and the imminent return of Jesus Christ (Neff and Packull 1987). After contact with a group of Anabaptists in Strasbourg in 1530, Hoffman founded his own Anabaptist sect that became known as the Melchiorites (Geortz 1996). He initially began baptizing adults, but after Hapsburg authorities executed nine of his followers, he suspended the practice and declared that in the final days true baptism would resume with the coming of the Holy Spirit (Stayer 1979). Hoffman believed and taught that Christ would soon return, Strasbourg would become the "New Jerusalem," and he and his 144,000 followers would meet Christ (Clasen 1972). Hoffman also believed that he was God's prophet tasked with revealing the secrets of Christ's second coming. Although Hoffman was not a pacifist—he believed that governments (including Christian rulers) could use violence—he did not believe Christians could use violence to advance the faith or hasten cosmic events (Stayer 1979). Hoffman was arrested in 1533 and sentenced to 10 years in prison, during which time he continued to write. However, his influence waned because his predictions about the end times failed to come true.

After Hoffman's arrest, Jan Matthys, a baker from Haarlem, assumed leadership of the Melchiorites (Stayer 1979), reinstated adult baptism (Klötzer 2007), and attracted a substantial following. He eventually moved to Münster in mid-February of 1534, but not until after hundreds of Anabaptists had migrated to the city where Anabaptist beliefs and practices were in ascendancy, largely because of the writings of the local Lutheran pastor,

Bernhard Rothmann, who embraced believer's baptism and condemned private ownership of property "divisive and contrary to God's will" (McDaniel 2007:66). Münster's Lutherans and Catholics grew increasingly uncomfortable with the growing power of the Anabaptists and as many as 2,000 non-Anabaptists left the city. Two of Matthys's followers, John van Leyden and GerritBoekbinder, visited Münster and reported that Rothmann was teaching doctrines similar to their own (Wikipedia 2015). This led Matthys to identify Münster as the "New Jerusalem" and send several of his disciples to Münster in January 1534, who baptized (or rebaptized) several prominent leaders, including Rothmann, along with another 1,000 adults (Wikipedia 2015; Williams 1975). They also introduced the apocalyptic teachings that would eventually lead the city down the path toward violence.

In early February, the city's Anabaptists gained political control of Münster, and when a perihelion appeared in sky, they interpreted this as a sign of the imminent redemption of God's chosen and the destruction of the damned, and in late February they began evicting those unwilling to be baptized (Klötzer 2007; Williams 1975). By this time Matthys had moved to Münster, and he and the other leaders sent out apostles to invite people to the "New Jerusalem." As many as 2,500 people migrated to the city and essentially replaced the Protestants and Catholics who had left (McDaniel 2007). After the Anabaptists gained control of Münster, the Prince-Bishop of the region,[4] Franz von Waldeck, amassed an army and began to lay siege to the city (Wikipedia 2015). On Easter Sunday in April, Matthys, who had previously prophesied that God's judgment would come to the wicked on that day, led a small band of followers and attacked the Prince-Bishop's army. Matthys was killed, and his head was cut off and placed on a pole outside the city gates (Krahn, van der Zijpp and Stayer 1987; McDaniel 2007).

After Matthys's death, John van Leyden gained control of the city and proclaimed himself King of Münster. He legalized polygamy, married Matthys's widow (along with 16 other women), and renamed Münster the "New Israel" because he believed he and the city's inhabitants were helping to usher in God's kingdom by punishing God's enemies (Klötzer 2007). He ruthlessly administered "justice," actively participating in the public executions of those who offended the kingdom or were perceived as a threat (Stayer 1979). His brutality led to numerous defections, and with the help of a few Anabaptist guards, the Prince-Bishop regained control of the city in June of 1535, killing hundreds of its inhabitants in the process (McDaniel 2007). In January 1536, van Leyden and several other leaders were tortured and then executed in Münster's marketplace. Their bodies were exhibited in cages, which hung from the steeple of St. Lambert's Church. The bones were later removed, but the cages remain (McDaniel 2007; Wikipedia 2015).

11.3 SOCIAL NETWORKS AND RELIGIOUS RADICALIZATION

All this raises the question, "What leads groups to radicalize?" Although there are numerous theories, we will test one here (with slight modifications) that draws on social network theory and takes into account religious factors (Everton Forthcoming). It takes as its point of departure Cass Sunstein's (2002, 2003, 2009) "law of group polarization," which holds that when like-minded individuals deliberate as a group, the group's opinion will move toward the extreme versions of its collective belief. Sunstein's law is similar to the echo-chamber effect, except that rather than simply holding those ideas and beliefs it can become amplified when a group meets regularly with little exposure to competing views, it contends that the beliefs of a group will gravitate to the views of its most extreme members. To be clear, the term does not mean that group members move to opposite ends of a pole on an issue, but rather that they collectively shift to a more polarizing view. As Sunstein notes, "The effect of deliberation is both to decrease variance among group members, as individual differences diminish, and also to produce convergence on a relatively more extreme point among predeliberation judgments" (Sunstein 2002:178).

Social Networks and Group Polarization

Sunstein's law implies that groups that distance themselves from the wider society and engage in intense social interaction are more likely to become radicalized (i.e., polarized) than are those that remain connected to the wider society and interact periodically. Reframed in terms of network analysis, this suggests that groups are more likely to radicalize if they become increasingly dense and more isolated, a process that scholars sometimes refer to as network closure. Figure 11.1 sketches a simple model of group radicalization. Although numerous factors undoubtedly affect network closure, here we focus on two: (1) coercion (social and political) and (2) sociocultural tension. Coercion refers to the degree that the political or social environment restricts the ability of groups to meet and deliberate. This can occur through governmental regulations, social sanctions, or outright repression (Grim and Finke 2010). Figure 11.1 suggests that the higher the level of coercion, the greater the likelihood that groups will seek to distance themselves from government authorities and society at large. The second factor, the degree of sociocultural tension that exists between a particular group and its surrounding society, results from the extent to which a group's beliefs and practices deviate from accepted cultural norms (Stark and Bainbridge 1985). Although coercion and sociocultural tension often go hand in hand, they are not the same. Coercion

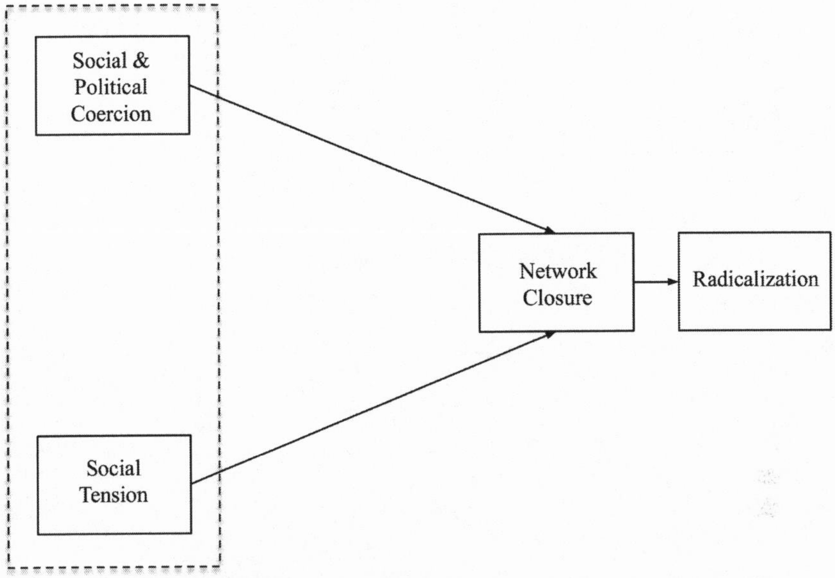

Figure 11.1 A Simple Model of Group Radicalization (adapted from Everton Forthcoming)

is a society-wide phenomenon, while tension is focused on the relation between specific groups and the larger society.

The model outlined in Figure 11.1 treats closure as a black box and does not identify the specific processes by which closure occurs. Figure 11.2 adds these processes into the model: (1) recruitment through strong (i.e., trusted), rather than weak, ties, (2) the limiting or severing ties to nonmembers, and (3) increased interaction among existing members. The first refers to tendency of groups to recruit new members through their social ties (Lofland and Stark 1965; McAdam 1986; McAdam and Paulsen 1993; Sageman 2004; Snow, Zurcher and Ekland-Olson 1980; Stark and Bainbridge 1980). Groups that feel pressure to distance themselves from the larger society tend to limit recruitment through ties of trust (i.e., strong ties) (Passy 2003), especially when the livelihood of the group is at stake. Recruiting primarily through strong ties can lead to an increase in network closure because it becomes more likely that ties will form between previously unlinked actors. This is the process known as triadic closure, which we illustrated earlier with Granovetter's forbidden triad.

Groups that seek to distance themselves from the wider community also tend to limit their ties with outsiders. Doing so limits the exposure that group members have to competing views, which is a concern for some groups. For example, the Branch Davidians forbade members to marry nonbelievers (Pitts 1995), and after Jim Jones led his congregation, Peoples Temple, to Guyana,

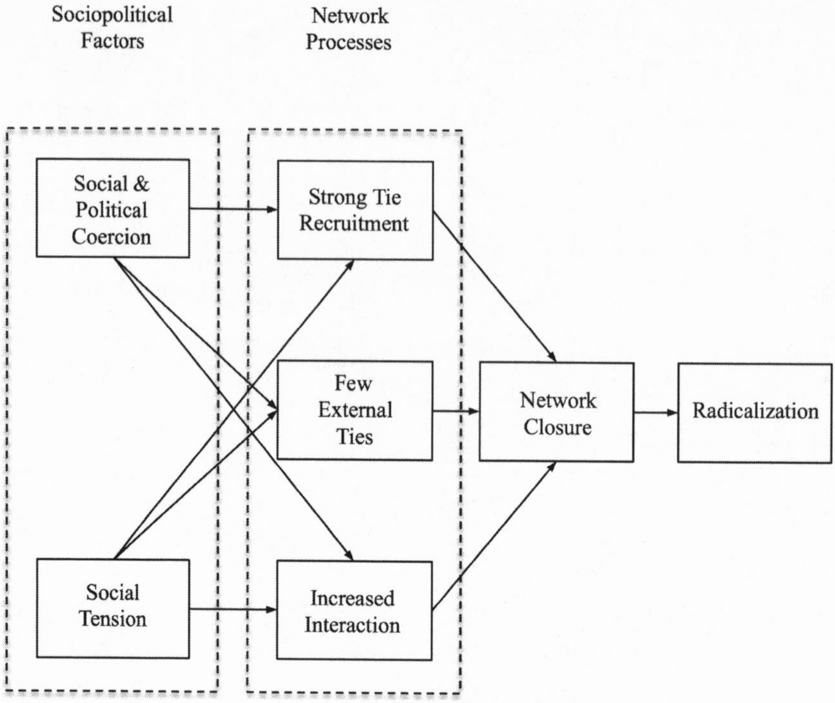

Figure 11.2 A Social Network Model of Group Radicalization (adapted from Everton Forthcoming)

he severed most of the group's external ties in order to further socialize "his followers to a leftist perspective on world events" (Hall 1987:237). Finally, and independent of these first two factors, network closure is characterized by increased interaction among existing group members. Not only do new ties among members form and ties to external members become less common, but also members who previously had ties to one another interact more frequently. This essentially describes the Hamburg Cell, which played a key role in the 9/11 terrorist attacks, once several of its members moved into the same apartment (Sageman 2004). Over the period of time that Mohamed Atta's name was on the apartment's lease,[5] 29 individuals listed it as their home address. It became the place where the cell met to practice their faith and discuss politics, and their discussions "became increasingly virulent" and talk about defeating "world-Jewry" and the United States "through jihad . . . became more prominent over time" (Sageman 2004:106).[6]

Religion, Social Networks, and Radicalization

Figure 3 captures the role that religion can play in the radicalization process. As it suggests, certain types of beliefs can either indirectly or directly affect

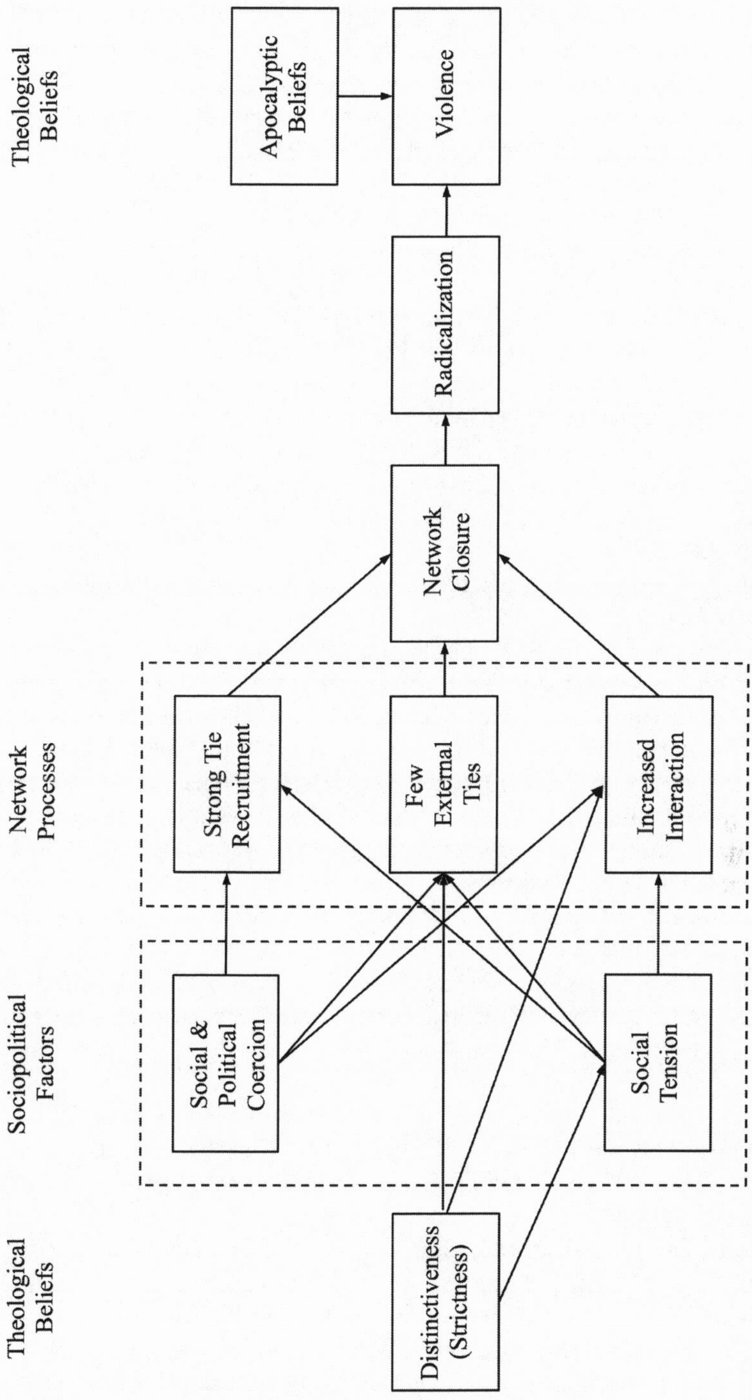

Figure 11.3 A Social Network Model of Religious Radicalization (adapted from Everton Forthcoming)

the degree of network closure or feed extremist beliefs about the surrounding world. Scholars have learned, for instance, that "social groups know who they are in large measure by knowing who is in and who is not. Ingroups establish what it means to be 'in' primarily by contrasting with outgroups whose members are 'out'" (Smith et al. 1998:91). This process can increase the tension between groups and the environment in which they are embedded (Alimi, Bosi and Demetriou 2012:13; Stark and Bainbridge 1985). And religious groups, in particular, those with theologically distinct beliefs, excel at demarcating who is in and who is out (Smith et al. 1998; Stark and Bainbridge 1985). Theologically distinct groups also place considerable demands on their adherents in terms of their finances and time, as well as restricting what they can wear, whom they can befriend, and what pleasures they can enjoy (Iannaccone 1994). Unsurprisingly, such demands reduce their ties with outsiders (Iannaccone 1994; Stark and Bainbridge 1985), not only because they encourage members to only socialize with other members, but also because they limit the time that members have to form and maintain ties with nonmembers.

Finally, it is far more likely for group radicalization to manifest itself violently if groups believe that the use of violence is divinely sanctioned. This often occurs in tandem with apocalyptic beliefs that hold that the final confrontation between good and evil. As Juergensmeyer (2001) notes, religious groups often resort to violence when they believe they are in the midst of a cosmic war between good and evil in which they are expected to establish order by destroying disorder (Gregg 2009). Indeed, "once a messianic advent is seen as imminent, particular elements of a messianic doctrine become critical in pulling a believer in the direction of terror" (Rapaport 1988:200). It is not uncommon for apocalyptic groups to embrace the belief that destruction can hasten the arrival of a new divine age. Such beliefs feed what Hafez (2003; 2004) calls antisystem frames, which see state and society (i.e., the system) as beyond redemption and therefore in need of annihilation. As Figure 11.3 indicates, apocalyptic beliefs play an independent role in the model. They increase the likelihood that radicalization will devolve into violence.

11.4 A LONGITUDINAL ANALYSIS OF THE ANABAPTIST LEADERSHIP NETWORK

As noted earlier, the network data we use for this analysis consists of 67 actors, 55 of whom were sixteenth-century Anabaptist leaders (McLaughlin 2015a). The remaining 12 were prominent Protestant Reformation leaders (e.g., Martin Luther, John Calvin, Ulrich Zwingli, Martin Bucer, and Philip Melanchthon), who had contact with and influenced some of the Anabaptist leaders included in the dataset. The original data were collected by Matthews et al. (2013) and consisted of 49 actors. Because the initial dataset did not include relational data on prominent Anabaptist leaders, such as Menno Simons (from whom the Anabaptist group, the Mennonites, take its name), McLaughlin (2015a, 2015b) drew on numerous other sources (e.g., Bender, Friedmann and Klassen 1990; Clasen 1972; Klötzer 2007; Krahn, van der Zijpp and Stayer 1987; Stayer 1979; Williams 1975) and expanded the dataset.

To illustrate the steps one might take to analyze a network longitudinally, we begin by first examining the network at various time points using network graphs and many of the topographical metrics discussed in chapter 4: density, average degree, cohesion, compactness, the global clustering coefficient, closure, and the E-I index. The only metric that we use here but did not discuss in the fourth chapter is closure, which is simply the average clustering coefficient of each actor weighted by their number of ties (Borgatti, Everett and Johnson 2013).[7] We begin with topographical metrics because although they are not as "sophisticated" as those produced by statistical models, they can still be quite informative. We then turn to our analysis of the data using SAOMs.

The basic approach for estimating an SAOM is to hypothesize as to what social processes gave rise to a particular network's global properties, and then build a model that takes these into account. As we noted above, local processes (i.e., endogenous factors) are operationalized in terms of the various micro-configurations found within a network (e.g., edges, stars, and open and closed triads), while actor attributes (i.e., exogenous factors) are operationalized in terms of actor covariates. In the following model we include two configurations—closed triads and alternating triangles (see Table 10.1 in the previous chapter)—that specifically test for increased network closure. Alternating triangles are simply a series of closed triads in which two actors share ties with numerous other actors in the network, so it is possible that one will be statistically significant but not the other. The estimated models also control for four additional micro-configurations—degree (edges), balance, actor popularity, and isolates. In SAOMs, the estimated degree coefficient is analogous to the intercept in standard regression models and usually not interpreted. The balance coefficient captures the tendency for actors to form ties with those who are structurally similar;[8] the actor popularity coefficient measures the degree to which one or a handful of actors form numerous ties; and the isolates coefficient reflects the effect of isolates in the network. We also test for whether apocalyptic beliefs played a role in tie formation, as well as control for three other exogenous factors: in particular, whether or not a leader identified as a Melchiorite, participated in the Münster Rebellion, or embraced believer's baptism.

Results

We begin with graphs of the entire network along with some descriptive network graphs and statistics. Figure 11.4 presents the entire Anabaptist Leadership network. In the network in the upper left, gray actors indicate individuals who were Anabaptists, while white actors indicate non-Anabaptist Protestant Reformers. An interesting aspect of the network is that without the non-Anabaptist Protestant Reformers, the Anabaptists leaders would be cut off from one another. Put somewhat differently, at the leadership level Protestant Reformers functioned as brokers between different sets of leaders. This is somewhat more obvious in the network in the upper right, where gray actors continue to indicate Anabaptists, white actors indicate Protestant Reformers, and black actor leaders associated with the Anabaptist Melchior Hoffman, who had a profound influence, including those who later participated in the Münster Rebellion. This last group is captured in the network graph in the lower center. Here the black actors indicate those involved in the Münster Rebellion, gray actors, Anabaptist not involved in the Münster Rebellion, and the white actors, Protestant Reformers. What is clear is that the leaders of the rebellion were deeply embedded in the network of Melchiorite Anabaptists.

Now let us consider some graphs of the leadership network at five different points in time Figure 11.5: 1525, 1530, 1535, 1540, and 1545. Here, black-colored actors indicate Melchiorites, gray indicate non-Melchiorite Anabaptists, and white indicate Protestant Reformers. Isolated actors (i.e., those with no ties) are hidden. In 1525 there is only one "Melchiorite": Melchior Hoffman himself, who had yet to convert to Anabaptism. By 1530, however, he had attracted some followers, and by 1535, the time of the Münster Rebellion, it is clear that the Anabaptist Leadership Network is essentially divided in two distinct groups with a few Protestant Reformers acting as intermediaries. The post-rebellion network in 1540 and 1545 is quite fragmented with the remaining Melchiorites forming a separate clique (Menno Simons, Dirk and Obbe Philips, and David Joris), except for Hoffman who was in jail and CornelisAppelman (not shown) who by 1540 was an isolate (i.e., unconnected to the rest of the network). Interestingly, none of the members of this clique were apocalyptic, which may explain, at least in part, why going forward the Anabaptist movement abandoned the beliefs and practices of the Münsterites.

We now turn to some basic SNA interconnectedness statistics of the leadership network over the five time periods: size, density, average degree, cohesion, compactness, the global clustering coefficient (standard and weighted), and the E-I index (Table 11.1). Readers can probably recognize by now that we cannot rely on the standard measure of density because each network is of a different size. In the table, the highest score has been set in bold with the exception of the E-I index for the Melchiorite Anabaptists because in 1525

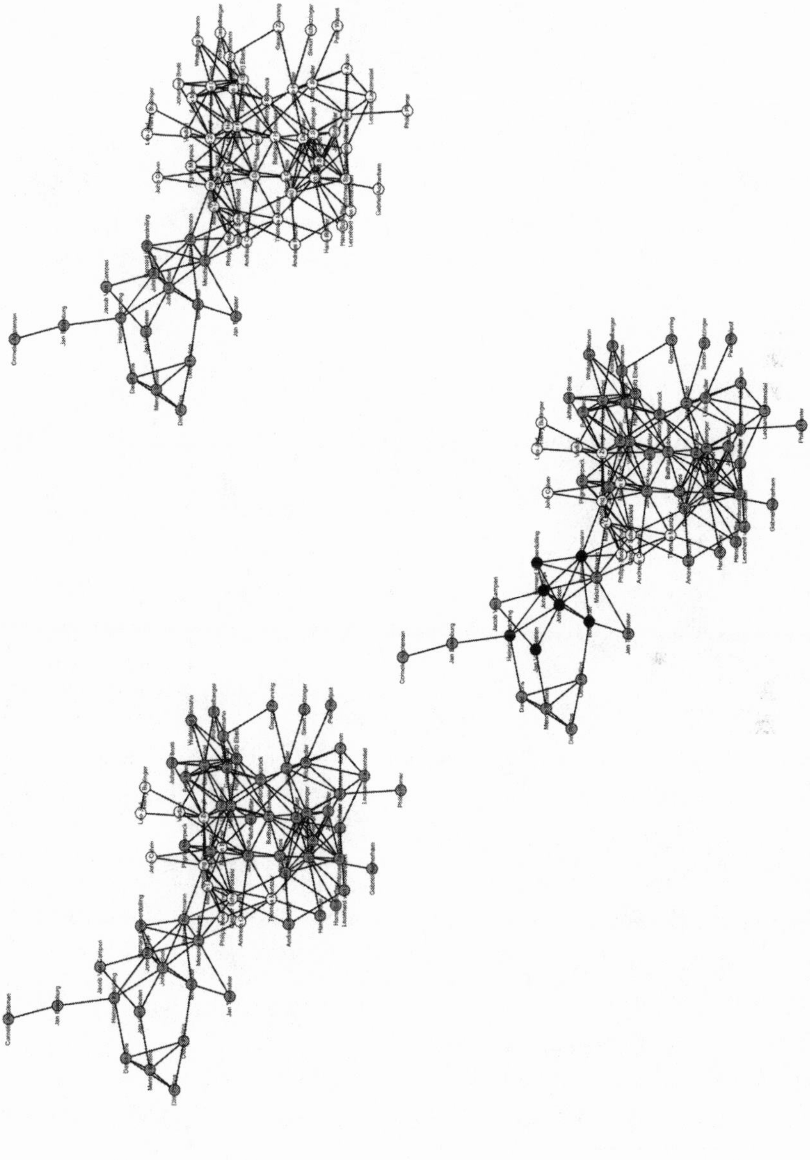

Figure 11.4 Anabaptist Leadership Network: Anabaptists, Melchiorites, and Münsterites

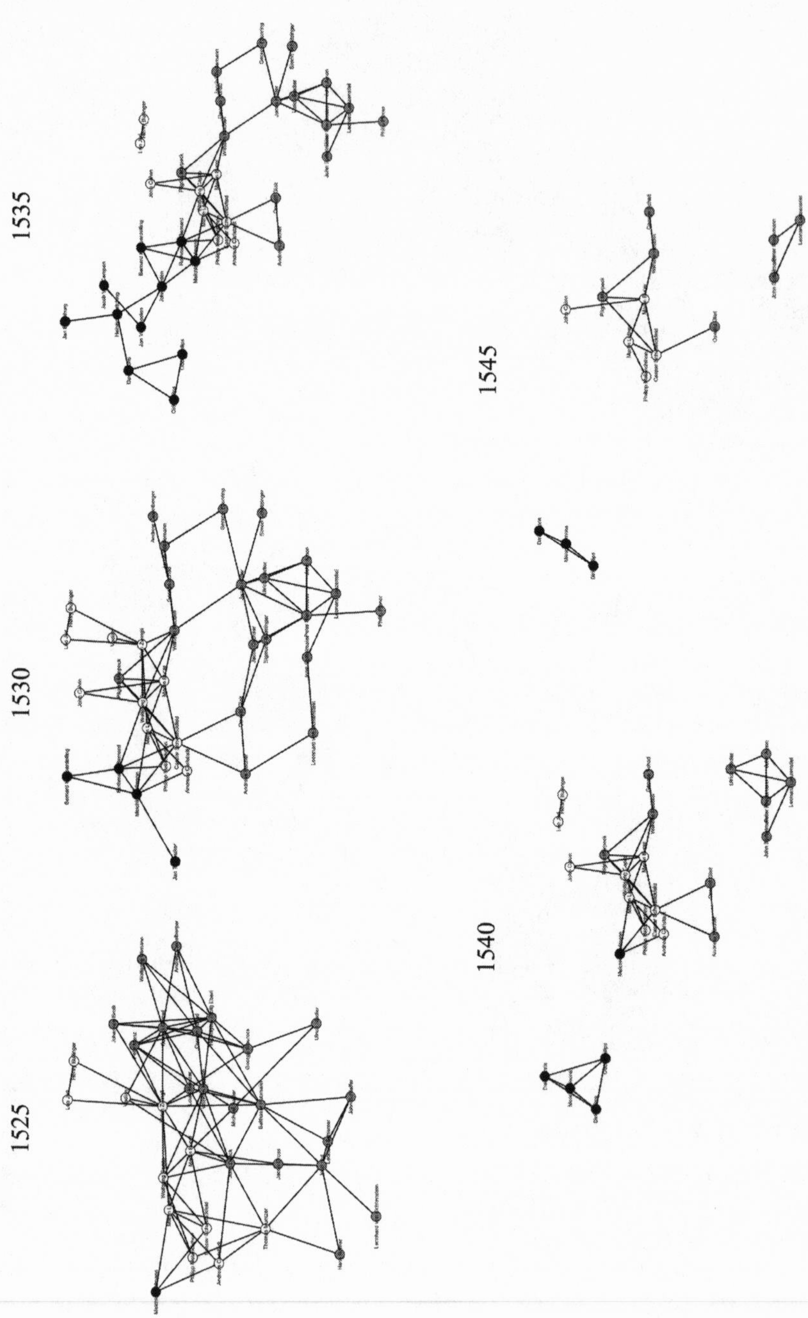

Figure 11.5 Anabaptist Leadership Network Over Time

Table 11.1 Measures of Anabaptist Leadership Network Interconnectedness, 1525–1545

	1525	*1530*	*1535*	*1540*	*1545*
Size	33	36	37	28	21
Density	**0.161**	0.102	0.086	0.098	0.076
Average Degree	**5.152**	3.556	3.081	2.643	1.524
Cohesion	**0.939**	0.890	0.794	0.251	0.200
Compactness	**0.475**	0.365	0.288	0.164	0.129
Global Clustering Coefficient	0.486	0.374	0.381	**0.534**	0.236
Closure (Weighted Global Clustering Coefficient)	0.369	0.372	0.407	**0.556**	0.414
E-I Index (Anabaptists)	–0.586	–0.650	**–0.671**	–0.524	–0.556
E-I Index (Non-Melchiorite Anabaptists)	–0.630	**–0.758**	–0.689	–0.481	–0.333
E-I Index (Melchiorite Anabaptists)	1.000	–0.143	**–0.647**	–0.600	–1.000
% Apocalyptic (Melchiorites/ Non-Melchiorites)	100/9.52	100/4.76	72.73/0.00	33.33/0.00	25.00/0.00

Source: McLaughlin (2015a).

there was only one "Melchiorite" in the dataset—Melchior Hoffman—and in 1545 there were only three (not including isolates). Thus, we focus on the E-I index of Melchiorite Anabaptists in the intervening years and highlight the year in which it reached its highest peak. The metrics paint an interesting picture. The density, average degree, cohesion, and compactness scores suggest that the leadership network reached its highest level of density in 1525, while the two global clustering coefficients (standard and weighted) indicate that it reached its peak in 1540. What these scores suggest, and which is born out of the network maps presented in Figure 11.5, is that the network's overall interconnectedness did peak in 1525 and began to decline thereafter as Anabaptist leaders were killed or executed. The decreasing cohesion and compactness scores perhaps best capture this decline (note the huge drop in the network's level of cohesion from 1535 to 1540). However, as the network fragmented, it broke into small groups in which almost everyone had ties to everyone else, which is why the clustering coefficient peaked in 1540.

Perhaps, more instructive for our purposes here are the three sets of E-I indices for all Anabaptists, non-Melchiorite Anabaptists, and Melchiorite Anabaptists. Recall that the index ranges from –1.00 to 1.00, where a score of –1.00 indicates that group members only have ties to other members (i.e., all internal ties), a score of 1.00 indicates that group members only have ties to nonmembers (i.e., all external ties), and a score of 0.00 indicates that in the aggregate members have an equal number of internal and external ties. What these scores tell us is that the non-Melchiorites reached their highest level of internal interconnectedness (i.e., when its E-I index reached its lowest level) in 1530, while Melchiorites (and Anabaptists as a whole) reached their highest level of internal interconnectedness in 1535. These trends, in particular that of the Melchiorites, coincided with the Münster Rebellion and is entirely consistent with the theory outlined above, which argued that as groups turn in on themselves and limit their ties to outsiders, there is an increased likelihood that the group will radicalize.

Nevertheless, observant readers will note that the E-I index of non-Melchiorites is actually lower than the E-I index of the Melchiorites, which raises an obvious question, "Why didn't the non-Melchiorite Anabaptists embrace violence?" The answer, we believe, lies in the final statistic listed in the table: the percentage of members (Melchiorite and non-Melchiorite) who held apocalyptic beliefs. As one can see, in the lead up to the Münster Rebellion the percentage of Melchiorites who held apocalyptic beliefs was quite high, especially when compared to non-Melchiorites, which once again is entirely consistent with the theory outlined earlier: namely, that apocalyptic beliefs combined with group radicalization increase the likelihood that groups will engage in violent behavior.

It is now time to consider the results from the SAOMs (Table 11.2). We initially estimated two models that included four and five time periods, respectively: 1525, 1530, 1535, 1540, and 1545; 1525, 1530, 1535, and 1540. However, both models failed to converge, which led us to estimate a reduced model that included only three time periods (1530, 1535, and 1540). This converged adequately (the maximum convergence is less that 0.10), but unfortunately none of the estimated parameters are statistically significant (see Model 1 in Table 11.2). Thus, in our second and third models we dropped the balance and isolated the effects and estimated the models that included either the Melchiorite (Model 2) or the Münster Rebellion (Model 3) covariates because, as we observe in Figure 11.4, those involved in the Münster Rebellion were also Melchiorites. Neither transitive triads nor alternating triangles proved statistically significant when they were included in the second and third models. However, when we included them in the models separately, the estimated coefficient for transitive triads proved to be statistically significant but not the one for alternating triangles. Thus, the second and third models include only an effect for transitive triads. We also retained the degree effect because, as with the edge coefficients in ERGMs, it is analogous to the intercept in a multivariate regression model.

The results for models 2 and 3 are presented in Table 11.2. In both cases the overall convergence statistics improved upon the first model. This is especially true for Model 3. In both models the degree coefficient is negative and statistically significant, which indicates that there was an overall negative tendency to tie formation. This may sound counterintuitive, but keep in mind this is only true after taking into account the effects of the other variables in the

Table 11.2 Estimated Coefficients of Stochastic Actor-Oriented Models

	Estimate (SE)			
	Model 1	*Model 2*	*Model 3*	*Model 4*
Structural Variables				
Degree (intercept)	0.508	−1.146***	−1.259***	−1.278***
	(3.575)	(0.288)	(0.342)	(0.319)
Transitive Triads	−3.755	0.622***	0.715***	0.704***
	(7.205)	(0.213)	(0.251)	(0.234)
Balance	0.751			
	(1.199)			
Alternating Triangles	5.938			
	(11.216)			
Isolates	4.799			
	(6.998)			
Commonalities				
Melchiorite	2.616	0.892		
	(7.462)	(0.550)		
Münster Rebellion	−5.174		−1.807+	−1.958+
	(12.645)		(1.053)	(1.093)
Believer's Baptism	−0.105	0.587	0.556	
	(1.243)	(0.428)	(0.518)	
Apocalyptic	1.653	−0.117	1.431	1.632+
	(4.658)	(0.539)	(0.870)	(0.907)
Rate Parameters				
Rate Period 1	0.447	0.995	0.822	0.810
	(0.105)	(0.252)	(0.195)	(0.193)
Rate Period 2	0.120	0.200	0.187	0.190
	(0.060)	(0.099)	(0.092)	(0.092)
Overall Maximum Convergence	0.085	0.076	0.041	0.039

Note: + = $p < 0.10$; *** = $p < 0.001$ (two-tailed).

model. More importantly, at least for our purposes here, in both models the transitive triads parameter is positive and statistically significant. This indicates that the over time the network tended toward network closure, which our theory suggests increases the likelihood that a group will radicalize.

In Model 2, the Melchiorite coefficient is positive but not statistically significant, so we cannot draw conclusions one way or another as to any effect identifying as a Melchiorite might have had. By contrast, the Münster Rebellion coefficient is statistically significant. However, it is negative, which at first blush may seem to run counter to our expectations. What this result indicates is that the majority of those in the leadership network avoided forming ties with those who eventually participated in the Münster Rebellion, and this may help to explain why its beliefs and practices were not embraced in the years after the rebellion. The two remaining coefficients in both the models are not statistically significant. It is perhaps unsurprising that the believer's baptism parameter is not since the majority of those in the network embraced believer's baptism. Thus, it probably had little or no effect on time formation among network members. It is somewhat surprising that the estimated apocalyptic coefficient is not statistically significant since it seems to be a defining feature of some network members.

That said, the apocalyptic effect is "almost" statistically significant in the third model at the $p < 0.10$ level.[9] Thus, in our fourth and final model we included the Münster Rebellion and apocalyptic effects but dropped the effect for believer's baptism. This led to a slight improvement in the model's overall convergence, and the estimated degree, transitive triad, and Münster Rebellion coefficients remain statistically significant and relatively unchanged. What has changed is that the apocalyptic coefficient has become statistically significant, which indicates that those who shared apocalyptic beliefs were more likely to form ties with one another than those who did not. In other words, the result suggests that shared apocalyptic beliefs may have had a positive effect on tie formation among the Melchiorites. This dynamic is not captured in theory outlined in Figure 11.3, but it is suggestive nonetheless.

Summary

In short, our analysis of the leadership network is, for the most part, consistent with the theory being tested here. We saw evidence that groups within the Anabaptist Leadership Network became increasingly closed in on themselves over time. We also saw that those who later became associated with the Münster Rebellion were far more likely to hold apocalyptic beliefs than those who were not. What our theory did not anticipate was that people who help apocalyptic beliefs were more likely to form ties with one another than those who did not. This result is not all that surprising, and it does not invalidate the theory. It merely suggests that apocalyptic beliefs may have had both a direct and indirect effect on the outbreak of violence in Münster. Directly it may have divinely sanctioned the use of violence by those in Münster, who saw their use of violence as a mechanism for purifying the world in anticipation of Christ's return. Indirectly, it may have contributed to the level of network closure among the Melchiorites, which in turn facilitated the radicalization of the group. Keep in mind that our results do not "prove" the theory being tested here. They are, however, consistent with it.

What can we apply from this analysis for dealing with contemporary dark networks? If we were to boil it down to a single phrase, it would be: stay connected. Prevent them from becoming isolated. That is, adopt a strategy that seeks to maintain ties with groups that could possibly radicalize or has already radicalized. According to Goldman (2011), this approach has been successful in several settings. For example, when Chen Tao, a Taiwanese group that settled in a Dallas suburb in August 1997 in anticipation of God's arrival on a flying saucer in March 1998 (Kleiver 1999), "Police and popular media in Garland, Texas, developed ongoing dialogue with Chen Tao representatives that facilitated the group's calm departure after their prophecy failed. Members of these groups . . . avoided violence because they cultivated external social networks and diminished their social isolation" (Goldman 2011:313). She also notes that the State of Oregon took similar approach with the Rajneeshpuram —an intentional community that settled in central Oregon in the 1980s that possessed a large cache of semi-automatic weapons—and as a consequence may very well have prevented widespread violence.

Of course, sometimes groups have already become isolated themselves, so we need to consider strategies that reintegrates them back into to the wider society (Tilly 2004, 2005). Although this can be accomplished in various ways, perhaps in today's world (not necessarily sixteenth-century Westphalia) the most effective approach is granting access to the political system because it encourages them to "become more like political parties and interest groups, and less like social protest movements or revolutionary groups" (Hafez 2003:208). This could "explain why communist and green parties in Western Europe were willing to make 'historical compromises' and abandoned revolutionary strategies, even if some of them did not completely abandon revolutionary rhetoric" (Hafez 2003:209). It may also explain why the founding of the Irish Free State in 1922 essentially marked the beginning of the end of the Southern wing of the Irish Republican Party (IRA). Although it did not grant Ireland complete sovereignty, it provided political access to those who had fought for Ireland's independence, and IRA membership fell from 14,541 members in August 1924 to 5,042 by November 1926 (English 2004:46). In short, what we are arguing for is a strategy of reintegration, except here it is aimed at the group rather than individual level. That is, rather than seeking to reintegrate specific individuals back into society, here we are arguing that a viable strategy is to reintegrate groups back into civil society (Tilly 2004, 2005).

11.5 SUMMARY: LESSONS LEARNED

In this chapter we have considered a variety of approaches for examining longitudinal data but have focused primarily on one: stochastic actor-oriented models (SAOMs). As we saw, these model network dynamics on the basis of observed longitudinal network data and are similar to the ERGMs that we examined in chapter 10, in that they assume that the observed network structure is, in part, a function of local patterns of ties that reflect endogenous social processes. Like ERGMs, they test whether a particular configuration occurs more frequently than one would expect given the other configurations included in the model, but they differ in that they are designed for longitudinal social network data and explicitly assume that actors "control their outgoing ties and to make changes in these ties according to short-term goals and restrictions" (Snijders and Koskinen 2013:138). The basic approach for estimating an SAOM is to hypothesize as to what social processes gave rise to a particular network's global properties, and then build a model that takes these into account.

11.6 QUESTIONS

1. Which of the following is not a method for examining longitudinal network data?
   a. Social network change detection.
   b. Stochastic actor-oriented models.
   c. Quadratic assignment procedure.
   d. Descriptive statistics.
   e. All of the methods listed above are for examining longitudinal network data.
2. In SAOMs, endogenous effects are structural characteristics that may predict a change in state such as an added or dissolved tie.
   a. True.
   b. False.
3. Which of the following is not an example of an endogenous effect?
   a. Popularity (degree of actor).
   b. Homophily.
   c. Intermediary (betweenness).
   d. Friend of a friend is a friend (triadic closure, transitivity).
   e. All of the above are examples of endogenous effects.
4. SAOMs do not include options for specifying exogenous effects in the form of actor and dyadic covariates.
   a. True.
   b. False.
5. Which of the following is an example of an exogenous effect?
   a. Popularity (degree of actor).
   b. Homophily.
   c. Intermediary (betweenness).
   d. Friend of a friend is a friend (triadic closure, transitivity).
   e. All of the above are examples of exogenous effects.
6. When would you want to use an SAOM rather than an ERGM?

11.7 ANSWERS

1. Quadratic Assignment Procedure (c).
2. True.
3. Homophily (b).
4. False.
5. Homophily (b).
6. We use SAOMs, rather than ERGMs, for examining longitudinal social network data.

11.8 FURTHER READING

Unlike for ERGMs, at present there is no book that provides an overview of stochastic actor-oriented models. There are, however, numerous articles that have applied the method to a variety of social network data. Some of these are listed below, but a more complete list can be found at the SIENA website.[10] A gentle (and short) introduction to SAOMs can be found on pp. 145–47 in Borgatti et al.'s *Analyzing Social Networks* (Thousand Oaks, CA: SAGE Publications, 2013). Tom Snijders offers a more in-depth (but still relatively short) introduction in his 2011 chapter on network dynamics in *The SAGE Handbook of Social Network Analysis*, edited by John Scott and Peter J. Carrington (Los Angeles and London: SAGE Publications, pp. 501–13). A helpful guide to building an SAOM is the SIENA manual, which has been written and continually updated by Ruth Ripley, Tom Snijders, ZsófiaBoda, AndrásVörös, and Paulina Preciado.[11] Readers who want to dig into the nuts and bolts of building and estimating an SAOM may find some of the following readings helpful:

- Jacob E. Cheadle and Philip Schwadel. 2012. "The 'Friendship Dynamics of Religion,' or the 'Religious Dynamics of Friendship'? A Social Network Analysis of Adolescents Who Attend Small School." *Social Science Research* 41:1198–212.
- Christina Prell. 2011. Pp. 238–48 (Appendix 2) in *Social Network Analysis: History, Theory & Methodology*. London and Thousand Oaks, CA: SAGE Publications.
- Tom A. B. Snijders. 2005. "Models for Longitudinal Network Data." Pp. 215–47 in *Models and Methods in Social Network Analysis*, edited by Peter J. Carrington, John Scott, and Stanley Wasserman. New York: Cambridge University Press.
- Tom A. B. Snijders, Gerhard G. van de Bunt, and Christian Steglich. 2010. "Introduction to Stochastic Actor-based Models for Network Dynamics." *Social Networks* 32:44–60.

• Christian Steglich, Tom A. B. Snijders, and Michael Pearson. 2010. "Dynamic Networks and Behavior: Separating Selection from Influence." *Sociological Methodology* 40:329–93.

NOTES

1. For a more nuanced explanation of the objective function and other aspects of stochastic actor-based models, see Snijders (2001, 2005).

2. Other models are available for undirected networks if the UIRC fails to converge (Ripley et al. 2015).

3. See the book's website for how this is done.

4. Prince-bishops were both leaders in both the secular and religious realms.

5. Readers will recall that Atta was the leader of the 9/11 team (9/11 Commission 2004).

6. Unbeknownst to the cell, German authorities had inserted a microphone in the apartment and occasionally monitored their conversations.

7. As Borgatti et al. (2013:156) note, the weighted global clustering coefficient is identical to transitivity, which is simply the ratio of closed triads over the number of triads containing at least two (undirected) ties.

8. Here, structural similarity refers to actors who share the same or similar patterns of ties to others and is often used to express similarities in tie patterns that result from similar job functions (e.g., middle managers are expected to have patterns of ties that are similar to one another).

9. In fact, in some estimations of the second model, the apocalyptic coefficient was statistically significant at the $p < 0.10$ level.

10. See https://www.stats.ox.ac.uk/~snijders/siena/

11. See https://www.stats.ox.ac.uk/~snijders/siena/RSiena_Manual.pdf

Part IV

CONCLUSION

Chapter 12

Lessons Learned

In putting this text together, we have tried to offer a somewhat more conceptual tone to what is frequently treated as a very technical topic. The application of social network analysis as a set of analytic tools requires at least some degree of technical detail. We have found, however, that interpretation tends to be the greatest hurdle for those who are first learning to apply social network analysis to understanding dark networks. We have presented some concrete examples of how we have analyzed dark networks and some of the inference we have gained. But those examples are, by necessity, somewhat fragmented. After all, our presentation was thematic and it would not do to have multiple themes running through a single chapter. A full analysis could benefit from any mix of the tools that are presented in the preceding chapters. But we strongly recommend that anyone preparing to analyze a dark network first give a great deal of thought to what they ultimately hope to learn. Specific research objectives are the best guides in that search. Without some thought as to what the measures and methods should ultimately reveal, it becomes easy to simply run a few centrality measures and a community detection algorithm hoping that something truly obvious will pop out.

Although we have provided tables at the beginning of several chapters for ease of reference and navigation, it is still best to try out many, if not most, of the covered topics. We understand that some readers may feel overwhelmed by the sheer number of techniques and concepts that are covered in this book. But their use becomes more natural with application and practice. This is also far from a complete collection of methods available through social network analysis. We encourage readers to continue to expand their knowledge of social network analysis by seeking out what others have done with these tools in other contexts. And, by all means, innovate. Social network analysis is a perishable set of skills, with much to forget, and these tools are best when they are well matched to a particular context or inferential goal. It is also easy to fall into the trap of misusing these tools or using the same set over and over.

This brief and final chapter, therefore, provides several lessons that readers (hopefully) can take away with a careful reading of this book. If you take nothing else away from this book, hopefully you will at least understand the need for upfront planning and preparation. For those of you who feel comfortable with that notion, we have also prepared a list of some of the greatest additional takeaways that we would like analysts to consider. While this is certainly not an exhaustive list of potential lessons learned, we find the following to be some of the more important lessons to have benefitted analysts that we have trained and colleagues with whom we have collaborated.

Lesson 1: What Dark Networks Have in Common Is that They Are Unique

The nature of dark networks (i.e., illegal and covert) provides several challenges to analysts conducting social network analysis (see chapter 1). They can evolve very rapidly, which makes having relevant network data quite challenging. This challenge is more acute in hostile environments where actors are constantly making alliances, severing ties, and dropping out of the network. Also, given that they are covert by definition, it is difficult to collect and record accurate and timely data about them (see chapter 3). Second, setting network boundaries can be challenging given that differentiating features can be short-lived among intersecting dark networks and even their alliances can be unclear (e.g., transnational groups). These challenges characterize dark networks as a whole. Also, dark networks are not uniform. For example, criminal organizations will behave differently than terrorist organizations in many situations given their different goals, motivations, and contexts. Even among terrorist organizations, there is a great deal of heterogeneity in terms of motivations, methods, and background. However, it is also important to keep in mind that, depending on the context, it is not unheard of for some dark networks function as allies in certain contexts. Żegota, for example, is one such "good" dark network (see Introduction).

Lesson 2: Social Network Analysis Is Unique

Social network analysis differs from link analysis, probabilistic statistical analysis, and social media analysis (see chapter 1). Unlike link analysis, it allows analysts to quantify aspects of dark networks in a manner that is inappropriate for link analysis. There are also strong advantages to clarity of depicting "social space" by using social network analysis, as opposed to link analysis, which tends to simultaneously consider multiple social and nonsocial links between actors. Similarly, traditional statistical analyses can be quite useful for their strengths in generalizing about populations, based on simple random samples. But if one hopes to develop a deeper understanding of the inner workings of group and individual behavior, there is a strong advantage to be had from the perspective offered through social network analysis and its ability to account for the patterns of interaction in which people are embedded. An individual's characteristics such as their ethnicity, socioeconomic status, and hair and eye color will remain more or less unchanged across various contexts, such as at work, with their family, or with their friends. Their behavior, however, will change in each context due to the relationships in which they are embedded. It is uncommon for anyone to behave in the same manner with family as they do with friends or at work. This is due to social constraints and contexts, and such forces can govern the behavior of a society. Social media, or social media analysis, by contrast, offer a much more superficial and limited context. Although, social network analysis can be used to better understand the relational data collected from social media platforms and applications, the analysis differs markedly from the tracking, monitoring, and reporting characteristic of social media analysis. While each of the above methodologies can offer strong contributions when they are used, social network analysis offers compelling visualizations and an approach that is tailored specifically for understanding human interactions and the order that emerges from such processes, which is also what supports the argument that social network analysis holds strong potential for understanding dark networks.

Lesson 3: Follow the Process

It is generally best for analysts to select their analytic objectives early in the analytic processes. Once a strategic approach is chosen (see chapter 2), social network analysts should at least try to clearly articulate what they hope to learn before conducting any analyses (see chapter 3). These pointers apply to both exploratory and explanatory network analytic approaches. Some situations dictate that analysts will need to develop their own question or in a team, while in others, their leadership, intelligence gaps, or a specific event (e.g., crime), will drive which question an analyst needs to explore. In both cases, especially the latter, analysts need to prod others about the concepts embedded within the question to ensure they do not begin analysis without a clear understanding of the question at hand. It can sometimes take a great deal of time for social network analysts to conduct even moderate to advanced techniques, such as ERGMs or SAOMs, if they hope to produce a meaningful analysis. That time would be wasted, however, if they have not taken the time to ensure that their data and methods are appropriate to the original question. The development of a clear, concise question could therefore save analysts time in the end. In fact, the time spent on this front-end step should be seen as an investment of one's time, and not a trivial and tedious step.

The development of a clear, concise question—or set of questions—should drive analysts' workflow as they analyze dark networks. Although the process of isolating problem elements and structuring problems to the point that they can be investigated may seem somewhat tedious to some, it is an investment that will, in turn, help them to identify which perspectives will add the most to the investigation they are constructing, and which would add little. We presented a suggested workflow model for analyzing dark networks in chapter 3. Note that roughly two-thirds of it is dominated by preparation. Analyses only appear in the last third, followed closely—or perhaps simultaneously—by interpretation. What this means for analysts is this: the better the preparation, the better the outcome. Being detail oriented will save time and frustration in the end. And at one point or another, analysts will have to return to the need for a hypothesis. It is much better for this to happen before there has been a substantial investment in data collection, cleaning, and analysis. To recap:

- Develop working hypotheses about network disruption
- Revisit background research regarding actors, their culture, and other factors
- Ask thoughtful analytical questions (exploratory and/or explanatory)
- Weigh the relative costs and benefits of various kinetic and nonkinetic actions
- Identify, define, and record relationships of interest
- Create a codebook
- Identify boundaries
- Collect and record data
- Clean and format data
- Analysis and Interpretation
- Select methods (descriptive or confirmatory analyses)
- Recast and present strategies for the disruption of the network
- Fuse with other data and information
- Make recommendations

Lesson 4: Codebooks, Codebooks, Codebooks

This lesson is embedded in the previous one; however, it deserves to be reiterated, particularly for practitioners. Some researchers can get away without developing a well-thought-out codebook before collecting data and conducting analysis (although this is not a good practice). Practitioners, however, need to be particularly aware of the potential consequences of not developing and adhering to one. Some of the consequences, on the one hand, are poor data quality, and analysts forced to "reinvent the wheel" by restarting collection when they do not trust or understand how others have collected or recorded data. Some of the benefits, on the other hand, include consistent data between analysts (also between teams, organizations, etc.), and quality data during changes in personnel (see chapter 3).

Lesson 5: Avoid Overreliance on Centrality and Brokerage Measures

Analysts should incorporate centrality and brokerage into larger analyses that incorporate other metric categories, such as network topography and cohesive subgroups. Central actors and brokers are embedded in larger networks (see chapters 6 and 7), and their relative importance depends largely on other network characteristics, such as the overall structure and levels of clustering. For instance, what it means to be central in a very centralized network differs from what is means to be central in a decentralized network. Moreover, many of the data management systems available to practitioners have built-in SNA tools that are quite limited in terms of social network analysis. Many of them only provide users with the ability to run four commonly used centrality measures: degree, betweenness, closeness, and eigenvector (perhaps one or two others as well), and they sometimes take into account objects that should not be. This trend is problematic because strategies, and questions based on those strategies, should drive the choice of appropriate metrics. Falling back on the big four centrality measures time and again, by contrast, is an overly simplistic approach that may not fit the particular scenario well. Ultimately, it is the analysts who should drive the analysis and not the platform.

Lesson 6: Network Actors Have Agency!

Analysts should not forget that the actors in dark networks are dynamic entities and not static or one-dimensional. It is common for analysts new to network analysis to want to "see what happens when actor A" is removed from the network. Although this can provide a nice side-by-side comparison in a briefing (i.e., a sort of "before and after"), it can also be extremely misleading. Dark network actors, just like the rest of us, have "agency," and they react to those around them and the environment in which they operate. Something as extreme as the removal of one of their neighbors will cause them to suddenly change their behavior, and a series of removals will likely cause the network to look completely different from what the initial investigation revealed.

Lesson 7: Know the Limitations of Exploratory and Explanatory SNA

Chapters 4–8 outline several exploratory techniques for analyzing dark networks. These techniques can help identify central actors, highlight aspects about a network's structure, locate clusters, illuminate brokers and bridges, and find structurally equivalent actors. Nevertheless, they only help analysts describe their network data. They do not allow analysts to understand the underlying causes of observed patterns and trends. Explanatory analyses (see chapters 9–11) are more focused on verification of findings that arise from exploratory and qualitative analyses. In other words, exploratory analyses can assist analyst with developing hypotheses, while explanatory approaches, such as QAP, CUGs, ERGMs, and SAOMs, help analysts test them. As we saw in this book's later chapters, they are built on hypothesis testing, which allows analysts to consider alternative points of views during statistical analyses, test their assumptions, and, therefore, provide greater confidence in their analysis. To some degree, they even allow analysts to delve deeper into the causes and motivations of those in the network. They do not, however, produce objective "truth."

Lesson 8: Fancy Visualizations Are No Substitute for Substance

The emergence of new tools and technologies that can help analysts produce stunning visualizations is very exciting, and very beneficial to social network analysts. Gephi, for example, is a relatively new program that can provide excellent network maps, even for very large data sets for which such a thing was not really possible before. Visualization, however, can only take one so far. Without the context with which to interpret the network's structure, the visualization itself will often be unhelpful. The overall goal for social network analysts should be to produce quality, relevant analyses that answer a specific question, and ultimately, help inform decision-making regarding dark networks. Excellent visualizations should be a part of this, but analysts should not rely on them alone.

Lesson 9: Avoid the "I Know" Trap with Dark Networks

Obtaining a strong understanding of dark networks (all networks, really) is often more difficult than one may think. There exist far too many interrelated aspects of dark networks for analysts to develop a complete understanding of their inner dynamics. All too often, however, people overestimate their ability to understand patterns and characteristics of networks using intuition or link analysis alone. This "I Know" trap even applies to those who already have a background in network analysis, which is why a strong grasp of the materials outlined in this book should be seen only as part of a larger, continual process of education. For instance, the International Network of Social Network Analysis (INSNA) hosts annual conferences for researchers and analysts from a range of backgrounds (e.g., sociologists, anthropologists, security experts) to present and share new ideas, techniques, and software within the realm of social network analysis. Most have a relatively strong grasp of the materials, and many are "lifers" in the sense that they are true experts within the application of social network analysis (many of whom are cited in this book). Even with relatively high levels of social network analytic competency, however, the most highly skilled have adopted the mentality that they can always learn more. For example, many of the interesting techniques that we have learned were not only after years of conducting SNA, but also from experts in different fields. In other words, the more you know, the more you realize you don't know. Also, the only thing stopping an analyst from growing in these techniques is generally either a lack of time or a lack of inventiveness.

Lesson 10: Commitment and Resources Required

So, what is the way forward? Introducing oneself to social network analysis, at least in terms of financial resources, is relatively cheap. The majority of the programs discussed throughout this book are free (with the exceptions of the new ORA version and UCINET) (see Appendix 3 for a brief summary of the packages used in this book).[1] Several organizations, within law enforcement and at the national level, have demonstrated this by incorporating social network analysis (to varying degrees) into their regular activities at a low cost. Some use social network analysis on a regular basis (and do it quite well), while others have dabbled in its application. The use of social network analysis, however, does not appear to be a norm among organizations that deal with dark networks.

We recommend that organizations consider institutionalizing social network analysis into a regular practice. Generally speaking, interested parties within those organizations must prioritize at least two things if they hope to successfully adopt these tools. The first is to commit to continual social network analysis education, which does not necessarily refer to attending a training session. Too often, organizations take the mentality that a training course and certification in social network analysis—something that is becoming more popular in consulting organizations—is all that is required to develop the capacity they seek. Training can be a helpful kick-starter, but it is not all that is required for competency. Education is a longer-term process that requires working with experts in the field, continued research, and the exploration of new social network analysis tools and techniques. It is not at all uncommon for some training courses to mislead analysts into oversimplifying social network analysis into a few simple metrics and processes. Though, it is really more of a way of thinking. The second is to commit analysts to conduct social network analysis on a regular basis. Many organizations move those capable of conducting social network analysis around into different functionalities. As we have seen, entire organizations are focused on other types of analysis (e.g., National Geospatial Intelligence Agency), but there does not appear to be such an organization for understanding networks. This is particularly worrisome given networks, including dark networks, are everywhere and it is unlikely they are going anywhere.

NOTE

1. UCINET remains relatively inexpensive. Other programs that have adopted some SNA metrics but that are not SNA-specific programs are often quite expensive.

Appendix 1

Data Description and Codebook

A1.1 AFGHAN TRIBAL NETWORK

This dataset includes tribes that reside within the geographic boundaries of the active U.S. RC South Area of Operations (AO), which is located in southern Afghanistan, covering six provinces and 63 districts. Based on a fusion of research products created by RC South analysts[1] and the Naval Postgraduate School (NPS) Program for Culture and Conflict Studies,[2] a list of 91 tribes was compiled. The unit of analysis is at the tribal level and is bounded between the sub- and super-tribe variant due to loss of fidelity in the data past either of the two extremes. Four types of ties were coded: biological (kinship), sentiment (positive and negative), and geographic movement. Please cite the data as follows:

Aschenbrenner, Mark, Jason Koo, and Daniel Toshner. 2014. *Afghan Tribal Network* [Machine-readable data file].

1. KINSHIP TIES

Definition of Kinship

A tie exists between two tribes based on their familial ties. This familial system of carefully memorized genealogy serves as the foundational social structure around which the indigenous population organizes.[3] Due to the pervasive importance of the familial ties within their culture and their role in establishing a social hierarchy derived from ancestral lineage, the Kinship tie provides a baseline for a Tribal Hierarchal tie as well. An example is the direct familial tie between the Popalzai tribe, which descended from the Zirak tribe; therefore, not only is there a Kinship tie, but also a Hierarchal tie, as the Popalzai is relationally subordinate to the greater Zirak Tribe. The data for this Kinship network was derived from a combination of written records spanning from 2009 to 2011 produced by the Program for Culture and Conflict Studies and the Tribal Analysis Center.[4]

One-mode matrix, 91 × 91

2. POSITIVE SENTIMENT

Definition of Positive Sentiment: Where a tribe that either has or had an alliance with another tribe, or participated in a cooperative act or endorsement that resulted in a positive sentiment by either actor. An example of a positive tie can be found in the CCS–Kandahar study, which states the Popalzai tribe "are still close to the Barakzai tribe and have formed political alliances with the Barakzai."[5] These data were compiled using an indirect collection methodology from a combination of research written records spanning from 2009 to 2011 produced by the Tribal Analysis Center, the Program for CCS, as well as an article published by Courage Services Inc. on the tribal dynamics in Afghanistan.[6] Ties were coded as directional because another tribe may not be aware of, or reciprocate, the sentiment.

One-mode matrix, 91 × 91

3. NEGATIVE SENTIMENT

Definition of Negative Sentiment: Where a tribe is documented as either having or had an open disagreement or conflict with another tribe that resulted in a negative sentiment being retained by either tribe. An example is the Alikozai tribe, which had a negative experience with Kabul's monarchs that resulted in the evolved confrontational posture and negative sentiment of the Alikozai tribe toward the rest of its kinship tribe, the Durranis.[7] In this case, because the text did not state that the sentiment was reciprocated, it was not assumed and the tie was coded as a directional tie from Alikozai to Durrani. Another example is the tie between the Achakzai tribe and Noorzai tribe, who are documented enemies, having clashed with each other continually throughout history.[8] In this case, the tie was coded a reciprocal. The data were compiled using the same methodology and data sources stated for the positive sentiment ties.

One-mode matrix, 91 × 91

4. GEOGRAPHIC PROXIMITY

Definition of Geographic Proximity: This tie assumes that a greater length of common geographic border between adjacent tribes indicates a greater potential for cross-border movement and exchange. Tribes share ties with those that they have a common border with, and the strength of the tie equals the length of the shared border. Tribal borders are not determined by administrative district borders, but rather they are defined by land where the tribe physically resides or exerts direct control over. Data for this relational tie was derived through the NPS Program for CCS website.[9,10] Tribal maps were broken down by province based on 2008 data. These individual province maps were combined to form an overlay and placed over a Google Earth map of Afghanistan, ensuring that the borders matched as closely as possible. Shared border space was measured using the Google Earth measurement tool in miles. If a tribe occupied multiple distinct areas, the border lengths of each distinct area were simply added together to represent the total border length for that tribe, as each section still represented the opportunity space for cross-border movement and exchange with another tribe. The diagonal of the network matrix represents the total amount of border length for that tribe, as each tribe effectively shares its entire border length with itself.

One-mode matrix, 91 × 91

A1.2 ANABAPTIST LEADERSHIP NETWORK

The dataset includes relational data of 67 actors, 55 who were sixteenth-century Anabaptist leaders. The remaining 12 were prominent Protestant Reformation leaders (e.g., Martin Luther, John Calvin, Ulrich Zwingli, Martin Bucer, and Philip Melanchthon), who had contact with and influenced some of the Anabaptist leaders included in the dataset. Drawing on numerous sources (e.g., Bender, Friedmann and Klassen 1990; Clasen 1972; Klötzer 2007; Krahn, van der Zijpp and Stayer 1987; Stayer 1979; Williams 1975), it expands network data collected by Matthews et al. (2013), which included 49 actors but did not include relational data on prominent Anabaptist leaders, such as Menno Simons. Please cite the data as follows:

McLaughlin, John M. 2015. *Anabaptist Leadership Network* [Machine-readable data file].

1. MET WITH

Definition of Met with

Ties between leaders reflect that they met, but they do not indicate theological agreement. In many cases, they worked or went to school together, but in others, they were at odds with one another (McLaughlin 2015b).

One-mode symmetric matrix, 67 × 67

2. ATTRIBUTES

1. *Believer's Baptism*
2. *Violence*
3. *Münster*
4. *Apocalyptic*
5. *Anabaptist*
6. *Melchiorite*

A1.3 FARC TFMC (TEOFILO FERERO MOBILE COLUMN) NETWORK

This dataset contains anonymized relational and attribute data on the special operations front (Teofilo Ferero Mobile Column—TFMC) of the Revolutionary Armed Forces of Colombia (FARC). It consists of twelve types of one-mode, undirected relations along with three types of attributes about the TFMC and several other FARC columns and affiliates. These data have been coded from unclassified, primary source documents that were given to the CORE Lab from Colombian officials, and they cover the network from 2000 to 2011. This detailed and in-depth information has been supplemented with additional open-source literature.

1. COLLABORATION

Definition of Collaboration

Collaboration relations are defined as two or more actors who are explicitly stated as collaborating in some unspecified (i.e., no specific event) nefarious activity (not including finances, see "Finance" ties). For example, two cabecillas (i.e., leaders) who worked together on narcotics trafficking in an unspecified time and at an unknown location would be coded as having this type of relationship.

One-mode symmetric matrix, 445 × 445

2. COLLEAGUES

Definition of Colleagues

Colleague relations are defined as two or more actors who are clearly affiliated with one another at the component level (i.e., submobile column), but who are not stated as collaborating, or working with one another in some manner. For example, company leaders have been recorded as having colleague relations with their deputy leaders even if there is no evidence of any direct interaction, or presence of any other type of relationship.

One-mode symmetric matrix, 445 × 445

3. COMMUNICATION

Definition of Communication

Communication ties are defined as direct communication between actors through some sort of medium, such as a cell phone or a radio. This option does not include direct, in-person communication. See "Met with" ties. Superior-Subordinate ties are also coded separately even though they likely indicate direct and indirect communication.

4. CO-WORKERS

Definition of Co-Workers

Co-worker relations are defined as two or more actors who worked with one another at the same non-FARC institution at the same time.

One-mode symmetric matrix, 445 × 445

5. FINANCE

Definition of Finance

Finance ties are defined as two or more actors directly involved in the transfer of money for any purpose except payments from an employer to an employee for normal compensation.

One-mode symmetric matrix, 445 × 445

6. FRIENDSHIP

Definition of Friendship

Friendship relations are defined as two or more actors who are explicitly stated as "friends," or some sort of trusted confidants.

One-mode symmetric matrix, 445 × 445

7. KINSHIP

Definition of Kinship

Kinship is defined as any family connection such as brother, brother-in-law, and nephew. Kinship will also include current marriages and past marriages due to divorces and/or deaths.

One-mode symmetric matrix, 445 × 445

8. MISCELLANEOUS

Definition of Miscellaneous

Miscellaneous relations are defined as two actors who have a relationship, but the nature of that relationship is unclear and does not meet any other definitions outlined in this codebook.

One-mode symmetric matrix, 445 × 445

9. MET WITH

Definition of Met with

Met with ties are defined as two or more actors who directly met one another at some point.

One-mode symmetric matrix, 445 × 445

10. NEGATIVE TIES

Definition of Negative Ties

Negative relations are defined as two actors who have perpetrated violence against one another, or who have been explicitly stated as having negative sentiment toward one another.

One-mode symmetric matrix, 445 × 445

11. ORGANIZATIONAL AFFILIATION

Definition of Organizational Affiliation

Organizational affiliation relations are defined as two or more actors who are members of the same FARC column, company, and/or squad.

One-mode symmetric matrix, 445 × 445

12. SUPERIOR-SUBORDINATE

Definition of Communication

Superior-subordinate relations are defined as a relationship between immediate superiors and subordinates, which accounts for the formal structure within the mobile column. This option also includes relationships in which one member is explicitly stated as giving orders to another.

13. ATTRIBUTES

1. *Formal Role/Title*

Definition of Formal Role/Title

Formal Role/Title attributes are defined as the highest-ranking title an individual assumes in the network.

2. *Organizational Affiliation*

Definition of Organizational Affiliation

This attribute is defined as an actor's most micro-level affiliation within the FARC. For example, an actor's relationship to a squad would be recorded as opposed to the actor's affiliation with a front.

3. *Status*

Definition of Status

This attribute is defined as an actor's physical status.

Coding Scheme

1. Alive
2. Detained
3. Demob
4. Dead

A1.4 KOSCHADE BALI I BOMBING NETWORK

This dataset was coded from Stuart Koschade's (2006) article on the first Bali bombing. It contains relational data on 17 individuals involved in the bombing. Two relational networks were coded: Binary and valued.

1. BINARY RELATIONAL DATA

Definition of Binary Relational Data: Combination of numerous types of interactions, including direct or indirect contact and the exchange of information through various means such as telecommunications, internet, and letters (Koschade 2006:564, 565). Differs from valued data in that the frequency and duration of the interactions are not reflected in tie strength.

One-mode symmetric matrix, 17 × 17

2. VALUED RELATIONAL DATA

Definition of Valued Relational Data: Combination of numerous types of interactions, including direct or indirect contact and the exchange of information through various means such as telecommunications, internet, and letters (Koschade 2006:564, 566). Differs from binary data in that the frequency and duration of the interactions are reflected in tie strength on a scale from 1 to 5.

One-mode symmetric matrix, 17 × 17

A1.5 NOORDIN TOP TERRORIST NETWORK

The foundation of the Noordin Top Terrorist network data were extracted from two International Crisis Group (ICG) reports (International Crisis Group 2006; International Crisis Group 2009b), which contain rich one- and two-mode data on a variety of relations and affiliations (friendship, kinship, meetings, etc.) along with significant attribute data (education, group membership, physical status, etc.). Because a single source for any network data raises the possibility of bias, the data were supplemented with additional open-source literature in order to fill gaps in the data and in order to generate monthly time codes from January 2001 through December 2010, which allow us to account for when actors enter and leave the network and examine the network longitudinally. The data were initially structured and analyzed by Defense Analysis students at the NPS in the course "Tracking and Disrupting Dark Networks' under the direction of Professors Sean Everton and Professor Nancy Roberts. Dan Cunningham reviewed, cleaned, and updated the data, in particular the time code information. Please cite these data as follows:

Everton, Sean F., Nancy Robert, and Dan Cunningham. 2013. *The Noordin Top Terrorist Network* [Machine-readable data file].

1. ORGANIZATIONAL AFFILIATION

Definition Terrorist/Insurgent and Affiliated Organizations

A terrorist/insurgent organization is defined as an administrative and functional system, whose primary common goal is the operational conduct of terrorist/insurgent activities, consisting of willingly affiliated claimant members. For the purpose of this exercise, factions and offshoots will be considered separate from their parent organization in order to prevent from coding redundant ties. In other words, the most micro-level affiliations are coded, while an individual is only coded in the parent organization if he or she is not listed as being affiliated with a component organization. Terrorist/insurgent affiliated organizations, such MMI and FPI, are also coded in this matrix.

Note: JI Central Command is considered a subcomponent but is not necessarily more or less "micro" than other JI subcomponents such as Mantiqi I or even JI wakalahs. Consequently, an individual affiliated with Mantiqi I and JI Central Command will get a tie in both columns.

List of Terrorist/Insurgent Organizations

1. AMIN (Full name—Angkatan Mujahidin Islam Nusantara—not listed)
2. Abu Bakar Battalion
3. Al-Qaeda (AQ)
4. Cimmangis Group (CG)
5. Darul Islam (DI)
6. Darul Islam Banten Battalion for Region IX (DI)
7. Darul Islam in Maluku (DI)
8. Darul Islam West Java Division (DI)
9. Islamic Defenders Front (FPI)-Pekalongan Branch
10. JI Central Command
11. JI Central Java Wakalah
12. JI East Java Wakalah
13. JI Johor Wakalah
14. JI Mantiqi I
15. JI Mantiqi II
16. JI Mantiqi III
17. JI Wakalah Hudaibiyah
18. Jemaah Islamiyah (JI)
19. KOMPAK Charity
20. KOMPAK Mujahidin
21. KOMPAK-Ambon Office
22. KOMPAK-Solo Office
23. KOMPAK-Waihong
24. Komando Jihad
25. Kumpulan Mujahidin Malaysia (KMM)
26. Laskar Jihad
27. Laskar Jundullah
28. Laskar Khos
29. Majelis Mujahidin Indonesia (MMI)
30. Mujahidin Kayamanya
31. Ring Banten (DI)
32. STAIN Group

Two-mode 139 × 32

2A. EDUCATIONAL AFFILIATION

Definition of Educational Relations:
Educational relations are defined as schools where individuals receive formal education, serve as an employee (teacher, admin etc.), and/or involve in additional educational or religious instruction at the institution.

List of Schools

1. Adelaide University
2. Airlangga University
3. al-Husein—*pesantren* (Islamic boarding school), Indramayu, West Java
4. al-Irsyad High School, Pekalongan
5. al-Islam—*pesantren*, Lamongan
6. al-Mutaqien, Indramayu
7. al-Muttaqien, Jepara
8. Bogor Agricultural University
9. Brawijaya University in Malang
10. Darul Fitroh
11. Darusysyahada—*pesantren*, Boyolali
12. Gontor
13. Luqmanul Hakeim—*pesantren*, Johor, Malaysia
14. Miftahul huda—*pesantren*, Cikampek
15. Pesantren, Isykarima, Solo
16. Pondok Ngruki/al-Mukmin—*pesantren*, Ngruki, Central Java
17. Reading University, UK
18. Serang Islamic High School
19. STAIN in Solo
20. Sukabumi
21. The Christian University of Malang
22. Universitas an-Nur/Mahad Aly—*pesantren*, Solo
23. Universitas Negeri, Malang
24. University of Technology, Malaysia
25. Unknown Name of School in Bangil, East Java

Two-mode matrix, 139 × 25

2B. CLASSMATES/EDUCATIONAL COLLEAGUES

Definition of Classmate Relations

Classmates/educational colleagues are defined as individuals who receive formal education, serve as an employee (teacher, admin etc.), and/or involved in additional educational or religious instruction at the same institution and at the same time. This relationship is more likely to reflect accurate relationships than the two-mode "Educational Affiliation" matrix since it considers the time in which individuals are present at a school.

Note: The coding on the master sheet will differ from coding based solely on the ICG report. The former used information outside of the ICG "Noordin's Networks" report for establishing if individuals could be considered classmates/educational colleagues based on the definition.

One-mode symmetric matrix, 139 × 139

3. COMMUNICATION TIES

Definition of Internal Communication

Internal communication is defined as the relaying of messages between individuals and/or groups inside the network through some sort of medium.

One-mode symmetric matrix, 139 × 139

4. KINSHIP TIES

Definition of Kinship

Kinship is defined as any family connection such as brother, brother-in-law, and nephew. Kinship will also include current marriages and past marriages due to divorces and/or deaths.

One-mode matrix, 139 × 139

5. TRAINING EVENTS

Definition of Training Relations

Participation in any specifically designated activity that teaches the knowledge, skills, and competencies of terrorism and insurgency. Training does not include participation in a terrorist sponsored act or mujahedeen activity in places such as Afghanistan, Bosnia, Chechnya, or Iraq unless the individuals' presence was to participate in a specifically designated training camp or base in one of these areas.

Note: Individuals who participated in the "Australian Embassy Religious Training" and/or the "Training for Bali II in the 'Selera' Restaurant" may reflect redundant ties with the "Operations Network" since some individuals participated in these trainings specific to the Australian Embassy (Sep 04) and the Bali II (Oct 05) operations.

List of Training Locations

1. 01–02 Ujunj Kulon Training
2. 03 Mindanao Training
3. 03 Rois Training
4. 99 Mindanao Training
5. Australian Embassy Religious Training
6. Azhari Apprenticeship
7. Jan 04 Bomb-Making
8. Jul 04 West Ceram
9. Jun 04 Bomb-Making
10. May 04 Training
11. Oct 99 Waimurat, Buru Training
12. Post-Bali Mil Refresh Training
13. Solo course
14. Training for Bali II in "Selera" restaurant
15. 08–01 to 09–01 Training

Two-mode matrix, 139 × 15

6. BUSINESS AND FINANCE AFFILIATION

Definition of Business Relations

Defined as profit and nonprofit organizations that employ people (includes Durassalam Foundation).

Types of Businesses

1. Al-Bayan Magazine
2. Clothing Business—making and selling clothing
3. CV Courier Business—business that specializes in transfer of information and products
4. Darussalam Foundation
5. Indonesian Muslim Workers Union
6. Mushroom Processing Company
7. Novotel Hotel-Surabaya
8. Sawt al-Jihad Online Magazine
9. Shock Absorber Repair Shop—the automobile shop that repaired shock absorbers.
10. Small Trading Business—exchange of goods
11. Tobacco Business—firm that grows tobacco
12. Used Cloth Business—the collection and sale of used cloth for industrial purposes

Two-mode matrix, 139 × 12

7. OPERATIONS

Definition of Operations

Operational relations are defined as individuals who are knowingly involved in preparing, executing, and/or providing postoperation support. Preparation must directly relate to the operation and can include surveying targets, providing a safehouse for preparation, contributing to religious and/or physical training, and participating in a robbery where proceeds fund a subsequent attack. Providing postoperation support, such as hiding fugitives and disposing of explosives, must also be directly related to the operation.

List of Operations

1. Atrium Mall Bombing (Aug 01)
2. Attack on Brimbob Post in West Ceram (May 05) (Note: Brimbob are paramilitary police and will be listed as so in the document)
3. Australian Embassy Bombings (Sep 04)
4. Bali Bombing I (Oct 02)
5. Bali Bombing II (Oct 05)
6. Bombing Attack on the Philippine Ambassador in Jakarta (Aug 00)
7. Christmas Eve Bombings (Dec 00)
8. Marriott Bombings (Aug 03)
9. Mosque Bombing in Yogyakarta (2000)
10. Murder of Palu Prosecutor Fery Silalahi (May 04)
11. Rizal Day Bombing (Dec 00)
12. Robbery of Medan Bank (May 03)
13. Robbery of Mobile Phone Store in Pekalongan (Sep 03)
14. Robbery to Raise Funds for Bali I (Aug 02)

Two-mode matrix 139 × 14

8. FRIENDSHIP TIES

Definition of Friendship Relations

Friendship relations are defined as close attachments through affection or esteem between two people. Friendship ties are not defined solely as meetings and/or school ties.

Note: Friendship relations can be extremely subjective if they are not explicitly stated in the document. Typically, the implicit relationships are based on consistent and close relationships across time. The relationship between Noordin Top and Azhari Husin, for example, is not explicitly stated as a friendship in the document, but they were close associates for many years.

One-mode matrix, 139 × 139

9A. RELIGIOUS AFFILIATION

Definition of Religious Relations

Religious relations are defined as an association with a mosque, church, synagogue, or religious study circle. Religious study circles are only coded if they are separate from other religious entities (i.e., mosque). We do not include Islamic schools even though we assume that the schools have mosques. Not using the schools prevents duplication of effort with the team constructing the school ties. Additionally, we listed the mosques by the town in which it is located. If there was more than one in a city, we added a numerical identifier plus the name of nearest location.

List of Mosques

1. Banten Mosque
2. Cipayung Mosque Surabaya Mosque I (al-Ikhsan Mosque)
3. Kedire Mosque
4. Pekalongan Pengajian (Religious Study Circle)
5. Solo Mosque (an-Nur School)
6. Surabaya Mosque I al Ikhsun
7. Surabaya Mosque II (Airlangga University)
8. Synagogue in Surabaya

Two-mode matrix, 139 × 8

9B. SOULMATES

Definition of Soulmate Relations

Soulmate relations are defined as individuals who are affiliated with the same religious institution at the same time. This relationship is more likely to indicate accurate religious ties than the "religious affiliation" since it considers the timeframes in which individuals are affiliated with religious institutions.

Note: The coding on the master sheet will differ considerably from coding based solely on the ICG report. The former used information outside of the ICG report for determining timeframes in which individuals were affiliated with a religious institution.

One-mode matrix, 139 × 139

10. LOGISTICAL PLACE

Definition of Logistical Relations

Logistical relations are defined to mean a Key Place within the archipelago where logistical activity occurred. Logistical activity is defined as providing "safe houses" for meeting/hiding, providing material support in terms of explosives, providing weaponry, or facilitating transportation of personnel or equipment.

List of Places Where Logistical Support Is Given

1. Ambon
2. Anyer
3. Bandung
4. Bengkulu
5. Blitar
6. Boyolali
7. Bukittinggi
8. Buru
9. Cianjur
10. Cotabato
11. Datu Piang
12. Dumai
13. Indramayu
14. Jakarta
15. Kartosura
16. Kuta
17. Malang
18. Medan
19. Mojoagung
20. Mojokerto
21. Palabuhanratu
22. Pasuruan
23. Pekalongan
24. Pekanbaru
25. Poso
26. Sekudai
27. Semarang
28. Solo
29. Surabaya
30. Surakarta
31. Tawau
32. Ungaran
33. Wonosobo
34. Yogyakarta
35. Zamboanga

Two-mode matrix, 139 × 35

11. LOGISTICAL FUNCTION

Definition of Logistic Functions

Logistical functions are defined as the support for terrorist/insurgency operations by providing materials, weapons, transportation, and safehouses.

List of Logistic Functions

1. Material
2. Safehouses
3. Transportation
4. Weapons

Two-mode matrix, 139 × 4

12. MEETINGS

Definition of Meetings

A preplanned, coordinated event between two or more individuals. Meetings do not include all styles of communications. Rather, meeting refers to a certain location at a certain date with specific individuals. Meetings infer the necessity of a decision, but the data does not specifically identify the decision or meeting subject.

List of Meetings

1. Page 5 ICG. Noordin met the secretary of the central command. 7 June in a hotel
2. Page 5 ICG. After the bombing, talked late into the evening in Bandung in late August
3. Page 6 ICG. At a prearranged spot in the city Mojoagung
4. Page 6 ICG. To discuss electronics training, in Solo, Indonesia, date unknown
5. Page 7 ICG. Meeting in Solo to discuss the protection of Azhari and Noordin
6. Page 8 ICG. Region; Surabaya Location at a house owned by Abu Fida to develop concept for construction of a new Islamic boarding school
7. Page 8 ICG. Noordin met Rois in Ambon or Mindanao
8. Page 8 ICG. Urwha ordered to reestablish contact with Rois and determine his willingness to take part in Jihad
9. Page 8 ICG. Delivery of a letter at a Mosque in Solo
10. Page 10 ICG. June 22 in Surabaya Discussion of readiness of three suicide bombers by Noordin

11. Page 11 ICG. October 2004 in Pekalongan Central Java, Noordin tasking to lobby for a revolver
12. Page 14 ICG. Lobbying meeting, Loc; Air Kuning May 2001
13. Page 15 ICG. Meeting to request det cord, RP 500K and find possible suicide bombers. Loc; Surabaya
14. Page 15 ICG. Arrangement of lodging for Noordin, Loc; Pekalongan
15. Page 15 ICG. Arrangement for a meeting between Noordin and Sunata Loc; Pekalongan
16. Page 15 ICG. Discussion for a program of cooperation with KOMPAK. Loc; Pekalongan
17. Page 16 ICG. Set up a meeting between Noordin and Sunata. Loc Yogyakarta
18. Page 16 ICG. KOMPAK meeting—The big one, Loc; Kartosuro at Joko's House Date Jan 2005
19. Page 17 ICG. Recruitment of university student. Loc; Solo, May 2005
20. Page 18 ICG. Discussion to develop a computer networking cite; Sep. 2005 Loc; Pekalongan

Two-mode matrix 139 × 20

13. ATTRIBUTES

1. *Education Level:* Defined as highest degree attained, level taught at, studied, participated in, or attended.

   Coding Scheme

   0) Unknown
   1) Elementary Education
   2) Pesantren (Luqmanul Hakiem, Ngruki, al-Husein, Indramayu, Jemaah Islamiyah)
   3) State High School
   4) Some University (University an-Nur, Univeristi Teknologi Malaysia, Adelaide University, Bogor Agricultural University)
   5) BA/BS Designation
   6) Some Graduate
   7) Masters
   8) PhD (includes Reading University)

2. *Contact with people outside Indonesia:* Defined as contact with people in different countries outside Indonesia.

   Coding Scheme

   0) Unknown
   1) Afghanistan

2) Australia
3) Malaysia
4) Pakistan
5) The Philippines
6) Singapore
7) Thailand
8) United Kingdom
9) Afghanistan and Malaysia
10) Afghanistan and Pakistan
11) Afghanistan and the Philippines
12) Afghanistan, Malaysia, and the Philippines
13) Australia and Malaysia
14) The Philippines and Malaysia
15) Afghanistan, Pakistan, Egypt
16) Iraq, Afghanistan, and Pakistan

3. *Military Training:* Defined as the country where an individual received military training and attained veteran status in fighting in known insurgent/conventional wars.

Coding Scheme

0) Unknown
1) Afghanistan
2) Australia
3) Indonesia
4) Malaysia
5) The Philippines
6) Singapore
7) Afghanistan and Indonesia
8) Afghanistan and the Philippines
9) Indonesia and Malaysia
10) Indonesia and the Philippines
11) Afghanistan and Iraq

4. *Nationality of individual:* Defined as country of birth, citizenship, or residence.

Coding Scheme

1. Afghanistan
2. Australia
3. Indonesia
4. Malaysia
5. The Philippines

6. Singapore
7. Saudi Arabia
8. Jordan
9. Egypt

5. *Current Status per ICG Article:* Defined as the physical condition of the individual.

   Coding Scheme

   0. Dead
   1. Alive
   2. Jail

6. *Current Status (Updated):* Defined as the physical condition of the terrorist/insurgent updated through spring 2011.

   Coding Scale

   0. Dead
   1. Alive
   2. Jail

7. *Role (Original):* Defined as the role an individual assumes in the terrorist/insurgent network.

   Coding Scheme

   0. no info/unclear
   1. strategist: high-level planner of a terrorist/insurgent network
   2. bomb maker: individual who constructs bombs
   3. bomber/fighter: individual who participates in bombing attacks or who is described as a fighter
   4. trainer/instructor: individual who trains or instructs new members of a terror network
   5. suicide bomber: individual who plans to or already has performed a suicide attack
   6. recon and surveillance—engaged in the surveillance and recon of targets
   7. recruiter—engaged in identifying and recruiting new members (to include bombers)
   8. courier/go-between—used in communications between members
   9. propagandist—developed information campaigns
   10. facilitator—assisted in the operation of the network (especially with materials and finances)
   11. religious leader—provided religious training and support

12. commander/tactical leader—in charge of operations at the local/tactical level

8. *Role Expanded (Primary and Secondary):* Defined as the role an individual assumes in the terrorist/insurgent network (includes primary and secondary roles).

   Coding Scheme

   1. Bomb Maker
   2. Bomber/Fighter
   3. Courier
   4. Facilitator
   5. Leader
   6. Liaison
   7. Local Leader
   8. Propagandist
   9. Recruiter
   10. Religious Leader
   11. Religious Teacher, Mentor, Motivator
   12. Resource Provider
   13. Strategist
   14. Suicide Bomber
   15. Sympathizer
   16. Trainer
   17. Missing

9. *Logistics Function:* Defined as the provision of safe houses, weapons, transportation, and/or material to the operational network.

   Coding scheme

   1. Providing a safe house
   2. Providing weapons
   3. Providing transportation
   4. Providing material
   5. Providing weapons, transportation, material
   6. Providing weapons, material
   7. Providing transportation, material
   8. Providing safehouse and transportation
   9. Providing safehouse, transportation, material
   10. Providing safehouse, weapons, material

10. *Technical Skills:* We chose to code technical attributes based on explicit skill sets mentioned within the ICG report. In contrast to an attribute

like "roles," we chose only to code the specific technical skills listed below and did not consider such things as "cell leader" or "financier" as a technical role. Basically, we were looking for skills related to electronics, bomb-making, web page design, etc. Below is a list of the roles and the corresponding number each individual received. In instances where someone had multiple technical skills, we chose to code the one that is subjectively the most relevant to terrorist operations. For instance, Azhari Husin has a mechanical engineering background but also has explosives training. We would code him under "bomb-making." Those with no identified technical skills receive a 0 in the matrix.

Coding Scheme

1. Bomb-making
2. Propaganda (production of videos and video CDs, magazines, web page design, etc.)
3. Military skills instruction (martial arts, shooting, etc.)
4. Other advanced degree (mechanical engineering, agriculture, etc.)
5. Religious instructions

11. *Primary Group Affiliation:* Defined as the primary group affiliation of each member of the network, generally.

Coding Scale

0. None (Noordin)
1. Darul Islam (DI)
2. KOMPAK
3. Jemaah Islamiyah (JI)
4. Ring Banten Group (DI)
5. Al-Qaeda

12. *Noordin's Network:* An individual is considered a member of Noordin's splinter group (*Tanzim Qaedat al-Jihad—Organization for the Basis of Jihad*), as opposed to simply being linked, if the individual knowingly participated in a Noordin-led operation during any stage, he or she is explicitly stated as a member of Noordin's inner circle, and/or he or she is tied to Noordin through kinship or friendship.

Coding Scheme

0. Nonmember
1. Member

13. *Original 79:* Defined as the 79 individuals listed in the appendix of the 2006 ICG Report, "Noordin's Networks"

Coding Scheme

0. Not listed in Appendix
1. Listed in Appendix

NOTES

1. International Security Assistance Forces—RC South link analysis diagram illustrating the RC (S) Tribal Structure, 2010.

2. The Naval Postgraduate School's program for Culture and Conflict Studies (CCS) uses the study of anthropological, ethnographic, social, political, and economic data to inform U.S. policies at both the strategic and operational levels. CCS is the result of a collaborative effort to provide current open-source information to Provincial Reconstruction Teams (PRT), mission commanders, academics, and the general public. Covering tribes, politics, trends, and people, this website—a twenty-first-century gazetteer provides data, analysis, and maps not available anywhere else.

3. Tribal Analysis Center, "Pashtun Tribal Dynamics," http://www.tribalanalysiscenter.com/PDF-TAC/Pashtun%20Tribal%20Dynamics.pdf (accessed October 28, 2014).

4. The Tribal Analysis Center, LTD is based in Williamsburg, Virginia, and uses an indirect anthropological approach to collect data obtained from a wide variety of sources, both current and historical in order to compile and analyze existing research and documents on tribal societies.

5. Program for Culture and Conflict Studies, "Kandahar Province," Naval Postgraduate School, http://www.nps.edu/programs/ccs/Kandahar.html (accessed October 28, 2014).

6. Courage Services Inc, "Tribal Dynamics in Afghanistan: A Resource for Analysts," http://stabilityinstitute.com/wp-content/uploads/AFGHAN-TRIBAL-DYNAMICS.pdf (accessed October 29, 2014).

7. Tribal Analysis Center, "Putting it Together in Southern Afghanistan," http://www.tribalanalysiscenter.com/PDF-TAC/Putting%20It%20All%20Together.pdf (accessed November 1, 2014).

8. Tribal Analysis Center, "Achakzai Tribe," http://www.tribalanalysiscenter.com/PDF-TAC/Achakzai%20Tribe.pdf (accessed October 27, 2014).

9. Program for Culture and Conflict Studies, "Afghanistan Tribal Maps," Naval Postgraduate School, http://www.nps.edu/programs/ccs/Tribal_maps.html (accessed October 28, 2014).

10. Program for Culture and Conflict Studies, "Afghanistan Tribal Shapefiles V_1," Naval Postgraduate School, https://cle.nps.edu/xsl-portal/site/993b50bf-0751-4f9e-8f75-fa145bbf7908/page/8faf6a43-6466-4d5f-801c-d5d11926c44f (accessed November 5, 2014).

Appendix 2

Glossary of Terms

Actor: An actor can be a person, subgroup, organization, collectivity, community, nation-state, etc. An actor is sometimes referred to as a node or vertex.

Affiliation Network: An affiliation network is two-mode network consisting of one set of actors and one set of events.

Arc: An arc is directed tie that connects one actor to another actor. See edge.

Attribute: Attributes are nonrelational characteristics of the individual actors in the network. Examples of attributes of individuals include gender, race, ethnicity, years of education, income level, age, and region/country of birth. Examples of organizational attributes include total sales, net income, age of the corporation, and number of employees/members. Examples of country attributes include GDP per capita, population size, and continent.

Automorphic Equivalence: With automorphic equivalence two actors are considered structurally similar if they occupy indistinguishable positions in a network.

Average Degree: Average degree equals the average number of ties among all actors in a network. It is sometimes used an alternative measure to network density because unlike density, it is not sensitive to network size.

Average Distance: Average distance refers to the average length of all the shortest paths (i.e., geodesics) between all connected actors in a network and could indicate the speed that information (and other resources) diffuses through a network.

Betweenness Centrality: Betweenness centrality measures the extent to which each actor lies on the shortest path between all other actors in a network.

Bi-Component: Formally, a bi-component is a component without a cutpoint. They are the sections of a network where the removal of a single actor does not create a new component.

Blocks, Blockmodels, and Blockmodeling: A set of structurally equivalent actors is referred to as a "block," the process by which blocks are identified is referred to as blockmodeling, with the resulting partition of actors into blocks as a blockmodel.

Bridge: Formally, a tie is said to be a bridge if deleting it would cause a network to disconnect into different components. Less formally, it refers to a tie that bridges a gap (i.e., structural hole) in a network. Edge betweenness centrality is sometimes used to identify bridges in a network.

Broker: An actor that is in a position to broker the flow of material and nonmaterial goods through a network. Analysts have developed numerous algorithms to capture brokerage, including betweenness centrality, structural holes (i.e., the additive inverse of Burt's measure of constraint), cut points, cut sets (i.e., key players), and Gould and Fernandez's brokerage roles.

Brokerage Role: A brokerage role of an actor (e.g., consultant, coordinator, gatekeeper, itinerant broker, liaison, and representative) is a function of the combination of a pattern of ties and group affiliation.

Centrality: Centrality measures give a rough indication of the social power of an actor based on their position within the network. A central actor can be someone who has numerous ties to other actors (*degree centrality*), who is closer (in terms of path distance) to other actors in a network (*closeness centrality*), who lies on the shortest path (geodesic) between any two actors in a network (*betweenness centrality*), who has ties to actors who are highly central (*eigenvector centrality*).

Centralization: Centralization uses the variation in actor centrality within the network to measure the level of centralization. More variation yields higher network centralization scores; less variation yields lower scores. In general, the larger a centralization index is, the more likely it is that a single actor is very central while the other actors are not, so they can be seen as measuring how unequal the distribution of individual actor values are. Centralization scores need to be interpreted in light of the type of centrality (e.g., degree, betweenness, closeness, and eigenvector) being estimated.

Clique: A clique is maximal complete subnetwork containing three or more actors. The term "maximal" means that no other actor can be added to the clique without destroying its defining characteristic, which in this case is means that each actor must be tied to each other actor.

Closeness Centrality: Closeness centrality captures how close (in terms of shortest path distance—i.e., geodesic distance) each actor is to all other actors in a network.

Constraint: Constraint measures the extent to which each actor does not lie in triadic brokerage positions.

Community Detection: Community detection algorithms are a series of clustering algorithms that detect subgroups such that there are more ties within the subgroups than across them than one would expect in a random graph of the same size with the same number of ties. The optimal number of subgroups generally uses modularity as a measure of fit.

Component: A component is a subnetwork in which members have ties to one another but do not have ties with members of other subnetworks. In directed networks, you can identify two types of components: strong and weak. Strong components take into consideration the direction of ties, whereas weak components do not. In a strong component each pair of actors is connected by a (directed) path and no other actor can be added without destroying its connectedness. By contrast, in a weak component each pair of actors is connected by an undirected path (i.e., a semi-path) and no other actor can be added without destroying its connectedness.

Complete network: See whole network.

CUGs (Conditional Uniform Graphs): A conditional uniform graph (CUG) test is a bootstrapping procedure where simulated networks are generated in a manner that is *conditional* on some specified aspect of the network being tested. The simulated networks are then used to calculate a null distribution of statistics that are then compared to the statistics generated using the actual network. If the actual statistics differ from a substantial proportion of those in the null distribution, then an analyst may conclude that the observed statistics could not have occurred by chance. CUGs are used to test the global (topological) network measures. See QAP (quadratic assignment procedure).

Consultant: See brokerage roles and itinerant broker.

Coordinator: Mediation between members of one group where the mediator is also a member of the group. See brokerage roles.

Cutpoint: A cutpoint is an actor whose removal increases the number of weak components in a network. Put differently, it disconnects the network. Also known as cut-vertex, articulation point, and boundary spanner (ORA).

Cutset: A cutset is the optimal set of actors whose (1) removal most effectively fragments a network (as compared to other sets of actors of the same size) or (2) reaches the greatest number of other actors (as compared to other sets of actors of the same size). See key player.

Dark Network: Dark networks are defined as a covert (or clandestine) and illegal networks (Milward and Raab 2006; Raab and Milward 2003) and is a term that (can) include terrorist, criminal, and insurgent networks. The term "dark" should not be interpreted normatively. Rather, it is simply a term that seeks to capture the fact that dark networks are those networks that, by definition, try to remain hidden (Tilly 2005).

Degree Centrality: Formally, degree centrality of an actor equals the number of lines incident with it. More simply, it is the count of the number of an actor's ties.

Density: Conceptually, density refers to the degree to which a network is connected. Formally, it is the number of ties in a simple network, expressed as a proportion of the maximum possible number of ties. It is inversely related to network size (i.e., the larger the network, the lower the density) because the number of possible lines increases exponentially as actors are added to the network, while the number of ties that each actor can maintain tends to be limited. That is why analysts will sometimes turn to other measures, such as average degree, for getting a handle on this dimension of network topography. See average degree.

Diameter: The diameter of a network refers to a network's longest geodesic (see below) and could be interpreted as how spread out a network is.

Directed Network (Graph): Also known as a diagraph (from directed graph), a directed network where one or more ties (arc) are directed from one actor to another.

Directed Tie: A directed tie is commonly known as an arc, which is simply a line that points from one actor to another.

Dyad: A type of two-mode network consisting of two sets of actors.

Edge: An edge is an undirected tie that connects one actor to another actor. See arc.

Edge Betweenness Centrality: Edge betweenness is similar to (node) betweenness centrality (see above), except that edge betweenness estimates the betweenness centrality of edges (i.e., ties) in the network, while node betweenness estimates the betweenness centrality of actors. Like node betweenness, edge betweenness measures the extent to which each edge in a network lies on the shortest path linking all pairs of actors (i.e., geodesic) in the network.

Ego Network: An ego network is an actor's (i.e., ego's) immediate social environment: the set of actors to which the actor has ties (i.e., alters and neighbors) and the ties among those actors. There are generally two ways of obtaining ego network data. One way is to use whole network data (see below) and then extract the ego networks of an actor or set of actors. The other is to survey a sample of individuals from whom ego-network data are then collected. Each person surveyed is generally asked for a set of contacts, using questions such as "Looking back over the last six months, who are the people with whom you discussed matters important to you?" After providing a list of contacts, they are then asked about the ties (if any) between their contacts (e.g., do they know one another, are they friends, and so on), as well as their contacts' various attributes of the alters (e.g., gender, race, and education level).

Ego-Network Density: Ego-network density is the ratio of actual number of ties between ego's alters (i.e., contacts) and the total possible number of ties between ego's alters. Same as the local clustering coefficient.

Eigenvector Centrality: Eigenvector centrality assumes that ties to central actors are more important than ties to peripheral actors and thus weights each actor's summed connections to others by their (i.e., the others) centrality scores. With an undirected network, eigenvector centrality scores are the same as hubs and authorities scores.

Exponential Random Graph Models (ERGMs): Exponential random graph models assume that observed social networks are built upon local patterns of ties, sometimes called micro-configurations (e.g., reciprocal ties and closed triads), that are a function of local social processes (e.g., homophily and closure). They are designed to predict the probability of tie formation in an observed network, while taking into account the network's properties as well as any covariates that pertain to the network's actors and the ties among them. In particular, they test whether a particular configuration occurs more frequently than one would expect given the other configurations included in the model. They are similar to the general linear models, except that they include important modifications in order to account for the dependencies between observations. See stochastic actor-oriented models (SAOMs).

Faction: A faction is a subnetwork where each actor is tied to all other actors within their own subnetwork but have no ties to actors in other subnetworks.

Fragmentation: Network fragmentation captures the extent to which a network is fragmented. In ORA, fragmentation equals the proportion of all pairs of actors that are not tied with one another. UCINET calculates both this measure of fragmentation and a distance-weighted one that takes into account the shortest path distance between pairs of actors.

Fruchterman Reingold: The Fruchterman Reingold algorithm attempts to simulate a system of mass particles where the vertices simulate mass points repelling each other, while the edges simulate springs with attracting forces. It then tries to minimize the "energy" of this physical system. It differs from the Kamada-Kawai algorithm in that it is able to distribute points in both two-dimensional and three-dimensional space. See also Kamada-Kawai, multidimensional scaling, and spring-embedded algorithms.

Full network: See whole network.

Gatekeeper: Mediation between two groups where mediator regulates the flow of information or goods to his or her group. See brokerage roles.

Geodesic: A geodesic is the shortest path between two actors. The longest geodesic in a network is the network's diameter.

Global Clustering Coefficient: The global clustering coefficient equals the sum of each actor's clustering coefficient divided by the number of actors in the network. Some software packages only divide by the number of actors with two or more contacts, while others divide by the number of actors in the network. See local clustering coefficient.

Graph: A graph is a visual model for a social network with ties between pairs of actors (vertices). A tie can be either present or absent between each pair of actors.

Hubs and Authorities: The hubs and authorities algorithm was initially designed for identifying which web pages functioned as hubs and which ones functioned as authorities where a good hub was defined as one that points to many good authorities, and a good authority is one that is pointed to by many good hubs. Consequently, the algorithm is designed to work with directed networks, but when used with undirected networks, it generates identical scores as eigenvector centrality.

Indegree (Outdegree) Centrality: Indegree (outdegree) centrality is the count of direct incoming (outgoing) ties. See degree centrality.

Input Domain: Input domain is a measure of prestige that counts all people by whom someone is chosen whether directly or indirectly. Restricted input domain only counts indirect ties at a prespecified maximum distance, which is chosen by the analyst. A restricted input domain of one is the same as indegree centrality because it only counts direct ties.

Itinerant Broker/Consultant: Mediator between members of one group where the mediator is not a member of the group. See brokerage roles.

Kamada-Kawai: A spring-embedded algorithm that assumes an attraction between adjacent points (vertices), repulsion between nonadjacent points and allocates points in two-dimensional space. See also Fruchterman Reingold, multidimensional scaling, and spring-embedded algorithms.

Key Player: There are two types of key player algorithms. One seeks to fragment a network; the other seeks to diffuse information through it. The former identifies the optimal set of actors that either completely disconnects the network or at least fragments it to such an extent that it makes the flow of resources across the network (e.g., communication) more difficult. The latter is designed to find the optimal set of actors that reaches the highest number of other actors. See cutset.

***K*-Core**: Formally, a *k*-core is a maximal group of actors, all of who are connected to some number (*k*) of other group members.

Liaison: Mediation between two groups where mediator does not belong to either group. See brokerage roles.

Local Clustering Coefficient: The local clustering coefficient is the ratio of actual number of ties between ego's alters (i.e., contacts) and the total possible number of ties between ego's alters. Same as ego-network density.

Loop: A loop is a tie that connects an actor with itself. It is the diagonal in a network matrix.

Longitudinal Network: A longitudinal network is network data measured over time. See stochastic actor-oriented models (SAOMs).

Modularity: A measure of fit used with faction analysis and community detection algorithms to identify the optimal number of subgroups within a network. See faction analysis and community detection algorithms.

Multidimensional Scaling: Multidimensional scaling is a method for locating a social network's actors in *k*-dimensional space (e.g., 2D and 3D). It is used primarily for visualization purposes. See Fruchterman Reingold, Kamada-Kawai, and spring-embedded algorithms.

Network Size: The size of a network equals the number of actors in the network.

Actor: Vertex, node.

One-mode Network: A one-mode network is a network that consists of a single set of actors. See also two-mode network.

Outdegree (Indegree) Centrality: Outdegree (indegree) centrality is the count of direct outgoing (incoming) ties. See degree centrality.

Partition: A network partition is a discrete classification or clustering of vertices that assigns each vertex to exactly one class or cluster.

Path: A path is a walk (i.e., a sequence of actors and ties) in which no actor and no tie in between the first and last actor of the walk occurs more than once. The one exception is that the first and last actor in a path can be the same actor.

Path Distance (Length): The distance between pairs of actors in a network. The shortest path between a pair of actors is known as the geodesic.

Positional Analysis: Positional analysis differs from the relational approach in that rather than focusing on the ties between actors, it seeks to identify actors who hold similar positions in the social structure. Why are positions seen as important? A position (e.g., student) is typically connected to a particular role or set of roles and located within a larger system of positions, which is why some social network analysts believe that actors occupying a particular position/role will exhibit similar types of behavior.

Proximity Prestige: A measure of prestige that for each actor in a network, divides its input domain by the average distance between it and all actors with which it is connected (directly or indirectly).

QAP (Quadratic Assignment Procedure): QAP is similar to bootstrapping in that it involves the random rearrangement of a network's rows and columns thousands of times in order to calculate a null distribution of statistics that are then be compared to the statistics generated using the actual network. If the actual statistics differ from a substantial proportion of those in the null distribution, then an analyst may conclude that the observed statistics could not have occurred by random chance and are "statistically significant." See CUG (conditional uniform graphs).

Regular Equivalence: With regular equivalence actors do not have to have identical ties to identical other actors (i.e., structural equivalence) or occupy indistinguishable positions in a network (automorphic equivalence). Instead, they must have identical ties to and from regularly equivalent actors. See automorphic and structural equivalence.

Relational Analysis: Relational analysis focuses on the direct and indirect ties between actors and seeks to explain behavior and social processes in light of those ties. It highlights the importance of the topography of networks, the centrality of actors, the cohesiveness of subgroups, and the brokers and bridges between such groups.

Representative: Mediation between two groups where mediator regulates the flow of information or goods from his or her group. See brokerage roles.

Social Network: A network consists of a graph with additional information concerning the graph's vertices and/or lines.

Social Structure: Social structure is the enduring patterns of behavior and relationships within social systems (e.g., roles) or the social institutions and norms that have become embedded in social systems in such a way that they shape behavior. Within SNA, social structures are seen in terms of enduring patterns of ties between actors (i.e., social networks).

Spring-Embedded Algorithms: Spring-embedded algorithms are graph-drawing algorithms that treat points (vertices) as pushing and pulling on one another that seeks to find an optimum solution where there is a minimum amount of stress on the springs connecting the whole set of points. See also Fruchterman Reingold, multidimensional scaling, and Kamada-Kawai.

Statistical Significance: Social scientists use measures of statistical significance in helping to decide whether a variable has a significant effect or not. A variable's effect is generally considered to be statistically significant if the probability (p-value) that it could have occurred by random chance falls below a particular threshold, typically 0.05. If the p-value of a particular variable's coefficient falls below 0.05 ($p < 0.05$), then the probability that the result could have occurred by random chance is less that 5.0 percent. Similarly, if $p < 0.01$, then the probability that the result could have occurred by random chance is less than 1.0 percent, and if $p < 0.001$, then the probability is less than 0.1 percent.

Stochastic Actor-Oriented Models (SAOMs): Stochastic actor-oriented models attempt to model network dynamics on the basis of observed longitudinal network data and evaluate these according to the paradigm of statistical inference. They are similar to exponential random graph models (ERGMs) in that they assume that the observed network structure is, in part, a function of local patterns of ties (e.g., closed triads) that reflect endogenous social processes (e.g., network closure). Like ERGMs, they test whether a particular configuration occurs more frequently than one would expect given the other configurations included in the model. They differ in that they are designed for longitudinal social network data and assume that actors control and change their ties according to short-term goals and constraints. They are similar to the general linear models, except that they include important modifications in order to account for the dependencies between observations. See exponential random graph models (ERGMs).

Strong Component: In a strong component, each pair of actors is connected by a (directed) path and no other actor can be added without destroying its connectedness. See component and weak component.

Structural Hole: A structural hole is a gap in the social structure. See constraint.

Structural Equivalence: Two actors are said to be structurally equivalent when they have exactly the same relationships to all other actors.

Tie: A tie is a relation between two actors. A tie can be either directed (arc) or undirected (edge). They can also vary in terms of strength.

Topography: Network topography refers to the overall structure of the network. Commonly used measures include density, fragmentation, network size, and centralization.

Trail: A trail is also a walk but a particular tie can only be used once. Thus, while all trails are walks, not all walks are trails.

Triad: A triad is a set of three actors that may or may not have ties between them.

Two-Mode Network: A network that consists of two sets of actors (i.e., dyadic network), or one set of actors and one set of events (i.e., affiliation network). See one-mode network.

Undirected Tie: An undirected tie is a line that connects two actors but does not point from one actor to another.

Vector: A vector is a numerical (continuous) value assigned to each actor in a network.

Walk: A walk is a sequence of actors and ties that begins and ends with actors that can involve the same actor and the same tie more than once.

Weak Component: In a weak component, each pair of actors is connected by an undirected path (i.e., a semi-path) and no other actor can be added without destroying its connectedness. See component and strong component.

Whole Network: A whole network that includes not only all relevant actors but also all relevant ties between actors. Also known as a full or complete network.

Appendix 3

Analytic Software

Gephi: Gephi is a free, open-source, Java-based software written for Mac, PC, and Linux. It is an interactive visualization and exploration program for a range of networks, small and large. It was developed in 2008 by a French research team at the University of Technology of Compiegne (UTC), and the Gephi Consortium, which is a French nonprofit corporation, supports and manages its development. Its interface is available in several languages, including English, Spanish, French, and Japanese, and it has an online forum in which users can request updates, and contribute to the open-source spirit of the program. Much of Gephi's functionality relies on "plugins," which are essentially add-ons that allow researchers and programmers to develop additional tools and techniques, and subsequently share them with a larger community. Gephi provides users with a of range visualization options (via plugins and base options), including a customizable "Preview" tool in which users can make "finishing touches" on their network maps before dissemination. It accepts several network file formats (e.g., .net files), and it is great for visualizing large networks, such as social media networks. However, it currently does not include several of the measures discussed in the book, and it provides unique challenges in terms of working with multiplex data.

NetDraw: NetDraw runs on Windows-compatible computers and can be downloaded for free from the Analytic Technologies website. It was developed by one of the masterminds (Steve Borgatti) behind the SNA package, UCINET 6 (see below) in order to draw networks (i.e., sociograms, network maps) using a variety of visualization algorithms. Network maps created by NetDraw can be rotated, flipped, resized, and stored in several different formats. In addition to its visualization algorithms, NetDraw also includes a handful of other algorithms for calculating centrality, detecting subgroups, identifying sets of key players, and so on. While it is technically a stand-alone program, it essentially functions as an extension of UCINET: it is distributed with UCINET, it can be opened from within UCINET, and it reads UCINET files without the need for using any importing and/or exporting functions. While NetDraw's initial iterations did not handle large networks very well, more recent versions seem to perform much better. Moreover, if you save network data in NetDraw's native .vna format, it can handle very large network files. Still, it is not as robust as Pajek (see below). Like UCINET, NetDraw is continually updated with new procedures, routines, and bug fixes.

Organizational Risk Analyzer (ORA): ORA was developed by Kathleen Carley, a former student of Harrison White who teaches at Carnegie Mellon University. It is user-friendly and designed to find those actors, types of skills or knowledge, and tasks that are critical to a network's performance. Lying at the heart of ORA's approach is the notion of a meta-matrix of networks (Carley 2001–2015; Carley, Lee and Krackhardt 2002) that includes not only social networks but also knowledge networks (who knows what), information networks (what ideas are related to what), assignment networks (who is doing what), need networks (what knowledge is needed to do the task), and so on. Unlike most SNA programs, ORA is report based. Instead of providing a single metric, ORA produces a report containing a series of related metrics. For example, if you wish to identify central actors using ORA, you would probably request ORA's "Standard Network Analysis" report, which provides the estimated scores of the most commonly used centrality measures. ORA includes both a main screen, where you can analyze networks using a variety of algorithms, and a draw screen, where you can visualize networks using different mapping algorithms in either two or three dimensions. A nice feature of ORA's draw screen is that it includes its own analytic capabilities. ORA also includes functions for simulating various scenarios (e.g., the effect of removing or isolating various actors from a network at different points of time), geospatially analyzing and mapping social networks that can then be plotted in various geospatial programs, creating different types of charts (e.g., histograms, bar charts, and scatter plots), and analyzing changes over time with its "View Measures Over Time" feature. As with all programs, ORA has its weaknesses. For example, its reports sometimes include metrics that are inappropriate for a particular network, such as estimating closeness centrality (Freeman 1979) when analyzing a disconnected network, or calculating Krackhardt's (1994) measure of hierarchy when examining an undirected (i.e., symmetric) network. And while its visualization capabilities are adequate and offer some useful options, the network maps it produces tend not to be as robust as other packages.

Pajek: Pajek, which means "spider" in Slovenian, was created by Vladimir Batagelj and Andrej Mrvar in 1996 and is designed to handle very large datasets. While it does not include as many algorithms as UCINET, it still offers most of those that analysts use. In particular, it includes routines that lend themselves to the visualization and simplification of large networks as well as allowing users to visualize networks in two or three dimensions. It runs on Windows-compatible computers, can be downloaded for free, and is routinely updated by its developers. Pajek stores network data as an edge list, which as we saw in chapter 3, is simply a list of vertices (i.e., actors/actors) and edges/arcs (i.e., ties). Pajek allows users to load and keep multiple networks and other data objects (e.g., partitions) in memory at the same time, which can then be stored in what Pajek calls a "project file." Being able to save all of one's work in a single file reduced the likelihood that you will have to later "recreate the wheel" of one of your analyses. Pajek's primary drawback is that it contains fewer algorithms than UCINET, and its network manipulation features are somewhat limited. Thus, many analysts sometimes use UCINET for data manipulation and then turn to Pajek for visualization. To Pajek's credit, however, it allows users to call other statistical packages, such as "R" and "SPSS," to perform procedures unavailable in Pajek.

PNet (MPNet): PNet is a suite of programs developed for the simulation and estimation of exponential random graph models (ERGMs) for social networks. Currently, several variations of PNet exist: (1) PNet, which is for one-mode networks, (2) BPNet, which is for two-mode networks, (3) MPNet, which is for multi-level networks, (4) XPNet, which is for bivariate analysis, (5) SnowPNet, which is for snowball sampled networks, (6) IPNet, which is for social influence models, (7) and LPNet, which is for longitudinal models. All of these programs are available free for noncommercial use. Currently, PNet does not offer as many options as the statnet package, ergm, does in terms of available micro-configurations. Nevertheless, it is a powerful program that offers analysts a somewhat gentle entry way into the world of ERGMs. It is the package that is used in the monograph on ERGMs by Lusher et al. (2013).

UCINET 6: UCINET was developed by Linton Freeman at the University of California, Irvine, which is where the "UCI" in "UCINET" comes from and later refined by others, in particular, Steve Borgatti and Martin Everett. It is the best known and most widely used SNA software, primarily because it includes a large number of SNA metrics and data management tools. For example, not only does it contain most of the routines needed for estimating measures of network topography, identifying subgroups, calculating actor centrality, detecting brokers and bridges, identifying structurally equivalent actors, and correlations and multivariate regression, but it also includes tools for selecting subsets of files, merging and stacking data sets, transposing and/or recoding data, and the importing and exporting of data in a variety of formats. UCINET is menu driven. Its commands open dialog boxes that specify the inputs needed for it to run its various routines; results are displayed using Window's *Notepad* program and saved in log files. UCINET's comprehensiveness is what makes it so valuable. In UCINET social network data are recorded in matrix format. Users can enter data using either UCINET's internal spreadsheet functions or with a Microsoft Excel wrapper that calls up an Excel spreadsheet within UCINET. UCINET also reads edge and actor lists, which are quite useful when working with large datasets. For storing data UCINET uses a dual file system: one containing the actual data (extension .##d) and the other containing information about the data (extension .##h). Both files are needed in order to analyze social network data in UCINET, and this can occasionally lead to problems, such as when one of the files ends up in one folder and the other in different folder. Because UCINET's creators regularly provide updates to the program in order to fix bugs and glitches, problems such as these are generally corrected relatively quickly.

R: R is a programming language and software environment for statistical computing and graphics that is widely used among statisticians for developing statistical software and data analysis, including social network analysis. There are two primary suites of social network analysis software available in R: *statnet* (Handcock et al. 2003) and *igraph* (Csárdi and Nepusz 2006). The *statnet* library includes a number of interrelated programs, such as (1) *ergm*, which unsurprisingly is designed to estimate exponential random graph models, (2) *network*, which is designed to create, store, modify, and plot network data, and (3) *sna*, which is set of tools for traditional social network analysis. Most of the graphics and much of the analysis found in this book were created using either the *statnet* or the *igraph* package. Also available is *RSiena* (Ripley et al. 2015), which we used for estimating the stochastic actor-oriented models in chapter 11. All of these packages possess a tremendous amount of power and include most of the SNA metrics and algorithms that we cover in this book. That said, there is a steep learning curve with R. We suspect that most analysts will gravitate to the stand-alone SNA packages, such as UCINET, ORA, Pajek, and PNet. Nevertheless, we have uploaded the scripts we used for the analyses contained in this book to the book's website so that interested analysts will have a place from which to begin.

References

9/11 Commission. 2004. *The 9/11 Commission Report*. New York: W. W. Norton & Company.

Akaike, Hirotugu. 1974. "A New Look at the Statistical Model Identification." *IEEE transactions on Automatic Control* 19:716–23.

Alimi, Eitan Y., Lorenzo Bosi, and Chares Demetriou. 2012. "Relational Dynamics and Processes of Radicalization: A Comparative Framework." *Mobilization: An International Journal* 17(1):7–26.

Arquilla, John. 2009. *Aspects of Netwar & the Conflict with al Qaeda*. Monterey, CA: Information Operations Center, Naval Postgraduate School.

Arquilla, John, and David Ronfeldt. 2001. "The Advent of Netwar (Revisted)." Pp. 1–25 in *Networks and Netwars*, edited by John Arquilla and David Ronfeldt. Santa Monica, CA: RAND.

Asal, Victor, and R. Karl Rethemeyer. 2008. "The Nature of the Beast: Organizational Structures and the Lethality of Terrorist Attacks." *The Journal of Politics* 70(2):437–49.

Asch, Solomon E. 1951. "Effects of Group Pressure Upon the Modification and Distortion of Judgment," in *Groups, Leadership and Men*, edited by Harold S. Guetzkow. Pittsburgh, PA: Carnegie Press.

______. 1955. "Opinions and Social Pressure." *Scientific American* 193:31–35.

Austin, David. 2011. "How Google Finds Your Needle in the Web's Haystack." *Feature Column*. http://www.ams.org/samplings/feature-column/fcarc-pagerank

Azarian, G. Reza. 2005. *The General Sociology of Harrison C. White: Chaos and Order in Networks*. New York: Palgrave Macmillan.

Baker, Wayne E., and Robert R. Faulkner. 1993. "The Social-Organization of Conspiracy: Illegal Networks in the Heavy Electrical-Equipment Industry." *American Sociological Review* 58(6):837–60.

Bakker, René M., Jörg Raab, and H. Brinton Milward. 2011. "A Preliminary Theory of Dark Network Resilience." *Journal of Policy Analysis and Management* 31(1):33–62.

Barabási, Albert-László. 2002. *Linked: The New Science of Networks*. Cambridge, MA: Perseus Publishing.

Barabási, Albert-László, and Reka Albert. 1999. "Emergence of Scaling in Random Networks." *Science* 286:509–12.

Batagelj, Vladimir, and Andrej Mrvar. 2015. *Pajek 4.06*. Lubjlijana, Slovenia: University of Ljubljana.

Bavelas, Alex. 1948. "A Mathematical Model for Group Structure." *Human Organizations* 7:16–30.

______. 1950. "Communication Patterns in Task-Oriented Groups." *Journal of the Acoustical Society of America* 22:725–30.

Becker, Gary S. 1976. *The Economic Approach to Human Behavior*. Chicago: University of Chicago Press.

Bender, Harold S., Robert Friedmann, and Walter Klassen. 1990. Anabaptism. *Global Anabaptist Mennonite Encyclopedia Online*. http://gameo.org/index.php?title=Anabaptism&oldid=128087

Berman, Eli. 2009. *Radical, Religious, and Violent: The New Economics of Terrorism*. Cambridge, Massachusetts: The MIT Press.

Boivan, Rėmi. 2014. "Drug Trafficking Networks in the World Economy." Pp. 182–94 in *Crime and Networks*, edited by Carlo Morselli. London: Routledge.

Bonacich, Phillip. 1972. "Factoring and Weighting Approaches to Status Scores and Clique Identification." *Journal of Mathematical Sociology* 2:113–20.

______. 1987. "Power and Centrality: A Family of Measures." *American Journal of Sociology* 92(5):1170–82.

Boorman, Scott A., and Harrison C. White. 1976. "Social Structure for Multiple Networks II: Role Structures." *American Journal of Sociology* 81(6): 1384–446.

Borgatti, Stephen P. 1988. "A Comment on Doreian's Regular Equivalence in Symmetric Structures." *Social Networks* 10:265–271.

______. 2005. "Centrality and Network Flow." *Social Networks* 27(1):55–71.

______. 2006. "Identifying Sets of Key Players in a Social Network." *Computational, Mathematical and Organizational Theory* 12:21–34.

Borgatti, Stephen P., Kathleen M. Carley, and David Krackhardt. 2006. "On the Robustness of Centrality Measures under Conditions of Imperfect Data." *Social Networks* 28:124–36.

Borgatti, Stephen P., and Martin G. Everett. 1989. "The Class of All Regular Equivalences: Algebraic Structure and Computation." *Social Networks* 11:65–88.

______. 1992. "Notions of Position in Social Network Analysis." *Sociological Methodology* 22:1–35.

______. 1993. "Two Algorithms for Computing Regular Equivalence." *Social Networks* 15:361–76.

______. 2006. "A Graph-Theoretic Perspective on Centrality." *Social Networks* 28(4):466–84.

Borgatti, Stephen P., Martin G. Everett, and Linton C. Freeman. 2002a. *UCINET for Windows: Index File*. Harvard, MA: Analytical Technologies.

______. 2002b. *UCINET for Windows: Software for Social Network Analysis*. Harvard, MA: Analytical Technologies.

Borgatti, Stephen P., Martin G. Everett, and Jeffrey C. Johnson. 2013. *Analyzing Social Networks*. Thousand Oaks, CA: SAGE Publications.

Boucek, Christopher. 2008. The Sakinah Campaign and Internet Counter-Radicalization in Saudi Arabia. *CTC Sentinel*, 1(9): 1–4. http://carnegieendowment.org/files/CTCSentinel_Vol1Iss9.pdf

Bouchard, Martin, and Richard Konarski. 2014. "Assessing the Core Membership of a Youth Gang from its Co-offending Network." Pp. 81–93 in *Crime and Networks*, edited by Carlo Morselli. London: Routledge.

Brandes, Ulrik, and Thomas Erlebach (Eds.). 2005. *Network Analysis: Methodological Foundations*. Berlin, Germany: Springer.

Brandes, Ulrik, Jörg Raab, and Dorothea Wagner. 2001. "Exploratory Network Visualization." *Journal of Social Structure* 2(1).

Breiger, Ron, Kathleen M. Carley, and Philippa Pattison (Eds.). 2003a. *Dynamic Social Network Modeling and Analysis: Workshop Summary and Papers*. Washington DC: National Academy of Sciences / National Research Council: National Academies Press.

Breiger, Ronald L., Gary A. Ackerman, Victor Asal, David Melamed, H. Brinton Milward, R. Karl Rethemeyer, and Eric Schoon. 2011. "Application of a Profile Similarity Methodology for Identifying Terrorist Groups That Use or Pursue CBRN Weapons." Pp. 26–33 in *Social Computing and Behavioral-Cultural Modeling*, edited by J. Salerno, S. J. Yang, D. Nau, and S-K. Chai. New York, NY: Springer.

Breiger, Ronald L., Kathleen M. Carley, and Philippa Pattison (Eds.). 2003b. *Dynamic Social Network Modeling and Analysis: Workshop Summary and Papers*. Washington DC: National Academy of Sciences / National Research Council: National Academies Press.

Breiger, Ronald L., Eric Schoon, David Melamed, Victor Asal, and R. Karl Rethemeyer. 2013. "Comparative Configurational Analysis as a Two-Mode Network Problem: A Study of Terrorist Group Engagement in the Drug Trade." *Social Networks* 36(1):23–39.

Brin, Sergey, and Lawerence Page. 1998. "The Anatomy of a Large-Scale Hypertextual Web Search Engine." *Proc. 7th International World Wide Web Conference*:107–17.

Burt, Ronald S. 1992a. "The Social Structure of Competition." Pp. 57–91 in *Networks and Organizations: Structure, Form and Action*, edited by Nitin Nohria and Robert G. Eccles. Boston: Harvard University Press.

______. 1992b. *Structural Holes: The Social Structure of Competition*. Cambridge, MA: Harvard University Press.

Butts, Carter. 2011. "Bayesian Meta-analysis of Social Network Data via Conditional Uniform Graph Quantiles." *Sociological Methodology* 41:257–98.

Butts, Carter T. 2014. "sna: Tools for Social Network Analysis." *R package version* 2.3–2. http://CRAN.R-project.org/package=sna.

______. 2015. "Package 'sna'." *R package version* 2.3–2. http://CRAN.R-project.org/package=sna.

Carley, Kathleen M. 2001–2015. *Organizational Risk Analyzer (ORA)*. Pittsburgh, PA: Center for Computational Analysis of Social and Organizational Systems (CASOS): Carnegie Mellon University.

______. 2003. "Dynamic Network Analysis." Pp. 133–45 in *Dynamic Social Network Modeling and Analysis: Workshop Summary and Papers*, edited by Ronald L. Breiger, Kathleen Carley, and Philippa Pattison. Washington DC: National Academy of Sciences / National Research Council: National Academies Press.

______. 2006. A Dynamic Network Approach to the Assessment of Terrorist Groups and the Impact of Alternative Courses of Action. *Visualizing Network Information Meeting Proceedings RTO-MP-IST-063*. http://www.vistg.net/documents/IST063_PreProceedings.pdf

Carley, Kathleen M., Matthew Dombroski, Maksim Tsvetovat, Jeffrey Reminga, and Natasha Kamneva. 2003. "Destabilizing Terrorist Networks," in *8th International Command and Control Research and Technology Symposium*. National Defense War College, Washington DC: Evidence Based Research, Track 3, Electronic Publication: http://www.dodccrp.org/events/2003/8th_ICCRTS/pdf/021.pdf.

Carley, Kathleen M., Ju-Sung Lee, and David Krackhardt. 2002. "Destabilizing Networks." *Connections* 24(3):79–92.

Carley, Kathleen M., J. Reminga, and N. Kamneva. 2003. "Destabilizing Terrorist Networks," in *8th International Command and Control Research and Technology Symposium*. National Defense War College, Washington DC: Evidence Based Research, Track 3, Electronic Publication, WebSite:http://www.dodccrp.org/events/2003/8th_ICCRTS/pdf/021.pdf.

Cartwright, Dorwin, and Frank Harary. 1956. "Structural Balance: A Generalization of Heider's Theory." *Psychological Review* 63:277–92.

Chaves, Mark. 1997. *Ordaining Women: Culture and Conflict in Religious Organizations*. Cambridge, MA: Harvard University Press.

Childress, Deak, and John Taylor. 2012. "A Better Way to Fight IEDs." *Armed Forces Journal* April: 8–11, 30.

Chwe, Michael Suk-Young. 2001. *Rational Ritual: Culture, Coordination, and Common Knowledge*. Princeton and Oxford: Princeton University Press.

Clasen, Claus-Peter. 1972. *Anabaptism: A Social History,* 1525–1618. Ithica, NY: Cornell University Press.

Clauset, Aaron, Mark E. J. Newman, and Cristopher Moore. 2004. "Finding Community Structure in very Large Networks." *Phys. Rev. E* 70, 066111.

Clayton, Philip, and Paul Davies (Eds.). 2006. *The Re-Emergence of Emergence: The Emergentist Hypothesis from Science to Religion*. Oxford and New York: Oxford University Press.

Coleman, James S. 1964. *Introduction to Mathematical Sociology*. New York: Free Press.

Collins, Randall. 2004. *Interaction Ritual Chains*. Princeton, NJ: Princeton University Press.

Cook, Karen S., and Richard M. Emerson. 1978. "Power, Equity and Commitment in Exchange Networks." *American Sociological Review* 43:712–39.

Cook, Karen S., Richard M. Emerson, Mary R. Gilmore, and Toshio Yamagishi. 1983. "The Distribution of Power in Exchange Networks." *American Journal of Sociology* 89:275–305.

Cook, Karen S., Mary R. Gillmore, and Toshio Yamagishi. 1986. "Point and Line Vulnerability As Bases For Predicting the Distribution of Power in Exchange Networks: Reply to Willer." *American Journal of Sociology* 92(2):445–48.

Cook, Karen S., and J. M. Whitmeyer. 1992. "Two Approaches to Social Structure: Exchange Theory and Network Analysis." *Annual Review of Sociology* 18:109–27.

Creswell, John W. 2014. *Research Design: Qualitative, Quantitative, and Mixed Methods Approaches*. Thousand Oaks, CA: SAGE Publications.

Cronin, Audrey Kurth. 2009. *How Terrorism Ends: Understanding the Decline and Demise of Terrorist Campaigns*. Princeton and Oxford: Princeton University Press.

Csárdi, Gábor, and Tamás Nepusz. 2006. "The igraph Software Package for Complex Network Research." *InterJournal* Complex Systems 1695. 2006. http://igraph.org.

Cunningham, Daniel, Sean F. Everton, and Philip J. Murphy. 2015. "Casting More Light on Dark Networks: A Stochastic Actor-Oriented Longitudinal Analysis of the Noordin Top Terrorist Network." Pp. 171–85 in *Illuminating Dark Networks: The Study of Clandestine Groups and Organizations*, edited by Luke M. Gerdes. Cambridge and New York: Cambridge University Press.

Cunningham, Daniel, Sean F. Everton, Gregory Wilson, Carlos Padilla, and Douglas Zimmerman. 2013. "Brokers and Key Players in the Internationalization of the FARC." *Studies in Conflict & Terrorism* 36(6):477–502.

Dalkey, Norman, and Olaf Helmer. 1963. "An Experimental Application of the Delphi method to the Use of Experts." *Management Science* 9(3):458–67.

Davis, James A. 1967. "Clustering and Structural Balance in Graphs." *Human Relations* 20(2):181–87.

de Nooy, Wouter. 2011. "Networks of Action and Events over Time: A Multilevel Discrete-Time Event History Model for Longitudinal Network Data." *Social Networks* 33(1):31–40.

de Nooy, Wouter, Andrej Mrvar, and Vladimir Batagelj. 2011. *Exploratory Social Network Analysis with Pajek*. Cambridge, UK: Cambridge University Press.

Degenne, Alain, and Michael Forse'. 1999. *Introducing Social Networks*. Thousand Oaks, CA: Sage Publications.

DiMaggio, Paul J., and Walter W. Powell. 1983. "The Iron Cage Revisited: Institutional Isomorphism and Collective Rationality in Organizational Fields." *American Sociological Review* 48(2):147–60.

Doreian, Patrick. 1987. "Measuring Regular Equivalence in Symmetric Structures." *Social Networks* 9:89–107.

______. 2001. "Causality in Social Network Analysis." *Sociological Methods & Research* 31(1):81–114.

Doreian, Patrick, and F. N. Stockman (Eds.). 1997. *Evolution of Social Networks*. Amsterdam: Gordon and Breach Publishers.

Emerson, Richard M. 1962. "Power-Dependence Relations." *American Sociological Review* 27(1):31–41.

______. 1972a. "Exchange Theory, Part I: A Psychological Basis for Social Exchange." Pp. 38–57 in *Sociological Theories in Progress*, edited by Joseph Berger, Morris Zelditch, and B. Anderson. Boston: Houghton-Mifflin.

______. 1972b. "Exchange Theory, Part II: Exchange Relations and Network Structures." Pp. 58–87 in *Sociological Theories in Progress*, edited by Joseph Berger, Morris Zelditch, and B. Anderson. Boston: Houghton-Mifflin.

______. 1976. "Social Exchange Theory." Pp. 335–62 in *Annual Review of Sociology*. Palo Alto, CA: Annual Reviews Inc.

Emirbayer, Mustafa, and Jeff Goodwin. 1994. "Network Analysis, Culture, and the Problem of Agency." *American Journal of Sociology* 99(6):1411–54.

Enders, Walter, and Paan Jindapon. 2010. "Network Externalities and the Structure of Terror Networks." *Journal of Conflict Resolution* 54(2):262–80.

Enders, Walter, and Todd Sandler. 2006. *The Political Economy of Terrorism.* Cambridge and New York: Cambridge University Press.

English, Richard. 2004. *Armed Struggle: The History of the IRA.* London, UK: Pan Books.

Erickson, Bonnie H. 1981. "Secret Societies and Social Structure." *Social Forces* 60(1):188–210.

______. 2001. "Social Networks." Pp. 314–26 in *Blackwell Companion to Sociology.* Oxford, UK: Blackwell Publishing, Ltd.

Everett, Martin G., and Stephen P. Borgatti. 1998. "Analyzing Clique Overlap." *Connections* 21(1):49–61.

______. 2005. "Extending Centrality." Pp. 57–76 in *Models and Methods in Social Network Analysis*, edited by Peter J. Carrington, John Scott, and Stanley Wasserman. New York: Cambridge University Press.

Everett, Martin G., John Paul Boyd, and Stephen P. Borgatti. 1990. "Ego-Centered and Local Roles: A Graph Theoretic Approach." *Journal of Mathematical Sociology* 15:163–72.

Everton, Sean F. 2012a. *Disrupting Dark Networks.* Cambridge and New York: Cambridge University Press.

______. 2012b. "Network Topography, Key Players and Terrorist Networks." *Connections* 31(1):12–19.

______. Forthcoming. "Social Networks and Religious Violence." *Review of Religious Reasearch.*

Everton, Sean F., and Daniel Cunningham. 2012. "Detecting Significant Changes in Dark Networks." *Behavioral Sciences of Terrorism and Political Aggression* 5(2):94–114.

______. 2014. "Terrorist Network Adaptation to a Changing Environment." Pp. 287–308 in *Crime and Networks*, edited by Carlo Morselli. London: Routledge.

______. 2015. "Dark Network Resilience in a Hostile Environment: Optimizing Centralization and Density." *Journal of Criminology, Criminal Justice, Law & Society* 16(1):1–20.

Famis, Andrea Giménez-Salinas. 2014. "Illegal Networks or Criminal Organizations: Structure, Power, and Facilitators in Cocaine Trafficking Structures." Pp. 131–47 in *Crime and Networks*, edited by Carlo Morselli. London: Routledge.

Faulkner, Robert R., and Eric Cheney. 2014. "Breakdown of Brokerage: Crisis and Collapse in the Watergate Conspiracy." Pp. 263–84 in *Crime and Networks*, edited by Carlo Morselli. New York and London: Routledge.

Faust, Katherine. 1988. "Comparison of Methods for Positional Analysis: Structural and General Equivalences." *Social Networks* 10:313–41.

Fernandez, Roberto M., and Roger V. Gould. 1994. "A Dilemma of State Power: Brokerage and Influence in the National-Health Policy Domain." *American Journal of Sociology* 99(6):1455–91.

Fink, Naureen Chowdhury, and Ellie B. Hearne. 2008. "Beyond Terrorism: Deradicalization and Disengagement from Violent Extremism." New York: International Peace Institute.

Finke, Roger, and Rodney Stark. 2005. *The Churching of America, 1776–2005: Winners and Losers in Our Religious Economy*. New Brunswick, NJ: Rutgers University Press.

Flynn, Michael T., Matt Pottinger, and Paul D. Batchelor. 2010. "Fixing Intel: A Blueprint for Making Intelligence Relevant in Afghanistan," in *Voices From the Field*. Washington DC: Center for a New American Security.

Frank, Kenneth A., and J. Y. Yasumoto. 1998. "Linking Action to Social Structure Within a System: Social capital Within and Between Subgroups." *American Journal of Sociology* 104(3):642–86.

Freeman, Linton C. 1977. "A Set of Measures of Centrality Based on Betweenness." *Sociometry* 40:35–41.

______. 1979. "Centrality in Social Networks I: Conceptual Clarification." *Social Networks* 1:215–39.

______. 2000. "Visualizing Social Networks." *Journal of Social Structure* 1(1).

______. 2004. *The Development of Social Network Analysis: A Study in the Sociology of Science*. Vancouver, Canada: Empirical Press.

______. 2011. "The Development of Social Network Analysis—with an Emphasis on Recent Events." Pp. 26–39 in *The SAGE Handbook of Social Network Analysis*, edited by John Scott and Peter J. Carrington. Los Angeles and London: SAGE Publications.

Freeman, Linton C., Stephen P. Borgatti, and Douglas R. White. 1991. "Centrality in Valued Graphs: A Measure of Betweenness Based on Network Flow." *Social Networks* 13:141–54.

Fridovich, David P., and Fred T. Krawchuck. 2007. "Special Operations Forces: Indirect Approach." *Joint Forces Quarterly* 44(1):24–27.

Friedkin, Noah E. 1991. "Theoretical Foundations For Centrality Measures." *American Journal of Sociology* 96(6):1478–504.

Fruchterman, T., and E. Reingold. 1991. "Graph Drawing by Force-Directed Replacement." *Software--Practice and Experience* 21(11):1129–64.

Galula, David. [1964] 2006. *Counterinsurgency Warfare: Theory and Practice*. Westport, CT: Praeger Security International.

Geortz, Hans-Jürgen. 1996. *The Anabaptists*. London and New York: Routledge.

Gerdes, Luke M. (Ed.). 2015. *Illuminating Dark Networks: The Study of Clandestine Groups and Organizations*. New York and Cambridge: Cambridge University Press.

Girvan, Michelle, and Mark E. J. Newman. 2002. "Community Structure in Social and Biological Networks." *Proceedings of the National Academy of Sciences USA* 99(12):7821–26.

Goldman, Marion S. 2011. "Cultural Capital, Social Networks, and Collective Violence." Pp. 307–23 in *Violence and New Religious Movements*, edited by James R. Lewis. New York and Oxford: Oxford University Press.

Gondal, Neha, and Paul D. McLean. 2013a. "Linking Tie-Meaning with Network Structure: Variable Connotations of Personal Lending in a Multiple-Network Ecology." *Poetics* 41:122–50.

______. 2013b. "What Makes a Network Go Round? Exploring the Structure of a Strong Component with Exponential Random Graph Models." *Social Networks* 35(4):499–513.

Goodreau, Steven M., Mark S. Handcock, David R. Hunter, Carter T. Butts, and Martina Morris. 2008. "A statnet Tutorial." *Journal of Statistical Software* 24(9):1–27.

Gould, Roger V. 1989. "Power and Social-Structure in Community Elites." *Social Forces* 68(2):531–52.

______. 1991. "Multiple Networks and Mobilization in the Paris Commune, 1871." *American Sociological Review* 56:716–29.

______. 1993. "Trade Cohesion, Class Unity, and Urban Insurrection: Artisanal Activism in the Paris Commune." *American Journal of Sociology* 98(4):721–54.

Granovetter, Mark. 1973. "The Strength of Weak Ties." *American Journal of Sociology* 73(6):1360–80.

______. 1974. *Getting a Job*. Cambridge, MA: Harvard University Press.

______. 1979. "The Theory-Gap in Social Network Analysis." Pp. 501–18 in *Perspectives on Social Network Research*, edited by Paul W. Holland and Samuel Leinhardt. New York: Academic Press.

______. 1983. "The Strength of Weak Ties: A Network Theory Revisited." *Sociological Theory* 1:201–33.

______. 2005. "The Impact of Social Structure on Economic Outcomes." *Journal of Economic Perspectives* 19(1):33–50.

Gregg, Heather S. 2009. "Fighting Cosmic Warriors: Lessons from the First Seven Years of the Global War on Terror." *Studies in Conflict & Terrorism* 32(3):188–208.

Grim, Brian J., and Roger Finke. 2010. *The Price of Freedom Denied: Religious Persecution and Conflict in the Twenty-First Century*. New York and Cambridge: Cambridge University Press.

Hafez, Mohammed M. 2003. *Why Muslims Rebel: Repression and Resistance in the Islamic World*. Boulder, CO: Lynne Rienner Publishers.

______. 2004. "From Marginalization to Massacres: A Political Process Explanation of Violence in Algeria." Pp. 37–60 in *Islamic Activism: A Social Movement Theory Approach*, edited by Quintan Wiktorowicz. Bloomington and Indianapolis: Indiana University Press.

Hall, John R. 1987. *Gone from the Promised Land: Jonestown in American Cultural History*. Piscataway, NJ: Transaction Publishers.

Hamilton, Lawrence C. 1996. *Data Analysis for Social Scientists*. Belmont, CA: Duxbury Press.

Handcock, Mark S., David R. Hunter, Carter T. Butts, Steven M. Goodreau, and Martina Morris. 2003. "**statnet**: Software tools for the Statistical Modeling of Network Data."

Hanneman, Robert A., and Mark Riddle. 2005. "Introduction to Social Network Methods." Riverside, CA: University of California, Riverside.

______. 2011. "Concepts and Measures for Basic Network Analysis." Pp. 340–69 in *The SAGE Handbook of Social Network Analysis*, edited by John Scott and Peter J. Carrington. Los Angeles and London: SAGE Publications.

Harper, Walter R., and Douglas H. Harris. 1975. "The Analysis of Criminal Intelligence." *Human Factors and Ergonomics Society Annual Meeting Proceedings* 19(2):232–38.

Harris, Jenine K. 2014. *An Introduction to Exponential Random Graph Modeling*. Los Angeles and London: Sage Publications.

Heider, Fritz. 1946. "Attitudes and Cognitive Organization." *Journal of Psychology* 21:107–12.

Hoivik, T., and N. P. Gleditsch. 1975. "Structural Parameters of Graphs: A Theoretical Investigation." Pp. 203–22 in *Quantitative Sociology*, edited by H. M. Blalock. New York: Academic Press.

Holland, Paul W., and Samuel Leinhardt. 1976. "Local Structure in Social Networks." *Sociological Methodology* 7:1–45.

Horgan, John. 2009. *Walking Away from Terrorism: Accounts of Disengagement from Radical and Extremist Movements*. New York: Routledge.

Hosmer, David W., and Stanley Lemeshow. 1989. *Applied Logistic Regression*. New York, NY: Wiley.

Hu, Daning, Siddharth Kaza, and Hsinchun Chen. 2009. "Identifying Significant Facilitators of Dark Network Evolution." *Journal of the American Society for Information Science and Technology* 60(4):655–65.

Hubbell, Charles H. 1965. "An Input-Output Approach to Clique Identification." *Sociometry* 28(4):377–99.

Hubert, Lawrence, and James Schultz. 1976. "Quadratic Assignment as a General Data Analysis Atrategy." *British Journal of Mathematical and Statistical Psychology* 29:190–241.

Hunter, David R., Steven M. Goodreau, and Mark S. Handcock. 2008. "Goodness of Fit of Social Network Models." *Journal of the American Statistical Association* 103(481):241–58.

Hunter, David R., and Mark S. Handcock. 2006. "Inference in Curved Exponential Family Models for Networks." *Journal of Computational and Graphical Studies* 15(3):565–83.

Hwang, Julie Chernov, Rizal Panggabean, and Ihsan Ali Fauzi. 2013. "The Disengagement of Jihadis in Poso, Indonesia." *Asian Survey* 53(4):754–77.

Iannaccone, Laurence R. 1994. "Why Strict Churches are Strong." *American Journal of Sociology* 99(5):1180–211.

Iannaccone, Laurence R., Roger Finke, and Rodney Stark. 1997. "Deregulating Religion: The Economics of Church and State." *Economic Inquiry* 35(2):350–64.

International Crisis Group. 2006. "Terrorism in Indonesia: Noordin's Networks." Brussels, Belgium: International Crisis Group.

______. 2009a. "The Hotel Bombings." Brussels, Belgium: International Crisis Group.

______. 2009b. "Indonesia: Noordin Top's Support Base." Brussels, Belgium: International Crisis Group.

______. 2010. "Indonesia: Jihadi Surprise in Aceh." Brussels, Belgium: International Crisis Group.

Jackson, Matthew O. 2008. *Social and Economic Networks*. Princeton, NJ: Princeton University Press.

Jackson, Maurice, Eleanora Petersen, James Bull, Sverre Monsen, and Patricia Richmond. 1960. "The Failure of an Incipient Social Movement." *Pacific Sociological Review* 3:35–40.

Johnson, Byron R. 2011. *More God, Less Crime: Why Faith Matters and How It Could Matter More*. West Conshohocken, PA: Templeton Press.

Juergensmeyer, Mark. 2001. *Terror in the Mind of God*. Berkeley, CA: University of California Press.

Kadushin, Charles. 2005. "Who Benefits From Social Network Analysis: Ethics of Social Network Research." *Social Networks* 27:139–53.

______. 2012. *Understanding Social Networks: Theories, Concepts, and Findings*. Oxford and New York: Oxford University Press.

Kamada, T., and S. Kawai. 1989. "An Algorithm for Drawing General Undirected Graphs." *Information Processing Letters* 31:7–15.

Katz, Leo. 1953. "A New Status Index Derived from Sociometric Data Analysis." *Psychometrika* 18(1):34–43.

Katz, Leo, and James Powell. 1957. "Probability Distributions of Random Variables Associated with a Structure of the Sample Space of Sociometric Investigations." *The Annals of Mathematical Statistics* 28(2):442–48.

Kenney, Michael. 2007. *From Pablo to Osama: Trafficking and Terrorist Networks, Government Bureaucracies, and Competitive Adaptation*. University Park: Pennsylvania State University Press.

Kerlinger, Fred N., and Howard B. Lee. 2000. *Foundations of Behavioral Research*. Orlando, FL: Harcourt Inc.

Kilcullen, David. 2009. *The Accidental Guerrilla: Fighting Small Wars in the Midst of a Big One*. Oxford and New York: Oxford University Press.

______. 2010. *Counterinsurgency*. Oxford and New York: Oxford University Press.

Kleinberg, Jon. 1999. "Authoritative Sources in a Hyperlinked Environment." *Journal of the ACM* 46(5):604–32.

______. 2000. "The Small World Phenomenon: An Algorithmic Perspective." *Proc. 32nd ACM Symposium on Theory of Computing*:163–70.

Kleiver, Lonnie D. 1999. "Meeting God in Garland: A Model of Religious Tolerance." *Nova Religio* 3:45–53.

Klerks, Peter. 2001. "The Network Paradigm Applied to Criminal Organisations: Theoretical Nitpicking or a Relevant Doctrine for Investigators? Recent Developments in the Netherlands." *Connections* 24(3):53–65.

Klötzer, Ralf. 2007. "The Melchiorites and Münster." Pp. 217–56 in *A Companion to Anabaptism and Spirtualism*, edited by John D. Roth and James M. Stayer. Leiden and Boston: Brill.

Knoke, David, and Song Yang. 2007. *Social Network Analysis*. Thousand Oaks, CA: Sage Publications, Inc.

Kolaczyk, Eric D., and Gabor Csardi. 2014. *Statistical Analysis of Network Data*. New York, NY: Springer.

Korte, Charles, and Stanley Milgram. 1970. "Acquaintance Linking Between White and Negro Populations: Application of the Small World Problem." *Journal of Personality and Social Psychology* 15(2):101–18.

Koschade, Stuart. 2006. "A Social Network Analysis of Jemaah Islamiyah: The Applications to Counterterrorism and Intelligence." *Studies in Conflict & Terrorism* 29:559–75.

Krackhardt, David. 1987a. "Cognitive Social Structures." *Social Networks* 9:109–34.

______. 1987b. "QAP Partialling as a Test of Spuriousness." *Social Networks* 9:171–86.

______. 1988. "Predicting with Networks: Nonparametric Multiple Regression Analysis of Dyadic Data." *Social Networks* 10:359–81.

______. 1992. "The Strength of Strong Ties: The Importance of Philos in Organizations." Pp. 216–39 in *Networks and Organizations: Structure, Form and Action*, edited by Nitin Nohria and Robert G. Eccles. Boston: Harvard University Press.

______. 1994. "Graph Theoretical Dimensions of Informal Organizations." Pp. 89–111 in *Computational Organization Theory*, edited by Kathleen M. Carley and Michael J. Prietula. Hillsdale, NJ: L. Erlbaum Associates.

Krahn, Cornelius, Nanne van der Zijpp, and James M. Stayer. 1987. Münster Anabaptists. *Global Anabaptist Mennonite Encyclopedia Online*. http://gameo.org/index.php?title=M%C3%BCnster_Anabaptists

Krebs, Valdis. 2002. "Mapping Networks of Terrorist Cells." *Connections* 24(3):43–52.

Kuhn, Thomas S. 1970. *The Structure of Scientific Revolutions*. Chicago: University of Chicago Press.

Laumann, Edward O., Peter V. Marsden, and David Prensky. 1983. "The Boundary-Specification Problem in Network Analysis." Pp. 18–34 in *Applied Network Analysis*, edited by Ronald S. Burt and Michael Minor. Beverly Hills, CA: Sage.

Leavitt, Harold J. 1951. "Some Effects of Communication Patterns on Group Performance." *Journal of Abnormal and Social Psychology* 46:38–50.

Lempert, Robert J., Horacio R. Trujillo, David Aaron, James A. Dewar, Sandra H. Berry, and Steven W. Popper. 2008. Comparing Alternative U.S. Counterterrorism Strategies: Can Assumption-Based Planning Help Elevate the Debate? http://www.rand.org/pubs/documented_briefings/2008/RAND_DB548.pdf

Levitt, Steven D., and Stephen J. Dubner. 2005. *Freakanomics: A Rogue Economist Explores the Hidden Side of Everything*. New York: Harper Collins.

Lewin, Kurt. 1951. *Field Theory in the Social Sciences*. New York: Harper.

Lewis, Ted G. 2009. *Network Science: Theory and Applications*. Hoboken, NJ: John Wiley & Sons, Inc.

Lin, Nan. 2001. *Social Capital*. Cambridge: Cambridge University Press.

Lindelauf, Roy, Peter Borm, and Herbert Hamers. 2009. "The Influence of Secrecy on the Communication Structure of Covert Networks." *Social Networks* 31:126–37.

Linstone, Harold, and Murray Turoff (Eds.). 1975. *The Delphi Method: Techniques and Applications*. Reading, MA: Addison-Wesley Publishing Company.

Lofland, John, and Rodney Stark. 1965. "Becoming a World-Saver: A Theory of Conversion to a Deviant Perspective." *American Sociological Review* 30:862–75.

Lusher, Dean, Johan H. Koskinen, and Garry L. Robins (Eds.). 2013. *Exponential Random Graph Models for Social Networks*. New York and Cambridge: Cambridge University Press.

Magouirk, Justin, Scott Atran, and Marc Sageman. 2008. "Connecting Terrorist Networks." *Studies in Conflict & Terrorism* 31:1–16.

Mantel, Nathan. 1967. "The Detection of Disease Clustering and a Generalized Regression Approach." *Cancer Research* 27:209–20.

Marks, Steven, Thomas Meer, and Matthew Nilson. 2005. "Manhunting: A Methodology for Finding Persons of National Interest," in *Defense Analysis Department*. Monterey, CA: Naval Postgraduate School.

Marsden, Peter V. 1987. "Core Discussion Networks of Americans." *American Sociological Review* 52(1):122–31.

Matthews, Luke J., Jeffrey Edmonds, Wesley Wildman, and Charles Nunn. 2013. "Cultural Inheritance or Cultural Diffusion of Religious Violence? A Quantitative Case Study of the Radical Reformation." *Religion, Brain & Behavior* 3(1):3–15.

Mayhew, Bruce H. 1980. "Structuralism versus Individualism: Part I, Shadowboxing in the Dark." *Social Forces* 59(2):335–74.

______. 1981. "Structuralism versus Individualism: Part II, Ideological and Other Obfuscations." *Social Forces* 59(3):627–48.

McAdam, Doug. 1986. "Recruitment to High Risk Activism: The Case of Freedom Summer." *American Journal of Sociology* 92:64–90.

______. 1988a. *Freedom Summer*. New York and Oxford: Oxford University Press.

______. 1988b. "Micromobilization Contexts and Recruitment to Activism." *International Social Movement Research* 1:125–54.

______. 1999 [1982]. *Political Process and the Development of Black Insurgency, 1930–1970*. Chicago: University of Chicago Press.

McAdam, Doug, and Ronnelle Paulsen. 1993. "Specifying the Relationship Between Social Ties and Activism." *American Journal of Sociology* 99:640–67.

McAdam, Doug, Sidney Tarrow, and Charles Tilly. 2001. *Dynamics of Contention*. New York and Cambridge: Cambridge University Press.

McCloskey, Deirdre. 1995. "The Insignificance of Statistical Significance." *Scientific American* April:32–33.

McCloskey, Donald N. 1985. "The Loss Function Has Been Mislaid: The Rhetoric of Significance Tests." *American Economic Review* 75(2):201–5.

McCormick, Gordon. 2005. "The Diamond Insurgent/COIN Model." Monterey, CA: Department of Defense Analysis, Naval Postgraduate School.

McCormick, Gordon, and Guillermo Owen. 2000. "Security and Coordination in a Clandestine Organization." *Mathematical and Computer Modelling* 31:175–92.

McCulloh, Ian, Helen Armstrong, and Anthony Johnson. 2013. *Social Network Analysis with Applications*. New York, NY: Wiley.

McCulloh, Ian, and Kathleen M. Carley. 2011. Detecting Change in Longitudinal Social Networks. *Journal of Social Structure*, 12(3). http://www.cmu.edu/joss/content/articles/volume12//McCullohCarley.pdf

McDaniel, Charles A., Jr. 2007. "Violent Yearnings for the Kingdom of God: Münster's Militant Anabaptism." Pp. 63–80 in *Belief and Bloodshed: Religion and Violence Across Time and Tradition*, edited by James K. Wellman. Lanham, MD: Rowman and Littlefield.

McFarland, Daniel A. 2004. "Resistance as Social Drama: A Study of Change-Oriented Behaviors." *American Journal of Sociology* 109(6):1249–318.

McLaughlin, John M. 2015a. "Anabaptist Leadership Network." Monterey, CA: Defense Analysis Department, Naval Postgraduate School.

______. 2015b. "Factors of Religious Violence and a Path to Peace," in *Defense Analysis*. Monterey, CA: Monterey, CA: Naval Postgraduate School, Department of Defense Analysis.

Meyer, John W., John Boli, George M. Thomas, and Francisco O. Ramirez. 1997. "World Society and the Nation-State." *American Journal of Sociology* 103(1):144–81.

Meyer, John W., and Brian Rowan. 1977. "Institutionalized Organizations: Formal Structure as Myth and Ceremony." *American Journal of Sociology* 83(2):340–63.

Milgram, Stanley. 1967. "The Small-World Problem." *Psychology Today* 1(May): 61–67.

______. 1974. *Obedience to Authority*. Princeton, NJ: Princeton University Press.

Milward, H. Brinton, and Jörg Raab. 2006. "Dark Networks as Organizational Problems: Elements of a Theory." *International Public Management Journal* 9(3):333–60.

______. 2008. "The Resilience of Dark Networks in Modern Protectorates – The Case of Liberia," in *Workshop on Modern Protectorates, Culture, and Dark Networks*. University of Konstanz, Germany.

Moody, James. 2005. "Fighting a Hydra: A Note on the Network Embeddedness of the War on Terror." *Structure and Dynamics* 1(2).

Moreno, Jacob L. 1953a. *Who Shall Survive? Foundations of Sociometry, Group Psycholtherapy and Sociodrama*. Beacon, NY: Beacon House.

______. 1953b. *Who Shall Survive? Foundations of Sociometry, Group Psychotherapy and Sociodrama*. Beacon, NY: Beacon House.

Morselli, Carlo. 2009. *Inside Criminal Networks*. New York: Springer.

Nadel, Siegfried F. 1957. *The Theory of Social Structure*. London: Cohen and West.

Nagl, John A. 2005. *Learning to Eat Soup with a Knife: Counterinsurgency Lessons from Malaya and Vietnam*. Chicago: University of Chicago Press.

Neff, Christian, and Werner O. Packull. 1987. Melchior Hoffman. *Global Anabaptist Mennonite Encyclopedia Online*. http://gameo.org/index.php?title=Hoffman,_Melchior_(ca._1495–1544%3F)&oldid=128083

Newman, Mark E. J. 2004. "Detecting Community Structure in Networks." *European Physical Journal* 38(2):321–30.

______. 2006. "Modularity and Community Structure in Networks." *Proceedings of the National Academy of Sciences* 103(23):8577–82.

Nohria, Nitin. 1992. "Is the Network Perspective a Useful Way of Studying Organizations?" Pp. 1–22 in *Networks and Organizations: Structure, Form, and Action*, edited by Nitin Nohria and Robert G. Eccles. Boston: Harvard Business School Press.

Onnela, Jukka-Pekka, Jari Saramaki, J. Hyvönen, Szabó. G., David Lazer, Kimmo Kaski, J. Kertész, and Barabasi, Albert-Laszlo. 2007. "Structure and Tie Strengths in Mobile Communication Networks." *Proceedings of the National Academy of Sciences of the USA* 104(18):7332–36.

Papachristos, Andrew V., Anthony A. Braga, and David M. Hureau. 2012. "Social Networks and the Risk of Gunshot Injury." *Journal of Urban Health: Bulletin of the New York Academy of Medicine* 89(6):992–1003.

Papachristos, Andrew V., David M. Hureau, and Anthony A. Braga. 2013. "The Corner and the Crew: The Influence of Geography and Social Networks on Gang Violence." *American Sociological Review* 78(3):417–47.

Passy, Florence. 2003. "Social Networks Matter. But How?" Pp. 21–48 in *Social Movements and Networks: Relational Approaches to Collective Action*, edited by Mario Diani and Doug McAdam. Oxford and New York: Oxford University Press.

Pedahzur, Ami, and Arie Perliger. 2006. "The Changing Nature of Suicide Attacks: A Social Network Perspective." *Social Forces* 84(4):1987–2008.

Pescosolido, Bernice A., and Beth A. Rubin. 2000. "The Web of Group Affiliations Revisited." *American Sociological Review* 64(1):52–76.

Pitts, William L., Jr. 1995. "Davidians and Branch Davidians." Pp. 20–42 in *Armageddon in Waco: Critical Perspectives on the Branch Davidian Conflict*, edited by Stuart A. Wright. Chicago and London: Chicago University Press.

Pons, Pascal, and Matthieu Latapy. 2005. "Computing Communities in Large Networks Using Random Walks." Pp. 284–93 in *Computer and Information Sciences-ISCIS 2005*, edited by P. Yolum, T. Gungor, and F. Gurgen. Berlin, DE: Springer-Verlag afXiv:physics/0512106v1.

Popielarz, Pamela A., and J. Miller McPherson. 1995. "On the Edge or in Between: Niche Position, Niche Overlap, and the Duration of Voluntary Association Memberships." *American Journal of Sociology* 101(3):698–720.

Popkin, Samuel L. 2007. "Discussion," in *Terrorist Organizations: Conference Sponsored by the University of California Institute on Global Conflict and Cooperation.* La Jolla, CA.

Powell, Walter W. 1985. "Hybrid Organizational Arrangements: New Form or Transitional Development." *California Management Review* 30(1):67–87.

______. 1990. "Neither Market Nor Hierarchy: Network Forms of Organization." Pp. 295–336 in *Research in Organizational Behavior: An Annual Series of Analytical Essays and Critical Reviews*, edited by Barry M. Staw and Larry L. Cummings. Greenwich, CT: JAI Press, Inc.

Powell, Walter W., and Paul J. DiMaggio (Eds.). 1991. *The New Institutionalism in Organizational Analysis*. Chicago and London: University of Chicago Press.

Powell, Walter W., and Laurel Smith-Doerr. 1994. "Networks and Economic Life." Pp. 368–402 in *The Handbook of Economic Sociology*, edited by Neil J. Smelser and Richard Swedberg. Princeton, NJ: Princeton University Press.

Prell, Christina. 2011. *Social Network Analysis: History, Theory & Methodology*. London and Thousand Oaks, CA: SAGE Publications.

Raab, Jörg, and H. Brinton Milward. 2003. "Dark Networks as Problems." *Journal of Public Administration Research and Theory* 13(4):413–39.

Radcliffe-Brown, Alfred R. 1940. "On Social Structure." *Journal of the Royal Anthropological Society of Great Britain and Ireland* LXX:1–12.

Raftery, Adrian E. 1995. "Bayesian Model Selection in Social Research." *Sociological Methodology* 25:111–63.

Ramakrishna, Kumar. 2005. "Delegitimizing Global Jihadi Ideology in Southeast Asia." *Contemporary Southeast Asia* 27(3):343–69.

______. 2012. Engaging Former JI Detainees in Countering Extremism: Can it Work? *RSIS Commentaries*, 003/2012. http://www.rsis.edu.sg/publications/Perspective/RSIS0032012.pdf

Rapaport, David. 1988. "Messianic Sanctions for Terror." *Comparative Politics* 20(2):195–213.

Rapoport, Anatole. 1953a. "Spread of Information Through a Population with Socio-Structural Bias I: Assumption of Transitivity." *Bulletin of Mathematical Biophysics* 15(4):523–33.

______. 1953b. "Spread of Information Through a Population with Socio-Structural Bias II: Various Models with Partial Transitivity." *Bulletin of Mathematical Biophysics* 15(4):535–46.

Rapoport, Anatole, and William J. Horvath. 1961. "A Study of a Large Sociogram." *Behavioral Science* 6:279–91.

Reed, Brian J. 2007. "A Social Network Approach to Understanding an Insurgency." *Parameters* 38:19–30.

Reed, Brian J., and David R. Segal. 2006. "Social Network Analysis and Counter-insurgency Operations: The Capture of Sadadam Hussein." *Sociological Focus* 39(4):251–64.

Reichardt, Jörg, and Stefan Bornholdt. 2006. "Statistical Mechanics of Community Detection." *Phys. Rev. E* 74(016110).

Ressler, Steve. 2006. Social Network Analysis as an Approach to Combat Terrorism: Past, Present, and Future Research. *Homeland Security Affairs*, 2(2). http://www.hsaj.org/?article=2.2.8

Ripley, Ruth M., Tom A. B. Snijders, Zsófia Boda, András Vörös, and Paulina Preciado. 2015. *Manual for RSiena*. University of Oxford: Department of Statistics: Nuffield College.

Roberts, Nancy, and Sean F. Everton. 2011. Strategies for Combating Dark Networks. *Journal of Social Structure*, 12(2). http://www.cmu.edu/joss/content/articles/volume12//RobertsEverton.pdf

Robins, Garry L. 2013. "A Tutorial on Methods of the Modeling and Analysis of Social Network Data." *Journal of Mathematical Psychology* 57:261–74.

______. 2015. *Doing Social Network Research: Network-based Research Design for Social Scientists*. London: SAGE.

Robins, Garry L., Philippa E. Pattison, Yuval Kalish, and Dean Lusher. 2007. "An Introduction to Exponential Random Graph (p*) Models for Social Networks." *Social Networks* 29:173–91.

Rodriguez, José A. 2005. The March 11th Terrorist Network: In Its Weakness Lies Its Strength. *EPP-LEA Working Papers*. http://citeseerx.ist.psu.edu/viewdoc/summary?doi=10.1.1.98.4408

Roethlisberger, Fritz J., and William J. Dickson. 1939. *Management and the Worker*. Cambridge, MA: Harvard University Press.

Ronfeldt, David, and John Arquilla. 2001. "What Next for Networks and Netwars?" Pp. 311–61 in *Networks and Netwars*, edited by John Arquilla and David Ronfeldt. Santa Monica, CA: RAND.

Sade, Donald Stone. 1989. "Sociometrics of Macaca Mulatta III: N-path Centrality in Grooming Networks." *Social Networks* 11(3):273–92.

Sageman, Marc. 2003. "Statement to the National Commission on Terrorist Attacks Upon the United States." National Commission on Terrorist Attacks Upon the United States.

______. 2004. *Understanding Terror Networks*. Philadelphia, PA: University of Pennsylvania Press.

______. 2008. *Leaderless Jihad: Terror Networks in the Twenty-First Century*. Philadelphia: University of Pennsylvania Press.

Saxenian, AnnaLee. 1994. *Regional Advantage: Culture and Competition in Silicon Valley and Route 128*. Cambridge, MA: Harvard University Press.

______. 1996. "Inside-Out: Regional Networks and Industrial Adaptation in Silicon Valley and Route 128." *Cityscape: A Journal of Policy Development and Research* 2(2):41–60.

Schroeder, Robert, Sean F. Everton, and Russell Shepherd. 2012. "Mining Twitter Data from the Arab Spring." *Countering Terrorism Exchange* 2(4):56–64.

Scott, John. 2011. *Conceptualising the Social World: Principles of Sociological Analysis*. Cambridge and New York: Cambridge University Press.

______. 2013. *Social Network Analysis*. London and Thousand Oaks, CA: SAGE Publications Ltd.

Sepp, Kalev I. 2005. "Best Practices in Counterinsurgency." *Military Review* May-June:8–12.

Shadish, William R., Thomas D. Cook, and Donald T. Campbell. 2002. *Experimental and Quasi-Experimental Designs for Generalized Causal Influence*. Boston, MA: Houghton Mifflin Co.

Shermer, Michael. 2008. "Patternicity." *Scientific American*, (December). http://www.scientificamerican.com/article/patternicity-finding-meaningful-patterns.

Simmel, Georg. 1950a. "The Isolated Individual and the Dyad." Pp. 118–44 in *The Sociology of Georg Simmel*, edited by Kurt H. Wolf. New York: The Free Press.

______. 1950b. "The Secret Society." Pp. 345–76 in *The Sociology of Georg Simmel*, edited by Kurt H. Wolf. New York: The Free Press.

______. 1950c. "The Triad." Pp. 145–69 in *The Sociology of Georg Simmel*, edited by Kurt H. Wolf. New York: The Free Press.

______. [1908] 1955. *Conflict & The Web of Group-Affiliations*. New York: The Free Press.

______. [1908] 1971. *On Individuality and Social Forms*. Chicago: University of Chicago Press.

Smith, Christian S. 1991. *The Emergence of Liberation Theology: Radical Religion and Social Movement Theory*. Chicago: University of Chicago Press.

______. 2010. *What is a Person? Rethinking Humanity, Social Life, and the Moral Good from the Person Up*. Chicago and London: The University of Chicago Press.

Smith, Christian S., Michael O. Emerson, Sally Gallagher, Paul Kennedy, and David Sikkink. 1998. *American Evangelicalism: Embattled and Thriving*. Chicago: The University of Chicago Press.

Snijders, Tom A. B. 1981. "The Degree Variance: An Index of Graph Heterogeneity." *Social Networks* 3:163–74.

______. 2001. "The Statistical Evaluation of Social Network Dynamics." *Sociological Methodology* 31(1):361–95.

______. 2002. "Markov Chain Monte Carlo Estimation of Exponential Random Graph Models." *Journal of Social Structure* 3(2):1–40.

______. 2005. "Models for Longitudinal Network Data." Pp. 215–47 in *Models and Methods in Social Network Analysis*, edited by Peter J. Carrington, John Scott, and Stanley Wasserman. New York: Cambridge University Press.

Snijders, Tom A. B., Gerhard G. van de Bunt, and Christian Steglich. 2010. "Introduction to Stochastic Actor-based Models for Network Dynamics." *Social Networks* 32(1):44–60.

Snijders, Tom, and Johan H. Koskinen. 2013. "Longitudinal Models." Pp. 130–40 in *Exponential Random Graph Models for Social Networks*, edited by Dean Lusher, Johan Koskinen, and Gary Robins. New York and Cambridge: Cambridge University Press.

Snijders, Tom, Philippa Pattison, Gary Robins, and Mark S. Hancock. 2006. "New Specifications for Exponential Random Graph Models." *Sociological Methodology* 36(1):99–153.

Snow, David A., Louis A. Zurcher, and Sheldon Ekland-Olson. 1980. "Social Networks and Social Movements: A Microstructural Approach to Differential Recruitment." *American Sociological Review* 45:787–801.

Sparrow, Malcom K. 1991. "The Application of Network Analysis to Criminal Intelligence: An Assessment of the Prospects." *Social Networks* 13:251–74.

Stanovich, Keith E. 2007. *How to Think Straight About Psychology*. Boston, MA: Pearson Allyn and Bacon.

Stark, Rodney. 1996. *The Rise of Christianity: A Sociologist Reconsiders History*. Princeton, NJ: Princeton University Press.

______. 2000. "Rationality." Pp. 239–58 in *Guide to the Study of Religion*, edited by Willi Braun and Russell T. McCutcheon. London: Cassell.

______. 2007. *Sociology*. Belmont, CA: Wadsworth Publishing Company.

Stark, Rodney, and William Sims Bainbridge. 1980. "Networks of Faith: Interpersonal Bonds and Recruitment to Cults and Sects." *American Journal of Sociology* 85(6):1376–95.

______. 1985. *The Future of Religion*. Berkeley: University of California Press.

Stark, Rodney, and Laurence R. Iannaccone. 1994. "Rationality and the Religious Mind," in *Paper presented at the meetings of the Western Economic Association*. San Diego, CA: July, 1995.

Stayer, James M. 1979. *Anabaptists and the Sword*. Lawrence, KS: Coronado Press.

Steglich, Christian, Tom A. B. Snijders, and Michael Pearson. 2010. "Dynamic Networks and Behavior: Separating Selection From Influence." *Sociological Methodology* 40:329–93.

Stephenson, Karen, and Marvin Zelen. 1989. "Rethinking Centrality: Methods and Examples." *Social Networks* 11(1):1–37.

Sunstein, Cass R. 2002. "The Law of Group Polarization." *The Journal of Political Philosophy* 10:175–95.

______. 2003. *Why Societies Need Dissent*. Cambridge, MA: Harvard University Press.

______. 2009. *Going to Extremes: How Like Minds Unite and Divide*. New York and Oxford: Oxford University Press.

Taylor, Michael. 1969. "Influence Structures." *Sociometry* 32(4):490–502.

Tilly, Charles. 2004. "Trust and Rule." *Theory and Society* 33:1–30.

______. 2005. *Trust and Rule*. Cambridge and New York: Cambridge University Press.

Tomaszewski, Irene, and Tecia Webowski. 2010. *Code Name: Żegota: Rescuing Jews in Occupied Poland,* 1942–45*: The Most Dangerous Conspiracy in Wartime Europe*. Santa Barbara, CA: Praeger.

Travers, Jeffrey, and Stanley Milgram. 1969. "An Experimental Study of the Small World Problem." *Sociometry* 32(4):425–43.

Tucker, David. 2008. "Terrorism, Networks and Strategy: Why the Conventional Wisdom is Wrong." *Homeland Security Affairs*, 4:2 (June 2008), 1–18. http://www.hsaj.org

Turner, Jonathan H. 2006. *Sociology*. Upper Saddle River, NJ: Pearson Prentice Hall.

U.S. Director of Operations. 2006. Information Operations: Joint Publication 3–13. http://www.dtic.mil/doctrine/jel/new_pubs/jp3_13.pdf

U.S. Special Operations Command. 2003. Doctrine for Joint Psychological Operations: Joint Publication 3–53. http://www.dtic.mil/doctrine/jel/new_pubs/jp3_53.pdf

Uzzi, Brian. 1996. "The Sources and Consequences of Embeddedness for the Economic Performance of Organizations: The Network Effect." *American Sociological Review* 61(4):674–98.

______. 2008. "A Social Network's Changing Statistical Properties and the Quality of Human Innovation." *Journal of Physics A: Mathematical and Theoretical* 41:1–12.

Uzzi, Brian, and Jarrett Spiro. 2005. "Collaboration and Creativity: The Small World Problem." *American Journal of Sociology* 111(2):447–504.

Van de Bunt, G.G., M.A.J. Van Duijin, and Tom A. B. Snijders. 1999. "Friendship Networks through Time: An Actor-Oriented Statistical Network Model." *Computational and Mathematical Organization Theory* 5:167–92.

Wang, Peng, Garry L. Robins, and Philippa E. Pattison. 2009. "Exponential Random Graph (p*) Models for Affiliation Networks." *Social Networks* 31(1):12–25.

Wang, Peng, Garry L. Robins, Philippa E. Pattison, and Johan H. Koskinen. 2014. "MPNET User Manual (June)." Melbourne, Australia: Melbourne School of Psychological Sciences, The University of Melbourne.

Wasserman, Stanley, and Katherine Faust. 1994. *Social Network Analysis: Methods and Applications*. Cambridge, UK: Cambridge University Press.

Watts, Duncan J. 1999a. "Networks, Dynamics, and the Small-World Phenomenon." *American Journal of Sociology* 105(2):493–527.

______. 1999b. *Small Worlds: The Dynamics of Networks Between Order and Randomness*. Princeton, NJ: Princeton University Press.

______. 2004. "The "New" Science of Networks." *Annual Review of Sociology* 30:243–70.

Watts, Duncan J., Peter Sheridan Dodds, and M. E. Newman. 2003. "Identity and Search in Social Networks." *Science* 296:1302–4.

Watts, Duncan J., and Steven H. Strogatz. 1998. "Collective Dynamics of 'Small World' Networks." *Nature* 393:409–10.

Weiss, Neil A. 2008. *Introductory Statistics*. New York, NY: Pearson.

White, Douglas R. 1985. "REGE: A Regular Graph Equivalence Algorithm for Computing Role Distances Prior to Block Modelling." Irvine, CA: University of California, Irvine.

White, Douglas R., and Karl P. Reitz. 1983. "Graph and Semigroup Homomorphisms on Networks of Relations." *Social Networks* 5:193–235.

White, Harrison C. 1992. *Identity and Control: A Structural Theory of Social Action*. Princeton, NJ: Princeton University Press.

______. 2008. *Identity and Control: How Social Formations Emerge*. Princeton, NJ: Princeton University Press.

White, Harrison C., Scott A. Boorman, and Ronald L. Breiger. 1976. "Social Structure from Multiple Networks I: Blockmodels of Roles and Positions." *American Journal of Sociology* 81:730–80.

Wikipedia. 2015. Münster Rebellion. (September 23, 2015). https://en.wikipedia.org/wiki/Münster_Rebellion

Williams, George Huntston. 1975. *The Radical Reformation*. Philadelphia, PA: Westminster Press.

Ziliak, Stephen T., and Deirdre N. McCloskey. 2008. *The Cult of Statistical Significance*. Ann Arbor: The University of Michigan Press.

Zimbardo, Philip G. 1972. "Pathology of Imprisonment." *Society* 9:4–6.

Zimbardo, Philip G., Christina Maslasch, and Craig Haney. 2000. "Reflections on the Stanford Prison Experiment: Genesis, Transformations, Consequences." Pp. 193–237 in *Obedience to Authority: Current Perspectives on the Milgram Paradigm*, edited by Thomas Blass. Mahwah, NJ: Lawrence Erlbaum Associates, Publishers.

Index

About the Authors

Daniel Cunningham is an Associate Faculty for Instruction at the Common Operational Research Environment (CORE) embedded in the Department of Defense Analysis (DA) at the Naval Postgraduate School (NPS) in Monterey, CA. His areas of research include visual analytics and the application of social network analysis to real-world problem sets. He led the development of the CORE Lab's social network analysis outreach and education program, and he has worked with a wide range of practitioners, including U.S. Special Operations Forces (SOF), Law Enforcement, and international partners. He is currently working toward his PhD.

Sean Everton is an Associate Professor in the Department of Defense Analysis and the Co-Director of the CORE Lab at the Naval Postgraduate School (NPS). Prior to joining NPS in 2007 he served as an adjunct professor at both Santa Clara University and Stanford University. Professor Everton earned his MA and PhD in Sociology at Stanford University (2007) and wrote his doctoral thesis on causes and consequences of status on the economic performance of venture capital firms. He has published in the areas of social network analysis, sociology of religion, economic sociology, and political sociology and currently specializes in the use of social network analysis to track and disrupt dark networks.

Philip Murphy is an Assistant Professor in the Graduate School of International Policy and Management at the Middlebury Institute of International Studies at Monterey. Professor Murphy is co-founder and Director of the Mixed methods, Evaluation, Training, and Analysis (META) Lab at the Middlebury Institute and a Research Fellow at the NPS CORE Lab. Before coming to Monterey, Professor Murphy worked as an adjunct professor at the Graduate School of Public and International Affairs at the University of Pittsburgh, where he also held the position of Senior Policy Fellow at the Matthew B. Ridgway Center for International Security Studies. Prior to that, Professor Murphy served on the Faculty of Public Administration at Southeast European University, in Tetovo, Macedonia. His research includes work on identity formation and the use of network analysis and allied tools to analyze organizational as well as dark networks.